D1601070

Letters across Borders

The Epistolary Practices of International Migrants

Edited by

Bruce S. Elliott,
David A. Gerber,
and
Suzanne M. Sinke

Published in association with the
Carleton Centre for the History of Migration

LETTERS ACROSS BORDERS
© Bruce S. Elliott, David A. Gerber, and Suzanne M. Sinke, 2006.

Portions of David Gerber's essay were previously published as "Acts of Deceiving and Withholding in Immigrant Letters," *Journal of Social History*, 39 (Winter 2005): 8–23. The editors gratefully acknowledge the permission of *The Journal of Social History*.

Miguel Angel Vargas's essay is reprinted in translation from "Communication epistolar entre trabajadores migrantes y sus familias," *Aztlán* (2000), UCLA Chicano Studies Research Center, with permission of The Regents of the University of California. Not for further reproduction.

First published in 2006 by
PALGRAVE MACMILLAN™
175 Fifth Avenue, New York, N.Y. 10010 and
Houndmills, Basingstoke, Hampshire, England RG21 6XS
Companies and representatives throughout the world.

PALGRAVE MACMILLAN is the global academic imprint of the Palgrave Macmillan division of St. Martin's Press, LLC and of Palgrave Macmillan Ltd. Macmillan® is a registered trademark in the United States, United Kingdom and other countries. Palgrave is a registered trademark in the European Union and other countries.

ISBN-13: 978–1–4039–7101–2
ISBN-10: 1–4039–7101–3

Library of Congress Cataloging-in-Publication Data

Letters across borders : the epistolary practices of international migrants / edited by Bruce S. Elliott, David A. Gerber, and Suzanne M. Sinke.
p. cm.
Includes papers presented at the international conference, "Reading the Emigrant Letter: Innovative Approaches and Interpretations," sponsored by the Carleton Centre for the History of Migration and hosted at Carleton University in Ottawa, Canada, in 2003.
Includes bibliographical references and index.
ISBN 1–4039–7101–3
1. Emigration and immigration—History—Congresses.
2. Immigrants—Correspondence—Congresses. I. Elliott, Bruce S. II. Gerber, David A., 1944– III. Sinke, Suzanne M. IV. Carleton University. Carleton Centre for the History of Migration.

JV6011.L36 2006
305.9'06912—dc22   2006041594

A catalogue record for this book is available from the British Library.

Design by Newgen Imaging Systems (P) Ltd., Chennai, India.

First edition: August 2006

10 9 8 7 6 5 4 3 2 1

Printed in the United States of America.

Contents

Illustrations

Tables

Notes on Contributors

Helen Brown is a member of the Department of History at Malaspina University College in Nanaimo, British Columbia, where she teaches Canadian History and the History of Modern Childhood. She is the author of "Financing Nanaimo Schools' Local Resistance to Central Control," in *School Leadership: Essays on the British Columbia Experience, 1872–1995*, ed. Thomas Fleming (Mill Bay: Bendall Books, 2001). She serves on the editorial board of the *Canadian Bulletin of Medical History* and is currently working on a book on the Hutton-Pellett letters.

Bruce S. Elliott is Professor of History at Carleton University in Ottawa. As director of the Carleton Centre for the History of Migration, he organized the 2003 conference, *Reading the Emigrant Letter: Innovative Approaches and Interpretations*. Recent publications include " 'Settling Down': Masculinity and the Rite of Return in a Transnational Community" in *Emigrant Homecomings*, ed. M. Harper (Manchester University Press, 2005), 153–183, and "Regional Patterns of English Immigration and Settlement in Upper Canada" in *Canadian Migration Patterns from Britain and North America*, ed. B. Messamore (University of Ottawa Press, 2004), 51–90.

David Fitzpatrick is Professor of Modern History at Trinity College, Dublin, where he has taught since 1979. Born in Australia, he is a graduate of the Universities of Melbourne and Cambridge, and a Member of the Royal Irish Academy. His works include *Politics and Irish Life, 1913–1921: Provincial Experience of War and Revolution* (1977); *Irish Emigration, 1801–1921* (1984); *Oceans of Consolation: Personal Accounts of Irish Migration to Australia* (1995); *The Two Irelands, 1912–1939* (1998); and *Harry Boland's Irish Revolution* (2003). He is preparing a history of the Orange Order.

David A. Gerber is Professor of History at the University at Buffalo (SUNY), where he teaches American History. As an historian, his principal interest has been the study of personal and social identities among immigrants and ethnic groups. He is the author of *Authors of their Lives: The Personal Correspondence of British Immigrants to North America in* *the Nineteenth Century* (New York University Press, 2006) and a number of essays on aspects of the history of the personal correspondence of immigrants.

Ann Goldberg is Associate Professor of History at the University of California, Riverside. Her areas of expertise are Modern Europe, Germany, and Gender History. She is the author of *Sex, Religion, and the Making of Modern Madness* (Oxford University Press, 1999) as well as of articles on anti-psychiatry at the turn of the twentieth century, and on gender and race in the Stefan George literary circle in the Weimar Republic. She is currently writing a book on defamation law and the politics of honor in nineteenth and twentieth century Germany.

Wolfgang Helbich obtained a BA in History at Princeton in 1958 and his Dr. Phil. at Berlin's Free University. He taught North American History at the Universities of Heidelberg and later Bochum until 2000. His publications in German, English, and French cover German and Canadian (*Auswandererbriefsammlung* including Québec) History but center on the United States in the nineteenth century. He built up the largest existing collection of German immigrant letters (from North America), formerly in Bochum (Bochumer *Auswandererbriefsammlung*), now in Gotha (*Nordamerika-Auswandererbriefsammlung*), with the cooperation of Walter Kamphoefner, out of which grew the scholarly editions mentioned by the latter below.

Anna D. Jaroszyńska-Kirchmann is Associate Professor in the Department of History at Eastern Connecticut State University in Willimantic. She is the author of *The Exile Mission: Polish Political Diaspora and Polish Americans, 1939–1956* (University of Ohio Press, 2004) and a number of articles on postwar political immigrants. She is vice president of the Polish American Historical Association and serves on the editorial board of *Polish American Studies*. Her current research project involves a study of letters to the editor in a Polish language newspaper, *Ameryka-Echo*, between 1889 and 1969.

William D. Jones is Senior Lecturer in Welsh History at the School of History and Archaeology, Cardiff University, Wales, where he teaches Welsh and British History. He is a specialist in nineteenth and early-twentieth century Welsh emigration and Welsh communities overseas. He is the author of *Wales in America: Scranton and the Welsh, 1860–1920* (1993) and (with Aled Jones) *Welsh Reflections: Y Drych and America, 1851–2001* (2001).

Walter D. Kamphoefner earned his PhD at University of Missouri-Columbia in 1978 and is Professor of History at Texas A&M University, where he teaches in the fields of immigration, urbanization, and quantitative methods. He has published widely in the field of immigration and ethnicity, including his monograph, *The Westfalians: From Germany to Missouri* (Princeton University Press, 1987). With Wolfgang Helbich, he has coedited a collection of articles and German and English versions of two immigrant letter anthologies, including *News From the Land of Freedom: German Immigrants Write Home* (Cornell University Press, 1991).

Vadim Kukushkin is a postdoctoral fellow in the Department of History and Classics at the University of Alberta. His dissertation explored patterns of Ukrainian and Belarusan immigration from the Russian Empire to Canada. He is currently working on a project that examines the relationship between immigrants and the Canadian justice system on the Prairies. He is coeditor of the book *Mikhail Klochko: Soviet Scientist, Cold-War Defector, Canadian Storyteller* (Penumbra Press, 2002).

Karen Lemiski, after completing undergraduate studies at the Canadian Institute of Ukrainian Studies (University of Alberta), received her PhD in History from Arizona State University with her dissertation focusing on issues of Ukrainian nationalism. In recent years, her research has focused on Ukraine's medieval past and connections to Byzantium. She is currently the director of Pegasus Press, an academic publisher of student texts in Medieval and Renaissance History.

Daiva Markelis is Assistant Professor of English at Eastern Illinois University, where she teaches courses in writing, linguistics, composition theory, and myth and culture, and also directs the Writing Center. Her academic publications, creative nonfiction essays, and fiction have appeared in *Written Communication, Women and Language, Writing on the Edge, Other Voices, The Cream City Review, The Chicago Reader,* and *The Chicago Tribune Sunday Magazine.*

Eric Richards was born in Wales and educated at Nottingham University. He has been Professor of History at Flinders University in Adelaide since 1975. His recent books include: *Patrick Sellar and the Highland Clearances: Eviction, Homicide and the Price of Progress* (1999); *The Highland Clearances: People, Landlords and Rural Turmoil* (2000); and *Britannia's Children: Emigration from England, Wales, Scotland, and Ireland since 1600* (2004). He has also been editing the six-volume series on the history of Australian immigration entitled *Visible Immigrants* (Pandanus Books, Canberra).

Alexander Schunka holds a doctoral degree in Modern History. After working as a research assistant at the University of Munich, he now teaches at the University of Stuttgart, Germany. His publications include books on the social knowledge of the early modern rural population and on migration in seventeenth-century Europe. He has published articles on Early Modern German and Ottoman History and is currently preparing a book on ecclesiastical and political relations between Britain and Prussia at the beginning of the eighteenth century.

Suzanne M. Sinke, Associate Professor of History at Florida State University, is the author of numerous articles on gender and migration as well as a monograph, *Dutch Immigrant Women in the United States, 1880–1930* (2002). Her current research relates to marriage and international migration in the North American context, from "bride ships" to matchmaking web sites.

Miguel Angel Vargas is a psychologist and educational researcher. His work focuses on the culture of writing, literacy, and textbooks. He has written feature articles and textbooks on language. At present, he is involved in a national educational program supporting disadvantaged and poor schools in Mexico, ones that serve rural and indigenous children. In particular, he is evaluating thirteen years of government policies targeted at improving these schools.

Introduction

Bruce S. Elliott, David A. Gerber,
and Suzanne M. Sinke

Migrations, within and across international borders, have so characterized the modern world that it has seemed at times in the last five hundred years, and certainly today, that the world's people are on the move, changing jobs, residences, and citizenship and fitting themselves into new cultures and polities.[1] As narrative, the adventure that permeates migrants' stories, especially the stories of the international migrants, can be poetically attractive for its drama. Some migrant accounts seem to offer the promise of new beginnings amidst new circumstances, sometimes accompanied by an escape from danger, oppression, and exploitation into security, liberty, and the chance for a greater measure of justice. At other times, the new is strange, foreboding, and anything but just.

Even among those whom historians usually think of as voluntary migrants, the emphasis on new beginnings may work to deny us knowledge of the structural constraints that exist in the social, political, religious, and economic contexts that have comprised the immigrants' daily lives. These difficulties often appeared to pressure people to emigrate, and they significantly qualify our understanding of *voluntary*. The concept of voluntary is also strained in numerous other ways when applied to migration. As the obvious examples of women and children remind us, not all immigrants had the same power over migration or resettlement decisions.[2] Whether immigrants came voluntarily or were forced by circumstance to leave their homelands, many began these new lives toward the bottom of the social ladder, where they encountered low wages, dead end jobs, and poor living conditions, from which they struggled to extricate themselves and to come to terms with the host society.

Moreover, the narrative of new beginnings too easily lends itself to framing the immigrant experience in terms of assimilation. In consequence, it also may deny us the opportunity for a realistic appraisal of what some scholars, in analyzing the psychology of migrants, understand to be a need of individuals to continue to look backward even as they move forward through life.[3] To be sure, migration over long distances has been widely understood in many societies as a part of the normal course of life, especially for younger people.[4] In their lands of resettlement, furthermore, migrants have drawn on past personal connections and ethnic identifications based on shared origins to create networks and communities that have eased their transition to new lives. It is a rare individual who can accept a complete divorce from the central elements of a personal past: a home place, and the kinship and friendship relations associated with it.

As individuals, migrants have often looked backward as they looked forward. This dualistic stance seems especially overdetermined in the case of the international migrant, for the greater the tensions incidental to exposure to new social systems and cultures, the greater may be the desire to preserve a feeling of rootedness in a personal past. In addition, in these adjustments, as Homi Bhabha reminds us, people were not totally free to choose new identities.[5] States and individuals alike imposed racial, ethnic, national, and gender identities, among others. Depending on the circumstances, therefore, people might desire to call upon the past in many ways, to serve multiple ends.

For many international migrants such transnationalized rootedness could be maintained by keeping in contact with family and friends in the homeland, just as the desire for a break with the past could be seen in the refusal to maintain contact.[6] Today, with the availability of international long distance, fax, e-mail, and jet air travel, it is not difficult to imagine how such contacts are achieved. Internet cafes have become excellent sites for witnessing international migrants' quest for maintaining personal networks and expanding knowledge across borders, creating "virtual communities."[7] In the more distant past, however, the mechanisms for maintaining contact were fewer and hardly instantaneous, but they were utilized by millions of people on the move and have never gone completely out of fashion. The personal letter sent throughout interlinked national postal systems was the most widespread instrument of migrant communication through the nineteenth and most of the twentieth century. So common was the personal letter exchanged between immigrants and family and friends in the homeland that this genre, more than newspapers, pamphlets, and books, became the source of wisdom about life in the new location.[8] Recipients in Scandinavian lands titled some of these missives "America letters," a genre of particular interest to historians of migration because they often contained vivid descriptions and precise evaluations of the new setting.[9]

The cycle of correspondence prompted by immigration, along with the flood of international business communications, assisted over the course of the nineteenth century in giving birth to modern postal systems and to the postal conventions that have allowed for *mail*, the commodified form of postal communications, to circulate across the globe relatively unimpeded. Countries adopted standard postal rates within their borders to help create a "national" identity as well as to facilitate commercial and personal exchange. By identifying the nation and representing it iconographically, prepaid stamps became symbols of the nation. As international migration increased in volume in the nineteenth century, so did the flow of letters across borders, stimulating innovations that improved modernity's original technology of communications. This conjuncture of the movement of masses of international migrants desiring to keep connections with people in their homeplaces and the growth of postal arrangements, accounts for the fact that the letters immigrants sent to their homelands are the largest body of the writings of ordinary people of the past that historians and other researchers possess. We cannot begin to know how many such letters were actually sent. Nor can we know what percentage those currently archived in libraries and other repositories are of the total number sent. Nor can we know how many are still in private hands.

This is only the beginning of an imposing list of difficulties we face in confronting personal correspondence as a source for expanding knowledge of migration and migrants. Additional problems, both artifactual and social, frame the historicity of the personal letter. Rarely do we have access to both sides of a cycle of correspondence.[10] It is an artifact of an obscure process of collection, long neglected as a matter of inquiry but now addressed by Wolfgang Helbich and Walter Kamphoefner in this volume, that we have few collections in which letters sent to the immigrant from the homeland are represented. We are tuned into a one-way conversation. Nor can we know how complete these existing collections are. How many letters were destroyed by the correspondents or latter-day descendants, by neglect or inadvertence, or because they contained embarrassing content, is a pressing but unanswerable problem. Even authorship is an issue, for the signing of a letter does not necessarily authenticate the identity of its writer. A signature is a token of responsibility, but not necessarily the mark of whose labor actually produced the letter.

There is also the problem of making sense of the writings of the many poorly educated and marginally literate writers for whom the necessity of writing inspired an exercise that taxed their abilities to the limit. Decoding texts with inadequate paragraphing and punctuation, ungrammatical constructions, highly irregular spelling, and language that combines native regional dialect, borrowings from the tongue of the country of resettlement, archaic colloquialisms, and singular, individualized modes of expression is the common experience of those who read immigrant letters. Moreover, immigrant writers often struggle on from topic to topic rarely spending time with any one matter, so that coherence is at the mercy of thematic diversity.

Social selection is another problem. How widely may we generalize about immigrant experience on the basis of immigrant letters? Women, illiterates, children, and those who wish for whatever reason *not* to maintain contact with their homelands are underrepresented in the corpus of immigrant letters. They are often spoken for, if spoken for at all, by others who do engage in writing. Occasionally, through relatively complex narrative techniques that often greatly strained the abilities of the letter-writers, nonauthorial voices work their way near to the surface of letters, as these writers sought to represent the opinions, attitudes, and feelings of, for example, their wives or children. But such mediation obviously raises its own interpretive issues regarding the accuracy of representation.

Yet what we do know for certain is that many thousands of immigrant letters are available to researchers. However great the interpretive issues, they provide access to the immigrant's attitudes, values, aspirations, and fears as no other source has the potential to do. The intellectual puzzles presented by the gaps, silences, and textual inadequacies of these letters have added to the challenges of using them to explore the worlds of immigrants. As generations of historians and social scientists have come to understand, no casual reading of immigrant letters takes us very far in making sense of their meanings. Attempts to solve these multiple analytical problems and to read immigrant correspondence deeply have led to general contributions to methodology, conceptualization, and theory in the social sciences and humanities, and have expanded our abilities to contextualize individuals, cohorts, and groups in the immigrant population.

A Tradition of Inquiry

Knowledge of the analytical potential of immigrant letters, and the almost simultaneous awareness of the difficulties involved in studying them, have been present in immigration scholarship since academic disciplines began systematic engagement with immigration in the early twentieth century. Many of the early works were political polemics that debated whether immigration was an evil or a benefit to American society. Alongside this literature was social work ethnography, which focused on the social problems thought to be the consequence of mass immigration and industrialization, and often seen as compounded by the character of the immigrants themselves. The work that marked the passage from such value-laden literature to more objective studies was William B. Thomas and Florian Znaniecki's multivolume *The Polish Peasant in Europe and America* (1918–1921), which has been a central influence upon immigration studies and the discipline of sociology for almost a century.[11] At the center of this massive work were the writings, principally personal letters, of Polish immigrants to Chicago. Qualitative analysis of texts, let alone of texts authored by ordinary people, was hardly common in sociology at the time. Immigrant writings suggested themselves as a source to Thomas, the senior author of the study, because he was interested in how social solidarity was maintained within families among Polish peasants both in Poland and in the United States. He saw modernization as inducing social disorganization by loosening social bonds within the families of the peasantry. He held that this was greatly exacerbated by immigration to a society as dynamic as that of the United States. The process of reorganization was slow and painful, and in the meantime, the authors maintained, Polish immigrants in Chicago experienced significant degrees of marital discord, juvenile delinquency, alcoholism, and general cultural demoralization.[12]

Thomas also was interested in testing new concepts which might assist him in understanding how people took the measure of the world around them and drew a mental picture of that world that guided their actions within it. To this end, he formulated the concept of the attitude, and sought ways to study such transient mental phenomena. For Thomas, the project ultimately proved a disappointment, and at the center of his disappointment was his frustration with the first-person documents he had hoped would unlock the intricacies of the uprooted peasant's mind. The personal letters of the immigrants had proved much too complex to be boiled down to Thomas's formulation of the impact of modernization. They were filled with all sorts of details about other matters, and, hence, understanding any single theme within them required an awkward abstraction from the whole, diverse text. The language of the letter, moreover, did not yield easily to understanding, even when it touched upon matters relevant to Thomas's interests.[13]

But, its authors' frustrations aside, *The Polish Peasant in Europe and America* laid down some important pathways for immigration studies and the study of immigrant letters. In seeking to understand social disorganization, the study framed one of the abiding approaches for analyzing the consequences of international migration and resettlement. It also created an expectation that immigrant letters might be mined systematically to prove hypotheses derived from the study of more general issues, events, and processes. Finally, it created the understanding that immigrant letters were central documents through which human solidarity and affective bonds could be understood.

Almost simultaneous in time with the rise of the analytical tradition represented by the work of Thomas and Znaniecki was the emergence of another way of looking at immigrant first-person writings, one quite different in its origins and aspirations from the concerns of the two academic sociologists. The first generation of social historians of immigration in the United States, most prominently Marcus Lee Hansen, George Stephenson, Theodore Blegen, and Karl Wittke, began their careers in the 1920s and 1930s. They would continue writing history until well into the mid-twentieth century. Second-generation sons of Scandinavian or German immigrants, they were eager to change the character of the American historical narrative. They wished to democratize that narrative by integrating into it the stories of nonelite and non-Anglo-American peoples who came to North America as peasant and artisanal migrants from Scandinavia, Germany, and other continental European locations. In the early twentieth century these ethnic groups of the first, mid-nineteenth century mass migration to the United States from Europe were integrating themselves into positions of leadership in the major institutions of American society. As these ethnic historians embarked upon careers in mainstream academic institutions, their assumption of the role of reformer of the conventions of American self-understanding seemed fitting. They would integrate American historiography just as they were changing the ethnic character of university faculties.[14]

These social historians were attracted to the idea of writing the histories of the ordinary working people from whom they were descended, and they found in the immigrant letter an ideal source for capturing that experience. Immigrant letters enabled them to write about the processes of immigration from the perspective of the ordinary immigrant and in the immigrant's own words. In their work, for the most part, immigrant letters provided color for narratives constructed from other types of sources, especially official sources such as consular service reports and censuses, and public sources such as newspapers and guidebooks published for prospective immigrants. Nevertheless, it was believed that cultural authenticity was added to generalizations derived from such sources when that coloring was the voice of those who had experienced the epic drama of transatlantic migration. They considered finding that voice and seeking to interpret it as one of the immigration historian's highest callings.[15]

The quest for authenticity was underscored in published collections of letters, such as were edited by both Blegen and Stephenson. The collection format, which anthologized the letter series of individual immigrants or grouped the letters of a variety of individuals around themes or experiences growing out of immigration and resettlement, seemed an ideal way to give a voice to ordinary folk and broaden the subject-matter of scholarship and the narrative of the American past. Collections of immigrant letters became a fixture in historical scholarship in the United States and eventually in Europe, Canada, and Australia, too, throughout the twentieth century.[16] Such collections have perpetuated the idea, often proclaimed by their editors and advocates, that in letters we find the unmediated voice of the immigrant, the voice of pure experience. A moment's reflection, however, tells us that in fact this cannot be true, for immigrant writers were immersed in cultures which informed their often tentative writing. The language of church or politics, for example, found its way into their own language, and most probably they learned to write letters by reading the letters of others.[17]

These efforts by social historians in the early and mid-twentieth century to conceptualize the immigrant letter set patterns that are still with us in immigration historiography. Immigrant letters are still being anthologized in increasingly imposing collections. These collections add to the older tradition of systematic editing of texts ever broader social, cultural, and biographical contexts for understanding the letter-writer. Immigrant letters also continue to be used to add color or substantiation to narratives derived from other sources. Letters help to document the larger processes of immigration and resettlement, such as population movement, political integration and civic engagement, and cultural assimilation, but they also are used to shed light on larger developments beyond but involving the immigrant cohort, such as revolution, rebellion, war, and trends in the emergence of popular culture.

Emerging Perspectives

New developments in recent decades have begun to influence how immigrant letters are conceived and the uses to which they may be put. One of these developments grows out of the linguistic turn in historical scholarship through which the study of language, whether written or oral, has become central to our understanding of the past. Discourse theory, narratology, anti-behaviorist psychology, feminist literary criticism, and ethnic and cultural studies have advanced this trend. A second set of concerns, tied to disciplines in the social sciences, articulates immigrant life in transnational terms. This approach connects more closely to previous scholarship on immigrant letters, but expands the scope of social and cultural analysis. In both linguistic and transnational trajectories, historians, and more specifically historians utilizing immigrant letters, have borrowed and adapted across interdisciplinary lines.

Under the rubric of language, the letter can be the object to be studied rather than a source that advances the study of other phenomena. This applies both to novels written in the form of letters and to letters penned without literary aspirations. The study of letters as a literary form in European culture has a long lineage, but one that has gained renewed interest, for as Thomas Beebee points out, the use of letters as a fictional literary device increased in popularity in the late twentieth century, sparking interest in their predecessors.[18] Earlier scholarship identified the late seventeenth and eighteenth centuries as peaks for epistolary novels, with a number of key published works as exemplars. Beebee's *Epistolary Fiction in Europe* includes such works, but goes beyond the previous canon. Other scholars of language, such as William Merrill Decker, support this position, articulating that letters not designed for publication or even for broad circulation may be seen "as a marginal literary form."[19] Thus the study of correspondence in terms of literary style, form, and conventions, has gained strength.

Another type of analysis goes beyond the epistolary text to discuss reception, both whether and when people receive letters, and then how they read the work. Some scholars argue that there is always tension in this process of reception. The tension could be based on whether one literally received the text, for inevitably there was a degree of uncertainly embodied in the Dead Letter Office.[20] The almost teleological story of progress in communications, of fewer lost missives, as seen in the histories of national postal systems, still required a caveat of possible loss, perhaps more prevalent for migrant populations, whose mobility, different linguistic and cultural skills regarding correspondence, and at times legal status, made them more susceptible to lost letters.[21] One other element of tension in reception was how several people, reading the same material, might perceive different meanings. If a letter's author challenged the "power gradient" between writer and reader, for example asserting a close relationship across class lines, it could demonstrate that the power structure was not absolute.[22] Other scholars have explored the theme of different readings, particularly in terms of gender.[23]

How is gender, and for our purposes any form of identity, constituted through reading and writing? At times people assume that women and men write in distinct ways, and readers bring these assumptions to texts. Epistolary novels sometimes manipulate these gender conventions—a misunderstanding based on false gender attribution.[24] The literary ideals have real life counterparts, for education, experience, and example provide different models of correspondence at times. Nonfiction writers also seek to manipulate these expectations and thus to change reception. Lynne Magnusson describes the case of an elderly widow who sought to influence her sons and others with letters of advice, but knew that as a woman she needed more "linguistic capital"—rhetorical sophistication and evidence of greater learning—than was normally the case for an elite woman in order to be taken seriously.[25] An effective admonition or plea, according to this model, required having, or assuming, an appropriate epistolary voice.

Authors who explore circuits of correspondence, collections of letters between particular groups of people for particular purposes, offer multiple means of understanding reader reception. Martha Hanna's insights demonstrate this. She suggests how the letters of semi-literate French correspondents during World War I required the reader to establish the punctuation by speaking the text in the oral cadence of the writer, thus achieving "an element of intimacy not present in more grammatically precise prose." [26] Hanna explores the world of emotions, the shift in feeling tied to the exigency of writing. People are prompted to write by changes in geography and circumstance, and so are more likely to write in times of war and migration. The soldiers write home and their families write back, and in the process they both inscribe a vision of home. Unlike Hanna's soldiers, however, not all groups of migrants were as homogeneous in gender and age. Whether this made a difference in articulating visions of home deserves study. Hanna's analysis places literacy and orality at the center of our concerns in decoding letters. She notes that letter reading and writing took place within families and groups, something well-documented among scholars of immigrant letters. At the same time Hanna underscores the existence of discursive communities. Migrants learned the conventions of letter-writing and developed the capacity to use language to express ideas and emotions in such communities.

Letters crossing borders may be texts that serve to inscribe human relations and personal and social identities through the mobilization of language. Migration historians have long examined adaptation based on letter series. Recent scholarship focuses greater attention on the specifics of language, words and concepts, from learning to accept and espouse white identity within a racial hierarchy, to shifting national identification. Tracing who the "other" is in a migrant's writings across time has been central to this process.[27] In one study of German letters in the period 1830 to 1930 Wolfgang Helbich highlighted seven different types of adaptation as seen in immigrant letter series, including one he described as full Anglo-assimilation within an immigrant's lifetime.[28] Whether these categories are useful for non-European immigrants remains a major question.

Emerging understandings of the origin and nature of discursive communities have sensitized historians of immigrant letters to the place of these letters in the emerging immigrant public square. In the nineteenth century, immigrant letters that appeared to be personal in nature were informally shared within communities, or ended up being published in newspapers and guidebooks. This highlights the permeable boundaries of public and private space within immigrant communications networks and suggests how such networks were constructed. To explore the development of a public for letters, some scholars have turned to the philosophical insights of critical theorist Jürgen Habermas, particularly as articulated in *The Structural Transformation of the Public Sphere*.[29] For historians of migration, a vexing problem has been how to evaluate letters designed for publication and more generally how to approach the assumed division between texts addressed to the familial or friendship circle from those sent to a newspaper or official. Scholars of other genres of correspondence have demonstrated how letter writers adapted forms. Lucía Invernizzi Santa Cruz, for example, described how the letters that an eighteenth-century Dominican nun sent to her father confessor went beyond confessional discourse, turning much more to self-reflection and constructing a female identity.[30] Moving beyond societal expectations, and bridging public and private, are well known phenomena to scholars of gender.[31] One of the major difficulties facing those who study letters crossing borders is the longstanding bracketing of the private as outside scholarly purview. In some published collections this took the form of literal bracketing, letting the reader know that the editors were omitting a section of household news. This also means less attention—both in terms of saving and collecting—to women's writing when it related to family and household activities. When the editors of *News from the Land of Freedom* quantified how well their selections represented the overall population of Germans in the United States, they found that women were underrepresented by a factor of two—and that was after they over-selected women's writings from among the letters donated to the collection.[32] The politics of collection and publication of letters remains an issue to this day.[33]

The emphasis on letters as text has led some historians to explore the genealogy of letters: how did the standard forms develop? A key component of this inquiry has been to examine formal models crafted to provide instruction in letter-writing and published in popular guidebooks to epistolarity in European history.[34] This analysis went on to examine the physical character of letters, the envelope, paper, and handwriting, all of which exemplified social status.[35] By exploring the way in which texts construct and reinforce social identity, Roger Chartier and others have tried to balance the tensions that often inhabit analysis of discourse, most notably whether experience can be separated from discourse. In this Chartier has responded to critics who see textual analysis as too removed from material realities.[36] Attention to social identity in text may illuminate the relevance of gender, class, religion, and region in the cultural practices of immigrant letter-writing. As Leo Schelbert demonstrated for a Swiss migrant couple, even husband and wife, writing from the same location at the same time, might present diametrically opposed evaluations and descriptions of their situation.[37]

On a more mundane level, content analysis, whether in qualitative or more quantitative form, can allow scholars to explore ideological tropes. Two analyses of Irish migrant letters exemplify this trend. Kerby A. Miller posits the extensive use of "exile" in the letters of nineteenth-century Irish migrants in North America in *Emigrants and Exiles*. Miller goes on to argue that this trope pervaded Irish American life. David Fitzpatrick, using a slightly more systematic approach to content analysis, reports no comparable use of the term among the Irish migrants in Australia in *Oceans of Consolation*.[38] These examples at least suggest that a more quantitative approach may be warranted (even if the collection is not representative of the population), in order to make a better case.

Basic quantitative analysis of text can provide important insights. Herbert Brinks, using several Dutch American letter series where both sides of the correspondence across the Atlantic is present, demonstrated that there was a literal meaning to "old" and "new" world. The letters from the "old" world were more often from parents, the older generation, who reported many more deaths and illnesses, and few innovations. The "new" world correspondents, quite literally younger in demographic terms, tended to have more births, fewer chronic ailments, and many more "new" things to report.[39] Using this methodology to explore the epistolary tropes of migrant populations with other demographic characteristics holds promise. It may be of particular use in comparing transnational groups past and present.

Transnational analysis of immigration, which developed in the late twentieth century in efforts to conceptualize contemporary international migrations, has attempted to find alternatives to assimilation theory. Underlying it is the belief that today's technologies of communication and transportation allow immigrants to avoid making final decisions about abandoning their homelands and original culture. Migrants are conceived as participating in two societies simultaneously, often balancing off their economic opportunities in the lands of resettlement with the cultural habits and understandings and familial loyalties that lead them back, mentally, emotionally, and physically, to their homelands.

The study of links across borders over time existed from the outset among historians studying migration, but the emphasis on transnationality has spurred additional research along these lines. In particular it has assisted in creating space academically for scholars whose research crosses borders. Because academic positions in the field of history are typically organized geographically according to nations, or at the most regions, scholarship in North America that crosses the Atlantic or Pacific (or even national borders within North America) has, until recently, been hard to place on a number of levels. Scholars risked not getting jobs, their work rejected, if they did not target a particular national constituency.[40] Transnational scholarship also required linguistic skills and research funding not typical for North American topics. Yet the increase in interest in history from the bottom up along with an upsurge in immigration in the late twentieth century fueled attention to immigration history. Letter collections developed in areas of out-migration, at least once the interest in social history made collecting the works of nonelite populations an archival goal in Western Europe.

The initial statements of transnational theory by behavioral scientists in the early 1990s saw transnationality as a wholly new phenomenon that only contemporary technologies could advance, but historians have argued effectively that immigrants of the past engaged in similar activities within the contexts and limitations of past technologies.[41] The growth of both international postal exchange in the nineteenth century and the emergence of fast and efficient transoceanic sailing and especially steam vessels provided the basis for immigrant letters, a central mechanism of transnationality among international migrants in that era. Conceived transnationally, the letter becomes a unique social space that exists neither in the homeland nor the land of resettlement, but in a third place that is, in effect, in both simultaneously.[42]

Transnational analysis supplements the analysis of immigrant discursive communities in helping us to conceptualize the nature of communication in immigrant networks. This endeavor also requires unpacking social identities. In this, transnational perspectives have shared with linguistic ones insights into how people express their positions. In this volume David Gerber explores the rise of transnational gossip—social intelligence—across the Atlantic for migrants in the mid-nineteenth century. Identity was not just a matter of self-evaluation. Unwanted as well as desired aspects of one's past could accompany a migrant back and forth across borders. Moreover, ascribed identity could change in new circumstances. In part due to the prodding of ethnic studies scholars, historians of European migrations to North America are now exploring how racial inequality is related to self-identification, using letters as sources.

Some transnational scholarship, by asking questions of people in the present, offers new questions for the past. Miguel Angel Vargas, in this collection, suggests that in the context of several alternative methods of communication, physical letters (or *snail mail* in today's terminology) are linked to affective relations, what others might call "care work," or emotional transnationalization.[43] This remains a topic for exploration in the twentieth century, as paper letters faced increasing competition from the telephone and later electronic communications. Migration patterns have shifted in the twentieth century to include more women, particularly mothers, in migration crossing borders.[44] How people create and maintain family ties across borders through letters deserves greater study for the past as well.

Both of these new perspectives, the linguistic and the transnational, point us toward the letter as text to be decoded, something that must be analyzed rather than simply read as an aid in the analysis of other phenomena. Both invite us to examine the ways in which the cultural practices constitutive of letter-writing and embedded in language are utilized to form and maintain networks. Such new developments enrich an already venerable tradition of inquiry into immigrant correspondence. It seems an appropriate time to reconsider the potential of the immigrant letter.

The Essays in Context

The essays in the current volume address a number of these long-standing theoretical and practical conundrums that impact the use that scholars have made of immigrant letters. The title of the opening section, "Limits and Opportunities," could well apply to the whole. Donald Akenson once remarked that surviving immigrant letters are an unknown subset of a universe whose perimeters are themselves unknown.[45] The degree to which archived letters are representative of the full range of the immigrant experience is a problem most scholars encounter, but one that is not entirely capable of resolution. Helbich and Kamphoefner's sample of relevant data for addressing this question is much smaller than the impressive archive of 7000 German-American letters from which it is drawn, but they nonetheless present a valuable first attempt at probing some elusive questions.

They compare their letter-writers with the German population of the United States at the time of the 1870 census, and explore how the demographic profile of the letters' donors may have affected their availability. They verify that continuity of residence contributes heavily to letters' survival, and that the educated are more likely to respond to academics' advertisements. Beyond this, their tables reveal trends for which they suggest a multiplicity of explanations. Were emigrants better educated than the average stay-at-home, or does the donor profile favor that impression? Were women less likely to write, or less likely to emigrate? The regional over-representation of Prussia is explained by the location of the collecting institution, but the authors hypothesize that the underrepresentation of south and southwestern Germany, traditionally areas with high rates of departure, may also result from partible inheritance practices that contributed to a lesser degree of persistence on the land.

Though quantitative comparisons confirm that letters written by some classes of immigrant are more likely to come before the eyes of historians than others, one can still select letters for published editions in ways that even out the representation, as in fact Helbich and Kamphoefner have done in their own well-known volumes. If one is interested in a representative profile of emigrant opinion at a national level, as these authors are, then one may well encounter the law of diminishing returns that they assert: after a time the positions taken on any one question begin to seem familiar. Not all researchers, however, use samplings of letters as a surrogate opinion poll. If one is exploring regional migration processes, for example, then one hopes for letters from specific locations and from specific groups of people, and here the archives still come up empty far too often.

Eric Richards outlines both the limits and the possibilities of the Australian emigrant letter. The singular form is deliberate, for Richards argues that Australian letters—or at least nineteenth-century British Australian and Irish Australian letters—form a distinctive category within a wider genre. Despite their colonies' convict origins, Australians wrote more letters than North Americans (post office statistics on the volume of mail suggest this) and they were major consumers of print literature. In part, this was because Australian immigrants at every level of society and from every region were more literate than their home populations. (The same was true of Russian labor migrants, as Vadim Kukushkin explains later in the volume.)

Richards's analysis is less resolutely quantitative than the essay by Helbich and Kamphoefner, but suggests that similar biases were at work in Australia. Letters from convicts, Irish Catholics, and women under-represent their populations, though the two most well-known published collections share an Irish focus. Richards laments a temporal bias in archiving that over-emphasizes the 1850s gold-rush years and leaves the twentieth century to the oral historians. Impressionistic evaluations give rise to contradiction, however: are failed emigrants more likely to write, as Richards observes, or more likely to keep silent till their fortunes turn, as Gerber suggests? Richards also regrets the lack of communication between scholars collecting immigrant letters and those seeking life-writings of the poor. Though the former reveal much of the mentality and moral economy of the working classes, they are preoccupied with "family solidarity, reunification, and consolation." They are not "the plea of 'the powerless to the powerful' " that one finds in recent publications drawing upon petitions to English poor-law authorities. For letters between emigrants and agents of the state we can, however, turn to the contributions of Alexander Schunka and Vadim Kukushkin in the current volume.

Suzanne M. Sinke's essay, by contrast, explores how the most intimate of human relationships have been negotiated by correspondence. She brings our survey into the computer age, and in a broader sense her essay explores how changing technologies create both limits and opportunities for historical actors, but at the same time she demonstrates how correspondence has been central to courtship for centuries. Illiteracy, cost, and lengthy turnaround times limited the use of the post as a mechanism for recruiting a potential spouse in the age of sail, but it was the necessary means of reuniting betrothed couples and for arranging the brideships that brought parties of marriageable females to many a resource frontier. Costs and lengthy voyages discouraged mere love letters until the nineteenth century when steam packets, railroads, the telegraph, and photography leant a new immediacy to intimate correspondence. State subsidies further reduced postal rates to derisory levels by 1900, creating national and transnational communities in which literary matchmaking flourished and commercialized, and affirming a popular acceptance of impersonal governmental agencies that some scholars see as diagnostic of modernity. In various cultures, traditional institutions adapted to the new infrastructure, but growing markets became susceptible to deception and fraud. Sinke reminds us, too, that while marriage arrangement across borders has been facilitated by technological innovation for some, communications remain subject to the constraints of power, privilege, and patriarchy, even in our electronic age.

Three authors explore writing conventions and practices in different national contexts, and in different ways provide support for the urging of Eric Richards that we undertake more comparisons of ethnic or national epistolary experiences. David Fitzpatrick muses on the origins of the structure, and especially the rhetorical conventions, of Irish vernacular letters surviving from the nineteenth century. He points out that the most common opening, "I take this favorable opportunity to write these few lines hoping the arrival of this letter finds you in good health as it leaves me at present, thanks be to God for his kind mercies to us all," considered by earlier scholars a quaint and quintessentially Irish formulation, was one ridiculed in English writing manuals of the period. Similarly, the five elements he commonly finds in Irish salutations closely resemble those in the "bowing section" identified in the pioneering study of Polish peasant letters by Thomas and Znaniecki in the 1920s, and discussed further by Kirchmann and alluded to by several of our other contributors. Neither structure nor phrasing was therefore of Irish origin, or at least not uniquely so.

Fitzpatrick finds little evidence that didactic writing manuals had any discernible influence on most emigrant correspondents, and the Irish vernacular model owed equally little to formal education or to a recognized coterie of professional scribes. Fitzpatrick reminds us that both composition and reading were collective acts, transgressing the neat dichotomization of public and private spheres questioned by so many of our contributors. He concludes that vernacular letter forms developed and evolved through repeated usage in such semi-public spaces, and that some international parallels are simply the result of coincidence based on "commonsense and practicality"—similar solutions to a common problem. Similar cultural parallels with the English case may be observed elsewhere: the close resemblance of the ritualized forms of agrarian protest in nineteenth-century Ireland and England is seldom remarked upon, but Captain Rock and Captain Swing were variants on a common symbolic motif of peasant power found in many countries. We can add vernacular rhetorical devices to the growing list of subjects upon which we might profitably be informed by the folklorists.

Our second contribution on writing conventions comes from Daiva Markelis who bridges the gap observed by Richards between letters research and oral history by interviewing Lithuanian nuns about their epistolary experiences as children. Lithuanians were among the least literate of American immigrants. Lack of literacy was a product of state policy in the homeland, and their laboring jobs abroad put no premium on education, but the ability to write home became a powerful motivation for literacy in a culture that valued the extended family. The act of writing was more important than what was said, and the ritual importance of the act was signified by the employment of formal stock phrases, which also enhanced the comprehensibility of the message. Lithuanians stressed neatness over grammar, and commercial interests marketed writing services, typewriters, and a variety of pre-printed message cards to cater to this disposition. As in Ireland, school-age children often read or wrote for their elders. Like Fitzpatrick, Markelis argues that excising ritual greetings when publishing letters diminishes our awareness that the primary function of the letter was to reinforce family ties. Unlike Fitzpatrick, she suggests that writing manuals were used in this culture, the content variously catering to the Lithuanian fixation on penmanship and appearance, or plagiarizing American guides. She agrees, however, that letters were composed primarily in a collective, intergenerational context that served important social functions.

Miguel Angel Vargas explores the letter-writing practices of another neglected population, undocumented/illegal Mexican migrants in the United States during the 1980s. He finds a basic consistency of format but little regard for the conventions promoted by educational institutions; in this his findings echo those of Markelis on the letters of Lithuanian workers.

This is a population that seldom reads for pleasure or information, but which writes to maintain links with home. They seldom bother, however, with the writing manuals that seem to have been more valued in the Lithuanian culture. Vargas's community of 375 families generated some 2,000 to 3,000 letters a month, which he thinks a considerable volume for such a population. Most letters went to women. Women migrants corresponded with a variety of female relations and friends whereas men wrote mostly to their mothers. It is unclear, however, what proportion of the migrant community was female. Writing persisted alongside the telephone, the only other form of communication much used, with poverty limiting employment of the latter. Perhaps most interesting is his conclusion that letter-writing is linked with "the affective sphere," and that remittances, generally small, were as much tokens of regard as of real economic value.

What is left unsaid can be as significant as what is addressed openly, especially in family letters. David Gerber and Ann Goldberg address epistolary silences in distinctive contexts, Gerber that of nineteenth-century Anglo-American immigrant letters, and Goldberg that of letters written under a totalitarian regime. Though some immigrant letters were written to convey promised information to a range of acquaintances, often on a one-time basis, Gerber is most interested in sequences of letters that functioned primarily to reconfigure personal relationships made vulnerable by distance. Unlike Stephen Fender,[46] Gerber does not view letters as narratives. The product of ongoing and ultimately unfinished negotiations, letter sequences normally lack the "closure which provides the poetic satisfaction for the narrative form." Gerber also disagrees with Steven Ozment's assessment that the emotional closeness of personal correspondence puts "clarity and truth" at a premium. Gerber counters that the emotional stakes are often too high: seeking to meet deep-seated emotional needs, family correspondents are especially tempted to indulge in lying and withholding. In as potentially wrenching a context as emigration, moreover, the commitment to maintaining contact takes precedence over truthfulness.

Gerber presents as examples types that will be familiar to students of migration: errant sons too embarrassed to write while parental expectations remained unmet, and others who found a way to secure personal space by postponing reports on courtship. Qualifying the picture painted by Sinke, the mails also became a place to *avoid* the discussion of marriage. Gerber goes beyond asserting the mere convenience of such silences, but also beyond claiming that truth was sacrificed at the altar of human relationships. Echoing Jerome Bruner, he argues the psychological necessity of continuity in constructing personal identities; if one agrees, then it follows that emigrants are especially likely to find "narrative truth," which can provide "a good, coherent story," more congenial than literal truth.

Ann Goldberg cites Jürgen Habermas on how individualist literary forms such as the letter, diary, and novel were formative in the construction of the modern self, in turn a prerequisite for the emergence of a bourgeois liberal public sphere. In her evocative analysis of the poignant correspondence of two sisters reaching out to one another in a divided Europe, she demonstrates how under Stalinism individuality, privacy, and authenticity were driven underground and communicated through fictional contrivances, obvious lies, and strategic silences. The strategies succeeded in part because they played upon the censors' understanding of liberal-bourgeois forms. Goldberg emphasizes nonetheless that every clever expedient was matched by one that was chillingly obvious. It was a "cat-and-mouse game" where evading detection depended equally upon the inattention or overwork of the Soviet censors. She reminds us, too, that all writing takes place within the parameters of accepted institutional contexts and conventions. Self-censorship therefore is not uniquely characteristic of totalitarian political contexts, as Gerber's essay further demonstrates, and letters are always culturally constructed performances. In this sense the Salomon correspondence is an extreme and self-conscious demonstration of universal practices.

Nor were letters in the most public of forums impervious to "strategies of duplicity." Bill Jones and Anna Jaroszyńska-Kirchmann address the now-familiar argument that letters in the public prints are suspect because they are unrepresentative, difficult to authenticate, and corrupted by editorial mediation. This position was advocated, for example, by our contributor David Fitzpatrick in his landmark 1994 book *Oceans of Consolation*.[47] While acknowledging the validity of concerns about authenticity, Jones argues that published letters assume additional significance as contributors to the emergence of a public sphere. Like Goldberg, Jones invokes Habermas in positing the emergence of fora for legitimate public debate as diagnostic of modernity—or a liberal democratic modernity at least.

By the mid-nineteenth century, the Welsh newspapers that are the subject of Jones's analysis had proliferated and were catering to an increasingly working-class, Welsh-speaking readership. This mass market press consisted, however, of numerous papers serving localized markets rather than a small number of metropolitan journals with a huge subscription base. The press therefore was particularly welcoming to emigrant letters, acknowledging demand for news of local people as well as providing reassurance that Welsh institutions were taking root abroad in an increasingly transnational era. Modernity, however, wielded a two-edged sword: publishers first promoted participation in the public sphere by male industrial workers and farmers, and then reclaimed editorial space as journalism professionalized later in the century. Jones remains unsure that emigrant correspondents during this "discrete phase" in emigrant communications strove consciously to mold the public sphere to the extent that editors did. He posits that popular influence to some extent arose organically out of correspondents' more obvious personal goals, but emigrants appear at the very least to have sought to influence discourses on emigration itself. The question remains whether the columns of the provincial press were "a forum for debate in which . . . individuals could come together as equals" or whether the censorious pen ensured that the editorial voice was heard most loudly.

Jones regrets that in the Welsh case the originals of printed letters have not survived to facilitate a closer investigation of editorial intervention. Anna Jaroszyńska-Kirchmann has uncovered just such a trove in a different national context and proceeds with just such an analysis. Her conclusions, of course, are specific to her case, a long-standing letters column in the Polish-American newspaper *Ameryka-Echo*. Here the editorial pen was wielded by a series of employees, rather than by the paper's owner, the self-made publishing tycoon Antoni Paryski, the "Polish Hearst." His minions nonetheless upheld Paryski's pro-working-class and anti-clerical stance, tempered by a wariness about disseminating criticisms of American government policies, until the paper was sold to postwar immigrants in 1956. The editors seldom intervened in print or entered into editorial debate with individual correspondents, but they did offer advice for future communications and they regularly deleted passages and, more rarely and controversially, added them. Comparison of the printed letters with their manuscript originals allows Kirchmann to assess how much historians can lose when they have only the former to work with. This fortunate archival survival allows her to explore the blurring of public and private spheres at a level Jones could not.

Helen Brown and Karen Lemiski find novel ways to explore how identity is negotiated through emigrant correspondence. The act of writing may stimulate self-reflection, a necessary prerequisite for constructing both personal and national identities. The process can become overt when these constructions are negotiated between correspondents as well as internally. Brown's research into the Hutton-Pellett correspondence addresses national identity but, like David Gerber, she is more interested in how displacement affects personal identity formation and the reconfiguring of human relationships. Brown's is also the only essay in the collection that explores the specific character of children's letters. As a small boy, John Hutton was removed by the exigencies of war from the bosom of his English family and the land he knew, and left to negotiate a place in an unknown and unrelated family an ocean away. John resolved the contradictions inherent in his situation in creative ways, and the adult participants in the three-way correspondence (John's English father, and

Canadian "mother") were moved by the pressures of circumstance to unusual levels of self-reflection and self-revelation.

Karen Lemiski is the only author apart from Suzanne Sinke to direct our attention to the means of transmission of letters. All our other contributions derive their evidence, in one way or another, from letters' content. Lemiski explores how a sense of national identity and shared historical memory were promoted by the quasi-postal products created by the Ukrainian Government-in-Exile. She reminds us that communications play multiple roles in forging identity. Postal services facilitate national integration, and postage stamps are an educational medium. But here we see a government-in-exile appropriating one of the functions of a sovereign state, employing it to preserve a claim to national status, promulgate knowledge of iconic symbols and historical events, and raise revenue for the nationalist cause. Lemiski explains how the post became "a weapon in the ongoing domestic and international political struggles," why the Ukrainian experience stands as unique among similar nationalist projects, and how the example of the Government-in-Exile was emulated by other Ukrainian diaspora organizations and, eventually, by the post-Soviet state.

Alexander Schunka and Vadim Kukushkin elaborate Lemiski's focus on eastern Europe and on the state, reminding us that emigrants corresponded not only with relatives and friends but also with the government. Letters to officials differ most obviously from personal correspondence in the extent to which writers package what they imagine the recipients want to hear. This is the main argument advanced by Schunka, who warns that we should not take entirely at face value the tales of oppression and suffering penned by (or for) seventeenth-century émigrés from Catholic to Protestant principalities in early modern Europe. Gerber's essay on silences and prevarications reminds us, however, that in this respect personal and official correspondence vary in degree rather than in kind. Kukushkin reviews the correspondence received from temporary labor migrants by the Canadian consular representatives of the twentieth-century Russian czarist state. For workers isolated from fellow countrymen and from community institutions, the consuls were representatives of an accustomed power structure that could be approached using familiar strategies.

Both Kukushkin and Schunka explore how the structure and language of submissions to ancien regime paternalist states reinforced their supplicatory function. Indeed many of the letters to the Russian consuls assumed the archetypal form of the petition between subject and ruler, which is more overtly the object of Schunka's analysis. Written mostly by supplicants of peasant background, the language in the consular files, while sycophantic, was often innocently unorthodox. It aimed to further personalize a relationship founded not upon legal strictures and formal regulations dictating predictable outcomes, as in the modern state, but upon a sense of entitlement rooted in the czar's moral authority, and an understanding that rulers or their agents stood in relation to their subjects as a father to his children. Schunka's earlier supplicants came from more varied levels of society and were more dependent upon a coterie of professional scribes in the Saxonian capital Dresden, and so their petition letters demonstrated a greater acquaintance with state policy and with what the ruling elites regarded as appropriate language. But in both contexts the distinction between public and private discourse fades. Kukushkin's archive records extravagantly emotional examples of personalizing discourse ("I kiss your sweet lips"), and Schunka notes that the familial model of government was understood so literally that women often petitioned the wife of the Elector of Saxony, and young people his son. In both states, centuries apart, the writers adopted strategies of "moral self-empowerment" by retailing vividly pathetic details and casting themselves in a variety of tried-and-true roles, varying incarnations of the deserving subject. One grizzled veteran of the Thirty Years War even enclosed to the ruler of Saxony a portrait mapping the wounds he had suffered in state service. The theatricality of the paternalist state was evident at the peasant as well as at the official level.

A number of the essays published here were first presented at an international conference, *Reading the Emigrant Letter: Innovative Approaches and Interpretations*, sponsored by the Carleton Centre for the History of Migration and hosted at Carleton University in Ottawa, Canada, by the Centre's director, Bruce Elliott, in August 2003. Additional essays were solicited by coeditor Suzanne Sinke for the present collection. The conference enjoyed the financial backing of the Shannon Fund, which supports a number of initiatives in social and immigration history at Carleton University. This publication is assisted by the Jackman Foundation through the generosity of Rev. Edward Jackman.

Notes

1. Organization of Economic Cooperation and Development, *Trends in International Migration* (Paris: OECD, 2005); Stephen Castles and Mark J. Miller, *The Age of Migration: International Population Movements in the Modern World* (New York: Guilford Press, 1993); Timothy J. Hatton and Jeffrey G. Williamson, *The Age of Mass Migration: Causes and Economic Impact* (New York: Oxford University Press, 1998); Robin Cohen, *Global Diasporas: An Introduction* (Seattle: University of Washington Press, 1997); Leslie Page Moch, *Moving Europeans: Migrations in Western Europe since 1650* (Bloomington: Indiana University Press, 1992).
2. See for example Suzanne M. Sinke, *Dutch Immigrant Women in the United States, 1880–1920* (Urbana: University of Illinois Press, 2002), pp. 36, 44.
3. David A. Gerber, *Authors of Their Lives: The Personal Correspondence of British Immigrants to North America in the Nineteenth Century* (New York: New York University Press, 2006).

4. On the ubiquity of movement see the introduction to Dirk Hoerder, *Cultures in Contact: World Migrations in the Second Millennium* (Durham, NC: Duke University Press, 2002).

5. Homi Bhabha, "Between Identities," in *International Yearbook of Oral History and Life Stories, vol. III: Migration and Identity* (Oxford: Oxford University Press, 1994), p. 196.

6. On this, see David Fitzpatrick, *Oceans of Consolation: Personal Accounts of Irish Migration to Australia* (Ithaca: Cornell University Press, 1994), p. 503.

7. For example, see K.V. Rao, "The First Case Study of a Virtual Community," *Computer Communications* 20, no. 16 (January 1998): 1527–1533.

8. For a comparison of the volume of business correspondence and private letters, see Wolfgang Helbich, "The Letters They Sent Home," *Yearbook of German-American Studies* 22 (1987): 1–20.

9. "America letter" has often referred to letters containing descriptions of the United States by recent immigrants, sometimes with the qualification that it had to be destined for wide circulation. But scholars have not always agreed. See for example Axel Friman, "The Growth of an 'American Letter' Collection," *Swedish Pioneer Historical Quarterly* 19, no. 3 (1968): 158–161.

10. A notable exception is *Iowa Letters: Dutch Immigrants on the American Frontier*, new edition edited by Robert P. Swierenga and translated by Walter Lagerwey (Grand Rapids, MI: William B. Eerdmans Publishing, 2004). (Expanded and edited version of Johan Stellingwerff, ed., *Amsterdamse emigranten: onbekende brieven uit de prairie van Iowa, 1846–1873* [Amsterdam: Buijten & Schipperheijn, 1975.])

11. William I. Thomas and Florian Znaniecki, *The Polish Peasant in Europe and America*, 5 volumes, vols. 1 and 2 (Chicago: University of Chicago Press, 1918), vols. 3, 4, and 5 (Boston: Badger Press, 1919–1920). On the influence of this classic work, see, Lester R. Kurtz, *Evaluating Chicago Sociology: A Guide to the Literature with an Annotated Bibliography* (Chicago: University of Chicago Press, 1984), pp. 12, 84; Norbert Wiley, "Early American Sociology and the Polish Peasant," *Sociological Theory* 4 (Spring 1986): 20–34; Herbert Blumer, *Critiques of Research in the Social Sciences, I, An Appraisal of Thomas and Znaniecki's "The Polish Peasant in Europe and America"* (New York: Social Science Research Council, 1939); Kathleen Neils Conzen, "Thomas and Znaniecki and the Historiography of American Immigration," *Journal of American Ethnic History* 16 (Fall 1996): 37–46; Eli Zaretsky, ed., "Editor's Introduction," *The Polish Peasant in Europe and America* (Urbana: University of Illinois Press, 1984), pp. 23–35.

12. Wiley, "Early American Sociology and the Polish Peasant"; Zaretsky, "Editor's Introduction," pp. 1–23; Dorothy Ross, *The Origins of American Social Science* (New York: Cambridge University Press, 1991), pp. 347–353; Stowe Persons, *Ethnic Studies at Chicago, 1905– 45* (Chicago: University Chicago Press, 1987), pp. 45–59.

13. "Comment by W.I. Thomas," in Read Bain et al., "Part Two: Proceedings of the Conference on Blumer's Analysis," in Blumer, *Critiques of Research in the Social Sciences*, pp. 82–87. See also Evan Thomas, "Herbert Blumer's Critique of 'The Polish Peasant': A Post-Mortem on the Life History Approach in Sociology," *Journal of the History of the Behavioral Sciences* 14 (April 1978): 124–131; Stephen O. Murray, "W.I. Thomas, Behaviorist Ethnologist," *Journal of the History of the Behavioral Sciences* 24 (October 1988): 381–391.

14. Jon Gjerde, "New Growth on Old Vines—The State of the Field: The Social History of Immigration and Ethnicity in the United States," *Journal of American Ethnic History* 18 (Summer 1999): 40–65; O. Fritiof Ander, "Four Historians of Immigration," in *In the Trek of the Immigrants: Essays Presented to Carl Wittke* (Rock Island, IL: Augustana College Library, 1964), pp. 17–32; Moses Rischin, "Marcus Lee Hansen: America's First Transethnic Historian," in *Uprooted Americans: Essays to Honor of Oscar Handlin*, ed. Richard Bushman et al. (Boston: Little, Brown, 1979), pp. 319–347; Theodore Blegen, *Grass Roots History* (Minneapolis: University

of Minnesota Press, 1947), pp. 9–14, 18–20, 65–67, 144, and Blegen, ed., *Land of Their Choice: The Immigrants Write Home* (Minneapolis: University of Minnesota Press, 1955), pp. v–vii.

15. On claims of authenticity for immigrant letters, and the general utility of letters as the voice of the ordinary people, see Blegen, *Grass Roots History*, pp.18–20, and Blegen, *Land of Their Choice*, pp. v, viii, xi, xii; Arnold Barton, "As They Tell It Themselves: The Testimony of Immigrant Letters," in *Nordics in America*, ed. Odd S. Lovell (Northfield, MN: Norwegian-American Historical Association, 1993), pp. 143, 144–145; Alan Conway, ed., *The Welsh in America: Letters from the Immigrants* (Minneapolis: University of Minnesota Press, 1961), pp. vii, 7, 13; Marcus Lee Hansen, "Migration Old and New," in *The Immigrant in American History*, ed. Arthur M. Schlesinger (Cambridge: Harvard University Press, 1940), p. 4; Lloyd Husvedt, "Immigrant Letters and Diaries," in *The Prairie Frontier*, ed. Sandra Looney, Arthur R. Huseboe, and Geoffrey Hunt (Sioux Falls, SD: Nordland Heritage Foundation, 1984), pp. 38–51; Rudolph Jensen, "The Story Told in Denmark Letters: Correspondence from the Old Country," in Lovell, *Nordics in America*, p. 199; Walter D. Kamphoefner, Wolfgang Helbich, and Ulrike Sommer, eds., *News from the Land of Freedom: German Immigrants Write Home* (Ithaca: Cornell University Press, 1991), p. 30; William Mulder, "Through Immigrant Eyes: Utah History at the Grass Roots," *Utah Historical Quarterly* 22 (January 1954): 42–52; George Stephenson, "When America Was the Land of Canaan," *Minnesota History* 10 (September 1929): 237, 245.

16. Among the significant collections published over the course of many decades are: Samuel L. Bailey and Franco Ramella, eds., *One Family, Two Worlds: An Italian Family's Correspondence across the Atlantic, 1901–1922* (New Brunswick: Rutgers University Press, 1988); Blegen, ed., *Land of their Choice*, and Blegen and Pauline Forseth, eds. and trans., *Frontier Mother: The Letters of Gro Svendsen* (Northfield, MN: Norwegian-American Historical Association, 1950); Arnold Barton, ed., *Letters from the Promised Land: Swedes in America, 1840–1914* (Minneapolis: University of Minnesota Press, 1975); Herbert J. Brinks, ed., *Dutch American Voices: Letters from the United States, 1850–1930* (Ithaca: Cornell University Press, 1995); Wendy Cameron, Sheila Haines, and Mary McDougall Maude, eds., *English Immigrant Voices: Labourers' Letters from Upper Canada in the 1830s* (Montreal and Kingston: McGill-Queen's University Press, 2000); Conway, *The Welsh in America*; Charlotte Erickson, ed., *Invisible Immigrants: The Adaptation of English and Scottish Immigrants in Nineteenth Century America* (Coral Gable, FL: University of Miami Press, 1972); David Fitzpatrick, ed., *Oceans of Consolation: Personal Accounts of Irish Migration to Australia* (Ithaca: Cornell University Press, 1994); Frederick Hale, ed., *Danes in America* (Seattle: University of Washington Press, 1984), and Hale, *Their Own Saga: Letters from the Norwegian Global Migration* (Minneapolis: University of Minnesota Press, 1986); Kamphoefner et al., *News from the Land of Freedom*; Kerby A. Miller, Arnold Schrier, Bruce D. Boling, and David N. Doyle, *Irish Immigrants in the Land of Canaan: Letters and Memoirs from Colonial and Revolutionary America, 1675–1815* (New York: Oxford University Press, 2003); Patrick O'Farrell, ed., *Letters from Irish Australia, 1825–1929* (Sydney and Belfast: New South Wales University Press and Ulster Historical Foundation, 1984); Leo Schelbert and Hedwig Rapport, eds., *Alles Ist Ganz Anders: Auswandererschicksale in Briefen aus Zwei Jahrhunderten* (Freiberg: Walter-Verlag, 1977); Adolph E. Schroeder and Carla Schulz-Geisberg, eds., *Hold Dear As Always: Jette, A German Immigrant Life in Letters* (Columbia: University of Missouri Press, 1988); Ronald Wells, ed., *Ulster Migration to America: Letters of Three Families* (New York: Peter Lang, 1991); Josephine Wtulick, ed. and trans., *Writing Home: Immigrants in Brazil and the United States, 1890–1891* (Boulder: Eastern European Monographs, 1986); Selveig Zempel, ed., *In Their Own Words: Letters from Norwegian Immigrants* (Minneapolis: University Of Minnesota Press, 1991).

17. Joan W. Scott, "The Evidence of Experience," *Critical Enquiry* 17 (Summer 1991): 773–797; Orm Øverland, "Learning to Read Immigrant Letters: Reflections toward a Textual Theory," in *Norwegian American Essays*, ed. Øyvind Gullicksen, David C. Mauk, and Dina Tolfsby (Oslo: Norwegian Emigrant Museum, 1996), pp. 207–225; Stephen Fender, *Sea Changes: British Emigration and American Literature* (New York: Cambridge University Press); Gerber, *Authors of Their Lives*.

18. On epistolary fiction see Thomas O. Beebee, *Epistolary Fiction in Europe, 1500–1850* (Cambridge: Cambridge University Press, 1999).

19. William Merrill Decker, *Epistolary Practices: Letter Writing in America before Telecommunications* (Chapel Hill: University of North Carolina Press, 1998), p. 20.

20. John Durham Peters, *Speaking into the Air: A History of the Idea of Communication* (Chicago: University of Chicago Press, 1999), pp. 169–171. Peters and others who discuss this typically take Jacques Derrida's *The Postcard: From Socrates to Freud and Beyond*, trans. Alan Bass (Chicago: University of Chicago Press, 1987) as an intellectual building block.

21. See for examples of how letter-writers still must verify that they receive letters, or express their dismay that others may not be writing, or that they may not have received correspondence: Larry Siems, ed. and trans., *Between the Lines: Letters Between Undocumented Mexican and Central American Immigrants and Their Families and Friends* (Tucson: University of Arizona Press, 1992), pp. 119, 187.

22. Beebee, *Epistolary Fiction*, p. 22.

23. For example the forms of address used between spouses in Rebecca Earle, "Briefe und die Liebe in kolonialen Spanisch-Amerika (16. bis 18. Jahrhundert)," in *Briefkulturen und ihr Geschlecht*, pp. 135–162.

24. See for example Janie Vanpée, "Reading Differences: The Case of Letter 141 in Les Liaisons Dangereuses," *Eighteenth-Century Studies* 27, no. 1 (Autumn 1993): 85–110.

25. Lynne Magnusson, "Widowhood and Linguistic Capital: The Rhetoric and Reception of Anne Bacon's Epistolary Advice," *English Literary Renaissance* 31, no. 1 (2001): 3–33.

26. Martha Hanna, "A Republic of Letters: The Epistolary Tradition in France during World War I," *American Historical Review* 108, no. 5 (2003): 1349.

27. In general on using letter series to identify patterns of adaptation see Wolfgang Helbich, "Immigrant Adaptation at the Individual Level: The Evidence of Nineteenth-Century German-American Letters," *Amerikastudien* 42, no. 3 (1997): 407–418. For an example of using letters to examine national and racial identity, see Orm Øverland, "Becoming White in 1881: An Immigrant Acquires an American Identity," *Journal of American Ethnic History* 23, no. 4 (2004): 132–141.

28. Wolfgang Helbich, "Immigrant Adaptation at the Individual Level: The Evidence of Nineteenth-Century German-American Letters," *Amerikastudien-American Studies* 42, no. 3 (1997): 407–418.

29. Jürgen Habermas, *The Structural Transformation of the Public Sphere*, trans. Thomas Burger (Cambridge, MA: MIT Press, 1989).

30. On the manipulation of confessional form see Lucia Invernizzi Santa Cruz and Josefa de los Deloros Peña y Lillo, "El discurso confesional en el epistolario de Sor Josefa de los Dolores Peña y Lillo (siglo XVIII)," *Historia* 36 (2003): 179–190.

31. On this see Dana D. Nelson's review article, "Women and Gender in the State of Sympathy," *Feminist Studies* 28, no. 1 (2002): 175–187.

32. Kamphoefner et al., *News from the Land of Freedom*, pp. 34–35.

33. See the introduction to Marie-France Silver and Marie-Laure Girou Swiderski, eds., *Femmes en toutes lettres: Les épistolières du XVIIIe siècle* (Oxford: Voltaire Foundation, 2000); and the introduction to Christa Hämmerle and Edith Saurer, eds., *Briefkulturen und ihr Geschlecht: Zur Geschichte der privaten Korrespondenz vom. 16. Jahrhundert bis heute, L'homme Schriften* 7 (Vienna: Böhlau, 2003).

34. Roger Chartier, "Introduction," to *Correspondence: Models of Letter-Writing from the Middle Ages to the Nineteenth Century*, ed. Roger Charier, Alain Boureau, and Cécile Dauphin, trans. Christopher Woodall (Princeton: Princeton University Press, 1997 [1991]), pp. 1–23.

35. Cécile Dauphin, "Letter-Writing Manuals in the Nineteenth Century," in Charier et al., *Correspondence*, pp. 138, 143; see also Sara Jayne Steen, "Reading Beyond the Words: Material Letters and the Process of Interpretation," *Quidditas* 22 (2001): 55–69.

36. See in particular Roger Chartier, *On the Edge of the Cliff: History, Language and Practices*, trans. Lydia G. Cochrane (Baltimore: Johns Hopkins University Press, 1997), pp. 4–5; see also the extended discussion of this book in a special issue of *French Historical Studies*, of which the most persistent on this topic is William H. Sewell, Jr., "Language and Practice in Cultural History: Backing Away from the Edge of the Cliff," *French Historical Studies* 21, no. 2 (Spring 1998): 241–254.

37. "On Interpreting Immigrant Letters: The Case of Johann Caspar and Wilhelmina Honegger-Hanhart," *Yearbook of German-American Studies* 17 (Lawrence: University of Kansas Press, 1981): 141–152.

38. Kerby A. Miller, *Emigrants and Exiles: Ireland and the Irish Exodus to North America* (New York: Oxford University Press, 1985); David Fitzpatrick, *Oceans of Consolation*, p. 617.

39. Herbert J. Brinks, "Impressions of the 'Old' World, 1848–1940," *European Contributions to American Studies* 20 (1991): 34–47.

40. Donna R. Gabaccia, "Is Everywhere Nowhere? Nomads, Nations, and the Immigrant Paradigm of United States History." *Journal of American History* 86, no. 3 (1999): 1115–1134.

41. The most well-known of this social science literature is Linda Basch, Nina Glick Schiller, and Cristina Blanc-Szanton, eds., *Towards a Transnational Perspective on Migration* (New York: New York Academy of Sciences, 1992); for the use of transnational analysis by historians see David A. Gerber, "Theories and Lives: Transnationalism and the Conceptualization of International Migrations to the United States," *IMIS-Beiträge* 15 (2000): 31–53; Suzanne M. Sinke. "Crossing National Borders: Locating the United States in Migration History," *OAH Magazine* 19, no. 3 (May 2005): 58–62; and Donna R. Gabaccia and Franca Iacovetta, "Introduction," in *Women, Gender, and Transnational Lives: Italian Workers of the World* (Toronto: University of Toronto Press, 2002), especially pp. 4–7; Peter Kvisto, "Theorizing Transnational Immigration: A Critical Review of Current Efforts," *Ethnic and Racial Studies* 24, no. 4 (2001): 549–577.

42. On this see David A. Gerber, "Forming a Transnational Narrative: New Perspectives on European Migrations to the United States," *History Teacher* 35, no. 1 (November 2001): 61–77.

43. Arlie Russell Hochschild, "Love and Gold," in *Global Woman: Nannies, Maids, and Sex Workers in the New Economy*, ed. Barbara Ehrenreich and Arlie Russell Hochschild (New York: Metropolitan Books, 2002), pp. 15–30; Diane L. Wolf, "There's No Place Like 'Home': Emotional Transnationalism and the Struggles of Second-Generation Filipinos," in *The Changing Face of Home: The Transnational Lives of the Second Generation*, ed. Peggy Levitt and Mary C. Waters (New York: Russell Sage Foundation, 2002), pp. 255–294.

44. See for example Rhacel Salazar Parreñas, *Servants of Globalization: Women, Migration, and Domestic Work* (Stanford: Stanford University Press, 2001), p. 133.

45. D.H. Akenson, "Reading the Texts of Rural Emigrants: Letters from the Irish in Australia, New Zealand, and North America," *Canadian Papers in Rural History* VII (1990): 387.

46. Stephen Fender, *Sea Changes: British Emigration and American Literature* (Cambridge: Cambridge University Press, 1992).

47. Fitzpatrick, *Oceans of Consolation*.

Part I

Limits and Opportunities

How Representative are Emigrant Letters? An Exploration of the German Case

Wolfgang Helbich and Walter D. Kamphoefner

Of the millions of letters sent to Europe by immigrants to the United States in the nineteenth century, only a tiny, infinitesimal fraction has been preserved and is available to researchers. The lion's share has been forgotten, discarded, destroyed, or left in place when the bulldozers moved in. But besides the few letters accessible in archives and collections, there must be far more still in the hands of individuals who, for various reasons, could not be reached by any public appeal to make their treasures available and have them professionally preserved or were not convinced that they should.

The huge discrepancy between the number of letters written and the few available to scholars is probably the major reason why historians interested in utilizing emigrant letters have long wondered how representative these letters and their writers may be for the sum total of emigrants. It is well known that fairly large groups of emigrants generally did not write letters at all: those who died soon after arrival, the illiterates,[1] entire families that left no close relatives behind, individuals who deliberately broke off contact with home,[2] and a considerable portion of those who failed in one way or another.[3] Of course there are no statistics on these nonwriters, but it would be surprising if they constituted much less than 20 percent of adult immigrants. The crucial question is how similar or different the socioeconomic and demographic profile of these individuals was, compared to those who did write.

The question of representativeness impinges directly on several major issues of immigration historiography. Assessing the degree of social mobility was one of the prime concerns of the erstwhile new urban history, which quickly metamorphosed into a new social and ethnic history as well.[4] The issue of whether the American venture was worth the cost for immigrants from the lower rungs of German society, and indeed whether they had a realistic picture of the risks involved when they departed, looms large in both popular and scholarly images of emigration on the German side. On the American side and among U.S. scholars, the ease of acculturation or the strength and endurance of ethnic identity, in both their cultural and political manifestations, have been major areas of concern.[5] If letter-writers are highly unrepresentative of immigrants generally, their writings may give an overly optimistic picture of the potential for social mobility. However, scholars may also be led to underestimate the persistence of ethnicity (regardless of whether one views it positively or negatively), if letters are concentrated among those best equipped on the basis of education and exposure to foreign languages and cultures to navigate the channels leading into the American mainstream.

The problem of representativeness is, of course, closely connected with the questions of which sort of letters survived and surfaced, what may distinguish them from those that did not, and which part of the chain composed by writer, recipient, preservers, and finally donor may have been most essential. David Fitzpatrick, one of the scholars most knowledgeable about emigrant letters, makes an important point in this context: the underlying "population" is defined by preservers rather than by writers or readers.[6]

Dealing with German letters, we arrived at the impressionistic results that by far the largest two groups of our preservers and donors were professionals or other well-educated people, and farming families who had stayed on the same farm for several generations. The emphasis on the educated and on sedentary farmers is shared by David Fitzpatrick and Charlotte Erickson.[7] David Gerber would seem to agree, though he is pessimistic about the chances of verification; H. Arnold Barton and Stephen Fender, by contrast, find the quality or attractiveness of the letters or of the writers to be most important for preservation, but there is very little in our material to support such a position.[8]

It is not hard to find other intelligent guesses and interesting speculations. What has been missing thus far is an attempt to tackle empirically the problems of preservation and representativeness. What induced us to venture onto this untrod path was the existence of two bodies of sources that promised to shed light on the question—a light all the brighter because the material could be investigated from two different perspectives. The core element of both approaches is a collection that used to be called the Bochumer Auswanderbriefsammlung (BABS), and in its new repository in Gotha has been renamed to a more accurate Nordamerika-Auswandererbriefsammlung (NABS).[9] Built up mainly in the 1980s, the NABS now holds more than 7000 letters (originals or copies of originals), including some 350 sequences of three or more letters from the same writer or family group, that German immigrants sent back home from the United States during the nineteenth and early twentieth centuries. Almost all of the sequences and some of the single letters have been transcribed, and the biographies of the writers researched, a huge task that could be performed only with the help of generous grants from the Volkswagen Foundation. The collection provides ample information on the letter-writing emigrants, from the data the donors contributed, from the contents of the letters, and from our subsequent research.[10]

This is certainly the largest and most accessible collection of German emigrant letters, but for the purpose of the present study, another aspect is even more important. Because the bulk of the material was acquired by solicitation in the media, and incoming documents were immediately followed up by a standard questionnaire sent to donors in order to elicit as much information on the writers as possible, a substantial and sometimes quite lengthy correspondence with the donor often ensued. For about two out of three donors of letters, this correspondence contains enough information on the donors themselves that they, not just writers and recipients, can be included in this study. This is one aspect that makes our collection probably unique, and it is the one that allowed the approach from the German side, which factored in practically all the information available in NABS, including the content of letters.

The approach from the American side is also based in part on the NABS material, though here it did not involve donors, and letter content was only relevant for tracking writers across time and space. One important characteristic of the NABS collection and the editions we published from it is the fact that we were able to research the letter-writers in individual-level sources on both sides of the Atlantic, in particular in the U.S. Manuscript Census. This helped place letter-writers in a broader social context, allowed us to verify many of the assertions in the letters, and often to trace careers and fortunes beyond the point where a letter series ended. Thanks to a burgeoning genealogical market, census indexing has lately been growing by leaps and bounds, to the point where there is now a CD-ROM indexing all Germans in the 1870 census and permitting "intelligent" searches to allow for variant name spellings, or restricting the search to certain states or cities or persons of a specific age group or German state of birth. This index is now available on the web and linked to digitalized census microfilm images, further facilitating the tracing process.[11] Besides the writers we had previously located in the census, we were able to track down a number of "stragglers" with the help of this new technology for this essay.

But to know how representative our letter-writers are, we needed a cross-section of German immigrants to compare them with. Here the IPUMS project at University of Minnesota came to our aid.[12] It offers, freely downloadable to anyone, random samples of all U.S. manuscript censuses, including a 1:100 sample of the 1870 census that forms the basis of subsequent analyses. Besides having the best indexes, this census is the last one to enumerate the property holdings of individuals, thus making possible detailed economic comparisons between our letter-writers and a cross-section of German immigrants present in 1870. The availability of information on writers and donors in the Gotha collection, and of the easily accessible 1870 census profile, make it possible to look at the dossiers from two different sides, each providing different data and yielding different yet, as it turned out, mutually supporting results.

Who Are the Donors?

From a total of the over 7000 individual letters including some 350 sequences, we selected the sample dossiers on the basis of the following criteria, which were tailored to practical needs, but also meant to exclude subjectivity in the selection: sequences of three or more letters; the writer was present in the USA in 1870; only letters sent to Germany, and only German donors (material from the United States is atypical for preserved letters sent to Germany); sufficient information on writer and donor; and only if letters have been transcribed.

Ninety-five dossiers met these criteria and were used for this study. Of those, five had been obtained from German archives, 17 were donated by what one might call indirect or mediating donors,[13] and 73 by direct donors, that is, persons who were in possession of the letters, almost exclusively by inheritance. Of the latter category, about two thirds were related to the letter-writer or the recipient and usually both in a direct line (most frequently, the donor was the grandchild or great-grandchild of a writer's sibling), one third in a more tenuous way, while only three were totally unrelated.[14] Of the 70 related direct donors, 18, or one fourth, still bore the last name of the writer.

The itinerary of the letters, and the connections between writers and donors, is further illuminated by pointing out that the writer's birthplace and the donor's residence were identical in 31 of our 70 relevant dossiers (including 11 farms where the letters had rested from receipt to donation, six other villages, as well as ten larger towns and four cities). Another 24 places were different, but within a 25-mile radius of the writer's birthplace. Of the remaining 15, 11 birthplaces were in East Germany or Western Poland, where the moving was usually the result of postwar upheavals and not entirely voluntary. In other words, hardly more than five percent of the donors (or their ancestors) had moved far away from the letter-writer's home of their own free will.

It is hardly surprising that the educational level of the mediating donors is very high, with seven out of the 17 holding graduate degrees, four the equivalent of a BA, and none who did not finish secondary school. But it is remarkable that the same tendency, though not to the same degree, applies to direct donors as well. Of the 69 for whom we have reliable data, 23, or 34 percent, belong to the top group, and another 12 or 18 percent to the second one. Thus more than half of the (direct) donors were at least college-educated.[15] But the top-heaviness of our sample becomes especially striking when one compares these figures with those of the average of their age cohorts. Table 1.1 contains a more detailed breakdown as well as the comparative educational levels attained by Germans aged 60–65 in 1985 (three-fourths of donors were over age 55 in the mid-80s, when most of the letters were collected).[16] The index of representation in the far right column shows the degree of deviation of our 68 direct donors with reliable data from the educational levels of the general population.[17]

Table 1.1   Educational Level of Direct Donors Compared to German General Public

	All Letter Donors		1985 Micro-Census	Index of Representation
	N	Valid %	Valid %	
Primary (incl. Dropouts)	5	7.4	79.0	9
Some Secondary	10	14.7	9.8	150
Secondary Diploma	18	26.5	5.1	519
Bachelor Level	12	17.6	2.4	735
Professional or Graduate Degree	23	33.8	3.7	914
(No Data)	5			
Total	N = 73	100.0	100.0	100

Thus, statistically our sample of 68 would be expected to comprise 2.5 university graduates, plus 1.5 BAs. The actual figures are 23 and 12, which means an overrepresentation by a factor of nine and seven, respectively. At the other end of the spectrum, we have the mirror image. Statistically, 53 of our 68 donors should have no more than an elementary-school education. In fact, there are only five such persons in our sample B, more than a tenfold underrepresentation![18]

How does the extremely high overrepresentation of well-educated direct donors affect the problem of representation? Does it simply mean that such donors are more inclined than others to donate letters, but the writers of the letters they donate are indistinguishable from the rest? Or are these letters and writers special in any way? More specifically, are there measurable differences between the writers of letters donated by the educationally privileged and those from the less educated donors? If we can discover no difference between the writers of the letters donated by the two groups, we may be fairly sure that the extreme bias applies only to the donors and does not demonstrably interfere with representativeness of writers or content. We compared the dossiers contributed by the more educated donors, numbering 35 ("Group A"), with the rest of the sample of direct donors, 38 ("Group B"), by five criteria:

1. occupational training and occupation in Germany
2. contentment or success in America
3. level of formal education
4. motivation for emigration
5. social position of letter-writer's father.

There is no need to present tabular results from the first two criteria, because letters and their writers from the two groups of donors show appreciable differences in only one or two items. With regard to occupations in Germany, the two are virtually equal except that the A group contains only two farmers as opposed to eight in B, and by contrast A has eight letter-writers with commercial training, whereas B has only three. And in the somewhat problematic attempt to gauge "contentment with one's lot in America" or even "success beyond expectations" from the contents of the letters, the "success" result is almost the same for both groups, but among those who were contented there is a slight majority for the B group, whereas seven of the ten "malcontents," were among the A writers.

The pairs of figures in the occupational breakdown both point to a somewhat more privileged position of the A group, since farming could be understood as "learned nothing but working on the family farm," and commercial training, while clearly no guarantee for success in America, indicates privilege in the sense that it was more difficult to come by than learning other trades and imparted skills in writing and calculating, an interpretation fully born out by the statistics presented below. The "contentment" results, on the other hand, seem to show the reverse. They can be easily explained away, however, by supposing the B group to have been more modest in their expectations, and the A writers more ambitious or more critical in their assessment.

In table 1.2, the level of formal education attained by letter-writers while still in Germany is compared between groups A and B as well as the remainder (letters obtained from archives and indirect donors).

Here, we have added a category in addition to the levels of formal education: "deficient" was marked on the grounds that the letters are rather difficult to understand because of chaotic spelling and syntax, regardless of whether writers had attended primary school or not. Of the letters from immigrants with only a primary education (or particularly with a deficient one), the majority was provided by donors in Group B. Such donors still maintain a slight edge among writers with some secondary education but no diploma. However, at the level of a secondary diploma or above, Column A is ahead in every category, not overwhelmingly so, but clearly and significantly. In fact, Column A holds a 12:4 lead over Column B at these higher levels of education.

Table 1.3 classifies the motives for writers' emigration by the educational level of the letters' donors. Admittedly these categories are somewhat subjective and overlapping, but in most cases the variety of available sources allowed a safe classification (and there is usually a clear difference between escaping actual or expected misery, as opposed to being

Table 1.2   Educational Level of Donors Relative to that of Letter-Writers

Education of Emigrant	A: Better Educated Donors	B: Less Educated Donors	Indirect Donors, Archives	Total
Deficient Primary	1	3	4	8
Primary	13	17	13	43
Some Secondary	7	9	2	18
Secondary Diploma	5	0	3	8
Bachelor Level	5	3	0	8
University or Professional School	2	1	0	3
No Data	2	5	0	7
Total	N = 35	N = 38	N = 22	N = 95

Table 1.3   Motivation for Emigration Relative to Educational Level of Donors

Motivation of Emigrant	A: Better Educated Donors	B: Less Educated Donors	Indirect Donors, Archives	Total
Escaping Misery	11	21	12	44
Improving Adequate Situation	8	6	3	17
Political	5	5	1	11
Family Discord	5	2	3	10
Escaping Military Service	1	1	2	4
Escaping Trouble	4	2	0	6
Religious Motives	0	0	1	1
Unknown	1	1	0	2
Total	N = 35	N = 38	N = 22	N = 95

Notes:
Escaping Misery includes both actual and anticipated economic misery;
Improving Adequate Situation: hope for economic improvement from a situation that is not uncomfortable;
Political: political discontent or persecution, in most cases with economic and family motives added;
Family Discord: serious family tension, mostly father-son, sometimes with a step-parent, combined with other motives;
Escaping Military Service: avoiding conscription to 3 years service, usually with other motives added;
Escaping Trouble: with the law, with creditors, with unwed mothers;
Religious Motives: (in this case: Old Lutheran group emigration from Pommerania, 1830s).

assured of a comfortable subsistence but wanting affluence). Nearly twice as many writers in Group B as in Group A were trying to escape misery, whereas there is a slight edge for Group A among people trying to improve on an adequate situation.

The other entries are more difficult to interpret. Motivation is rarely one-dimensional; it usually has several ingredients and is highly volatile. One may say that in almost every emigrant leaving misery behind there is at least a trace of political discontent, whereas none of the other reasons indicated should be read as "nothing but"; usually some economic factors come into play as well. While emigrants motivated by political considerations (being actually hunted by the police, more generally persecuted or discriminated against, or just unhappy with the political situation) and draft dodgers are equally distributed, there is a clear preponderance of the "privileged" in cases involving unbearable tensions or constant friction within the family in Germany as well as running away from bankruptcy, creditors, the law, or irate fathers of pregnant women. Thus if better educated donors were also indicative of higher family status at the time of emigration, this may be indicative of the "black sheep" of such families taking refuge or being shunted off overseas.

Table 1.4 Occupation of Fathers of Emigrants Relative to Educational Level of Donors

Emigrant's Father's Occupation	A: Better Educated Donors	B: Less Educated Donors	Indirect Donors, Archives	Total
Farmer	10	9	5	24
Skilled Crafts	3	5	6	14
Affluent and/or College-Trained	14	4	3	21
No Data	8	21	8	37
Total	N = 35	N = 38	N = 22	N = 95

Table 1.4 is in some ways the shakiest statistic, since there are no data for 40 percent of the dossiers, but it is also the most convincing one for demonstrating the privileged position of the letter-writers connected with the better-educated donors. A and B do not differ appreciably with regard to letter-writers' fathers who were farmers or craftsmen. But they differ strikingly in the categories "no data," and in a diverse high-status group comprising university graduates, affluent millers or innkeepers, large landowners or administrators. The high degree of "no data" with the B group might seem to throw doubt on the overall results, but it actually reinforces them. It is far more likely that information has been preserved in the A group, especially for the more illustrious ancestors, than for the probably undistinguished lot in the B group.

All in all, the 14:4 ratio in the high status group confirms conclusively, or as conclusively as can be with such a small sample, the impression growing all along that the letters provided by the more educated donors are not like all the others, but that the A group letter-writers range a notch or two, on average, above the B group as far as education, training, occupation, the economic dimension of emigration motives, and the position of fathers are concerned. Some upward social mobility can be observed across generations in most of the families documented in our sample; there is also some downward mobility; but above and beyond those secular trends our dossiers and calculations show rather clearly that privilege not inevitably, but frequently runs in families.[19] So one of our major questions seems to have found a clear-cut answer: letter-writers from the better-educated donors are at least slightly privileged over the others, and we can thus conclude that if roughly a third of our dossiers rather than the statistical mean of five percent were provided by well-educated people, there is a significant bias in favor of the better-off and better-trained emigrants in our sample.

The clear, if slight margin of difference between the two groups points to two further explanations, probably in combination. The better-educated families were probably more likely than others to have preserved, rather than discarded, emigrant letters over the generations. They might have a greater pride in the achievements of their ancestors and a stronger sense of family tradition. This may partly explain why obviously more A group donors provided their documents than others. Pride and sense of tradition may lead to the wish to have their letters published, or at least preserved in a public space under professional care. But apart from family pride, there is in some cases, particularly with ancestors involved in some sort of scandal, the wish to contribute to scholarship, an idea that is not self-evident and is usually enhanced by education.

A sense of family tradition is not, however, the monopoly of the well-to-do and college graduates, as is witnessed by the high percentage of letters that were kept in one place from original receipt to donation, usually in substantial farm buildings that stayed in one family for more than a century. Underprivileged families, rural or urban, would be less likely to develop a sense of family tradition, might have less interest in written remnants of the past, tend to have less space for storing memorabilia, and probably move more frequently, a situation almost proverbial as an occasion for clearing out the attic.

The second explanation for that breathtaking degree of overrepresentation of well-educated donors, not contradicting, but complementing the former, concerns the attitude of potential donors approaching the threshold of actually donating a bundle of letters rather than leaving them in the drawer. A lawyer or engineer usually has at least a vague sense of the value of old letters, has been exposed to and trusts university-affiliated institutions, does not fear approaching intellectuals, and is used to writing to authorities, whereas any or all of the above may prevent other people from contributing their documents. If these assumptions hold true, it would follow that a large number of emigrant letters is still being held by people reluctant to cross the threshold to become donors, despite having learned of the solicitation in the media (plus others who have not been reached), and inversely that there is such a massive overrepresentation of well-educated donors not because they possess so many letters, but because they are more apt to donate them.[20] Future collecting projects might focus their attention on ways to overcome these barriers and reach a larger spectrum of potential donors.

Letter-Writers and Population of Germany Compared

Let us now turn back in time and review tables 1.2–1.4 from the perspective not of donors but of letter-writers, and focus on the far right columns showing the total for all letter-writers. If the proportions in the last column of table 1.2 applied to German emigration in 2000, no one would raise an eyebrow. But 100 years earlier, when only 2.2 percent of the male population in Prussia attained the right to attend college, the 20 percent in our sample with that qualification would have been considered sensational.[21] Moving further back in time, to the first half of the nineteenth century when almost all of our emigrants were born, the statistical situation becomes increasingly fuzzy. Piecing together information from several sources, one arrives at a percentage hovering around one percent of the same group successfully finishing secondary school.[22] This group of emigrants, with more than ten percent having attended a college or university, is thus breathtakingly exceptional. Looking at this state of affairs naively, two interpretations are plausible: either emigrants were better educated than the source population as a whole, or our sample is grossly skewed in favor of diploma holders, or a combination of the two. Similar patterns are suggested from the occupational profiles presented in table 1.5 below.

Table 1.3 as a whole as well as the Total column is more problematic than the others, since it is based on such uncertain data as the memories of donors three or four generations removed, and the interpretation of bits and pieces contained in the letters. On top of this, as explained earlier, what appears as neat categories often involved rather fuzzy combinations of several reasons, like "escaping misery plus family discord" or "political plus a chance to improve economic situation." While fully aware of this difficulty, we saw no choice but to enter the one motive that seemed dominant.[23] Against the foil of conventional wisdom or what we think we know of the German mass emigration, all of the results with the exception of "religion" are somewhat surprising: only 44 for escaping misery (less

Table 1.5   Occupation and Training of Male Emigrants in Germany

	Germany 1871–1874		Württemberg 1854–1871	Letter-Writers	
	%	valid %	%	N	valid %
Farmers	34.3	46.6	36.0	19	23
Crafts & Industry	14.6	19.8	56.4	40	49
Trade & Transport	5.6	7.6	5.2	10	12
Laborers	18.2	24.7	—	4	5
Professions	0.9	1.2	2.3	8	10
No Data	(26.4)	—	—	(14)	—
Total	100.0	100.0	100.0	N = 95	100

than half), no less than 17 for improving a tolerable situation (almost one out of five), an amazing 11 with political reasons (we always thought it was a tiny minority), just four dodging the draft (that reason usually figures more prominently), but 16 leaving because of trouble with the family or trouble with creditors or the law (aspects too frequently ignored by scholars). Taken together, and considering the lack of any such statistics on emigrants overall, let alone reliable ones, it would seem that these figures, however representative they may be, also constitute an appeal to historians to reexamine their estimates of the composition and motivation of German emigration.

Still, from what we think we know about the migration in general, one would suspect that "misery" is at least somewhat underrepresented in our sample, whereas individuals with a modest to comfortable subsistence who are lured by the prospect of becoming affluent or rich are rather overrepresented. The political reasons might well be somewhat inflated, not only because of problems of definition (reaching from dislike of a prince or a tax to running for one's life), but also because in the family tradition such motives sound more honorable than many others, including tension within the family and conflict with the law. The latter two might not be too far off the mark in representation.

Better statistics on education epoch, but they relate to the occupational training and occupations of German emigrants rather than to the entire source population (see table 1.5). Unfortunately, they are either for the (slightly) wrong period (German Empire, 1871–1874)[24] or for a fairly small state making up less than one-tenth of German emigration (Kingdom of Württemberg, 1854–1871).[25] Yet we know that changes in the composition of emigration tended to be slow, and even though Württemberg's emigration had a structure different from that of other German states, the basic pattern was similar.

Apart from other handicaps, the two statistics are rendered more problematic by the different methods in calculating them, the most conspicuous being Württemberg's lacking the categories of "Laborers" and "No Data." This excludes a direct comparison between the two statistics, although the missing laborers can be taken into account by assuming they are included in "Crafts and Industry," and the "No Data" category, mostly involving dependents, can be safely calculated out of the percentages for Germany, with the other occupational groups inflated proportionally. While the adjusted percentages of the two statistics are almost ten points apart, the underrepresentation of farmers in our sample by a factor of about two is apparent. In the "Crafts and Industry" category, our 49 percent plus the five percent laborers, now totaling 54 percent, falls roughly between the adjusted figures for Germany (with the laborers added) and the Württemberg percentage. Looking at the category of "Laborers" separately, this group is clearly underrepresented in the sample compared to overall figures for Germany, although some "Laborers" in the latter column doubtless belong to the agriculture group. The two categories most seriously overrepresented among letter-writers are "Trade and Transportation" and "Professions," by factors of two and four, respectively if one takes the statistics at face value. (In fact, the "Trade and Transportation" figures for Germany and Württemberg must be cut at least in half because of all the blue-collar railroad and riverboat personnel and the teamsters that are included.) Thus, our sample is clearly top-heavy with respect to occupation, though not as much as with the level of education.

Several other aspects of representation can be considered without resort to tables. Religious affiliation presents a problem. Although nowhere officially recorded on either side of the Atlantic, the percentage of Catholics among German immigrants has been estimated at a minimum of one-third, and probably higher before 1870 when eastern Germany was little affected by emigration.[26] Our sample seems rather skewed: 73 Protestants (including Evangelical, Old Lutherans, Reformed, and even Baptists), 19 Roman Catholics, and three without data. This leaves plenty of room for speculation about the literacy level of Catholics, though as will be seen later, the deficit of South Germans explains at least part of the difference.[27] Here our data are clear and free from ambiguity, but the interpretation is all the more difficult given the lack of comparative material on immigrants generally.

The gender ratio is even more out of balance with the letter-writers than their religious makeup. Here we have just 11 women versus 84 men as primary writers, that is, those who wrote alone or, if other people wrote as well, those who wrote most of the letters. Nine of the 11 women had a man as a secondary writer. If one takes the analysis one step further, figuring that the gross imbalance can be partly corrected by women who were secondary writers together with a man, this helps, but not much: 19 of the men had a woman writing at their side, resulting in 30 women writing one way or the other. So only 30 of the 95 letter groups involve any women writing, even including secondary writers. One might add that 51 men were the sole writers in their dossier, while 14 men wrote with another man (brother, son, etc.). For once, we have a reliable statistic as a foil. For the years of emigration covered in our sample, 1830–1865, the portion of males among immigrant arrivals was about 61 percent, with a downward trend over time, (though given a higher return migration and possibly a higher mortality among males, Germans in the 1870 census were somewhat more balanced, only 55.7 percent male).[28]

So all too obviously, women in our sample are considerably underrepresented. This is interesting and may be culturally significant and reflective of the role of women in the nineteenth century. But it does not help in deciding between two possible scenarios: 1) our sample is grossly biased against women, who in fact wrote far more but whose letters were presumably preserved less and donated less, or 2) our sample is fully representative for the minority of women who did actually write. Either alternative could fully account for the imbalance, but one suspects that both came into play.

Internal evidence from the letter collection is somewhat ambiguous. There are instances such as the Lehmann family where a better educated husband wrote to his wife's relatives as well as his own, but in giving a resume of the Civil War, he dealt with a topic that was clearly part of a man's world, and his wife did add some lines on family matters.[29] Where siblings of both genders emigrated and settled in proximity, both males and females often wrote home, as with the Klinger and the Stille families.[30] In the latter case, in fact, not only did brother, sister, and brother-in-law write to the family back on the homestead, but even the latter's second wife did, although neither she nor her husband was related to the recipient. In this case it may be of significance that all originated from the same village and were personally acquainted.[31]

Often more important than the emotional role transatlantic correspondence played in maintaining family ties was the economic role it played in providing those left behind with pertinent information to facilitate the decision-making process about whether to follow. And this latter function belonged primarily to the "man's world": all the familiar price lists for land, farm animals, agricultural products or store goods; elaborate accounts of weather, climate, and harvests; information on transportation, schools, and churches; not to mention the sometimes heated elaborations and insinuations about inherited money and distributing it fairly. Women certainly had something to say about such things, but in the two dozen cases in which we have husband and wife both writing, the woman mostly leaves those matters to her man.

Another factor affecting the gender balance is education. Above the elementary level, and sometimes even there, boys had greater educational opportunities than girls in the society of origin. Women with a secondary education were very unlikely to emigrate, whereas the educated young men who figure disproportionately among these letter-writers frequently went alone, and often married down socially or married out into the Anglo-American community. However, considering that these educated young men were not seldom the black sheep of their families whose attainments were not always commensurate with their social and educational level, it is of greater relevance to examine how the socioeconomic profile of letter-writers on the American side compared with that of the average German immigrant at the time.

Letter-Writers and Other German Immigrants Compared

The following section compares the sample of immigrant letter-writers from NABS with a representative cross-section of German immigrants present in the 1870 census, obtained from the IPUMS. Because letter-writers were practically all adults, whereas the immigrant population (and the immediate families of the letter-writers) includes many children, these comparisons include all German natives among the immediate families of writers (or an adult subset of them when analyzing occupations).[32]

Given the fact that most of our letter collecting was carried out in the 1980s before the collapse of the GDR provided access to the German east, one might expect some regional concentrations rather than a uniform coverage of German places of origin. Indeed, as shown in table 1.6, a comparison of birthplaces reported by letter-writers and their immediate families in the 1870 census does reveal some contrasts with places of origin reported in the IPUMS sample, although not always in the direction one might expect. Since individual Prussian provinces are seldom reported in the U.S. census, the only unambiguous eastern states of origin are Saxony and Mecklenburg. They do in fact come in below quota as birthplaces of letter-writers, but not by much. Their index of representation compared to immigrants in the IPUMS sample is 73 (i.e. 73 percent of the expected proportion based on the IPUMS), a difference that with such small numbers could easily be due to random variation. The most surprising figure in the table is the serious underrepresentation of southern and southwest Germans, who make up barely half the expected numbers. The state most

Table 1.6   German States of Origin as Reported in the 1870 U.S. Census

	Letter-Writers		IPUMS Sample		Index of Representation
	N	%	N	%	
East: Saxony & Mecklenburg	9	4.7	972	6.4	73
South & Southwest (incl. Hessen)	46	24.0	6620	43.6	55
Prussia	107	55.7	5911	38.9	143
Other North & Northwest	30	15.6	1695	11.2	139
Total	219	100.0	15198	100.0	100

heavily overrepresented is Prussia, though unfortunately it stretches across the whole north of Germany, making it difficult to discern exactly which parts of Prussia are overrepresented. But other northwestern German states are only a fraction behind them in their relative presence among letter-writers, suggesting that the bulk of Prussian writers originated west of the Elbe.

Two possible explanations for this regional skewing come to mind, one involving letter collecting, the other involving letter survival. The University of Bochum, where the collecting was carried out, lies in former Prussian territory in northwestern Germany, and may have drawn a greater response from people living close by than from more distant letter owners in southern Germany. (Also, in the Palatinate, the most emigration-prone province of all Germany, a letter collection program was already underway before ours.) The public lecturing we did, often with the side-effect of recruiting letters, was confined almost entirely to Northwest Germany, including both Prussian and non-Prussian areas. Secondly, conditions for preserving letters were optimal on the farms of Northwest Germany, where a relatively prosperous peasantry practiced single-child inheritance, and a stem family often stayed on the same farmstead for centuries, in contrast to the greater fluctuation that characterized partible inheritance regions of much of southern Germany.

With respect to regional distribution across the United States shown in table 1.7, the letter-writers roughly reflect the national profile of German immigrants, but there are several differences worth noting. The region with the largest deficit among letter-writers is the Northeast, coming in at barely half its quota; the eastern Midwest and the South Atlantic regions are also slightly underrepresented. All three of these are heavily urbanized regions (Baltimore accounting for more than half of all Germans in the

Table 1.7   Place of Residence by Census Region as Reported in the 1870 U.S. Census

	Letter-Writers		IPUMS Sample		Index of Representation
	N	%	N	%	
Northeast	33	16.6	5367	32.2	52
E. North Central	79	39.7	7010	42.1	94
W. North Central	51	25.6	2410	14.5	177
South Atlantic	8	4.0	758	4.6	87
South Central	14	7.0	755	4.5	156
Mountain & Pacific	14	7.0	352	2.1	333
Total	199	100.0	16652	100.0	100

South Atlantic region). All other regions of the country are overrepresented (the West Coast, with the highest index, involves quite small numbers), but the farm country of the western Midwest stands out in both absolute and relative terms, coming in 77 percent above quota with one-fourth of all writers. In part, this may reflect the tendency of writers from rural backgrounds to settle in areas offerings access to agricultural land. Also, southern Germans, who are underrepresented in the collection, were more heavily concentrated in the east.[33] But a purely methodological factor could also be at work: poorer census coverage and greater difficulty of tracing people in the large urban areas, coupled with the fact that recent arrivals often stopped first in cities, even if they moved on later.

Given the strong tendency of farm families in Germany to preserve letters, one might expect an overrepresentation of immigrant farmers among letter-writers, and a corresponding deficit among urbanites. Such tendencies are indeed present; as shown in table 1.8, farmers make up 59 percent more than their share among the letter-writers, compared with the nationwide cross-section from IPUMS, and the non-farm population shows a 22 point deficit. Similar tendencies can be observed in the proportion of population living in large cities of over 100,000, shown in table 1.9. Nationwide, almost 30 percent of all German immigrants lived in big cities in

Table 1.8 Proportion of Immigrants Living in Farm Households, 1870

	Letter-Writers		IPUMS Sample		Index of Representation
	N	%	N	%	
Non-Farm	113	56.8	12127	72.8	78
Farm	86	43.2	4525	27.2	159
Total	199	100.0	16652	100.0	100

Table 1.9 Proportion of Immigrants Residing in Cities of over 100,000 Inhabitants, 1870

	Letter-Writers		IPUMS Sample		Index of Representation
	N	%	N	%	
Below 100,000	160	80.4	11655	70.1	115
Above 100,000	39	19.6	4964	29.9	66
Total	199	100.0	16619	100.0	100

1870; among letter-writers, the figure is less than 20 percent, only two-thirds of their quota, and the rural and small town share is correspondingly higher. So all in all, there is a substantial, though not overwhelming, bias in the letters toward the rural and farm population.

When one examines the occupational patterns displayed in table 1.10, the favorable position of letter-writers is more apparent. As suggested earlier, the agricultural sector as a whole is somewhat overrepresented; moreover, the letter-writers included more farmers and fewer farm laborers than Germans as a whole. But in general, the higher one goes on the occupational scale, the greater the overrepresentation of letter-writers. The white collar segment comes in with an index of 162, almost two-thirds above quota. Letter-writers make up just three-fourths their share of the mostly skilled blue collar category. And at the lowest rank, unspecified common laborers, the letter-writers come in at 71 percent of their quota. This is the strongest evidence so far of a positive selectivity among letter-writers.

Since the 1870 census includes figures on value of real estate and personal property, it is possible to examine how much this occupational skewing is reflected in the reported wealth of immigrants. Not surprisingly, the data on wealth show considerable discrepancy between letter-writers and run of the mill immigrants. As displayed in tables 1.11 and 1.12, the mean figures on real estate holdings and total wealth (the sum of real and personal property values) were in every instance one-half to two-thirds higher for letter-writers than for the cross section of German immigrants in the 1870 census. This is true regardless of whether the analysis is restricted to household heads (table 1.11) or includes all males aged twenty-one and above (table 1.12).

Similarly, the proportion reporting any amount of real estate or total wealth was higher by one-fourth to one-half for letter-writers than for

Table 1.10   Occupational Breakdown, 1870, German-Born Males Age 21+

	Letter-Writers		IPUMS Sample		Index of Representation
	N	%	N	%	
Non-Manual	25	22.9	1135	14.1	162
Farmers & Farm Laborers	37	33.9	2252	27.9	122
Skilled & Unskilled Manual	34	31.2	3358	41.7	75
Laborers, non-specified	9	8.3	942	11.7	71
Not in Labor Force	4	3.7	371	4.6	80
Total	109	100.0	8058	100.0	100

Table 1.11   Average Wealth Figures, 1870, German Males Age 21+

	Real Estate		Total Wealth	
	Letter-Writers	IPUMS Sample	Letter-Writers	IPUMS Sample
N	109	8071	109	8071
Mean Value	$2790	$1703	$3936	$2470
Writers' % of IPUMS Mean	164%		159%	
% with any Wealth	59.6	40.6	76.1	60.2
Writers' % of IPUMS Mean	147%		126%	

Table 1.12   Average Wealth Figures, 1870, German Male Household Heads Age 21+

	Real Estate		Total Wealth	
	Letter-Writers	IPUMS Sample	Letter-Writers	IPUMS Sample
N	89	6087	89	6087
Mean Value	$3417	$2195	$4810	$3101
Writers' % of IPUMS Mean	156%		155%	
% with any Wealth	73.0	51.9	92.1	75.2
Writers' % of IPUMS Mean	141%		122%	

Germans in general. No doubt some of this contrast is due to the "I wasn't doing well so I didn't write" phenomenon mentioned earlier. But there are some extenuating factors that make the letter-writers less exceptional than they initially appear.

Besides the occupational skewing, another reason why letter-writers were more prosperous than Germans in the average cross section is the fact that they were older and had been in the country longer and thus had more time and opportunity to accumulate wealth. In this context, Joseph Ferrie has documented annual wealth gains of close to 15 percent for immigrants in the mid-nineteenth century.[34] As table 1.13 shows, regardless if one looks at the mean or the median age, male German letter-writers were on average two to three years older than their compatriots nationwide.

Table 1.13   Age in 1870 Census, All German-Born Individuals

Sex	Letter-Writers			IPUMS Sample		
	Mean	Median	N	Mean	Median	N
Male	39.1	39.0	119	36.5	36.0	9283
Female	35.0	34.0	80	35.3	34.0	7369
Total	37.5	37.0	199	36.0	35.0	16652

Women letter-writers, by contrast, were right at the overall average, but it was primarily the men's earning power that determined the wealth of a family. In part, the apparent prosperity of writers simply reflects the fact that the most recent arrivals proved the most difficult to locate in the census—not surprising given the language barrier and the tendency to change residence frequently at the outset.[35] The year of arrival, which is available for most letter-writers, provides additional evidence that they had been in the country longer than the average German. Even without any controls for mortality, the mean year of arrival for all Germans who came between 1831 and 1869 was 1854; if this was restricted to persons alive in 1870, it would doubtless be a year or two later. For the letter-writers present in 1870, the mean and median year of arrival were 1853 and 1852 respectively. So some of the financial advantages of letter-writers was simply due to the longer time they had had to accumulate wealth in America. Letter-writers and their immediate families had a higher proportion of male immigrants than did immigrant Germans generally. While the IPUMS sample was 55.7 percent male, the figure for letter-writers is nearly five points higher, 60.5 percent male. This, too, would have favored their wealth accumulation. Moreover, a much higher proportion of immigrants in letter-writer households were in the prime decades of life: nearly 61 percent were in their thirties and forties, a figure 14 points higher than with the IPUMS group. These structural factors, then, explain some of the wealth advantages shown by this group of letter-writers.

There are also cultural indicators that can give us an idea of how well immigrants were integrated into the host society. Of these, intermarriage is one of the most telling, and also one of the most accessible from census information. As shown in table 1.14, here the letter-writers prove to be closely matched to the German immigration population, generally. Overall, the endogamy rate for German males was 80 percent; for letter-writers, it was just four points lower. With the minority that married outside their nationality, both letter-writers and Germans in the IPUMS sample showed a similar clear preference for the American-born over other

Table 1.14   Ethnicity of Spouse, All German-Born Family Heads

	Wife's Birthplace			
	Germany	United States	Other	Total
Letter-Writers	65	15	6	86
	76%	17%	7%	100%
IPUMS Sample	4524	829	319	5672
	80%	15%	6%	100%
Index of Representation	95	119	124	100

immigrants. In both cases, the exogamy rates shown here are somewhat exaggerated. In fact, many American-born women were second-generation ethnics, and France, Switzerland, and Austria were the three leading sources of "other foreign spouses" in all cases including many speakers of German. If male letter-writers appear to be slightly more acculturated than the German cross section, the opposite is true of the few women in the sample. Only one of 66 German women in the writers' families married outside her group, less than two percent; for the IPUMS sample it is close to nine percent. One explanation for this is that most of the exogamous women had probably come over in their youth with their families and had grown up in the New World; there are few letter-writers of this type in the collection, male or female. Moreover, young men were much more likely than young women to immigrate alone. So at least on the male side, the letter-writers were quite typical of Germans generally in their marriage patterns.

In summary, then, the figures presented here call upon us to use letter evidence with caution, but they do not show patterns that are wildly divergent from the general tendencies among German immigrants. In all the measures of socioeconomic status in America, there is not a single index of representation over 200 or under 50 (double or half the expected proportion). Some of the greater wealth of letter-writers can be attributed to a longer period of accumulation. One of the most surprising patterns to emerge is the preponderance of northern and northwestern German letter-writers and the deficit of south Germans. But all in all, the American data provide considerable reason for confidence in immigrant letter evidence.

Conclusions

From an empirical study one should expect more clear-cut results, less lee-way for alternative interpretations, and fewer loose ends. In defense of our experiment it might be said that even if many of our findings are open to various interpretations, without this study we and other scholars would not even have the facts and figures to speculate about. Looking at the German side alone, the huge overrepresentation of well-educated donors in a neutral sample of a large collection cannot be doubted, and the "privileged families through generations" hypothesis would seem to be confirmed to a certain degree. There is a very high overrepresentation of the privileged in education and property not just among the donors, but among the letter-writers as well, and inversely the underprivileged, although certainly present, are clearly underrepresented compared to emigrants in general. But putting these findings of misrepresentation into hard figures is most difficult, and turning them into something like a conversion table is impossible.

Still, although letter-writers reported somewhat more wealth in 1870 than the average German immigrant at the time, the discrepancy is not as great as might be expected given their social profile on the German side. Especially among immigrants of poorer origins, there was no doubt a greater tendency to write home in situations of prosperity than in times of want. But there is a compensating factor: at higher levels of society, it was often the black sheep of the family who chose or was encouraged to go to America. Sometimes the new environment brought a turnaround in habits and achievements, but more often it did not. Thus our letter collection includes a disproportionate number of these prodigal sons, begging for funds and/or forgiveness. Consequently, the concentration of letters from better educated writers (and donors) does not inflate the wealth and occupational profile of immigrant letter-writers to the degree that one might have expected.[36]

What conclusions can be drawn from this empirical exercise? Probably first and foremost that others might continue where we have left off by trying other samples, other nationalities, other approaches, and different methodologies to fill the gaps we have left and follow up the leads we have offered.[37] This way, more generalization ought to become possible, some of our conclusions may be confirmed and some questioned, almost certainly our methods refined. But it seems safe to claim that every letter-writer is representative or unrepresentative in so many different ways by age, place of origin, social background, education, occupation, financial circumstances, residence, personality, marital and family status, religion, politics, and so on but that the issue of representation depends heavily on what aspect is being researched.

It would be hard to use emigrant letters as a historical source without at least a rough idea of "how typical" they are, which is perhaps a better term in that it does not pretend to the exactness that "representation" usually connotes. But a rough measure, a tendency, would be sufficient in most cases. If letters are used to investigate clear-cut questions, for example in the Civil War context, "abolitionist," "enthusiastically pro-Union," "indifferent," "reluctant draftee," or "Copperhead"; or with regard to the Know-Nothing riots of the 1850s "shocked and scared," "considers remigration," "burning for revenge," or "playing down the danger," an interesting phenomenon should emerge. The French sociologist Daniel Bertaux discovered it a generation ago, to his great surprise, when he conducted a life history study of bakers in France. He found that in his oral history interviews, the law of diminishing returns was at work, and he learned less and less that was new, until full saturation was reached and nothing new at all was added.[38] There are great differences in methodology as well as content between interviews with bakers and emigrant letters, but they have one point in common: on any clearly defined question, there are only a limited number of positions taken by letter-writers, and after a while, no new position or type is added. Obviously, within those types, details and nuances will differ, but the point is that we may be confident after reading twenty or thirty letter-writers that we have obtained the three or five or, rarely, eight types of response that can be found.

Of course, in the light of the evidence presented here, it would not be justified to simply percentage the different positions and then project these proportions on the immigrant population overall. Granted, if a large majority of letters points in one direction, this may well reflect majority opinion, and if another position has a half-dozen letters to back it up, one cannot dismiss it as totally insignificant. But as important as what was being said is the question of who was saying what. Whenever opinions appear to vary by social origins, one must be cautious not to give the views of immigrants of privileged backgrounds more weight than they deserve. However, if the spectrum of opinions on a given issue bears no apparent relation to the social background of those expressing them, it probably comes closer to a "Gallup poll" of the immigrant community at large. A generation ago, the then "new social history" provided an important and far reaching impetus for historians to listen to the inarticulate, but more recent census indexing projects have given us additional tools that allow us to determine just how ordinary in fact were the presumably undistinguished Americans, immigrants or otherwise, from whom we have surviving primary documents in their own voices.

Notes

1. For an interesting exception see Walter D. Kamphoefner, Wolfgang Helbich, and Ulrike Sommer, eds., *News from the Land of Freedom: German Immigrants Write Home* (Ithaca: Cornell University Press, 1991), pp. 383–405, esp. n.1.

2. This is often apparent from transatlantic gossip; one emigrant wrote home in 1856, "You can reassure Johannes Durst's family and tell them that I myself put the letter into their son's hands, & every time I visited him I entreated him to write to his parents. If he hasn't done it yet, it's not my fault." Ibid., 156.

3. In the German letters we have worked with, there are dozens containing passages like the following, where emigrant Georg Heubach wrote to his siblings on October 20, 1863, a decade after his arrival "If I had stayed poor I would have been lost to you forever, and I couldn't write what was untrue, and I was ashamed of being poor, and that is why I didn't write to you in those first years." Translation of Wolfgang Helbich and Walter D. Kamphoefner, eds., *Deutsche im Amerikanischen Bürgerkrieg: Briefe von Front und Farm, 1861–1865* (Paderborn: Schöningh, 2002), p. 238. An English translation will be published as *Germans in the Civil War: The Letters They Wrote Home* (Chapel Hill: University of North Carolina Press, 2006).

4. See the historiographic overview in John N. Ingham, ed., "Comment and Debate: Thernstrom's *Poverty and Progress*: A Retrospective after Twenty Years," special issue, *Social Science History* 10, no.1 (Spring 1986), with comments by Edward Pessen, Michael Frisch, and Steven A. Reiss, and a response by Stephan Thernstrom.

5. For an insightful interpretive summary of this broad field see Jon Gjerde, *The Mind of the West: Ethnocultural Evolution in the Rural Middle West, 1830–1917* (Chapel Hill: University of North Carolina Press, 1997).

6. David Fitzpatrick, *Oceans of Consolation. Personal Accounts of Irish Migration to Australia* (Ithaca: Cornell University Press, 1994), p. 28.

7. Ibid., 28–29. Charlotte Erickson, *Invisible Immigrants. The Adaptation of English and Scottish Immigrants in Nineteenth-Century America* (Coral Gables, FL: University of Miami Press, 1972), pp. 6– 7.

8. David A. Gerber, "Theories and Lives: Transnationalism and the Conceptualization of International Migrations to the United States," *IMIS-Beiträge* 15 (2000): 31–53, cited 47–48. H. Arnold Barton, "As They Tell It Themselves: The Testimony of Immigrant Letters," in *Nordics in America: The Future of Their Past*, ed. Odd S. Lovell (Northfield, MN: The Norwegian-American Historical Association, 1993), pp. 138–139; Barton refers to his experience in editing *Letters From the Promised Land: Swedes in North America, 1840–1914* (Minneapolis, 1975). Stephen Fender, *Sea Changes. British Emigration & American Literature* (Cambridge University Press, 1992), pp. 18, 19.

9. Description (in German) and list of holdings: www.auswandererbriefe.de. The entire collection was microfilmed in 1998 by the Library of Congress Manuscripts Division, Accession # 21,732 (40 reels). This material was drawn upon for both of the anthologies published by Helbich and Kamphoefner that are cited in Kamphoefner et al., *News from the Land of Freedom* and Helbich and Kamphoefner, *Deutsche im Amerikanischen Bürgerkrieg*.

10. For more detail on background research see Kamphoefner et al., *News from the Land of Freedom*, pp. 36–42.

11. Heritage Quest, *World Immigration Series: Germans in the 1870 U.S. Federal Census* (CD; 2000); http://www.heritagequest.com/.

12. Steven Ruggles and Matthew Sobek et al., *Integrated Public Use Microdata Series: Version 3.0* (Minneapolis: Historical Census Projects, University of Minnesota, 2003); documentation at http://www.ipums.org/usa/index.html.

13. People who, as local or family historians or genealogists, solicited letters from holders for their own projects, and made copies available to the collection.

14. One donor found emigrant letters among the papers of his grandfather, who had been an auctioneer, and two found theirs in second-hand purchases, in the secret drawer of a desk and a flea market chest.

15. Ascertaining the level of formal education with the material at our disposal is often a hazardous endeavor, as we never asked donors about their own background but

drew our conclusions from the correspondence. But in order to exclude errors at least in the surprising figures at the top, we put donors and letter-writers in the top two categories only if there was clear evidence for their having earned such degrees.

16. German 1985 microcensus, 2, Bevölkerung und Erwerbstätigkeit, 2.8, Bevölkerung im Juni 1985 nach Altersgruppen und Bildungsabschluss. Statistisches Bundesamt Deutschland, www.destatis.de/basis/d/biwiku/ bildab1.htm, July 15, 2003.

17. The index of representation (or relative concentration) is a common social-scientific measure often used to gauge a subgroup's deviation from an overall population. It can be interpreted as a percentage of parity, where an index of 100 indicates representation in an educational category equal to that of the general population, and an index of 50 shows representation at half the expected rate, and index of 200, double the expected rate at a given educational level, etc.

Considering that roughly one-third of the donors (26 of 90) were women, and in the German mini-census, university graduates constitute 1.4 percent of the female age cohort, whereas for men it is 4.9 percent, the weighted average of 3.7 percent was used, rather than the 2.8 percent for both genders combined in the mini-census. Similar weighted averages were calculated for the other educational levels in table 1.1.

18. Including the 17 indirect donors would increase the imbalance by some percentage points, but they are of less concern because they would not involve the issue of social and educational status being passed down across generations.

19. For a sophisticated sociological discussion of status and occupational transmission and transmissibility in families, see Daniel Bertaux and Isabelle Bertaux-Wiame, "Heritage and its Lineage: A Case History of Transmission and Social Mobility over Five Generations," in *Pathways to Social Class: A Qualitative Approach to Social Mobility*, ed. Daniel Bertaux and Paul Thompson (New York: Oxford University Press, 1997), pp. 62–97.

20. Our collection experience sheds additional light on this problem. In 1981, we ran elaborate appeals for emigrant letters in *Die Zeit*, a highbrow weekly, and subsequently in *Hör Zu!* a mass-circulation TV guide. The former yielded close to 1500 letters, the latter only about 400, despite an eightfold advantage in circulation figures.

21. Peter Lundgren, *Sozialgeschichte der deutschen Schule im Überblick. Teil I: 1770–1918* (Göttingen, 1980), Table 22, p. 119.

22. Hartmut Titze with Hans-Georg Herrlitz, Volker Müller-Benedict, and Axel Nath, *Datenhandbuch zur deutschen Bildungsgeschichte, Band I: Hochschulen. Das Hochschulstudium in Preußen und Deutschland 1820–1944*, ed. (Göttingen: Vandenhoeck & Ruprecht, 1987), pp. 66, 172, 226.

23. Our published work provides illustrations of emigrants classified under most of these categories of motivation: Escaping Misery: Lenz, Hecks, Klingers, and Winkelmeiers in *News From the Land of Freedom*, pp. 122–148, 367–382, 532–568, 569–588; Improving Adequate Situation: *Deutsche im Amerikanischen Bürgerkrieg*, pp. 345–350, 396–409; Political: Heubach, Gerstein, *Deutsche im Amerikanischen Bürgerkrieg*, pp. 237–240, 330–345; Escaping Military Service: Krause, *Deutsche im Amerikanischen Bürgerkrieg*, pp. 254–277; Family Discord: Probstfield, *News From the Land of Freedom*, pp. 223–259; Religious: Pritzlaff, *News From the Land of Freedom*, pp. 299–318.

24. Peter Marschalck, *Deutsche Überseewanderung im 19. Jahrhundert. Ein Beitrag zur soziologischen Theorie der Bevölkerung* (Stuttgart: Ernst Klett, 1973), p. 80.

25. Wolfgang von Hippel, *Auswanderungs aus Südwestdeutschland. Studien zur württembergischen Auswanderung und Auswanderungspolitik im 18. und 19. Jahrhundert* (Stuttgart: Klett-Cotta, 1984), p. 228.

26. Kathleen Neils Conzen, "German Catholics in America," in *The Encyclopedia of American Catholic History*, ed. Michael Glazier and Thomas J. Shelley (Collegeville, MN: The Liturgical Press, 1997), pp. 571–583.

27. The underrepresentation of Catholics in the professions and institutions of higher learning in Prussia was considerable, though decreasing during the nineteenth century. For example, 18 percent of the students at Prussian universities in 1886 were Catholic; in 1905, with no territorial changes, it was 28 percent, while the 1910 census reported 36 percent of Prussians as Catholic. See G. Hohorst, J. Kocha, G.A. Ritter, eds., *Datenhandbuch zur deutschen Bildungsgeschichte*, I: 226; *Sozialgeschichtliches Arbeitsbuch II*, 2nd edn. (Munich, 1978), 55.

28. Marschalck, *Deutsche Überseewanderung*, 72, 73. Tabulations from the 1870 IPUMS.

29. Helbich and Kamphoefner, *Deutsche im Amerikanischen Bürgerkrieg*, pp. 492–517, here esp. 513–516.

30. Kamphoefner et al., *News From the Land of Freedom*, pp. 532–568, 62–94.

31. Ibid., 78–80, 90–93. With the Klinger family as well, a brother-in-law unacquainted with the home folks wrote along with his wife and several of her siblings. Ibid., 539–555.

32. Some letter series are restricted to a single writer who migrated alone; others may include several siblings and/or a number of dependants. But in the following analysis, each individual in letter-writers' families is given equal weight, so that some letter series have greater input into the average than others. Non-related household members are not included in this analysis; along the same lines, letter-writers who are boarders or servants are tabulated alone without reference to other members of the households where they reside. From the 95 dossiers, a total of 114 primary and secondary writers were located in the census: from 18 dossiers, no writers could be located in the census, 55 were represented by one writer, 14 by two, three by three, three by four, and two by five primary or secondary writers. Including all German born members of writers' families, 18 dossiers were represented by one person, 21 by two, 19 by three, and 24 by four or more (one reaching a maximum of fourteen members and two represented by nine each).

33. Walter D. Kamphoefner, *The Westfalians: From Germany to Missouri* (Princeton: Princeton University Press, 1987), pp. 75–81.

34. Joseph Ferrie, *Yankeys Now: Immigrants in the Antebellum U.S., 1840–1860* (New York and Cambridge: Cambridge University Press, 1999), pp. 101–116.

35. Of course, if someone escaped enumeration entirely, he would not show up in the IPUMS either, but if his name and other personal characteristics were simply too badly distorted to be recognizable, he would still figure in the overall averages.

36. For examples from our published work see letter-writer Bürkert, *News From the Land of Freedom*, pp. 406–419, and writers Richter, Francksen, Treutlein, and Gerstein in *Deutsche im Amerikanischen Bürgerkrieg*, pp. 157–166, 197–208, 287–295, 330–345.

37. Applying the same census tracing methods to letter-writers published in Erickson, *Invisible Immigrants*, reveals an even greater divergence from a cross-section of the British present in the 1870 census, even though the author shows a keen awareness of the issue of representativeness. Perhaps the biggest skewing is the "front loading": of the Erickson letter-writers who could be found in the 1870 census, more than 80 percent had arrived before 1850; by contrast, more than 70 percent of British immigration from 1800 through 1870 arrived during the last two decades of that era. Not surprisingly, writers were much older and more prosperous than the cross-section of Britons found in the 1870 IPUMS. With all British household heads aged 21 and over, the median age was 43; for Erickson's writers, the figure was 51.5 years. The mean real estate value of British household heads in 1870 was $2032; for Erickson's writers it was $5655, or 278 percent of the average (although more than half of the total holdings of the letter-writers were attributable to one man). The occupational profile of Erickson's writers was similarly skewed: eight of

17 writers reporting occupations were farmers, nearly double the proportion for British immigrants in general (only 25 percent of whom were employed in the agricultural sector in 1870). Erickson's group included just one common laborer and one factory worker, in contrast to three in white-collar occupations and four who were skilled artisans. Emigration figures were obtained from *Harvard Encyclopedia of American Ethnic Groups* (Cambridge: Harvard University Press, 1980), pp. 1047–1048; since these figures started in 1820, immigration for the previous twenty years was estimated by the generous assumption that it was twenty times the 1820 figure. Rough occupational breakdowns by nationality are found in Francis A. Walker, *Ninth Census, Vol. I: The Statistics of the Population of the United States, 1870* (Washington, DC: Government Printing Office, 1872), pp. 689–699.

38. Daniel Bertaux, "Note on the Use of the Life-History Approach to Study a Whole Sector of Production: The Artisanal Bakery in France," in *Biographie in handlungswissenschaftlicher Perspektive*, ed. Joachim Matthes et al. (Nürnberg: Verlag der Nürnberger Forschungsvereinigung, 1981), pp. 283–286.

2

The Limits of the Australian Emigrant Letter

Eric Richards

C.R. Fay, the Anglo-Canadian historian, occasionally wrote about British emigration in the nineteenth century, and remarked that

> Hundreds of letters no doubt crossed the ocean from every quarter of the globe to some farm or village of the British Isles; and if we had but one per cent before us, we could attempt a real history of emigration.[1]

Taking Fay literally we would need to read tens of thousands of letters.[2] Among the many challenges in reading the emigrant letter is the sheer quantity of the surviving material, even for so remote a destination as Australia. There are simply too many letters to digest and the problems of categorization and interpretation are severe, especially if we seek "a real history of emigration." The possibilities and the limits of emigrants' letters are the central questions in this essay.

The fact that Australia has some rich lodes of emigrant correspondence in the colonial period is perhaps surprising and serendipitous. It is fortunate because, for one thing, it provides the basis of comparison with the larger destinations of emigrants. It is surprising for several reasons related to the special circumstances of Australian immigration. Australia was a relatively small and extremely distant destination—only about 1.6 million people emigrated to Australia before 1900 (less than a tenth of the number coming to America) and of these 160,000 were convicts who dominated the inflow until 1840. Even when free emigration superseded the convicts, a large proportion, about half, were subsidized labor specifically recruited from the lower strata of the British population. They were laboring people with a high ratio of women, agricultural laborers, and domestic servants; they contained a high proportion of rural folk from the south of England, Scotland, and Ireland. In aggregate, more than half of Australia's immigrants were either convicts or assisted laborers. None of these were categories from which one would expect much in the way of letter-writing; they were not of the "letter-writing classes." Indeed Geoffrey Blainey claimed that 90 percent of the emigrants who voyaged to Australia during the nineteenth century traveled in the steerage class, and that most of them were illiterate.[3]

Representing the illiterate in history is, of course, an immovable problem. But what is surprising is that Australia rapidly outgrew its unpromising origins. By 1900, (and not counting the Aborigines who were literally not counted anyway), Australia had a very high level of literacy and was already one of the highest per capita consumers of books and magazines, of the printed word, in the world. In the 1880s Australians wrote and received more letters per capita than people in the United States, and twice as many as Canadians at that time. More than a million letters per annum were sent abroad from Australia at the end of the century. This probably reflected the high levels of income in Australia, but it remains surprising in a society that was still largely uncommercialized in the modern sense.[4] Australia had become a highly literate society that wrote vast numbers of emigrant letters, and many have survived.[5]

Categories of Australian letters

Using the emigrant letter for the "real history of emigration" is only one part to the agenda. In Australian colonial history the emigrant letter has also a special rescue function. In most countries the most important documentary sources in modern social history are the manuscript returns of the Censuses. In Australia, the census manuscripts have always been destroyed. Consequently, every other source, especially nominal data series, assumes great compensatory significance. It specifically means that the least affluent elements in Australian society are extremely difficult to retrieve in the general historical record. Happily there exist very detailed administrative convict records and also a good survival of immigrant shipping lists for the assisted after 1831. But the writing of "history from below" in the Australian context remains poorly documented, which gives "the emigrant letter" enhanced value.

A critical problem is, as always, the skewed representation among the emigrant letters. Emigrants who maintained no ties with home wrote no letters. Long ago, Charlotte Erickson identified such difficulties when she surveyed the letters of British emigrants in the United States. She spoke of the paucity of letters of laboring immigrants and observed that any sample of immigrant letters gives undue emphasis to people who failed as immigrants, and those who did not break their ties with the homeland. The illiterate are not represented at all: the poorest emigrants, those who emigrated for the most straightforward economic reasons, will not be found among the letter-writers. In her collection *Invisible Immigrants* Erickson conceded that "ordinary laborers from both town and country are clearly underrepresented." And common laborers were the "single largest group" of emigrants in the second half of the nineteenth century—perhaps up to two-fifths in the 1880s. "Few of the letters of this huge segment of British emigration . . . . have been found."[6]

One of the earliest searchers for Australian emigrants' letters was Margaret Kiddle, who also concluded that there was a systematic bias in the generation and survival of letter collections. In her British searches Kiddle found about 28 collections of emigrant letters from Australia and noted that "some of the best collections she had found were records of failure."[7] Since Kiddle's time the available corpus of emigrant letters in Australia has grown greatly and has begun to reach into the lower strata of immigrant life, though the general bias remains.

These problems are not exclusive to Australian sources or to migration history in general.[8] The search for emigrants' letters in many places has been successful but has been somewhat divorced from similar searches in adjacent fields of historical research. Thus parallel enterprises in British and European history have been devoted to the rescue of the "voices and strategies of the poor" as well as the longer standing quest for so-called working-class "ego-documents" and autobiographical writings. They are best exemplified in the remarkable collection of *Essex Pauper Letters, 1731–1837* written by, or on behalf of, paupers seeking support from the local poor law in the county of Essex.[9] They constitute "a direct rendering in idiomatic language and phonetic spelling of ordinary forms of speech, so that these letters are an invaluable record of the ways in which ordinary folk expressed their own views of their own lives, their various setbacks and disasters, and their expectations of support from the poor law." These letters, several hundred of them over a period of almost a century, have been edited with a scholarly reverence comparable to that invested in medieval bulls and royal charters.[10] They provide a first-hand record of the living conditions and experiences of ordinary people about, for instance, "the loss of a child or spouse, or about getting old . . . put down in their own writing, often under conditions of extreme necessity, privation and despair."[11] This, of course, is part of the urgent search for direct and unmediated plebeian documentation.[12] The *Essex Pauper Letters* are said to "represent the lowest level of recorded written communication"—people with "limited powers of alphabetical articulation" and "the most compelling type of record within the collective archive of the English poor."[13]

This is exciting research but there is no sign of any convergence with recent comparable work on emigrant letters. There has been little mutual awareness or intersection: they are historiographical ships that pass in the night even though their journeys are similar. Emigrant letters often reach into comparable levels of society: many emigrants were indeed from below decks and from the bottom of society. And convict letters are surely contenders in the competition for "the lowest level of recorded written communication." A post-E.P. Thompson literature on British working life histories has emerged, vigorous and penetrating into the lives of working people. But it seems almost entirely oblivious of the rich humus of emigrants' letters best exemplified in the wonderful collection of Irish-Australian letters assembled by David Fitzpatrick. Emigration, moreover, was itself one of "the strategies of the poor" and their letters open windows into conditions not only in their destinations but also in the home countries from which they departed.

Pauper letters form "an invaluable record of the ways in which ordinary folk expressed their views of their own lives, their various setbacks, and their expectations of support from the poor law." The same kind of exercise is often achieved with emigrant letters. Recreating the mental world of, say, an eccentric sixteenth century Italian miller by way of an inquisition, or that of a French village in the thirteenth century from another sort of Inquisition, or the mentality of Martin Guerre from an obscure trial in 1560, is not different from the reconstruction of the world of an emigrant from their letters. Self-documentation through family correspondence can equally reveal the inner world, even the moral economy, of the working emigrant in, say, 1835.

Many Australian emigrant letters were written by British working people who ordinarily had little inclination, occasion, or compulsion to put pen to paper. These letters give voice to proletarian colonial Australia as the immigrants adjusted themselves to remote overseas conditions. They are powerful and vivid examples of working-class life. They provide supreme illustrations of the process and realities of migration and, moreover, often constitute wonderful examples of plebeian literary achievement with an "intrinsic interest in both content and style."[14]

On the other hand the nineteenth century emigrant letter is usually contained within certain boundaries. The common horizons of the emigrant letter are interestingly and variably limited. Their key characteristics are their individuality, their localism, and their attachment to family. This can be paradoxical since emigrants' lives were commonly engaged directly with some of the most dramatic forces of their times—not only those of intercontinental dispersion, but also with the pressures transforming the contexts from which the emigrants departed, such as industrialization, political turmoil, and demographic change. Emigrant letters are usually silent on most of these larger forces. This is not surprising since most kinds of correspondence are circumscribed but the radius of the emigrants' world was significantly narrower than the distance they traveled.

Migrants normally focused on their immediate circumstances. They were hardly likely to discourse on Malthusian pressures or income differentials at large in the world economy, or on the impact of industrialization. Emigrants rarely had opportunity or inclination, or occasion to peer out of their domestic world: they could hardly be expected to take an historical or sociological or economic perspective of their place in the world. In the mid-nineteenth century British and Irish emigrants to Australia were more likely to make observations on rural change on a local scale at home—and they might allude to some of the symptoms of these issues— for example, land hunger, lack of opportunities, political instability, unemployment, and harvests. But they are much more vocal on matters such as the prospect of returning home, domestic economies, ways of coping, borrowing, and repatriating money. The emigrant letter was sometimes a channel of information but more often a channel of solidarity and consolation. Most of their correspondence was contained within "the little kingdom of the family" and its radius was mainly defined by the functions of the letter. Emigrant letters, unless they were negotiating family reunification, were mainly about reassurance and domestic news.

This genre of letters, therefore, exposes the social and political boundaries of the immigrant mind, the range of their points of reference, the scope of their dialogue with home. In other words there were interesting limits on the scope of the emigrant letter. They suggest mental worlds which are open to definition and can be read in terms of omission as much as inclusion. Few English emigrant letters, for instance, refer to the Reform Bill or to Chartism or the accession of the new Queen; in Irish letters there is surprisingly little allusion to the Famine; letters for the Scottish Highlands rarely relate in any way to the Clearances or make any murmur about landlords or evictions.[15] The scale of reference is narrow, for these are primarily domestic communications contained within the framework of the family. They were essentially nonpolitical, non-general. There is a general low self-awareness of their place in the wider world. The migrants, at least in their letters, are mostly unreflective about broader forces. Such letters may be compared with the oral record which, in the Scottish context, is often similarly particular and selective.[16] There is a marvelous density of interest about local realties but no generalized view of the world, which was probably left to accompanying newspapers if thought of at all.

When an ordinary emigrant takes a wider view of his or her context it comes as a jolt. For instance a convict, Richard Bowler, originally of Brill in Buckinghamshire, wrote from Van Diemen's Land that he liked the island very well. When he first arrived it had been a very beautiful and flourishing place. But by 1843 the convict colony, said Bowler, was in decline:

> this country is much altered and for the worse[,] Emigration Ruins this country . . . I can confidentially assure you there his scores unemployed . . . it was easier before Emigrants came here to get a farm that it is now to get a shilling, etc.[17]

Bowler indeed was identifying the opposition of interest between the emigrants and the convicts, and was evidently unable to see that the two streams might operate to their mutual benefit.[18]

Mostly migrants did not use their letters to reflect on the general context of their expatriation. The limited horizons of most emigrant letters also set limits to their explanatory value—for instance, one does not normally use them for their wider documentary content, though there are telling exceptions. Like most letters they were domestic documents whose purpose was that of maintaining contact, offering reassurance, begging and borrowing, conveying births and deaths, entertaining with local dramas, and sustaining loyalties and enmities too. They were not like an interrogation or a parliamentary investigation where the witness was questioned more broadly. Similarly the emigrant letter is different from the pauper letter—it was rarely the plea of "the powerless to the powerful," to use James Scott's phrase.[19] Emigrants were likely to have been much more literate than paupers (though some were both paupers and emigrants).

Is the Australian emigrant letter therefore limited to providing illustrative documentation and individual insights, narrative coloring, and windows into the lives of ordinary folk? Is there any systematic fashion in which letters can be harnessed for more directly explanatory purposes? In other words, how far does the emigrant letter reach? It may be argued that there are certain aspects of emigration analysis into which only the emigrant letter can penetrate. Several categories of Australian letters demonstrate their special utility while also raising questions about explanation in migration history, and these are the themes of the remainder of this essay.

Before, During, and After Emigration

Letters written before embarkation, before the moment of emigration, have crucial value. They provide special entry to the emigration decision and its context, usually inaccessible in the broader record. In the Australian sphere there are collections of family letters which document arrangements about who was to go, who was resisting, persuading, financing, denying, promoting, arguing, reassuring, and so on in the months before the actual emigration. They contain graphic documents about the psychology of emigration. In one set of letters, belonging to a working-class family, the Slocombes of Bristol, the correspondence arose because the younger generation was intent on emigration to Sydney in 1841 and the youngest daughter was in domestic service in Taunton. It featured the excruciating tensions that arose between the young would-be emigrants and the wife's parents. The correspondence is barely literate and is hot with anger and recrimination issuing from the core of the family politics. The resistance, however, failed, and the younger Slocombes sailed away to Sydney.[20] This kind of intra-family tussle may have been common and may have prevented some emigration, and diminished the outflows from the British Isles especially to Australia, a destination which always battled against the negative image inherited from the convict years.

Another category of pre-emigration correspondence—those of prospective emigrants at large—has rarely been studied. Many schemes of assisted emigration from the British Isles sprouted in the nineteenth century and Australia figured prominently in this field, since about 750,000 of them made successful application, and many others failed. Unfortunately, virtually all these applications for subsidized passages have been destroyed. There is one analysis in print of applicants who responded to an 1814 Colonial Office inducement to men of capital; 2500 responses were received from England and Wales, 400 from Scotland, and 300 from Ireland. Wealthy farmers from southern England dominated the pool, and over half the applicants were from the London area. To the extent that this migration actually took place, it selected from the top end of the market to a greater extent than did the programs that came afterwards.[21] Before the Australian colonial schemes (which began in earnest in the 1830s), there were other smaller schemes. In 1820 the British government voted £50,000 for an emigration scheme to assist settlers to the Cape of Good Hope, allowing for 4,000 places. In the outcome there were, reportedly, 80,000 applicants from all over the British Isles. This itself suggests an astonishing level of unsatisfied demand for emigration: there was even evidence of people (in Skye) selling up their farms in the vain, and overly optimistic expectation, of free passages.[22] This episode strongly suggests a large pent-up demand for emigration which the costs of passage left unsatisfied. None of this sort of correspondence appears to have survived. This is a shame because the rates and distribution of application for passages would furnish critical data about variations in the propensity to emigrate, their regional differences, and their shifts over time. Consequently, in this case, the utility of emigrant letters is limited by the vagaries of their survival.

Convict emigration to Australia was less about propensities than about coercion. The nominal and administrative documentation regarding the 160,000 convicts transported has been the basis for important studies.[23] They show for instance that the convicts were surprisingly literate by the standards of the time and this might arouse expectations of a substantial correspondence from the convicts. A recent volume from Tasmania carries the encouraging title of *Chain Letters*.[24] But, in terms of the genuine emigration letter, the convicts are disappointing. There were, it is true, many published convict narratives—30 published in Britain alone between 1816 and 1850, and a few more in Australia itself. But even here only half have been authenticated as written by actual convicts and all clearly pursued a sensationalist and commercial market. These narratives followed a formulaic tendency and were generally incurious about conditions of the colony, of convict society, or of the Aborigines.[25] Anne Conlon commented that the convict narratives include "every type of convict except the poor Papist Irishman" and no women—both very large exceptions in this context.[26] Of actual letters by convicts there are only a few.[27] It may be recollected that the best known set of Australian emigrant letters was a literary hoax from a prison—namely E.G. Wakefield's *Letter from Sydney*, written from Newgate Jail in 1829, which eventually formed a blueprint for the Australian assisted immigration schemes.

Of the fragments of convict writing that survive, most are of the "convict gentleman" category. But one classic sequence represents a larger span of Australian convict society. These are the letters of Richard Taylor and his brother Simon—six letters written between 1840 and 1859 to their father at home in Pontefract, in Yorkshire. They have the advantage of starting prior to their transportation to New South Wales, and they also show the supreme value of longitudinal coverage. Robert Hughes, the best-selling convictologist, blatantly distorted the Taylor story by his selective use of a particular part of this sequence of emigrant letters.[28] Hughes quoted only the early letters of the correspondence, which demonstrated the despair and remorse of the departing convicts and the wrench of departure from their father's home. Hughes chose not to use letters later in the sequence. In 1845 the brothers were still reacting negatively to the colony, remarking that they would "lose no time in coming home again, and I hope we never more will be separated in [t]his life . . . .Father I am longing for the day to come to behold you face once more."[29]

But in their subsequent letters the brothers began saying that the colony was wonderful, and that they would never return to England; after that they began their effort to recruit the rest of their Pontefract family into free emigration to Australia.[30] By 1850 Richard Taylor was clearly no longer keen to return to England and was advising his brothers and sisters to emigrate:

> as they could go a great deal better here than at home . . . a fine place for a Poor man and in fact for the rich as well as the Poor . . . plenty of work for the Poorer Class, that is the labouring classes—it was a land of perpetual summer, a land of plenty.

His step brother Simon had reached similar conclusions. He had "no intention of ever going home and as I am married and doing well here much better than I could do in England." He too encouraged his family to join them:

> we are doing very well we not know any hardships or what it is want we have plenty to eat and drink and a house to live in rent free and plenty of wood and water gratis, not taxes or poor rates. [31]

The Taylor letters chart the changing perception of the colony over the course of two decades. They are worth juxtaposing with two other surviving convict letters that have particular interest in the study of emigrant letter-writing. These are two individual letters relating to a convict in New South Wales from Bedfordshire, the least literate county in England in the mid-nineteenth century. The first letter was written on behalf of the barely literate convict and the other written in stuttering prose by the same convict himself. These two letters offer a case study in the difference that the mediation of an amanuensis might make in the process, an issue common in the wider study of the emigrant letter.[32] Other than these examples, the corpus of convict documentation is thin and may reflect the likely destruction of such stained correspondence in family archives over the intervening years—before a convict past in Australia became a matter of genealogical pride in place of shame.

Free emigration to Australia began in earnest in 1831 and in much larger numbers, eventually reaching about 1.6 million by 1900. As the century proceeded and literacy rates rose (possibly ahead of those in Great Britain), and the means of communication improved, so also the number of letters home rose. But there seems to be a clumping of surviving letters in the 1850s, the decade of the gold rushes and the great peak of self-financing emigration to Australia. For the rest of the century the inflows were dominated by the assisted immigrants who were generally more modest in their social pretensions, and in writing skills, too.

Literacy has a particular significance. The immigrants, on average, were more literate than each of the populations from which they were derived in the British Isles and also higher than the levels of literacy prevailing in the receiving colonial populations. The Australian immigration nominal literacy data, for tens of thousands of assisted immigrants, is of better quality than that for the home populations until the late nineteenth century. Australian immigrants were measurably more literate than those at home (from their respective counties, occupational groups, age groups, and from the general average). Thus, for instance, the assisted immigrants from, say, Suffolk to New South Wales, were more literate than the Suffolk population at large. Moreover, when we line up the lists of cohorts from each county we get a full league table of immigrant literacy—showing, predictably, that the Scots were most literate, the southern rural English less than their northern compatriots, and the Irish well down the table and declining from north east to south west. In England Bedfordshire was the least literate county but still higher than Ireland. More remarkable is the fact that the immigrant literacy league table corresponds almost exactly with the county rank ordering of the home countries.[33] This suggests, powerfully, that the immigrants were very broadly drawn from the upper echelons of their respective strata in the home populations. Emigrants to Australia seem to have chosen themselves partly by the factor of literacy—which carries implications for the way we read their letters.[34] The Australian immigrants therefore raised the rate of literacy in Australia and lowered it in Britain by their emigration.

Whether these findings apply to emigrant populations at large is not yet clear. It is likely, however, that there was a particular propensity among the more literate of each population to migrate. Literacy probably favored the potential immigrant. These Australian data relate to the literacy of the assisted immigrants, that is the least affluent, the most labouring section of the immigrant populations from the British Isles. Self-financing immigrants (about 50 percent of the total intake) were almost certainly more literate. Taken together, their capacity to write emigrant letters was greater than we might expect.

In the currently published Australian emigration letters there exists a predictable bias toward the more affluent families, the best example being the celebrated collection of the letters of Rachel Henning.[35] Emigrant letters are also sprinkled through the widening range of family histories, often in the form of incidental illustrative correspondence slipped in amongst the family trees and potted biographies. Occasionally they contain pure gold—that is, sequences of letters transcribed for their essential entertainment and antiquarian value as much as anything else. There are also some collections of women's emigrant letters and oddly enough a few letters from Bedfordshire emigrants.

The other significant bias in the available record, like so much else in the Australian sphere, is toward the Irish. The two most professional and fully authenticated collections of Australian letters are those dealing with Irish emigrants, edited respectively by Patrick O'Farrell and David Fitzpatrick.[36] The Irish of all groups in the incoming Australian population are the best celebrated and studied—their dominance is virtually imperial. But there also exist several hundred collections of English, Scottish, and Welsh emigrant letters in Australia and Britain, as well as fragments; some are fully articulated sequences but there are few two-way sequences.

The Australian emigrant letter is limited in its chronological reach since there appear to be few such collections for the mid- to late twentieth century.[37] Of these few some were the product of a special effort to garner them in 1960 by means of advertisements in many British newspapers: the response was sparse but contained some excellent documents of a very unusual character. For example, there were some seethingly angry letters remembering the 1920s and the alleged betrayal of British immigrant boys, as well as their foul treatment by Australian farmers during the years approaching the Great Depression. Another collection of letters derives from a man who emigrated as a boy from a good farming family in Oxfordshire in the 1920s, was broken by the Depression, returned home to flirt seriously with Fascists and the Black Shirts, and came back to Australia in 1945–1949. He later privately published a remarkably revealing volume of memoirs including a faithful transcription of his original letters. This was a rare voice among British emigrants.[38] In another collection there are a few letters relating to the short-lived premature revival of British emigration in the years just before the Second World War.[39]

For the Australian immigrant, therefore, the twentieth century has largely been the century of the tape recorder and there exist several well-organized collections of oral memories. The interviewer is able to interrogate the subject in a way rarely possible with the letter-writer. The two forms, written and oral, are evidently different in their provenance, and their relative characteristics deserve systematic comparison and contrast especially in their depiction and explanation of migrant psychology. In other words, they possess different limits and possibilities for migrant history.[40]

The Uses of the Australian Letter

One of the general questions that is unresolved in the study of migration is the degree of geographical mobility that commonly preceded the act of emigration. This is not easily discovered unless there is a longitudinal record of the family in question. Sometimes a good run of emigrant letters can expose the pre-emigration moves of the migrant better than most other sources, and the precise details of the context out of which the emigration took place, especially where it can be combined with birth certificates and diaries and journals.[41]

The best Australian example of this type of documentation is that of Henry Parkes, a very poor working man who wrote a superb series of letters about his emigration to New South Wales in 1838–1839, and continued to document his life as one of Australia's best known public figures for the remainder of the century. For the migration historian, however, the greatest interest is in the time when he was unknown, a cog in the Australian assisted emigration system, a statistic, and a voice for thousands of people who were part of the first free emigration to Australia in the 1830s. Moreover, his letters began several months before the critical moment of his emigration.

Parkes's letters provide a precise account of his pre-emigration career, a life of plebeian mobility in the extreme. He was born in Warwickshire in 1815 in a rural family of an impoverished small farmer who was pushed off his land by adverse economic forces, and moved to Glamorgan, then to Gloucester, and then went into a downward spiral to Cheltenham and Cirencester as a very casual laborer, and was in prison for a year, too. At 11 years of age Henry Parkes was digging in a brick pit for six shillings a week to support the family. He eventually trained as an ivory-turner, gravitating toward Birmingham by the 1830s, where he married in 1836. He was a failing small craftsman with a young wife and he decided to seek an assisted passage to Australia. He was not precisely a coerced emigrant, but he was responding to the pressure of economic adversity and this was converted effectively enough into exile. His letters cover the entire period from the decision in Birmingham to emigrate, through the waiting period in London, and then the voyage to Sydney, and their re-establishment in the colony. The letters perfectly chart the classic emigrant career down along a U-shaped curve that saw a continuing deterioration of Parkes's circumstances even after his arrival in Sydney. The upturn in the Parkes's fortunes was achieved only after a long transition in the receiving colony.[42]

Parkes's letters provide direct documentation of the accumulation of debts and promises to his family, the exhaustion of his resources while waiting for embarkation, mounting psychological pressures, the sickness of his wife in transit, and the petty corruption of the bureaucratized system of the Australian assisted emigration. "I shall be sure to go from England penniless," he wrote while still in London. His letters evoke a perfectly Dickensian setting for their departure.

Their arrival in Sydney was followed by further economic and emotional depression. The local labor market had turned into a severe recession and Parkes found that he had to leave the city and go into the distant bush to find work; he suffered the theft of his possessions and then ill health. In effect he proceeded along the bottom of the U-curve of emigrant life. He said that all his fellow immigrants wished that they had never come to Australia and he swiftly reversed all his previous advice to his family about coming to Australia.[43] "I have been disappointed in all my expectations of Australia, except as to its wickedness; for it is far more wicked than I had conceived it possible for any place to be."[44] This was the immigrant's nadir.

Four months later Parkes was somewhat more cheerful and had secured a job in the Customs Office. Six months later the Parkeses had turned the corner. They were at last joining the upward sector of the immigrant curve and reporting much happier prospects: "I have now a more comfortable home than it was ever my lot to possess in England," he wrote.[45] By mid-1843 he was saying that "Australia has afforded me a better home than my motherland, and I will love her with a patriot's love . . . . I am full of hope." This was his celebration of the upturn of the immigrants' U-curve, and he was perfectly conscious of its course. Parkes's letters traced the classic trajectory of the working immigrant, in his case much eased by the assisted passage, but also clouded by the parallel motion of the trade cycle which blighted the first year of his arrival and re-establishment in the colony. The span of the letters is vital to knowing the significance of the Parkes's story—individual letters taken out of the long sequence would convey totally different perceptions of his experience.

Emigrant letters are evidently limited unless they allow the full unwinding of the course of the emigrant enterprise. This is crucial, for instance, on the issue of returning home, one of the most common recurring themes in Australian emigrant letters. The idea of "possible return often began even before departure for the colonies and was played out in a series of variations on the psychology of departure, the earnest of return, the game of reassurance, the annual declaration of intent, the prevarications, and the apologies. In the outcome most emigrants did not return home. The discourse on return was a central function of many emigrant letters and probably skewed the survival of such letters. Emigrants with no family in Britain had much less likelihood of returning and therefore do not figure in the source at all, thereby defining one of the limits of the genre.[46]

Coping with Oceanic Migration

Of all the functions of Australian emigrant letters the central purpose was that of dealing with the emotional dislocation of migration, with the strategies of coping with the main dramas, hazards, and possibilities of intercontinental migration in the age of sail. They demonstrated the way in which people calculated the risks, which was the key to much migrant behavior, documenting how discussions were often made hurriedly and inconsequentially. Emigration's greatest effect, however, was that of dislocating the family and much of the correspondence is about the implications and solacing that this entailed.

James Adam emigrated to New Zealand in November 1847 from Scotland, having heard a lecture extolling emigration. He obtained a free passage from the Otago Association on condition he stayed in the colony for five years. His relatives tried to dissuade him and his wife persuaded the local minister of the church to withhold a certificate of character at least temporarily. Adam remarked, "I can honestly say that the greatest difficulty I ever experienced was breaking away from the loving hearts of a father's home." And there were very sorrowful quayside scenes—his 70-year-old father was in tears. Adam's five month passage with 260 other emigrants included a party of weavers from Paisley "who had never seen an American axe [and who] did not know how trees six and eight feet in circumference were to be removed." Adam declared that every emigrant should write home once a month. When he returned to Scotland he met "an aged mother [who] requested [a] prayer on behalf of a careless son in New Zealand who had *never* written to his sorrowing mother."[47]

In a wider perspective, emigration to Australia was one of the avenues by which the laboring poor coped with the problem of subsistence and reproduction, and the struggle to survive and rise in the world. For those who used the emigration option, always a minority, it was a high-risk speculative way of lifting a family out of poverty and insecurity, as the career of Henry Parkes shows. Mostly these migrants' strategies were played out in what Olwen Hufton called the "Economy of makeshifts."[48] Migrants confronted literal displacement and resettlement and the challenges of the U-shaped curve: running down their resources before departure, facing adverse circumstances which their letters illuminate. At their destination they had no poor law or gentry largesse on which to fall back, though they never seem to express regret about this. Their successful survival methods seemed to entail sloughing off their British past. Emigrants in extremis generally do not figure in these letters and consequently any portrait of immigrant life from this source is limited in its range. Emigrant letters penetrate best in the mechanisms of capital transfer, death, attitudes to race, the psychology of adaptation, intercommunal relations, solidarities of social and familial varieties, and immigrant networks.[49]

Emigrant letters are often considered in isolation, in segregated ethnic clusters, which tends to mask the sense of similarity or difference among migrants. The value of a control group in this sort of evidence is shown by the juxtaposition of letters written by German immigrants in the mid-nineteenth century. They were a small minority of non-English-speaking migrants in Australia and their preoccupations were significantly different from their British counterparts. A series of German letters, written in 1849, reveal a quite distinctive psychology at work.[50] According to their editor, George Nadel, the Germans possessed a special view of the world:

> Many English migrants had to reconcile themselves slowly to the fact that these English colonies were not really English; nor were they temporary stopping places in which to recoup a lost or denied fortune, or acquire precisely that station in life from which they were excluded at home . . . it was only when the English migrant became conscious of the fact that his migration was a total and not a temporary committal that his perception of the new country approximated the unbridled visions of these Germans.

While the German immigrant possessed "unbridled visions," the British were trapped in expectations which derived from the fact that they migrated within the privileged world of the *Pax Britannica*. One of the ways of transcending the limits of specific selections of emigrant letters is to juxtapose them with those of other groups, thus defining their exceptional and their common characteristics.

The Australian emigrant letter is most effective where it can be linked to a hypothesis, where it can be made to yield evidence toward explanation. Letters are able to penetrate into the means by which individuals, families, and other close groupings negotiated the complex trials of intercontinental migration. Their letters reach into the heart of the question of how they regarded themselves, whether as anguished victims expelled by their homelands, or enterprising spirits who took advantage of the opportunities which became manifest in the age of intercontinental migration.[51] It may be that on the larger questions of how it was that so many millions of people were activated to take these extraordinary steps out of western Europe, their letters are generally not central evidence. Nevertheless, in the Australian theater at least, there is rich evidence that the emigrant letter was indeed instrumental, and the family itself was often the primary vehicle in effecting emigration—sustaining and mediating the propelling psychology. The migrant was engaged with the largest forces in modern history, the intersection of intercontinental and multicultural exchanges. Their letters, for all their modesty and the limits suggested in this essay, showed that they were not merely respondents but agents in the transfer.

Notes

1. C.R. Fay, *Huskisson and his Age* (London: Longmans, 1951), p. 262.
2. David Fitzpatrick points out that "millions of letters were exchanged between Ireland and Australia in the nineteenth century." David Fitzpatrick, *Oceans of Consolation* (Carlton, Victoria: Melbourne University Press, 1995), p. vii. The Irish were no more than a third of all Australian immigrants.
3. Cited in N.M. Wace, "Settlers in Transit," in *Of Time and Space*, ed. J.N. Jennings and G.J.R. Linge (Canberra: ANU Press, 1980), p. 29.
4. See, *Victorian Year Book*, 1881–1882, p. 317; *Official Year Book of New South Wales*, 1904–1905, (1906), p. 155. In 1904 the Post Office of the State of New South Wales carried almost 100 million items of letters and 40 million newspapers for a population of about 1.3 million. Australia was a great book buyer for British publishers—accounting for 25 percent of exports by 1900. See Martyn Lyons, "Britain's Largest Export Market," in *A History of the Book in Australia, 1891–1945*, ed. M. Lyons and J. Arnold (St Lucia, Australia: University of Queensland Press, 2001), pp. 19–20.
5. Richard Broome, *The Victorians. Arriving* (1984) p. 23.
6. Charlotte Erickson, *Invisible Immigrants: The Adaptation of English and Scottish Immigrants in Nineteenth-Century America* (London: Leicester University Press for the London School of Economics, 1972), p. 7.
7. Ibid., p. 484, fn 17.
8. Fitzpatrick discusses the problem at length in *Oceans of Consolation*, esp. p. 29.
9. Thomas Sokoll, ed., *Essex Pauper Letters, 1731–1837* (Oxford: Oxford University Press for the British Academy, 2001).
10. Ibid., p. xii.
11. Ibid., Foreword and p. 4.
12. See, for instance, Tim Hitchcock, Peter King, and Pamela Sharpe, eds., *Chronicling Poverty: The Voices and Strategies of the English Poor, 1640–1840* (New York: St Martin's Press, 1997), pp. 7–8. Some excellent pauper emigrant letters are employed in D.J. Francis King, "From the Weald to Wellington: A History of Six Pauper Families who Emigrated from Stapleford in Kent to Port Nicholson in Wellington Arriving in April 1840" (dissertation in Local History, University of Kent, Canterbury, England, 1991, copy in National Library of New Zealand). For an early discovery of emigrant letters from Australia, see Eric Richards, "A Voice from Below: Benjamin Boyce in South Australia, 1839–1846," *Labour History* (November 1974): 61–72.
13. Sokoll, *Essex Pauper Letters*, pp. 4, 8.
14. See Fitzpatrick, *Oceans of Consolation*, viii and pp. 4–5, 25.
15. Fitzpatrick's collection of letters contains a few references to the famine—as in the Burke letters, p. 149, and the O'Sullivan letters, p. 176.
16. See, for instance, Eric R. Cregeen, "Oral Tradition and History in a Hebridean Island," *Scottish Studies* 32 (1998): 12–37, esp. 15, 27, 29.
17. Richard Bowler to John Bowler, eight mss letters, 1835–1843, Australian National Records Register MS 4253, NK 6451, National Library of Australia (NLA), Canberra. Richard Bowler had been transported to Tasmania for life in 1821; his brother John Bowler was a clockmaker in Brill.
18. See Amanda Laugesen, *Convict Words: Language in Early Colonial Australia* (South Melbourne, Australia: Oxford University Press, 2000), xiii–xvi and p. 73.
19. Quoted in Hitchcock, King, and Sharpe, *Chronicling Poverty*, p. 5.
20. Letters of William and Betsey Slocombe from their parents. May 1841. Holograph, Ae35/1, Mitchell Library, Sydney.

21. David S. Macmillan, "Commercial and Industrial Society in Great Britain and Ireland 1814–1824: A Study of Australian Immigrant Applications," *Histoire sociale/Social History* VI no. 12 (November 1973): 181–201. Macmillan analyzed the Scottish applications in his *Scotland and Australia, 1788–1850: Emigration, Commerce and Investment* (Oxford: Clarendon Press, 1967), chapter 3.

22. Ian Whyte, *Migration and Society in Britain, 1550–1830*, (Basingstoke, England: Macmillan, 2000), p. 136.

23. See for instance S. Nicholas and P. Shergold eds., *Convict Workers: Reinterpreting Australia's Past* (Cambridge, England: Cambridge University Press, 1988).

24. Lucy Frost and Hamish Maxwell-Stewart, eds., *Chain Letters: Narrating Convict Lives* (Carlton South, Victoria: Melbourne University Press, 2001).

25. See Anne Conlon, " 'Mine is a Sad yet True Story': Convict Narratives; 1818 –1850," *Journal of the Royal Australian Historical Society* 55 (March 1969): 43–82. On the problems relating to the convict narrative genre, see David Dunstan, ed., *Owen Suffolk's Days of Crime and Years of Suffering* (Kew, Victoria: Australian Scholarly Publishing, 2000), Introduction. Such doubts are not of course confined to convict narratives. For an example of the extreme doubts that can attach to emigrant letters in published places, see G.R.C. Keep, "A Canadian Emigration Commissioner in Northern Ireland," *Canadian Historical Review* 34 (1953): 156.

26. An important exception is offered by the very unusual journals of John Grant: Yvonne Cramer, *This Beauteous, Wicked Place: Letters and Journals of John Grant, Gentleman Convict* (Canberra: NLA, 2000). The important letters of the female convict Susannah Watson are used by Babette Smith in *A Cargo of Women* (Kensington, New South Wales: University of New South Wales Press, 1988). Another published convict letter, of John Slater, is reproduced in Geoffrey Chapman Ingleton, *True Patriots All* (Sydney: Angus and Robertson, 1952), pp. 81–82.

27. Irish convict letters are employed by Patrick O'Farrell, *Letters from Irish Australia, 1825–1929* (Sydney: University of New South Wales Press, 1984), chapter 2. Fitzpatrick in *Oceans of Consolation* employs one sequence of convict letters— Michael Hogan, 1853–1857, in chapter 5, pp. 161–173, though his convict origins were not identified in the correspondence. A better known collection is that of Alexandra Hasluck, *Unwilling Emigrants: A Study of the Convict Period in Western Australia* (Melbourne: Oxford University Press, 1959).

28. Robert Hughes, *The Fatal Shore* (New York: Knopf, 1986), pp. 134, 143.

29. Quoted by Bruce Hindmarsh, "Wherever I go I whill right to you," in Frost and Maxwell-Stewart, *Chain Letters*, p. 170.

30. Ibid., pp. 105–117.

31. Ibid., pp. 171–173.

32. These are the Cartwright letters in NLA 92, pp. 230–231. Andrew Underwood, ed., "Some Letters from Bedfordshire Pioneers in Australia, 1842–86," *Bedfordshire Historical Record Society* 40: 226–238. Letters relating to transported machine breakers are considered in Jill Chambers, *Hampshire Machine Breakers: The Story of the 1830 Riots* (Clifton, England: J. Chambers, 1990). On the role of the amanuensis see Fitzpatrick, *Oceans of Consolation*, p. 390.

33. See Eric Richards, "An Australian Map of British and Irish Literacy in 1841," *Population Studies* 53 (1999): 345–359.

34. Another cache of immigrant testimony is found in the "Voluntary Statements" collected by Caroline Chisholm and published as a an appendix to her pamphlet "Emigration and Transportation Relatively Considered," some of which are reprinted in Margaret Kiddle, *Caroline Chisholm* (Carlton, Australia: Melbourne University Press, 1969 [1950]), Appendix B.

35. Some of the better known collections of letters include: Alexandra Hasluck, *Unwilling Emigrants*. Edgar Beale, ed., *The Earth between Them: Joseph Beale's Letters Home to Ireland from Victoria, 1852–3* (Sydney: Wentworth Books, 1975); Nancy Bonnin, *Katie Hume on the Darling Downs, a Colonial Marriage: Letters of a Colonial Lady, 1866–1871* (Toowoomba: DDIP, 1985); Peter Cowan, ed., *A Faithful Picture: The Letters of Eliza and Thomas Brown at York in the Swan River Colony, 1841–1852* (Fremantle, Australia: Fremantle Arts Centre Press, 1977); J.M.D. Hardwick, ed., *Emigrant in Motley: The Journey of Charles and Ellen Kean in Quest of a Theatrical Fortune in Australia and America, as told in their Hitherto Unpublished Letters* (London: Rockliff, 1954); Valerie Ross, ed., *The Everingham Letterbook: Letters of a First Fleet Convict* (Wamberal, Australia: Anvil Press, 1985); Pamela Statham, ed., *The Tanner Letters: A Pioneer Saga of Swan and Tasmania, 1831–1845* (Nedlands, Western Australia: University of Western Australia Press, 1981); Patricia Clarke and Dale Spender, eds., *Lifelines: Australian Women's Letters and Diaries, 1788–1840* (North Sydney: Allen and Unwin, 1992); Patricia Clarke, *The Governesses: Letters from the Colonies, 1862–1882* (Melbourne: Hutchinson, 1985); David Adams, ed., *The Letters of Rachel Henning* (Ringwood, Australia: Penguin, 1969). Shipboard diaries are reproduced with some letters in Andrew Hassam, *Sailing to Australia* (Manchester: Manchester University Press, 1994). A good selection of women's letters over the early colonial period is found in Helen Heney, *Dear Fanny: Women's Letters to and from New South Wales, 1788–1857* (Canberra: ANU Press, 1985). Other colonial women are represented in Lucy Frost, *No Place for a Nervous Lady: Voices from the Australian Bush* (Melbourne: McPhee Gribble, 1984), though this mainly draws on diaries rather than letters. Another set of migrant letters was specially generated by a departing Lieutenant Governor, C.J. Latrobe in 1853 when he invited early squatters to recollect their experiences at the start of settlement at Port Phillip. This appeal produced a substantial collection of 50 letters of self-documentation (not to mention self-justification). They were later published with an introduction which referred to the thousands of letters written back home to Britain by the squatters in their day. T.F. Bride, ed., *Letters from Victorian Pioneers* (Melbourne: Heinemann, 1969 [1898]). Richard Broome, *Arriving* (McMahon's Point, Australia: Fairfax, Syme and Weldon, 1984), employs emigrants' letters in several places in his narrative, see pp. 25, 36–37, 86–87, 107, 109, 112, 117, 127. Letters from Australia turn up in many places: e.g. J.F.M. Macleod, "Notes on Waternish in the Nineteenth Century," *Transactions of the Gaelic Society of Inverness* 59 (1994–1996): 49–118.

36. Fitzpatrick, *Oceans of Consolation*, and Patrick O'Farrell, *Letters from Irish Australia*.

37. Letters from British emigrants to Australia 1900–1960, NLA 212/05/00049. Collections for the twentieth century are perhaps not yet in the "collectable" category.

38. Robert C. Keen, *Big Men, Little Man and Those In Between*, NLA MS 1767

39. Letters written by Mr. Albert Pace in 1939. NLA MS 644.

40. On this issue see A. James Hammerton and Eric Richards, eds., *Speaking to Immigrants. Oral Testimony and the History of Australian Migration* (sixth volume of *Visible Immigrants*) (History Program, R.S.S.S., ANU, Canberra, 2002).

41. A case in point is that of George Kershaw (1801–1878) a working man who with his wife, Selina, and their children emigrated to Sydney in 1841 and whose notebook records the time and place of the births of their children before and after their migration. They chart his peripatetic life—through Wakefield, Leeds, Manchester, York, Wellingborough, York again, then Sydney, Braidwood and Thornhill in New South Wales. Diary of George Kershaw, ML MSS 624, Mitchell Library, Sydney. See also Barrie Dyster, *Servant & Master: Building and Running the Grand Houses of*

Sydney 1788–1850 (Kensington, New South Wales: New South Wales University Press, 1989).

42. A W. Martin, *Henry Parkes*, (Carlton, Victoria: Melbourne University Press, 1980); Henry Parkes, *An Emigrant's Home Letters* (Sydney: Angus & Robertson, 1896), p. 51. The letters were subject to new editing against the originals in the 1980s and I am grateful to the late Prof. A.W. Martin for kindly showing me the restorations which he undertook in the new edition—which reflect well on the original edition of the 1890s.

43. Parkes, *An Emigrant's Home Letters*, p. 91.

44. Ibid., 86.

45. Ibid., 98.

46. On Australian return migration, see David Fitzpatrick, ed., *Home or Away? Immigrants in Colonial Australia: Visible Immigrants Three* (Canberra: Research School of Social Sciences, Australian National University, 1992) and Marjory Harper ed., *Emigrant Homecomings: the return movement of emigrants, 1600–2000* (Manchester University Press, 2004).

47. James Adam, *Twenty Years of Emigrant Life in the South of New Zealand* (Edinburgh, 1874).

48. See Laurence Fontaine and Jürgen Schlubohm, "Household Strategies for Survival: an Introduction," in *Household Strategies for Survival, 1600–2000: Fusion, Faction and Co-operation*, ed. Laurence Fontaine and Jürgen Schlubohm, *International Review of Social History*, Supplement 8 (2000): 1–19, citing on p. 3: Olwen H. Hufton, *The Poor of Eighteenth Century France, 1750–1789* (Oxford: Oxford University Press, 1974). More generally see Eric Richards, *Britannia's Children. Emigration from England, Scotland, Wales and Ireland since 1600* (London and New York, Hambledon and London, 2004).

49. For evidence of the transfer of class attitudes see Heney, *Dear Fanny*, esp. pp. 126–127.

50. George Nadel, "Letters from German Immigrants in New South Wales," *Royal Australian Historical Journal* 39 (1953): 253–266.

51. See Fitzpatrick, *Oceans of Consolation*, pp. 502, fn 82, 617.

3

Marriage through the Mail: North American Correspondence Marriage from Early Print to the Web

Suzanne M. Sinke

Searching for that special Philippine pen-pal? We can help! We list marriage minded ladies who are interested in being pen-pals with men all over the world. Their hope is to meet a nice gentleman and eventually marry. This relationship starts through being pen-pals, later your bride, and wife.

Snooky's Philippine Pen-Pals[1]

So begins one of several hundred web sites devoted to matchmaking across borders in 2004. It offers online pictures, addresses, and descriptions of women, international (telephone) calling cards, and a video people can order. At first glance the technology would appear to be driving a new form of marriage arrangement. Is this a new transnational world?[2] A better question is to what extent infrastructure, in the form of communications systems and education, creates opportunities or sets limits on making key personal connections across space and borders. To answer that, I suggest looking at the history of epistolary courtship across borders in North American history.

Letters are one form of courtship communication, a form that has shifted across time with variations in transportation and communications technology and with levels of literacy and the reach of postal systems. The ease of communication does not guarantee people will make contact, and certainly not that they will form enduring personal relationships, for not all want partners and ideas of who is a suitable partner come into play.

Would someone consider a person of a different nationality, race, or class, someone previously married, or of the same sex as a potential spouse?[3] Moreover, ideas of courtship, and who controls it, vary across time and from one cultural setting to another: arranged marriage, love match, economic or dynastic union. All can rely on letters. States also have a formal role, regulating (or trying to regulate) who can marry, who can migrate, and who can communicate, both through education and censorship. Popular perceptions may look at marriage by mail as a relatively new phenomenon, even one of the electronic age, but we have examples of people using letters to arrange marriage throughout North American history.

Not everyone marries, or wishes to marry, some try to avoid marriage, and others are not allowed to marry, but the majority of people across time in various cultures enter long-term relationships of marriage or its equivalent at some point in their lives, typically in young adulthood, the period also most likely for migration. Because migration is gendered, it often involves uneven sex ratios in the migration process. My question here is what role communication across borders, especially letters, plays in a key life transition—the process of finding a spouse—and how does it change over time. A concomitant question is what communications options are available to people across time, and how the available level of technology influences marriage choices. So I turn to a brief overview of marriage and the mail over four centuries, drawing my examples from North America.

Prior to European colonization we have no written history of marriage or marriage arrangements crossing borders, not because it did not happen, but because we have no written history. Instead we have oral traditions and later reports that suggest marriage across borders was at the very least a diplomatic tool for some indigenous societies, much as it was in Europe at the time of contact.[4] Arrangements had to be made face to face, though intermediaries could carry the messages verbally one to another, reinforced by symbols of power or specific trade goods. With European contact letters became a small part of marital arrangements as well, and a mix of oral and written marriage requests could exist. For example, when John Rolfe of Virginia wanted to marry Pocahontas, the daughter of Algonkian leader Powhatan, she had to convince her relatives *in person* that she wanted this arrangement, and Rolfe had to ask permission of her relatives *in person*. Both went by ship from Henrico (an English town in Virginia) to Werowocomoco (Powhatan's village), a distance of about fifty miles, to meet and discuss the issue. Since the two groups were at war, both sides were uneasy about trusting messengers or their messages.[5]

Meanwhile, Rolfe had written a lengthy (four sheets of paper!) and impassioned letter to Sir Thomas Dale, the English deputy governor of Virginia, asking for permission to wed.[6] Literacy was one of the tools of control.[7] In this case a physical letter was passed by hand from one English person to another in the colony to reach the royal representative. Even in England in 1614 the rudimentary postal network of stagecoaches and routes was developing primarily to serve the monarchy.[8] Ordinary people, who often were illiterate, were unlikely to use it. Not until 1657 did Parliament officially pass an act setting up the post office, and then it justified postal connections primarily for promoting trade and protecting national security.[9] At that time it set official rates for England, Scotland, and Ireland, as well as for a number of places abroad, from Scandinavia to the Levant—North America did not even make the list.[10] In the native Algonkian case, messages were relayed either face to face, or through messengers. These messengers had the advantage of extensive natural waterway connections in the Chesapeake, which facilitated travel, but they were largely confined to rowing/paddling or walking the paths from place to place.

Technologically, it was easier for the English to go back to England in the early 1600s than to go very far into the interior of the continent. And that is exactly what happened within a few years. The Virginia Company, after repeated complaints of the absence of women making it difficult to settle the new territory, arranged for several shipments of "young Maids to make wives" in 1620 and 1621.[11] Ninety women came on two ships in 1620, financed by public lottery money funneled through the Virginia Company. When that money was no longer available, the company recruited "magazines," investors who would sign on to a particular project for a profit. With this financing another 57 women were sent in 1621. At least on paper, the company tried to find young women of good reputation, though some of the earlier arrivals may not have fit this description. To *redeem* such a woman (the company made a point of not saying "sell"), a man had to pay 120 pounds of tobacco, a price soon raised to 150 pounds. Even the former figure was six times the price of a contract for a young male indentured servant. Despite shipments, the sex ratio was still seriously imbalanced for the English population, at 230 women to 1,250 men.[12] Though some of the male settlers had been reasonably well-to-do in England, and a number were literate, the rudimentary connections between England and North America, and the control of the Virginia Company on trade and communications, made sending for a spouse on their own nearly impossible. Except in rare cases of divorce where the husband "sold" his wife, neither was advertising for a spouse in the newspapers, something within English experience.[13] The women who arrived en masse were not in contact with their future spouses in advance of migration. They only knew they were coming to North America to marry. Letters exchanged by company officials to arrange such shipments were about population, unrest, and the business arrangements.

The corporate recruitment of wives was not limited to British North America in the early colonial era. The French government was even more active in sending shipments of female orphans, as well as poor women, known as "filles du roi" [King's daughters] to help balance the sex ratio and populate New France.[14] Forced migration of *épouseuses* (marriageable young women) to Louisiana in the early 1700s served a similar purpose. Like most of these organized endeavors, there were questions as to the virtue of the women involved, though one of the men handling the correspondence to the metropole requested that those in France find women on the basis of good physical appearance rather than morals after the 1713 "shipment" arrived.[15] There was little doubt that every woman would marry, given the imbalance in demographics. Moreover, though the numbers of women who were recruited by colonial officials were not large, they made a significant difference in grounding families, reinforcing the importance of European background, and challenging the role of non-white women and mixed race children, not to mention stemming "unnatural" sexuality of other types. Poor migrant women, in other words, were an important weapon in the arsenal of colonial power, helping to undergird European control and to reinforce official heterosexual marriage. Mass recruitment of women to migrate and become wives was an extreme, but one which continued sporadically in various areas suffering from an overabundance of men.[16] Company reports, governmental requisitions, and business letters were a far cry from love letters, but they were typical for corporate marital arrangement, and typical of the kinds of correspondence that crossed borders more generally in this period.

In the early colonial era individual settlers who wanted to write back to their homelands for spouses often could not have done so, literally. Literacy rates for most European migrants were high by homeland standards, but the majority of men and women could not write well if at all.[17] When and if colonial governments set up schools, they embodied ideas of who should learn, sometimes targeting native populations, slaves, and women, but often focusing primarily on the sons of elite European-descended families.[18] For example, in New Spain, colonial authorities tried to control which people could read and write and what they read and wrote, using not just the education system, but also the Inquisition to enforce social order and belief.[19]

Scholars tend to judge literacy in this period by whether one could sign one's name.[20] Various studies indicated that the percentage of adult men who could sign a will or deed (a select group of propertied individuals) ran from about 30 to 80 percent during the 1600s. Rates were less (and less studied) for women, in rural areas, and among the servant and slave populations.[21] This level of literacy still was sufficient to allow for some, often family and friends, to write for others if they had the necessary supplies. Some individuals served as scriveners for a modest price. James Mander wrote at least three letters for his neighbor Francis Chapple of Marblehead, who sought to convince his betrothed in England (who also was illiterate) to come to New England to wed him. In addition to the letters, Chapple sent a number of tokens of his love, though these he entrusted to returning friends.[22] The use of a third party to write letters, whether a formal scrivener or not, was a practice that would continue for migrants across time.[23]

A scrivener often had some standing in the community, and materials needed to write indicated why. Historian David Cressy listed a basic inventory for a scrivener in the early colonial era: 1) paper, an expensive imported item; 2) pen and ink, that people could make from local materials if they knew how; 3) a writing surface and adequate lighting, both problematic given the lack of furniture and other supplies, and 4) sufficient time and peace of mind. Once a letter was written it had to get to the port and then wait for the next ship headed in the right direction. Because there was no regular shipping, letters could wait for months before making the transatlantic crossing. Once the ship departed it typically took eight to twelve weeks to cross the Atlantic in the early 1600s.[24] People sent duplicate or triplicate letters on different ships in hopes that at least one would make it to the destination. The ability to get one message from a northeastern outpost to Europe and receive a reply during the normal spring to fall sailing season was a major accomplishment.[25] In other words, a typical exchange of letters took a year. With this time frame and level of uncertainty a man writing to attract a spouse, unless it was to convince an existing fiancée to join her betrothed, was a rare individual. Another option, to go back to find a spouse, was even less likely. According to one study of the early New England migrants from East Anglia, approximately eight percent of adult men who migrated from England in the 1630s also returned to England, though apparently few returned to the colonies again.[26] Though there is less information on women, it appears they were less likely either to be able to write or to return to Europe in this period, patterns that continued in courtship letters through the next two centuries.

By the mid-1700s the communication and transportation network was changing. Not only did the royal postal service run a regular packet service among New York, Charleston, and Falmouth, England by the 1760s, but there were also postal offices scattered along the coast.[27] Moreover, shipping companies sought to attract more emigrants by organizing their "trade in strangers," for example by outfitting ships for transatlantic passengers, especially German speakers leaving via Rotterdam, or later Irish from Ulster.[28] The number of correspondents also grew in some areas. For example, in Newport, Rhode Island the number of postal correspondents as well as the volume of mail doubled from 1749 to 1774. Though more of the poor or middling sorts and more women appeared as letter-writers, they apparently still relied on friends or other couriers for much of the transatlantic exchange.[29] Literacy rates for Europeans and the European-descended were slowly rising, at least in the *longue durée*, but it was an uneven climb, interspersed with setbacks, and tied to power. School systems and educational philosophies, economic opportunities, and political developments, changed opportunities for education, particularly for a nondominant language, such as in French-speaking Canada after the English Conquest of 1759. [30]

Literacy and transportation developments made corresponding and migrating a bit easier for some Europeans—at least when there was no war going on—but writing to find a spouse in the mid-1700s remained unusual. When James Metcalf wrote from Maccan River, Nova Scotia to Ann Gill in Yorkshire in the 1770s, it was a letter to convince someone with whom he already had an unofficial engagement that it now was the time for her to come. The General Post Office in London supervised mail, and this letter probably went through the Halifax office, that had opened in 1754.[31] Metcalf's marriage plea, like many letters meant to recruit others, balanced the advantages of joining him (focusing on elements that would be particularly enticing) with at least some negative aspects of life in the new setting.[32] In light of the ongoing nature of migration and news exchange between the two locations it was a reasonable strategy, for Gill was likely to hear reports from others about conditions in Nova Scotia, and too rosy a picture would appear false. After explaining in positive terms about the land he was farming and the nice people he met, Metcalf also anticipated some of the complaints of others in the area, in particular explaining that there were little bugs called mosquitoes that could be a bit difficult. He went on to request:

> Dear I Shall be very Glad to See you fulfill your promiss to mee and I will ful-fill mine to you if you Come I will be a kind Husband to you and will take you before aney other for I must Marry for I Cannot Live well as I am.[33]

Metcalf went on to offer to pay her passage, as well as to describe some items that might be useful to bring. The letter, dated August 1772, was successful. Ann Gill arrived the following spring and the two married.[34]

Metcalf's letter exemplified several aspects common in courtship correspondence even into the twentieth century. These were rarely love letters, the romantic epistles that began to populate the world of the elite by the mid-1800s. Rather, Metcalf stressed that he needed a wife, with a hint of desperation. While the corporate letters had stressed the impossibility under New World circumstances of "appropriate" marriage for groups of men, individual letters took the general demographics and added life course variations. Meanwhile, the rate to send a letter from the North American colonies to England had risen as part of the Post Office Act of 1765, angering those who raised the banner "no taxation without representation." As an antecedent to American independence some colonists began a private Constitutional Post in 1774.[35]

In the United States, postal connections grew exponentially after independence with the Postal Act of 1792. By the 1820s the United States had expanded the number of postal offices to several times that per capita in England or France, making the post office a key state institution. Post offices, both in the United States and Canada, were often the only governmental presence in rural areas.[36] With other improvements in roads and waterways, people discussed how the time to send letters was more than cut in half by the mid-1800s compared to a few decades earlier.[37] Historian Paul Starr described the late 1700s and early 1800s as the first American Information Revolution.[38]

When Martin Weitz wrote from Rockville, Connecticut to Philipina Fey in Gedern, Hesse to arrange a marriage in 1857 he could get letters back and forth within a few weeks—even in the winter—due to mail packet steamship service. Passengers might still take a sailing ship across the Atlantic due to slightly lower costs, but the expansion of the steam fleet made this increasingly unlikely by the late 1850s.[39] Not only was the postal transportation speed much greater, but the couple also took advantage of other new technologies. Weitz sent a photograph to his family that Fey could see when she visited them prior to coming to the United States. Commercial photography, introduced in 1839 in the United States, was becoming more common in some areas.[40] Moreover, she sent him a telegram when she arrived in New York so he could come to meet her.[41] Weitz also wrote about the transatlantic telegraph cable that went into place about the time his spouse arrived: "we never thought it would be possible to get news from Europe within a few minutes."[42] In other words, almost instantaneous messages around the United States and even across the Atlantic (though primarily for the newspapers he read rather than for personal messages) were a part of this migrant's life in 1858. A factory worker like Weitz would not use telegraphy or photography often, but it made the arrangement of a match across the Atlantic more feasible. Under these circumstances matchmaking via letters across borders began to increase for Europeans, who faced few barriers to marriage or migration.

The foremost functions of the post remained administration and business, but the percentage of private correspondence grew exponentially as well, aided by rate cuts and standardization of postal units on both sides of the Atlantic. The Hessian/German situation exemplified this trend. According to Weitz in 1854, to receive a standard letter typically cost him 22 cents, or about one-fourth of a day's wage.[43] Rate tables from 1855 indicated it cost 36 cents to pay full postage on a standard letter from New England to Hesse. Letters from Hesse arrived at the post office and the recipient had to ask for them and often pay the postage, because they did not need to be pre-paid; sometimes the ethnic press would list unclaimed letters.[44] In general correspondents in the United States still paid an escalating scale of charges based on weight and distance within the country, plus a fixed ship letter or packet ship fee for crossing the Atlantic. In 1863 the United States adopted the single rate system: one price by weight anywhere within the country.[45] Britain and Canada had already switched to this system in 1840 and 1851 respectively. Standardization of transatlantic rates followed, eliminating the necessity of paying the internal postage of all countries through which a letter traveled, and thus making it easier and cheaper to send mail.[46] With German unification in 1871 the new rate for a letter from the United States to Germany was six cents. [47]

Commentators argued that the dropping postal rates were creating national communities. People could write to others anywhere in the country and pay the same rate. By the 1850s, rail connections existed along much of the east coast of the United States, with mail cars serving on many routes. Railroad expansion westward also connected to steamships on major rivers.[48] As David Vincent put it: "[The] association of communication with locality was now challenged by the introduction of a flat-rate pre-paid charge for letters which, it was hoped, would eliminate the dimension of distance in contact between individuals. . . ."[49] While countries used this policy to promote a sense of nationality, it also worked to foster contacts across national borders.

Meanwhile, in 1851 Canada took over the administration of its postal service, and with the Confederation in 1867 the government took over full responsibility for the mail. The dominion post took on free home delivery in 1875 in Montreal, Hamilton, Ottawa, Quebec, and Saint John, not because of demand, but because they thought it would increase communications. It did—by 300 percent within six months.[50] Similar developments had taken place in major U.S. cities by the mid-1860s as well.[51] Railroad connections spreading through the Maritimes and then across the continent carried mail cars to assist in this process.[52] Postal and transportation infrastructure, in other words, made the movement of people and information faster, less expensive, and more reliable, at least along some routes. Inexpensive postal connections, like declining fares, were also in part a consequence of larger ships and increasing volume.

By the late nineteenth century several elements of communications had changed the likelihood that someone would use the mail to seek a spouse. First, the level of literacy had risen dramatically for much of the population of North America and Europe, though it remained tied to power relations, excluding or disadvantaging certain groups. International migration was likely to press people into using their literacy in order to maintain connections, or to make them across the international divide. Second, regular steamship service made transoceanic crossings more reliable and much faster. This connected to internal transportation networks, so that increasingly people could engage in transatlantic letter exchanges. Third, inexpensive postal connections, promoted in part to encourage immigration, made this period one where getting people and post to and from Europe into North America was relatively easy, certainly in comparison to earlier eras. At least as important, however, were the seriously imbalanced sex ratios of migrating populations, a strong desire to marry someone of similar background (especially linguistic and religious), and a general positive image of "America" among Europeans, contributed to make this a significant period of correspondence marriage.

When Dutch migrant Cornelis van der Vliet, wrote to ask Jantje Enserink in Eefde, Gelderland to marry him in 1907 he had already traveled from the Netherlands to South Africa to England to Canada—all within a five-year period. The frequency of his letters back to the Netherlands was at least as much a function of his interest in writing as in the possibility of sending mail. When he wrote to Enserink in 1907 he was working on construction of the Canadian Northern Railroad, which helped speed the communications connections inland.[53] When rural free delivery began in Canada in 1908 it followed the existing rail and stagecoach lines.[54] Van der Vliet's letter may have cost only five cents to cross the Atlantic, a rate introduced in 1907 by the Universal Postal Union.[55] Thin stationery, readily available in urban areas, though not perhaps at Fort William where Van der Vliet was based, made letter writing at this rate easier. As it was, governmental subsidies kept lowering postal rates in both the United States and Canada around the turn of the century when migration was high. With lower rates the number of letters rose.[56]

The increase in the number of letters crossing the Atlantic was not a direct reflection of the number of immigrants, rather, as the Bochum Emigrant Letter Project illustrated for German immigrants, individual people also wrote more letters.[57] A part of that increase related to literacy, as in the case of Van der Vliet and Enserink. In the Netherlands near total literacy prevailed among the young by 1900.[58] Enserink and Van der Vliet were part of an international marriage market. Men and women did not literally "sell" themselves, but they used correspondence in which men typically specified what they wanted in a spouse, and intermediaries or women themselves described their own characteristics and tried to gain information about the men as well. It was an exchange in which patriarchal custom still prescribed that men do the asking and women then make a yes or no decision. Van der Vleit had worked for Enserink's father briefly several years before they married, so their decision-making was based at least in part on face-to-face contact. This too was quite common for letter-writers: immigrant men who waited until they had the financial status to marry and then tried to attract women they had met in the homeland at some time in the past.[59]

People from various countries participated in this international marriage market, in part because they preferred spouses from their home-lands, in part because they had few choices locally, in part because they were used to letting others assist in finding spouses for them. The man who wrote back to a relative asking for a spouse could have been from Cape Verde, Russia, Italy, or Sweden.[60] The letter he wrote might take two weeks to reach its destination, which compared to a month was a big improvement. In cases where the man had the wherewithal and interest to go back to marry, he might do so, as did Cornelis van der Vliet (who recruited railroad workers as well as a wife). Ships devoted to migrant passage plied the Atlantic regularly, and by the early twentieth century had often increased their comfort level through greater speed (decreasing crossing time to a few days) and a switch to cabins even for steerage class passengers.[61] In other cases the couple married at the docks when the woman debarked, or immediately on her arrival in the man's location somewhere inland. In this period fears of white women being lured into prostitution through promises of marriage ran high as the press reported on "white slavery" and how single women should travel.[62] Both the United States and Canadian authorities strengthened their laws forbidding the transport of prostitutes, though in practice scrutiny was harshest for women from Asia.[63] For prostitutes who wanted to migrate, particularly those from Europe, marriage became a way to avoid the law. The xenophobic fear of Chinese wives joining husbands fueled both intense investigation at the borders and legal measures, such as the "head tax" on Chinese immigrants in Canada. The result could be men with wives in China and second wives/concubines in North America.[64] In general as immigration restrictions hardened, the category of spouse took on greater importance for the migration of young women.

The group of women recruited through the mail who received the most publicity was from Japan. The women labeled "picture brides" were similar to other women who joined spouses in North America. Men wrote to their families asking for a spouse, families searched for a suitable person, sometimes with the assistance of a matchmaker, and once they found a person the two might exchange pictures as well as other information. Both parties had to agree. In some cases the men returned for the wedding, perhaps relying on the Toyo Kisen Kaiska Line, which specialized in regular passenger service from Japan to San Francisco.[65] What differentiated the Japanese women from other women recruited by mail was the ability of Japanese immigrant men to register their marriages in Japan without being present at the ceremony. American officials sometimes called this "proxy marriage," and demanded remarriage at the docks, to the chagrin of Japanese commentators, who noted that people in valid marriages from other countries did not face this treatment.[66]

Under the Gentlemen's Agreement/Lemieux Agreement of 1907–1908, Japanese men in the United States and Canada could not legally send for fiancées, only for wives under family reunification provisions.[67] The women arrived already married to men they had never seen in a few cases. At times the pictures in the letters were deceptive: men were younger, dressed in clothing they could not afford, placed in settings that were not typical.[68] The deception could work both ways, as women chose flattering pictures that did not show their height or frizzy hair, and portrayed traditional clothing on rather progressive women.[69] The women usually had at least a basic education, in part because of the educational reforms of the Meiji government, but also because women with an education sometimes had to look hard to find a spouse. Moreover, those who received education from North American missionaries often had a font of knowledge about life across the Pacific that made it more likely they would consider migration.[70] Once again the combination of literacy and communications infrastructure made marriage arranged by letter a feasible option. The women had some ideas about the place to which they were going, even if the ideas were inaccurate. Racial animosity in both North American and Japanese cultures made it unlikely that Japanese men would look outside their ethnic background for spouses.

A tradition of third party matchmaking made correspondence marriage easier in many ways, for it often eliminated the expectation of meeting and knowing the individual prior to the wedding. The key, however, was the reliability of the matchmaker. The U.S. Braun Commission, which studied "white slavery," collected stories of procurers posing as Jewish matchmakers who came to Galicia with marriage offers—engagement cards preprinted in Hebrew—from rich but busy U.S. businessmen.[71]

One other avenue to correspondence marriage also made significant inroads in the period around the turn of the twentieth century: personal ads. Advertisements were widely distributed in ethnic newspapers that had circulations throughout the United States and Canada, and sometimes crossed oceanic borders as well. If you look through *De Volksvriend* [Friend of the People] a relatively conservative Dutch paper from Iowa, *Työmies* [The Worker] a left-leaning Finnish publication from northern Michigan, or the *Forverts* [Yiddish Forward] the ubiquitous New York paper from the early 1900s, you will find classified ads for marriage. Many were short, perhaps assuming various characteristics about the readers of a particular paper (e.g. religious, political), while others such as the following from *Y Drych* [The Mirror] a Welsh-language weekly out of Utica, provided more detail:

> WIFE WANTED!: I wish to commence correspondence with a young woman or a young widow; no objection if she has one young child. Must be of good character and religious. The intention is to make two into one in order to take up a farm in the West, and to make home comfortable. No deceit or frivolity.[72]

Personal ads were not entirely new, for even in the colonial era a few such advertisements existed, but they were much more common in this era.[73] The ads sometimes allowed people to exchange letters via the newspaper—which could provide a degree of anonymity at least initially, though many simply printed their names. In this way newspapers could take the place of a matchmaker in organizing correspondence between potential spouses, and like the matchmaker, the newspaper might be paid for providing this function.

By the late twentieth century people wrote once again of a communications revolution, a term Richard John used to describe the early national period in the United States.[74] Others spoke of telegraphy, steamships, railroads, and international postal connections of the later nineteenth century as eliminating distance. But the twentieth century version of "death of distance" facilitated by the telephone, television, and electronic computer has been at the heart of what many recent commentators describe as a transnational world.[75] In this context, letter-writing to find a spouse has—in some cases—gone electronic. But not everyone worldwide has electronic access, or even telephone access. And even within a national infrastructure power applies to communications as well; for example a father, husband, or village leader may control who has access to a telephone or computer in a family or a village and when they may use it.[76] Electronic letters, I suggest, differ in degree rather than kind. This is most easily seen in the shift of personal ads found in online ethnic newspapers and websites.

Of the 35 online ethnic papers or web sites I contacted in 2001, 18 replied, and of those 13 carried personal ads for marriage. One editor said they did not carry the ads "yet" and another asked whether I wanted to set up the service for them. Some of the papers without ads had other options, such as chat rooms for members only—with membership limited to those of a particular ethnic background. Many had simple advertisements, not unlike those that had appeared a hundred years earlier, though the more technologically savvy often included photographs. The breadth of national background and panethnic identification was striking: *Brazzil, Filipino Express, German Corner, India Abroad, Islamic Horizons, MundoHispanico, Russian Los Angeles, U.S. Africa Online,* and *Warsaw Voice.* Other websites were more specifically devoted to matchmaking: *Amigos Amores, Asian connections, Vietnetcity.* In 2004 there were "singles" sites devoted to most countries worldwide, but with an option to look for potential spouses in North America. These sites in most cases were aimed at members of a particular ethnic, panethnic, or religious background who wished to connect with others of the same background. As one testimonial posted on the Iranian Singles Network stated: "I live in a small city . . . The Iranian community is small and scattered . . . I truly hope that this service continues for others, who prefer to marry Iranian and to help preserve our culture and heritage."[77]

Intra-ethnic sites tended to differ from the numerous "foreign brides" sites where the goal was for U.S. and Canadian men to find women from other countries, most often from Asia or the countries of the former Soviet Union.[78] The foreign bride sites not only sold names, addresses and pictures, but organized tours as well. At the margins, some of these were basically sex tours. "Club of all nations" notes men could choose "ladies–girls" who want to meet American men "10, 20, or 30 years older for vacation dates, friendship, love & marriage."[79] Other sites were primarily for posting nude pictures or otherwise float into the spectrum of pornography. While selling descriptions of women, or at least some of their attributes, was not absent in the past, there was a greater degree of commercialization in the foreign brides sites. The Philippine government, beset by notorious examples of failed international marriages based on such matchmaking, sought to thwart such businesses by outlawing the agencies. But the companies simply changed their official task to finding cute, young, female "pen-pals" for North American men (like the one that opened this essay), a disguise that fooled no one but evaded the letter of the law. It was striking that Cherry Blossoms, one of the longest-running and most successful matchmaking agencies on the web, stressed that it was not a "mail order bride" service like those of the past, but rather an internet vehicle for posting "picture personal ads."[80] Moreover, the sites are often listed as foreign bride companies, that is, their emphasis is on providing "foreign" women for North American men, but rarely vice versa. This pattern was the product of and sought to create unions that would uphold patriarchal and heterosexual privilege.

One of the most striking elements of these cross-cultural courtship situations was language difference. While literacy was almost a prerequisite for taking part in these commercial endeavors, language differences often existed between potential spouses.[81] Few North American men made the effort to learn the languages of the women involved, and for some, the inability of the woman to speak effectively in English was at least part of the allure. Though the women were typically attracted to a view of American life which they knew from various media sources, many became linguistically and culturally dependent on their husbands for years to come.[82] The women, learning to function in a nonnative language, were likely to appear less intelligent. It was a situation that existed in earlier times through one spouse learning English while the other had little or no opportunity to do this, but it was intensified by the cultural distance a nonnative had to negotiate. The multiculturalism that made for more marriages across national lines, in other words, sometimes intensified gendered hierarchies of communication.

Another way in which matchmaking at the turn of the twenty-first century was a continuation of the past, though intensified, was in the way people used marriage to enter or remain in the United States. For same-sex couples this was notable, with American/ foreign gay couples seeking similar lesbian couples to arrange green card marriages for one another.[83] Green card marriages were present among heterosexuals as well, particularly for some national groups. Even when the marriage was meant to last, often one partner had a stereotypical view of opportunities and gender roles that awaited in North America, stereotypes which were not unraveled in premarital correspondence. For Usha, a woman from India who had an MBA and wanted to build a career, an arranged marriage brought her to the United States, only to dash her hopes when her husband demanded that she stay home and take care of the children they soon had.[84]

By the late 1990s e-mail might mean faster communication but not necessarily better communication. Electronic mail, like telephone connections, was not always available or affordable to new immigrants. Those coming from countries without technological infrastructure to make computers a widespread reality, might still rely on the postal system, which could get a letter to many places in the world, albeit at a varying pace. Marina Roxana Molino Fuente, writing from El Salvador to her fiancée, Adan Isael Lazo, in Los Angeles in the early 1990s, noted that she had not heard from him in five months, and that she suspected he might have married someone else in the meantime. It was a reasonable suspicion, given that other letters to Lazo indicated he had romantic contact with other women. But in this case the problems of correspondence intensified due to Lazo's undocumented status, which could rapidly lead to change of address or even deportation.[85] Mail delivery in El Salvador was also unreliable, leaving questions for both partners about whether the lack of correspondence was intended or due to infrastructure. The expectation of love letters between potential spouses, a much greater cultural demand for some groups in the late twentieth century than for many late nineteenth century migrants, helped create and reinforce the need for more frequent communication.

Improvements in airmail, introduced in 1918 in the United States and shortly thereafter in Canada, meant letters theoretically could arrive in a day in many parts of the world. In practice, however, the typical delivery time in 2000 compared to 1910 has diminished to one week from two.[86] Telephone connections, on the other hand, which existed early in the twentieth century for the elite few, were prohibitively expensive for most people through mid-century, and remained expensive even late in the twentieth century for many parts of the world. As one woman from Nigeria explained in 2000, there was only one telephone in her hometown, and people used it primarily for emergencies. Just as the telegraph was not something an average immigrant used late in the nineteenth century, neither was a telephone a typical means of international communication for many in the late twentieth century. This was changing in the 2000s, though perhaps not as quickly as some commentators suggest.[87] Travel mirrored other technological advances. Transpacific and transatlantic travel by air was much more readily available in 2000 than it was when it was introduced in the 1930s, but it remained prohibitively expensive for many migrants, particularly those outside the most important travel hubs.[88]

What this suggests is that air travel, telephones, and computers have not brought as much of a revolution in epistolary courtship in the late twentieth century as some would suggest. Migration has sparked many to seek spouses through the mail throughout North American history. Once the postal system and regular transportation systems were in place, those connections led a significant number of persons to look across international borders for spouses, first from their homelands, and later from other lands. The inequalities of communications technology between countries and among groups within North America remained, and the cultural expectations of courtship guided who could write what to whom. For some, arranged marriages went onto the web, and the primary shift was one of the distance people would travel to join the spouse. For others, the encounter with a North American version of companionate marriage, emphasizing love and the selection of one's own spouse, was more significant than the adoption of new technologies. To return to the advertisement for pen pals that opened this essay, the fact that people expected to select their own spouses, and that they wanted to love the other person, and that they had a sufficient education and wherewithal to correspond electronically, made online love letters a possibility. Moreover, their openness to persons of different cultural backgrounds was at least as important as their ability to use computers in creating a long-term link. Migration has spurred many to turn to the mail for contacts, and then to make major life decisions based on the limited repertoire of information that was contained in those communications.

Notes

The author wishes to thank David Gerber, Bruce Elliott, Eithne Luibheid, and Donna Gabaccia for their comments on drafts of this essay.

1. Online at <http://www.snookys-video.com/> Accessed July 30, 2004.
2. John J. McCusker provides a similar perspective by looking at the rise of business newspapers in "The Demise of Distance: The Business Press and the Origins of the Information Revolution in the Early Modern Atlantic World," *American Historical Review* 110, no. 2 (April 2005): 295–321.
3. On this topic see Gregory M. Pflugfelder, *Cartographies of Desire: Male-Male Sexuality in Japanese Discourses, 1600–1950* (Berkeley: University of California Press, 1999), p. 1.
4. William Engelbrecht, *Iroquoia: The Development of a Native World* (Syracuse: Syracuse University Press, 2003), p. 113. The practice of marriage as a means of alliance continued, for example in unions of fur traders and first nations women. See Sylvia van Kirk, *Many Tender Ties: Women in Fur-Trade Society, 1670–1870* (Norman: University of Oklahoma Press, 1983) and Jennifer S.H. Brown, *Strangers in Blood: Fur Trade Company Families in Indian Country* (Vancouver: University of British Columbia Press, 1983).
5. Camilla Townsend, *Pocahontas and the Powhatan Dilemma* (New York: Hill and Wang, 2004), pp. 122–123; 127–128.
6. Ibid., pp. 113–114.
7. On this theme see Bernardo P. Gallegos, *Literacy, Education, and Society in New Mexico, 1693–1821* (Albuquerque: University of New Mexico Press, 1992), p. 63.
8. Philip Harrison and Mark Brayshay, "Post-Horse Routes, Royal Progresses and Government Communications in the Reign of James I," *Journal of Transport History* 18 (1997): 116–133.
9. Ian R. Lee, "The Canadian Postal System: Origins, Growth and Decay of the State Postal Function," PhD dissertation, Ottawa, Ontario: Carleton University, 1989, p. 38.
10. Frank Staff, *The Transatlantic Mail* (Lawrence, MA: Quarterman Publications, 1980 [1956]), p. 19.
11. Records of the Virginia Land Company, quoted in David R. Ransome, "Wives for Virginia, 1621," *William and Mary Quarterly* 48 (1991): 5.
12. Ransome, "Wives," p. 5; and Brown, *Good Wives*, p. 82.
13. See Samuel Pyeatt Menefee, *Wives for Sale: An Ethnographic Study of British Popular Divorce* (Oxford: Basil Blackwell, 1981). See also E.P. Thompson, *Customs in Common* (New York: The New Press, 1993), chapter 7 "The Sale of Wives."
14. Yves Landry, "Les Filles du Roi Emigrees au Canada au XVIIᵉ siecle, ou un Exemple de Choix du Conjoint en Situation de Desequilibre des Sexes," *Histoire, Economie et Société* 11, no. 2 (1992): 197–216.

15. Clark Robenstine, "French Colonial Policy and the Education of Women and Minorities: Louisiana in the Early Eighteenth Century," *History of Education Quarterly* 32, no. 2 (Summer 1992): 205–206. On morality see also Nelson Dawson, "Les Filles du Roi: Des Polleuses? La France du XVIIe siecle," *Historical Reflections* 12, no.1 (1985): 9–38.

16. On mass recruitment of women as a strategy of empire see also Adele Perry, *On the Edge of Empire: Gender, Race, and the Making of British Columbia, 1849–1871* (Toronto: University of Toronto Press, 2001).

17. For English rates see David Cressy, *Literacy and the Social Order: Reading and Writing in Tudor and Stuart England* (Cambridge: Cambridge University Press, 1980), p. 73.

18. See Clark Robenstien, "French Colonial Policy and the Education of Women and Minorities: Louisiana in the Early Eighteenth Century," *History of Education Quarterly* 32, no. 2 (1992): 193–211; and Linda L. Arthur, "A New Look at Schooling and Literacy: The Colony of Georgia," *Georgia Historical Quarterly* 84, no. 4 (2000): 563–588.

19. Gallegos, *Literacy, Education, and Society*, pp. 68–71.

20. For a brief discussion of the meaning of signing rates see Bruce Curtis, "Some Recent Work on the History of Literacy in Canada," *History of Education Quarterly* 30, no. 4 (Winter 1990): 615.

21. F.W. Grubb, "Growth of Literacy in Colonial America: Longitudinal Patterns, Economic Models, and the Direction of Future Research," *Social Science History* 14/4 (Winter 1990): 453–455; Gallegos, *Literacy, Education, and Society*, p. 53; and see Ruth Wallace Herndon, "Literacy Among New England's Transient Poor, 1750–1800," *Journal of Social History* 29, no. 4 (1996): 963–965.

22. David Cressy, Coming over: *Migration and Communication between England and New England in the Seventeenth Century* (Cambridge: Cambridge University Press, 1987), p. 220.

23. See for example the description of Peter Klein's letters in Walter D. Kamphoefner, Wolfgang Helbich, and Ulrike Sommer, eds., *News from the Land of Freedom: German Immigrants Write Home* (Ithaca: Cornell University Press, 1991), pp. 383–384.

24. Ibid., pp. 217, 222–224.

25. Jane E. Harrison, *Until Next Year: Letter Writing and the Mails in the Canadas, 1640–1830* (Quebec; Canadian Postal Museum/ Canadian Museum of Civilization, 1997), p. 65.

26. Roger Thompson, *Mobility and Migration: East Anglian Founders of New England, 1629–1640* (Amherst: University of Massachusetts Press, 1994), p. 209.

27. Richard R. John, *Spreading the News: The American Postal System from Franklin to Morse* (Cambridge: Harvard University Press, 1995), p. 26.

28. See Marianne S. Wokeck, *Trade in Strangers: The Beginnings of Mass Migration to North America* (University Park: Pennsylvania State University Press, 1999).

29. Konstantin Dierks, " 'Let me Chat a Little': Letter Writing in Rhode Island Before the Revolution." *Rhode Island History* 53, no. 4 (1995): 120–133.

30. Literacy also underscored power, with categories of people—slaves, first nations, conquered European groups, the lower classes, and women—excluded at times from both learning to read or write, particularly in a non-dominant language, and from disseminating their views in writing. On Quebec see Michel Verrette, *L'Alphabétisation au Québec, 1660–1900: En Marche vers la Modernité Culturelle* (Quebec: Septentrion, 2002). A similar argument appears in Kenneth L. Steward and Arnoldo de Leon, "Literacy among Immigrants in Texas, 1850–1900," *Latin American Research Review* 20, no. 3 (1985): 180–187.

31. J.J. MacDonald, *The Nova Scotia Post: Its Offices, Masters and Marks 1700–1867* (Toronto: Unitrade Press, 1985), p. 9.
32. See Kamphoefner et al., *News from the Land of Freedom*, on this theme in emigrant recruitment generally, p. 20.
33. James Metcalf to Ann Gill, Maccan River, Nova Scotia, August 1772, in Barbara DeWolfe, ed., *Discoveries of America: Personal Accounts of British Emigrants to North America during the Revolutionary Era* (Cambridge: Cambridge University Press, 1997), p. 45.
34. Ibid., p. 44.
35. Lee, "Canadian Postal System," p. 48.
36. Ibid., p. 152.
37. John, *Spreading the News*, pp. 5, 17.
38. Paul Starr, *The Creation of the Media: Political Origins of Modern Communications* (New York: Basic Books, 2004), chapter 3.
39. Edward W. Sloan, "Collins Versus Cunard: The Realities of a North Atlantic Steamship Rivalry, 1850–1858," *International Journal of Maritime History* 4, no. 1 (1992): 83–100.
40. Susan Annette Newberry, "Commerce and Ritual in American Daguerreian Portraiture, 1839–1859," PhD dissertation, New York: Cornell University, 1999.
41. Kamphoefner et al., *News from the Land of Freedom*, p. 359.
42. Martin Weitz to Father et al., Rockville, CT to Schotten, Hesse, August 1, 1858, in Kamphoefner et al., *News from the Land of Freedom*, p. 364.
43. Martin Weitz to Father et al., Astoria, NY to Schotten, Hesse, July 16, 1854, in Kamphoefner et al., *News from the Land of Freedom*, p. 341.
44. Kamphoefner et al., *News from the Land of Freedom*, p. 350.
45. *The United States Postal Service: An American History, 1775–2002* (Washington, DC: United States Postal Service, 2003), p. 11.
46. John C. Arnell, *#1: Handbook on Transatlantic Mail* (Transatlantic Study Group Handbooks: British North America Philatelic Society, 1987), pp. 5–17.
47. Frank Staff, *The Transatlantic Mail* (Lawrence, MA: Quarterman Publications, 1980 [reprint of 1956]), pp. 162–163. Letters crossing the Pacific from China around the same period were more expensive and more prone to delay. The rate from Shanghai to the United States for a single sheet was ten cents. Richard Pratt, *Imperial China: History of the Posts to 1896* (London: Christie's Robson Lowe, 1994), pp. 168–170.
48. James H. Bruns, *Mail on the Move* (Polo, IL: Transportation Trails, 1992), p. 65.
49. David Vincent, *Literacy and Popular Culture: England 1750–1914* (Cambridge: Cambridge University Press, 1989), p. 43.
50. Lee, "Canadian Postal System," p. 154.
51. *The United States Postal Service*, p. 20.
52. Susan McLeod O' Reilly, *On Track: The Railway Mail Service in Canada* (Hull, Quebec: Canadian Museum of Civilization, 1992), pp. 26–28.
53. Frank Verbrugge, ed., *Brieven uit het Verleden*, Manuscript, Heritage Hall Collection, Calvin College, pp. 42, 78, 98.
54. A.W. Currie, "The Post Office Since 1867," *Canadian Journal of Economics and Political Science* 24, no. 2 (1958): 244.
55. John Gillis, "Immigrants and the Postal Service," Canadian Museum of Civilization, <http://www.civilization.ca/cpm/chrono/chc1900e.html>. Accessed October 5, 2005.
56. Frank Staff, *The Transatlantic Mail* (Lawrence, MA: Quarterman Publications, 1980 [reprint of 1956]), pp. 110, 173–176; see also Allan Poulin, "Floating the Ocean Lines: Transatlantic Mail Subsidies," *Archivist* 17, no. 4 (1990): 5–7.
57. Kamphoefner et al., *News from the Land of Freedom*, p. 27.

58. Hans Knippenberg, *Deelname aan het lager onderwijs in Nederland gedurende de negentiende eeuw. Een analyse van de landelijke ontwikkeling en van de regionale verschillen* (Amsterdam: Koninklijk Nederlands Aardrijkskundig Genootschap, 1986), pp. 51–52.
59. Frank Verbrugge, comp., *Brieven uit het Verleden*, [manuscript letter compilation] Heritage Hall Collection, Calvin College, Grand Rapids, MI. pp. 156–172.
60. Suzanne M. Sinke, "Migration for Labor, Migration for Love: Marriage and Family Formation across Borders," *OAH Magazine* (Fall 1999): 17–21.
61. Drew Keeling, "The Transportation Revolution and Transatlantic Migration, 1850–1914," *Research in Economic History* 19 (1999): 39–74.
62. See for example, H. Dekker, "Immigration Laws," *The Banner*, July 9, 1914, p. 422.
63. See John McLaren, "White Slavers: The Reform of Canada's Prostitution Laws and Patterns of Enforcement, 1900–1920," *Criminal Justice History* 8 (1987): 53–119. Marcus Braun, head of the white slavery committee in the United States, claimed 90 percent of Japanese women coming as spouses were prostitutes. U.S. National Archives and Records Administration (NARA), Files of the Immigration and Naturalization Service (INS), Record Group 85, Entry 9, 52484/1-A, "Memo for the Acting Commissioner General 19 Oct 1908 from Chief, Law Division."
64. See Denise Chong, *The Concubine's Children* (Toronto: Penguin Canada, 1994).
65. Michio Yamada Fune Ni Miru Nihonjin Iminshi: Kasato Maru kara kuruzu kyakusen e [Japanese Emigration History As Seen Through Ships: From the Kasato Maru to Passenger Cruisers], trans. Bob Barde, Jeff Bradt, Tomoko Negishi, Yuko Okubo, Ann Sokolsky, Wesley Ueunten, and R. Douglas Welch (Tokyo: Chuokoron-Sha, 1998).
66. On this see NARA, INS, Record Group 85, Entry 9, Box 107, especially Letter of H.H North, Commissioner of Immigration San Francisco, to Commissioner General of Immigration, June 24, 1908, 1456-I; and E.H. Van Dyke, Japanese Interpreter to John H. Clark, Commissioner of Immigration, Montreal, June 21, 1907.
67. Tomoko Makabe, *Picture Brides: Japanese Women in Canada*, trans. Kathleen Chisato Merken (North York: Multicultural History Society of Ontario, 1995), p. 18.
68. Eileen Sunada Sarasohn, *Issei Women: Echoes from Another Frontier* (Palo Alto: Pacific Books, 1998), p. 75. On the rise of matchmaking in Japan related to photography see Kei Tanaka, "Japanese Picture Marriage and the Image of Immigrant Women in Early Twentieth-Century California," *Japanese Journal of American Studies* 15 (2004): 115–138.
69. See for example Tami Nakamura's self-description in Makabe, *Picture Brides*, p. 131; Sarasohn, *Issei Women*, p. 30.
70. Midge Ayukawa, "Good Wives and Wise Mothers: Japanese Picture Brides in Early Twentieth Century British Columbia," *BC Studies* 105–106 (1995): 103–118.
71. NARA, INS, Record Group 85, Entry 9, 52484/1-D, Letter of Marcus Braun to Commissioner General, Berlin, June 18, 1909.
72. *Y Drych*, September 15, 1887, quoted in Aled Jones and Bill Jones, *Welsh Reflections: Y Drych and America 1851–2001* (Llandysul, Wales: Gomer, 2001), p. 73 [their translation].
73. Suzanne M. Sinke, *Dutch Immigrant Women in the United States, 1880–1920* (Urbana: University of Illinois Press, 2002), pp. 22–23.
74. John, *Spreading the News*, p. 63.
75. Frances Cairncross, *The Death of Distance: How the Communications Revolution Will Change Our Lives* (Boston: Harvard Business School Press, 1997); on the role of communications in transnational migration see Peggy Levitt, *The Transnational Villagers* (Berkeley: University of California Press, 2001), p. 22.

94   SUZANNE M. SINKE

76. Sarah Mahler, "Transnational Relationships: The Struggle to Communicate Across Borders," *Identities: Global Studies in Culture and Power* 7, no. 4 (January 2001): 583.
77. "ISN Successful Matches," <http://www.iraniansingles.com/happy.htm> Accessed April 18, 2001, p. 7 (of 10).
78. See Nicole Constable, *Romance on a Global Stage: Pen Pals, Virtual Ethnography & "Mail Order" Marriages* (Berkeley: University of California Press, 2003).
79. "Meet & Marry Foreign Single Women!" Online at <http://getgirls.com/foreign.htm> Accessed August 4, 2003.
80. "Cherry Blossoms" Online at <http://www.blossoms.com> Accessed August 4, 2003.
81. See for example the discussions of linguistic problems in Lynn Visson, *Wedded Strangers: The Challenges of Russian-American Marriages* (New York: Hippocrene Books, 1995), pp. 59–60.
82. Rosemary Breger and Rosanna Hill, "Introducing Mixed Marriages," in *Cross-Cultural Marriage: Identity and Choice* (Oxford: Berg, 1998), p. 22.
83. Chris Dueñas, "Coming to America: The Immigration Obstacles Facing Binational Same-Sex Couples," May 3, 2000, for Partners Task Force for Gay & Lesbian Couples. Online at <http://www.buddybuddy.com/duenas-1.html> Accessed July 14, 2003.
84. Sudha Sethu Balagopal, "The Case of the Brown Esahib: Issues that Confront Working South Asian Wives and Mothers," in *Emerging Voices: South Asian American Women Redefine Self, Family, and Community*, ed. Sangeeta R. Gupta (Walnut Creek, CA: Altamira Press, 1999), p. 153.
85. Larry Siems, ed., *Between the Lines: Letters Between Undocumented Mexican and Central American Immigrants and Their Families and Friends* (Tucson: University of Arizona Press, 1992), pp. 161–165.
86. Roger E. Bilstein, "Technology and Commerce: Aviation in the Conduct of American Business, 1918–29," *Technology and Culture* 10, no. 3 (1969): 392–411; F.J. Hatch, "Ship-to-Shore Airmail Services in the 1920's," *Canadian Geographic* 97, no. 1 (1978): 56–61.
87. Mahler, "Transnational Relationships."
88. Richard K. Schrader, "Bridging the Atlantic," *American History Illustrated* 24, no. 3 (1989): 34–47.

Part II

Writing Conventions and Practices

4

Irish Emigration and the Art of Letter-Writing

David Fitzpatrick

Historians of migration, though increasingly aware of the unique value of personal letters as a source for the mentality of emigrants, are still inclined to neglect the painful process by which such testaments were composed. Yet the process of composition, embedded in form and structure, was itself a vital element in the experience of migration. The letters exchanged between nineteenth century emigrants and their families at home served a variety of functions, which I have discussed in *Oceans of Consolation: Personal Accounts of Irish Migration to Australia.*[1] Apart from supplying both public and private information, they served to maintain material and emotional links between separated brethren, and helped to shape future migration. The arrival of a letter was in itself a token of solidarity, while the absence of an expected letter was an endemic source of anxiety, even a harbinger of death. Until the early twentieth century, when the new "Imperial Penny Post" quartered the charge for sending a basic letter between the United Kingdom and Australia, the cost of transoceanic postage was high enough to deter most plebeian correspondents from dashing off trivial notes. In the 1830s, such a letter had cost over half a crown, equivalent to a week's wages for a laborer in contemporary Ireland. Most surviving letters were carefully constructed, earnest in tone, and packed to capacity with messages, advice, and information. Typically, one or two folded sheets, densely inscribed, were charged with maintaining the fractured family group for a month or more. It is scarcely surprising that so momentous an enterprise would develop its own rhetorical conventions, to the point that vernacular letter-writing became an art form. My purpose in this essay is to identify some of the techniques used by these neglected artists of the "few lines," to establish whether Irish migratory correspondence conformed to a "type," and to unravel the process by which the conventions of letter-writing evolved. My main source for this enquiry is the collection of 14 sequences of Irish Australian letters analyzed in *Oceans of Consolation*, amounting to 111 letters sent between 1843 and 1906 of which almost equal numbers were sent to and from Australia. The letters were deliberately selected to represent the semi-educated, subliterate majority who, but for migration, would hardly have needed to compose a letter. In short, I chose, perhaps perversely, to exclude letters by the "letter-writing classes." Though my book concerned Australia, the language and flavor of the letters were overwhelmingly Irish, and the preoccupations of the emigrants who chose Australia probably differed little from those of the Irish in America or Canada. The degree to which particular streams of emigrants differed in their composition, education, outlook, and experience is, of course, one of the great unresolved issues of migration history. Likewise, we should not simply assume that the forms and structures detectable in Irish Australian letters were replicated elsewhere. However, any skeptics inclined to dismiss Irish Australian letters as an atypical curiosity should ponder the parallels with Irish American correspondence in the preceding century, as documented in Kerby Miller's prodigious dossier, *Irish Immigrants in the Land of Canaan*.[2] I shall return to such international echoes shortly.

Admittedly, the surviving correspondence between Ireland and Australia does not conform rigidly to a single "type," in the sense that the observable variations in calligraphy, format, rhetorical structure, and declamatory conventions are reducible to embellishments of one underlying or "dominant" pattern. These variations were partly governed by factors such as region of origin, gender, class, and education, glaringly obvious in that most basic of the epistolary arts, penmanship. Yet, even among the letters of the unlettered, the quirks and peculiarities of individual writers undercut all attempts to reduce their correspondence to uniformity. Michael Normile from Clare, like William Fife in Fermanagh, came from a small farm overcrowded with children, survived the ravages of the Great Famine, acquired a rather higher standard of literacy than most of his neighbors, and wrote memorable and moving letters which helped shape the lives of the recipients. Their letters nevertheless differed sharply in calligraphy, vocabulary, turns of phrase, and rhetorical ploys. What they had in common was a distinctive blend of ceremonial and conversational elements, and considerable skill in manipulating their distant kinsfolk through the written word. It is these common elements, utterly unlike any known style of modern correspondence but widely shared among Irish Australian letter-writers, which I shall now try to distil.

Such regularities often defy measurement, creating the risk that editors over-steeped in their beloved documents will impose ingenious but fanciful patterns on incoherent reality. One element of vernacular correspondence which does invite measurement is the use of ritualized phrases by way of salutation (and also farewell). For the letter-writing classes, of course, the choice of appropriate modes of address and salutation was minutely attuned to the relative status of sender and recipient. Any breach of the rules of polite address might be interpreted as a failure of etiquette, an exhibition of crass ignorance, or a deliberate provocation. In 1847, for example, a government enquiry into the administration of poor relief in Clare was diverted by a contretemps between a landlord (that of Michael Normile, as it happens) and an official, who had replied to a request chummily headed "Dear Sir" with a missive beginning "Sir, I beg leave to say . . ." The landlord fumed that this constituted a "discourtesy" on the part of a person who had dined at his house, implying that the abrupt salutation followed a disagreement. The official admitted that he had once been "on very intimate terms" with Cornelius O'Brien, having dined with him five or six times in the previous season, but that "it was my habit in writing to gentlemen above me in rank, to write so."[3] The canny correspondent trod a fine line between presumption and frigidity, the boundary being patrolled by an elaborate code of etiquette.

For unlettered correspondents, respect and courtesy were conveyed by other means than matching rank to the form of address. The formal greeting "Sir" was scarcely used, and even "Dear Sir" was usually set aside in favor of warmer expressions such as "my dear," "my very dear," or even "my very very dear." Warmth was expressed alike by male and female writers, and varied little according to relative seniority, except that seniors were always addressed by rank (such as "my dear father"), whereas juniors were always assigned a name. The greeting was only the first element of a complex routine of salutation, often occupying several lines of formulaic phrases, enquiries, declarations, and exhortations. My analysis of Irish Australian salutations distilled five elements, each detectable in a substantial proportion (between 33 and 82 percent) of the letters examined. These may be classified as introductory phrases, references to correspondence, references to health, affirmations of religious faith, and personal messages.

The simplest way to illustrate this widespread (though not universal) "type" of salutation is to quote a characteristic, if elaborate, example in a letter sent from Armagh to Victoria in 1845:[4]

I embrace this favourable opportunity of scribling these few Lines to you [*introductory phrases*]

once more hoping that the will find you Both in as Good Health as the leave
us all in at present [*discussion of health*]
thank God for all His mercies to us [*affirmation of faith*].
I received your Letter after a long silence on the 30th of May Being Dated the
29th of September 1844 [*reference to correspondence*]
which Gives us all a Great Deal of Comfort But sory to hear of your Loss But
content to Hear of you Being in a situation and your children in Good
Health [*message*].

The order of the five elements was not immutable; few salutations
embraced all five categories, and the conventional phrases were subject to
extensive and sometimes playful variation. Even so, the salutations are
sufficiently uniform to justify the inference of a conventional pattern.

There is nothing novel in my claim that Irish emigrant salutations conformed to a type, usually dismissed as quaintly characteristic of rural Irish
culture. Arnold Schrier, the pioneering analyst of Irish American letters
and one of Kerby Miller's coauthors, reported that the "usual opening
sentence," deployed by Protestant as well as Catholic writers, was as follows:
"Dear Father and Mother, I take this favorable opportunity to write these
few lines hoping the arrival of this letter finds you in good health as it
leaves me at present, thanks be to God for his kind mercies to us all." He
maintained that "nearly all were enhanced by a charm of expression inherent in the modes and manners peculiar to Irish speech," conveying "an air
of unlettered eloquence." "Beyond the standard opening sentence which
seemed to characterize a great majority of the letters and gave them a note
of stilted formality, they were almost conversational in tone."[5] Apart from
his more emphatic claim of uniformity, Schrier's analysis based on the
"American letter" differs little from mine. Schrier, while implying that
these forms were distinctively if not uniquely "Irish," did not enquire further
into the origins of the form. But texts included in *The Land of Canaan*
show that similar salutations were already prevalent among Ulster
Presbyterians in the late eighteenth century, as in a letter sent from New
Jersey to Armagh in 1796: "I take this opertunity of Letting you know that
I and My family are in good health at Pres[en]t thanks be to God for all his
Continued Mercies to us and trust you all share the Same Blessing."[6]

Schrier's stereotype was derived not only from actual letters, but also
from beliefs about the "American letter" which had passed into the supposedly collective memory by 1955, when he induced the Irish Folklore
Commission to circularize its collectors with queries about emigration
and correspondence. Several collectors duly reported the existence "in
those days" of "an unwritten code or usage, a fixed formula," which was the
subject of much rustic merriment. Strikingly similar examples were

elicited from Rossport in North Mayo and Grange in Tipperary, where the collector remembered "a local wag who used to make fun of the stereotype form of American letters":

> Dear Father and Mother I now sit down and take my pen in hand to write these few lines which I hope will find you both in good health as I am myself at present, thank God for his kind mercies to us all. [Tipperary]
>
> Dear so and so. I take my pen in hand hoping the arrival of these few lines will find you in a good state of health, as the departure of this letter leaves us in the same state, thanks be to God for his kind mercy to us all. [Mayo]

The Mayo folklorist asserted that "every American letter to and fro was prefaced with that introduction, and its omission would be considered a grave error of taste and courtesy."[7] This analysis uncannily resembles that of William Thomas and Florian Znaniecki when dissecting the "bowing letter" in their pathbreaking (but unemulated) study of the art of Polish American letter-writing (1918–1920).[8]

On the basis of these accounts of "folklore," one might be tempted to presume that the stereotype was quintessentially Irish, if also exportable to America. In fact, it conformed closely to the "general case of letter-writing as practised by uneducated persons," in the mocking view of an English manual (*Letter-Writing Simplified, for Those Who are not Used to It*) published in 1856. "Whatever be the subject of the letter or the occasion of writing, it is pretty sure to begin thus—'This comes hopping to find you all well, as it leaves us at present, thank God for it.' In the next letter the writer varies the commencement for the sake of change, and begins—'I take up my pen to write you these few lines.' " Four decades later, as in *The Letter-Writer's Handbook and Correspondent's Guide* (1895) English pedagogues were still protesting that it was "dreadfully illiterate" to begin a letter with the hope that "you are quite well, as this leaves me at present."[9] Although somewhat less ornate than the Irish parodies, these English vulgarisms are clearly variants of the same model. Whatever the origins of the Irish Australian stereotype, they were neither Australian nor merely Irish.

As Schrier observed, the formality of the salutation (as of the phrases expressing farewell) seems at odds with the typically easy, conversational manner of the letter proper. In many letters, an antiphonic effect was created by interspersing the text with further formulaic expostulations or wise sayings, whose gravity added further conviction to the intervening requests or admonitions. However, this contrast can be overdrawn. Until recently, Irish rural speech also alternated between formulaic greetings, pious exclamations, and often rambunctious vernacular (barely comprehensible to a visiting Australian when I first encountered County Clare in 1971). As

P.W. Joyce from Limerick observed in 1910, Irish conversation was punctuated by such utterances. "The people thank God for everything, whatever it may be His will to send, good or bad. 'Isn't this a beautiful day, Mike.' ' 'Tis indeed, thank God.' 'This is a terrible wet day, William, and very bad for the crops.' 'It is indeed, Tom, thanks be to God for all: He knows best.' "[10] Whether in person or in writing, such changes of register helped create intimacy with the audience, an essential precondition for effective persuasion. Irish Australian correspondents spared no pains to simulate conversation and personal immediacy in their letters, not only by choice of phrase but also by word-pictures conjuring up conversation. William Fife in Fermanagh told his children that he "must soon quit talking to yous for want of ro[o]m", and later that "I could talk to you for a year but I must say Farewell for a while." John McCance on the Ards peninsular drew his "long yarn to a close," and Biddy Burke in Brisbane sat down "to have a few words of conversation." Philip Mahony and Michael Normile made the artifice explicit. Mahony, writing from Melbourne to Cork, hoped that his letter might "have the effect of a Friendly chat between yourselves in that grand Old Homestead," while Normile exclaimed that "actualy my Dear Father I fancy I am speaking to you verbaly while I am writing this scroll to you but my grife I am not."[11] For the most part, however, the construction of conversation through letters was unsignposted.

When writing *Oceans of Consolation*, I was tempted (like Schrier) to attribute the conversational style of these letters to a distinctively Irish cultural trait. A comparative publication such as this seems an appropriate forum for confessing self-doubt. Since epistolary discourse first became a matter of study in the eleventh century, it has been commonplace for experts to urge correspondents to write as they spoke, the letter being a substitute for speech made necessary by separation. Far from coming naturally, the translation of speech into the written word requires care and imagination. Janet Gurkin Altman is responsible for coining the "paradox of temporal polyvalence," whereby correspondents are compelled to use elaborate devices for simulating immediacy when both parties know that the letter was written days, weeks, or months before receipt.[12] To Cécile Dauphine, one of a pioneering group of French scholars determined to rescue the vernacular letter from literary oblivion, we owe the term "illusion of orality", along with a dissection of the purposes served by creating this illusion.[13] In their attempts to bridge the ocean with talk, and talk about talk, Irish Australian correspondents were unconsciously acting on the precepts of the medieval *ars dictaminis*, the *secrétaires* and manuals which proliferated from Erasmus onwards, and the discourse theorists who briefly bewitched the fin-de-siècle intelligentsia with their dubious profundities. This admission does not, of course, demolish the hypothesis that the Irish created their own distinctive set of devices for pseudo-conversation, drawing on an unusually rich oral tradition.

So far, while sketching some elements of the Irish art of letter-writing, I have not established how its conventional forms came into being. Elsewhere, I have discussed the prescriptions of medieval rhetoricians, publishers of manuals, and modern educators. Oddly, the medieval tracts inspired by Cicero's treatise on oratory come closest in their advice to Irish Australian practice. The model letter was divided into an elaborate *salutation*, nicely graded according to the status of the recipient; an *exordium* setting the tone with a proverb or passage from scripture; a *narration* stating the purpose of the letter; a *petition* or specific request, deduced from premises buried in the preceding sections; a brief *peroration* unrelated to the request; and an authorizing signature or *subscription* from the person dictating the letter. Correspondents were urged (as in the *Rationes dictande* compiled at Bologna in 1135) to restrict themselves to a single theme, while avoiding full development of any argument, and to drop virtually any element except the salutation and petition, as circumstances demanded. Indeed, the most striking aspects of the *ars dictaminis* were its informality and flexibility, combined with its lack of discernible influence upon medieval letter-writers.[14]

Yet the recommended sequence is closely paralleled in the letters of Michael Normile from New South Wales to Clare. Writing in April 1855,[15] Normile used descriptive passages to prepare his father's mind for the absence of a remittance with the letter, in place of which he wished "them all an ocean of happiness." The rhetorical design is complex: first, an antiphonic sequence of *salutations* and facts about Australia; second, the general observation that "a man cant make a fortune here so very quick if he minds his Duty to God and keeps convenient to Chappel" (*exordium*); next, news of neighbors in the colonies and the recitation of names warmly remembered (*narration*); then, the abrupt and detailed enumeration of the costs of passage and clothing which made a remittance impracticable (*petition*); and finally, as a postscript to the *subscription*, some wry remarks by way of *peroration*:

> I wished to God you came to this Country when you was young and able to work as you were a good while ago. You would be a happy man. Dont forget in sending the children to shool and I will find a better place for them than to stop in Derry.

It is a tribute to the common sense and practicality of the medieval scholastics that their prescriptions were so closely matched by a Clareman in another age, searching for ways to maintain his family rights and duties in another hemisphere. The flexible rules of the *ars dictaminis* had a more direct influence on the flood of *secrétaires* and letter-writing guides catering for an increasingly plebeian readership from the sixteenth century onwards. In their prose and social affectations, however, the specimen letters published in these chapbooks and cheap manuals could scarcely have been more unlike Irish emigrant correspondence of the nineteenth century. Though typically recommending a conversational style as well as observance of epistolary etiquette, the manuals drew on styles of conversation and etiquette utterly alien to the "plain people" of Ireland and out of Ireland. As Cécile Dauphine and Roger Chartier have shown, the *secrétaires* of the *Bibliothèque Bleue* did not supply the model for vernacular letters of Frenchmen "without quality," instead providing entertainment for plebeian *voyeurs* into the intricate manners and mannerisms of the bourgeoisie and the aristocracy.[16]

The innumerable English manuals inspired by Samuel Richardson's *Familiar Letters*, first published in 1741 and still being plagiarized in 1906, were more humdrum and businesslike. Though originally intended to teach moral lessons to humble rustics through the medium of unaffected letters in "the common style," these manuals also invited middle-class *voyeurs* to savor the unsophistication of the semi-educated underclasses. The language attributed to plebeian letter-writers also had little in common with Irish Australian correspondence. Instead of giving uninhibited expression to their reserves of "untutored eloquence," the deferential tenant farmers of Richardson's imagination took great care to be correct in their utterances, like "your honest Tenant, and humble Servant" addressing his landlord:[17]

> Honoured Sir. The season has been so bad, and I have had such unhappy accidents to encounter with in a sick family, loss of cattle, etc. that I am obliged to trespass upon your patience a month or so longer.

In such publications, as I have shown, the forms of letter-writing practiced by Irish Australians only appeared as deplorable examples of how not to write a letter. Scarcely any surviving letters of the unlettered conform to the prescriptions of manuals designed to save plebeians from the embarrassing consequences of their lack of education.

Likewise, the type of the Irish emigrant letter cannot be traced to the "national" elementary education system, which transformed the subliterate Ireland of 1850 to a society in which almost every young adult could read and write by 1900. The near monopoly achieved by Vere Foster's copy-books in the last third of the century came too late to impose a uniform style of calligraphy on emigrants, most of whom had already departed. The same applied to the introduction of composition as a distinct subject, which did not occur even at senior level until 1872. Though indictment of "a simple letter on any subject suggested by the inspector" accounted for one-third of the examination, the few recorded model letters owed more to Richardson than to vernacular practice. Even so, the interest shown by pupils in the subject was often aroused by their respect for the "American letter" with its much anticipated enclosures. An official reported in 1889 that "if you go into one of the national schools any day, and ask a child to write an ordinary letter for you, the letter is invariably written to some friend either in the United States or Canada, or Australia, asking the person to send a ticket to take them out." As in France, where systematic instruction in letter-writing was not introduced until about 1890, formal training was a consequence rather than a cause of the widespread conviction that this skill was essential to success in life.[18]

Nor can the Irish art of letter-writing be attributed to the conventions adopted by some caste of professional scribes catering for an illiterate peasantry. Whereas this practice was widespread in rural France, the evidence of folklore and of surviving letters indicates a far less formal and regulated régime in nineteenth-century Ireland. Admittedly, subliterate correspondents routinely asked neighbors, teachers, or (increasingly) their own children to act as scribes or to correct their prose. But such letters are said by folklore collectors to have been dictated rather plucked from a folder of model compositions—sometimes in return for payment in kind, as reported from Galway:[19]

> Illiterates would bring letters to the school-master to read for them, and there was a woman in Barna . . . who used to read letters for them. She used also to write letters to their friends in America. She would write whatever they wished to say—put it into words on paper for them. They would make her a present of a dozen eggs for this service.

Such accounts remind us that both composition and reception were semipublic events, in which the forms as well as the content of letters were diffused within the kinship group. Like a dialect, the Irish art of letter-writing evolved through practice and imitation. From this perspective, it is scarcely surprising that no overt models for the Irish emigrant letter can be located in formal rhetoric, popular manuals, or elementary education. Just as dialects evolve and used to thrive in defiance of the standard languages taught in schools, so also the vernacular style of Irish correspondence resisted all attempts to discredit it through ridicule or contempt. So long as its forms and structures served the practical needs of correspondents, they endured. Emigrant letters were too important to be shaped or dictated by the letter-writing classes.

Notes

1. David Fitzpatrick, *Oceans of Consolation: Personal Accounts of Irish Migration to Australia* (Ithaca, NY: Cornell University Press, 1995).
2. Kerby A. Miller, Arnold Schrier, Bruce D. Boling, and David N. Doyle, *Irish Immigrants in the Land of Canaan: Letters and Memoirs from Colonial and Revolutionary America, 1675–1815* (New York: Oxford University Press, 2003).
3. David Fitzpatrick, "Famine, Entitlements and Seduction: Captain Edmond Wynne in Ireland, 1846–1851," in *English Historical Review*, cx, no. 437 (1995), pp. 596–619, esp. p. 604.
4. Fitzpatrick, *Oceans of Consolation*, p. 487.
5. Arnold Schrier, *Ireland and the American Emigration, 1850–1900* (Minneapolis: University of Minnesota Press, 1958), pp. 23–4.
6. Miller, *Irish Immigrants*, p. 198.
7. Fitzpatrick, *Oceans of Consolation*, pp. 489–490.
8. William I. Thomas and Florian Znaniecki, *The Polish Peasant in Europe and America* (New York: Dover Publications, 1958; 1st edn. 1918–1920).
9. Fitzpatrick, *Oceans of Consolation*, p. 490.
10. P. W. Joyce, *English as We Speak It in Ireland* (London: Longmans, Green, 1910), p. 197.
11. Fitzpatrick, *Oceans of Consolation*, p. 493.
12. Janet Gurkin Altman, *Epistolarity: Approaches to a Form* (Columbus: Ohio State University Press, 1982), pp. 118, 135.
13. Cécile Dauphine, "Les manuels épistolaires au XIXe siècle", in *La correspondance: Les usages de la lettre au XIXe siècle*, ed. Roger Chartier (Paris: Fayard, 1991), pp. 209–72, esp. pp. 229–231.
14. Fitzpatrick, *Oceans of Consolation*, p. 496.
15. Ibid., *Oceans*, pp. 22, 70–74.
16. Dauphine, "Les manuels"; Roger Chartier, "Des 'secrétaires' pour le peuple? Les modèles épistolaires de l'Ancien Régime entre littérature de cour et livre de colportage," in Chartier, *La correspondance*, pp. 159–207.
17. Samuel Richardson, *Familiar Letters on Important Occasions* (London: George Routledge, 1928; 1st edn. 1741), pp. 132–133.
18. Fitzpatrick, *Oceans of Consolation*, pp. 498–501.
19. Testimony of Micheál O'Cadhain of Rahoon parish (1955), in Collectors' Reports, Book 1409, f. 208, Irish Folklore Archive, University College, Dublin.

5

"Every Person Like a Letter": The Importance of Correspondence in Lithuanian Immigrant Life

Daiva Markelis

My mother couldn't write at all to her dying day. She couldn't even sign her name. She would sign x's.

William Wolkovich-Valkavicius[1]

At home we never made a man sign contract papers. We only had him make the sign of the cross and promise he would do what he said. But this was no good in Chicago.

Antanas Kaztauskis, *Lithuania to Chicago Stockyards*[2]

Published collections of letters written by specific immigrant groups to the United States offer a wealth of information from a number of different perspectives and have become a standard resource for both the scholar of immigration and the more "casual" reader, often a descendent of the particular group. The letters often convey a palpable sense of the mixed emotions involved in relocation, of beginning one's life anew, giving the reader a glimpse of the minutiae of everyday life. In addition, editors often provide useful historical background information in their introductions. The drawbacks to such volumes include the fact that few attempt to place letter-writing in a wider sociocultural perspective. Even in volumes where many different groups are represented, little effort is made to address the material conditions that encouraged or hindered correspondence. We may learn *why* immigrants wrote letters, and *what* they wrote about, but little about *how*.

There can be no question that letter-writing practices differ in significant ways according to the social, political, and economic circumstances of particular immigrant groups. That there is what amounts to a subfield of Swedish history devoted to the immigrant letter while Sweden's neighbors south of the Baltic have little epistolary data to show for themselves has less to do with numbers than with the successful literacy campaigns commenced in Protestant Sweden in the seventeenth century. It is thus likely that a Swede in the United States at the turn of the twentieth century found writing a letter a more or less "natural" process. Sitting down "with pen in hand" evoked less anguish for the Swede than it did for the peasant Lithuanian, for whom a pen was a fairly novel instrument, and for whom writing was often an activity that necessitated the help of family and friends.

The Swede might also have asked for advice and contributions from family members: the personal letter is the writing genre most conducive to collaboration. Cross-cultural and historical examples abound. Women in the United States, excluded from formal schooling before the mid-nineteenth century, urged each other to improve their letter-writing, providing recommendations concerning mechanics and style. In one instance we see an older sister assessing her younger sister's strengths as a writer and offering further encouragement.[3] We find other examples of familial collaboration in Thomas and Znaniecki's collection of letters written by Polish peasants to relatives in the United States.[4] Contemporary instances of personal collaboration in letter-writing occur in Shuman's study of adolescents in a Philadelphia high school and Farr's account of Chicago Mexicanos.[5]

For the Lithuanian immigrants who arrived in the United States during the period of mass migration, from 1880 to 1920, reading and writing were collaborative activities, not the individual, solitary acts that we often assume them naturally to be. Individuals often turned to more literate neighbors for assistance in tasks involving reading and writing, an extension of the concept of *talka*, the Lithuanian tradition of collective assistance. Parents also frequently engaged the help of sons and, especially, daughters in writing letters to relatives in Lithuania. Letter-writing thus not only fostered solidarity between immigrants and their relatives in Lithuania but also between Lithuanian immigrant parents and their increasingly literate, Americanized children.

One of the purposes of this essay is to examine Lithuanian immigrants and letter-writing within the frame of a more authentic definition of literacy, as a set of practices where an individual's reading and writing abilities are utilized for particular purposes in specific social situations. The questions that guide this work include the following: what social and personal functions did letter-writing perform in the lives of Lithuanian immigrants? How did Lithuanians, coming as they did to the United States with among the lowest literacy rates for immigrants of the time, undertake the seemingly daunting task of writing letters to the homeland?

Although there is no dearth of primary historical material on early Lithuanian immigration to the United States, most of it is in the form of government and parish records, newspapers, and informal, often self-published autobiographies. No substantial immigrant letter collections exist for Lithuanians, as they do for the Swedish or the Dutch.[6] The archives at the Balzekas Museum of Lithuanian Culture and the Lithuanian Pedagogical Research Center, both located in Chicago, do contain letters, though for the most part these are penned by individuals of literary or political importance. In research for this study I have examined some 15 letters written by Lithuanian immigrants. I was able to obtain several interesting letters from the Lithuanian Immigrant Research Center in Kaunas, Lithuania. I am also grateful to Giedrius Subacius and Father Tony Markus, who have provided me with important examples of correspondence.

A more significant source of information for this study comes from ethnographic interviews conducted with the children of Lithuanian immigrants. Among my most important participants were the sisters of the Order of St. Casimir, a Lithuanian congregation founded in Pennsylvania in 1907. I spent several afternoons at the motherhouse on Chicago's South Side talking to the sisters, most of whom are more than 80 years old, about their families, all of whom had emigrated from Lithuania around the turn of the century, their early childhood experiences with reading and writing, their educational backgrounds, as well as the kinds of reading and writing they engage in today. Although Lithuanian had been the first language for all of the sisters, most of them preferred talking in English. All of the participants in this study agreed to have their real names used.[7]

Historical Background

The quote in the title of this essay—"every person like a letter"—refers to an expression used by one of the participants in this study to talk about a practice used by shipping companies to make sure that immigrants did not get "lost in the mail." Company representatives would write the name, place of origin, and final destination of an immigrant on a piece of paper, and then pin it onto the immigrant's clothing or attach it to a string around his or her neck. This was especially important if a transfer from ship to train were involved. Sister Dilecta described how, when her father disembarked at Ellis Island, officials knew that his journey's end was his brother's residence in Chicago: "Nobody *asked* you where you were going, or where you were from. They looked at you, they read what was written, and then said something like, 'Don't go there. Stay here.' " In Dilecta's words, "Each person was like a letter. Like a human letter."

While the phrase resonates with a certain poetic whimsy, it also has more negative connotations, suggesting an objectification of the body, a Foucaultian preoccupation with order and efficiency that did, in fact, manifest itself in other bodily inscriptions at Ellis Island, such as the alphabetic marking of immigrant backs in chalk to signify disease. Such practices intimated future immigrant experiences with authoritarian discourse: the use of literacy tests for entrance into the country, the suspicion toward native-language schooling, and so on.

From 1881 to 1920, more than 300,000 of these "human letters" left Lithuania, the southernmost of the three countries often collectively referred to today as the Baltic States, and entered the United States. Actual immigration figures are problematic because there was no separate U.S. census category for Lithuanians until 1910; before that, they were grouped with the Russians, whose subjects they had been for more than a century.[8]

Although one of the reasons for emigration was, in fact, political—many young Lithuanian men left the country to avoid enforced and lengthy conscription into the army of the czar—the major causes were economic. The increase in the number of landless peasants brought about by the disintegration of feudalism in the mid-nineteenth century and the growth of industry that could not accommodate them resulted in high levels of unemployment. The majority of individuals who left Lithuania came from an agrarian background. Exceptions were Lithuanian Jews who, for the most part, were urban dwellers who worked as merchants and craftsmen.[9]

As was the case with other immigrant groups of the time, many Lithuanians arrived in the United States with the intention of returning to their home country once they had saved up enough money to pay off debts and to buy a farm. In speculating on the surprisingly small number of farmers among Lithuanian immigrants in the United States, historian David Fainhauz believes that it was largely this desire to return to their homeland that prevented Lithuanians from taking up agricultural pursuits in the United States to any significant extent; very few wanted to invest money in the land and machinery needed for farming. There were also those, such as Sister Angela Balchunas's grandparents, who had emigrated with the plan to remain, but who returned to Lithuania because they had problems adjusting to the American way of life.[10]

For the most part, Lithuanian immigrants arrived with little or no education. In nineteenth century Lithuania, economic motivations for learning to read and write were few. The long working hours and physically demanding labor typical of the agrarian nature of Lithuanian life made formal learning difficult. Literacy acquisition was also adversely affected by political oppression. The czarist press ban of 1863 had decreed the closing of Lithuanian schools and suppressed all books not written in Cyrillic, the national alphabet of Russia.

David Fainhauz contends that between 1899 and 1914, the rate of illiteracy among Lithuanian immigrants in the United States was 53 percent.[11] Literacy statistics for this time period, however, are difficult to calculate with any degree of accuracy. A major problem is that the term *literacy* encompasses a wide range of behaviors. There are individuals who read and write fluently, those who can read but not write, and those who neither read nor write. What constitutes "writing" is problematic as well, as seen in the ongoing debate as to whether a signature represents wider reading and writing abilities.[12]

Most of the participants in this study believe that their parents read well enough to follow their prayer books, and that they had probably acquired this basic reading competency from a type of home schooling that was popular during the press ban, where a traveling teacher gave informal lessons to a small group of neighboring children. Writing, however, was another matter. The sentiments inherent in the quotes at the beginning of this essay were echoed again and again by the participants in this study, suggesting an alternate reading of the phrase "every person like a letter": in such an interpretation, the letter is clearly an X.

Exceptions to these generally low rates of literacy were the Jews of Lithuania, whose traditions of learning went back centuries to the concept of the yeshiva, which Masha Greenbaum aptly describes as "a lifetime of scholastic endeavor in which notions such as 'completion' or 'graduation' were unknown." The majority spoke and wrote Yiddish, with many of the men (and some women) also literate in Hebrew. The more highly educated Jews often helped less-educated community members write letters to relatives who had emigrated to the United States. Polish, Lithuanian, and Russian were spoken by most Jews; of those who knew how to write in these languages, some worked as scribes for neighboring Poles, Lithuanians, and Russians, both Jewish and Gentile.[13]

It is unlikely that such inter-faith scribal relationships survived the crossing of the Atlantic. In general, Eastern European Jews tended to live in cultural, though not social, isolation from their non-Jewish neighbors. This pattern continued in the United States, strengthened by alliances based on religion, culture, and language. In Chicago, Lithuanian Jews tended to live among other Orthodox Jews, primarily on the west side of the city, where they engaged in a variety of mostly non-manual labor occupations.[14]

The first generation of non-Jewish Lithuanian immigrants settled in the coalmining regions of Pennsylvania and in the Stockyards neighborhoods of Chicago, where finding jobs depended not on literacy skills, nor even knowledge of English, but on strength, youth, and connections. Although it may have been occasionally necessary for an individual to read a contract for the fine print or skim a newspaper for the listing of the next meeting of the Daukantas Society, a lack of reading ability posed no significant problems in everyday life. Not only were practical, day-to-day transactions conducted orally, but also larger, more complex needs for affiliation were met through institutions such as the church and the local tavern, where communication was overwhelmingly oral. In many ways, writing was even less essential. The one exception, however, was the writing of letters to friends and relatives in Lithuania, and here it took on paramount importance.

The Social Importance of Correspondence

Although it was important for those who remained in Lithuania to be able to write to their relatives in the United States, the impetus for writing letters remained in the hands of those who emigrated. Lithuanian immigrants were prompted to write letters for many reasons. First and foremost, they knew that their loved ones would be anxious to hear the facts about this land of milk and honey. Letters allowed for the transmission of important practical information, especially concerning possibilities for employment in the United States. Letters were thus an important stimulus for emigration to the United States.[15] Immigrants also wrote letters to send money and announce significant life events. Tadas Kublickis penned a letter to his brother proclaiming his intention to marry. His brother wrote back stating his objections—in Kublickis' own words, "forbidding" him to carry out his plans.[16] Christine Konstant's father often dispatched money to his extended family, once sending $200, "a lot of money at that time in Lithuania." Konstant remembers her father talking about how providential his gift out to be because his own father had just lost two horses.[17] Sometimes even a disturbing dream could spur one on to write a letter, as in the case of Sister Dilecta Krauchunas's mother, who dreamt of a white horse and interpreted that to mean that a loved one had died in Lithuania. Dilecta helped her mother write a letter to the "bereaved," stating that a Mass was being ordered for the soul of the "deceased."

The most important reason for writing letters, however, one under which the others were more or less subsumed, was to reaffirm family solidarity. In Lithuania, day-to-day contact and extended visits with close relatives on ceremonial occasions made such artificial means of connection unnecessary. The significance of the extended family was deeply rooted in Eastern European peasant culture, and the threat of the dissolution of family bonds was a great incentive for writing frequently. Practical considerations played a role as well. Because many immigrants planned on returning to Lithuania once they had saved enough money for a farm, maintaining connection with those who might eventually assist them was especially important. Given the importance of family allegiance, what one wrote often was not as important as the fact that one wrote. Sister Cyril Krasauskas recounted that, as a young girl, when she was told by her mother to write letters to relatives in Lithuania, she would ask her mother just what it was she was supposed to communicate to them:

> I would say, "What should I tell them? I don't know what to tell them." "Praised be Jesus Christ," that's the first thing you write. "I kiss your dear hands." Then I would say, "What should I write about now?" "Write about the farm, how we live here, that we have animals."

Between the formal, ritualized greeting and the news about the farm, Krasauskas would have included a line or two about the family's health. The letters of Lithuanian immigrants followed a fairly fixed form, one that we see repeatedly in the letters of Polish peasants of the time collected by Thomas and Znaniecki. The greeting, a variation of "Praised be Jesus Christ," is followed by the information that the writer, with God's help, is in good health and is succeeding and wishes the same for the recipient and his or her family. These introductions were lengthy because family members were often mentioned by name, their health and happiness frequently inquired about individually; Thomas and Znaniecki have termed such letters "bowing letters" because of their emphasis on deference and politeness.[18]

One of the consequences of following these requirements was a definite sameness of tone in the letters. William Wolkovich-Valkavicius remembers that they "all sounded alike," an impression echoed by Sister Anita Petroshus:

> We would always write the same way. "As Tavo sesuo Elena, sveikinu jus su zodziais Tegu Bus Pargarbintas Jezus Kristus." [I, your sister Elena, greet you with the words "Praised be Jesus Christ."] We used to write the same things over and over again . . . "As Elena sveika esu, mano seima graziai auga." [I, Elena, am in good health. My family is doing well.] And, of course, when they wrote back, they would write more or less the same thing.

The expressions of respect and endearment inherent in bowing letters were probably customary in letters written by most immigrant groups of the time; ritualized beginnings are a common feature of letters in general. In published collections of immigrant letters, editors have almost always removed these elaborate introductions, as David Gerber points out, viewing them as superfluous to the "real" purpose of the correspondence. Since the declarations of sentiment we find in these openings functioned to highlight the significance of family bonds, the result of such editorial elisions is that readers obtain an incomplete picture of the immigrant experience, one where relationships take a back seat to more seemingly newsworthy concerns.[19]

The ritualized greeting also served the purpose of highlighting the importance of the letter-writing occasion itself, emphasizing it as "a social duty of a ceremonial character."[20] The more ceremonial an occasion, the more likely a highly specialized address will be used; letters of condolence are a good example. Such openings thus serve as markers, in a similar way that different greetings, salutations, and words of farewell work in speech. The generic forms in which we cast our speech allow others to more easily determine their ultimate significance in any given social context, as Bakhtin has shown us.[21]

The "I, your relative, greet you . . ." construction, as well as the traditional "bowing" to relatives, was not only a widespread feature of Lithuanian letters but also a persistent one. We find it in a letter written in 1961 by Jonas Juktonis to his brothers in Lithuania:

> I, Jonas Juktonis, along with my family, greet you my brother Antanas and your children, wishing you much happiness and good fortune in your lives and the best of health for you, and now we wish my brother Povilas much happiness and a long life, and now we thank him for the letter, heartily thank him that at least we can talk through letters.

The religious sentiment is absent; such expressions would have aroused the suspicion of the Soviet authorities that routinely opened mail from abroad. Although I have added punctuation marks and have capitalized the appropriate words in the English translation of Juktonis's letter, in the original handwritten Lithuanian they are practically nonexistent. There is no sense of paragraphing, and word choice and spelling are often nonconventional: the extended greeting would not have seemed out of place in a letter written 80 years earlier. In spite of what many might consider obvious flaws in the writing, Juktonis achieves his primary purpose: family connection is maintained at a time when, because of the Soviet occupation, physical visitation was impossible. The letter is neatly handwritten (a ruler may have been used to help form lines) and, most importantly, the appropriate expressions of greeting are present.

A Beautiful Hand

The emphasis on ritualized openings that we find in Lithuanian and Polish immigrant letters was paralleled in the stress placed on their visual appearance. A letter had to look the proper way, following current conventions of format, penmanship, and style. Proper penmanship was especially important, although what was "proper" did not go uncontested.

In the first decades of the twentieth century, according to Tamara Thornton, academic experts who argued for some measure of individuality in handwriting went head to head with penmanship educators who favored the push-pull drills of the Palmer Method. The foreign-born and their children would not have been immune to the social and cultural forces advocating for *good* handwriting; in fact, rigorous instruction in penmanship was often viewed by educators and government officials as a necessary step in immigrant assimilation.[22]

Many of the participants in this study spoke of writing in terms of penmanship, sometimes to my confusion, so firmly embedded in my mind was the conception of writing as school-based rhetoric. When I asked Sister Anita whether she had enjoyed writing as a young woman in the convent, her response was, "I was a good writer. The nuns sent me around the room showing my beautiful hand-writing." Sister Agnesine related how her mother's graceful and precise handwriting was the envy of others; she would be the one who would be asked to write words on the board at the school she attended in Chicago.

For many Lithuanian immigrants, writing was a new technology, one that many of them had been exposed to only minimally because social, personal, and economic circumstances had precluded formal learning. Like any new technology, it came with its own set of requirements. Although the children of Lithuanian immigrants would have been exposed to the rigors of handwriting instruction in American schools, their parents would have had no such training. Sister Cordia Vaisvilas, in explaining how she tried to teach her mother to write, emphasized that it was not grammar, word recognition, or sentence structure that her mother needed to learn, but hand movement: "I would take her hand, 'Mama, write it this way.' " Cordia mimicked these handwriting motions as she spoke.

The letters I examined showed a wide range of writing styles—from attempts at Spencerian with its fancy flourishes, to the bolder, simpler Palmerian script. Many writers resorted to printing. In one example of correspondence, each letter of the letter had been capitalized. Looking at the somewhat shaky printing, the switching between the lower and upper case *I*, one can only imagine the labor involved in such an undertaking. In addition, there was little correlation between beautiful handwriting and the qualities often associated with a more contemporary definition of good writing: grammatical and mechanical correctness, competent sentence structure, and appropriate word choice.

To side step the problems involved in handwriting, some Lithuanian immigrants resorted to pre-written and pre-printed letters to which they might have added a few words of their own. Sometimes the letters were in the form of poems, often with drawings to illustrate the theme of the poem. One typical message read (in Lithuanian): "Like an elk that thirsts for water from a brook, so my heart does for my dearest and most beloved friends." While such letter/poems could not have represented the details of a person's life, there were enough varieties to choose from to ensure a wide range of sentiments: warnings and advice about the United States, declarations of religious faith, expressions of longing.[23]

The difficulties involved in writing motivated some immigrants to turn to other forms of technology. The following advertisement in *Lietuva* [Lithuania] gives us a sense of the issues involved in this discussion. It appeared July 25, 1913, and announced the opening of a public stenographer's bureau in the offices of the paper:

> Many Lithuanians come daily to our office demanding that letters be written for them, etc. In order to help those who cannot write, or those who want to write a neat letter, we have established such an office . . . Each letter will be considered confidential.[24]

The Boston-based *Keleivis* [The Traveler] featured advertisements for a typewriter that would transform individuals into accomplished letter writers. The following advertisement in the April 20, 1905, issue was published in the form of a dialogue:

> "Philip, why aren't you writing letters to the Homeland?"
> "Well, brother, it's because I don't know how to write well, and it's better not to write at all than to write any old way."
> "Then why don't you buy yourself a little machine with which you can fashion a letter so beautifully, that even an unlearned person will understand what it is you're trying to say? You can get yourself such a thing for only nine dollars. And they'll even pay for delivery."[25]

The opening line of the advertisement provides a good example of the traditional marketing ploy of playing on personal guilt, in this case of a major kind—not fulfilling family obligations by writing letters to the Homeland. The ad also reveals the continued emphasis on correctness; "it's better not to write at all" than to submit something to loved ones that falls short of current standards of what is proper. It is difficult, of course, to assess the efficacy of such an ad; the implication that a typewriter will turn poor writers into good ones suggests a kind of "miracle cure" for gullible consumers along the lines of other products advertised in the pages of both immigrant and American newspapers of the time, such as hair-growth tonic and syphilis remedies. Given the cultural emphasis on neatness and correctness, however, it is entirely possible that Lithuanians living in the United States bought these machines in the hope that typewriter print would, in fact, make their sentiments more clearly understood.

Let's Learn to Write

Some Lithuanian immigrants, like immigrants from other groups, as well as native-born Americans, may have turned to correspondence manuals for assistance in writing letters. Hundreds of titles were published in the nineteenth century alone; some, such as *Hill's Manual of Social and Business Forms*, went through more than ten editions. The earliest exemplars of this genre were aimed at young men and women from upper-class families; in large part their purpose was to reinforce proper etiquette, especially in matters of courtship and matrimony, in order to maintain social status. Toward the latter end of the nineteenth century, the audience for such books broadened to include businessmen, college students, and would-be socialites. The books, often written by teachers at small business colleges, began to take on a decidedly utilitarian turn, evidenced in such titles as the *Standard Up-to-Date Practical Letter Writer*, written by E.J. Strong and published in 1902.[26]

Letter-writing manuals of the time straddled an often precarious line between an emphasis on direct language, of simplicity of expression, and a preoccupation with form, neatness, handwriting, and proper writing material. On the one hand, letter-writing was represented as within everyone's reach, a matter of not trying too hard to be eloquent: "The single purpose of a letter is to convey thought," writes Mary Crowther in *The Book of Letters*. "Come to your meaning at once. State the facts. Let every sentence bristle with points," suggests Alfred Chambers.[27] On the other hand, the endless rules and warnings must have made the seemingly simple process of writing a letter a discomfiting enterprise for the inexperienced writer. "It is just as bad and worse to scrawl illegible words as it is to speak indistinctly in your conversation," Strong cautions in the *Standard Up-to-Date Practical Letter Writer*. He also admonishes the writer against making "too many paragraphs" and writing in the margins, or "crosswise." His strongest criticism, however, is reserved for unsightly markings: "Never permit your letter to contain blots, even if you have to write it over a dozen times."[28]

The above mentioned advice could have been familiar to Lithuanian readers, for it appeared in both English and Lithuanian in a book called *Kaip Rasyti Laiskus Lietuviskoje ir Angliskoje Kalbose* [How to Write Letters in Lithuanian and English]. Advertisements for the book were a mainstay in the Chicago-based Lithuanian newspaper *Lietuva* [Lithuania], appearing in 1910 and in every successive issue. Several summers ago while working in the archives of the Lithuanian Immigrant Research Center in Kaunas, Lithuania, I came upon a copy of *Kaip Rasyti Laiskus*. The grammatically perfect English appeared on the verso, the Lithuanian translation on the right side. No author or place of publication was given. Upon my return to the United States, I discovered that the work was a word-by-word copy of Strong's book.

Other books purporting to teach Lithuanian immigrants writing skills, such as Paltanavicia's *Mokinkimes Rasyt* [Let's Learn to Write], concentrated on the mechanical skills of word formation, although their introductory statements suggest something more complex and dramatic. In the preface to *Mokinkimes Rasyt*, Paltanavicia exclaims, "My dear brothers and sisters, it is now time for all of us to carry out by hand our writerly duties; the era is past when man could live without writing; the times are gone when our parents would spin, weave, sew their own clothing." The main purpose of the book was to teach prospective writers how to move their hands on the paper so that the letters would emerge "clearly and beautifully." However, Paltanavicia did include "a little bit of grammar, showing by example when to use capitals and when to use lower case letters . . . as well as punctuation marks."[29]

The Personal Importance of Correspondence

Most Lithuanian immigrants did not rely on writing services, which cost money and entailed a trip to the newspaper bureau, or on writing manuals, which presupposed a basic level of literacy. A much more common solution was to ask for help from more literate neighbors. A neighbor woman used to write letters for Sister Anita's mother, who would return the favor in other ways, such as bringing over a meal. Wolkovich-Valkavicius's father, who was self-taught, wrote letters for friends and acquaintances while living in Lithuania. He continued doing so for neighbors after he had immigrated to the United States.

Having neighbors write letters was an extension of the concept of mutual aid or *talka* that Lithuanian immigrants had brought with them to the United States. Fainhauz defines *talka* as "a tradition of helping neighbors and of collective assistance," especially during the harvest or times of illness.[30] Christine Konstant remembers *talka* as an important part of life in her Lithuanian neighborhood in Chicago:

> If somebody was going to paint a house, the word got around, and everybody who had an older son would say, "You better be available for that day." You would help, and then when you needed something, people would help you.

The fostering of good neighborly relationships played a vital part in the forging of community cohesiveness, especially important in the light of the many adjustments immigrants had to make to the dominant Anglo culture.

The women I have interviewed stated that they had often felt a sense of importance as girls in performing these so-called adult writing tasks. Compared to other household duties, such as cooking meals, taking care of younger siblings, and even sewing, writing letters was an activity where they had expertise that their parents lacked. Parents occasionally allowed them to take responsibility for the actual composition of letters; Sister Cyril, for example, was told she could write what she wanted to about the animals the family kept. At their most productive, these collaborative sessions allowed both participants to contribute, as we see in the following excerpt from the interview with Sister Dilecta:

> My mother knew how to write, but very slowly . . . . I would have to write letters for her. "Praised be Jesus Christ for ever and ever. I kiss your little white hands." Like that. After a while, I knew how she started [a letter]. I had the beginning ready. I would say, "Ma, what else do you want me to write"? And so she'd tell me, and maybe sometimes I'd suggest something. Then she'd say, "Read me what you have." And so I would.

Many times, however, parents dictated in the literal sense of the word. Sister Angela Balchunas, who wrote letters for her father, "who wasn't much of a writer," clearly remembers her father being in charge. Their letter-writing followed the same routine. She would open the recently received letter from Lithuania, read it out aloud, then ask her father, "What do you want me to tell them?" He would then dictate, stopping after every phrase so that his daughter could write down his words. At the end of the session, she would hand the pen over to her father, who would then ceremoniously sign his name to the letter.

For the young women who were scribes for family members, letter-writing became important when many of them left their families in a way they would not have had they married. After completing their novitiate, all spent time at schools and hospitals outside of Chicago, sometimes for long periods of time. Sister Dilecta lived for many years in Argentina, where she became an avid letter-writer, writing in Lithuanian, English, and Spanish. Her father would write once a month; she later discovered that he would spend the entire day at this: "My mother told me that it was like a valley of tears around the house on those days."

Since coming back from Argentina, Sister Dilecta has kept up with her correspondence, writing to friends on a regular basis: "I've written about a hundred letters already. All in Spanish. I write all the time." She reads Spanish books and magazines on a variety of topics, as well as missionary magazines in English, though she states that one of the drawbacks is that they make her want to go back to Argentina.

The women in this study contend that the writing and reading they did with and for their families positively affected their reading and writing experiences as adults. Sister Cyril Krasauskas, for example, believes she enjoyed writing more than her peers in grammar and high school did, partly as the result of her role as family scribe. In her later career as a teacher of English, she emphasized grammar and clarity of style. Today, at 85, Sister Cyril writes letters to several nuns in Pazaislis, Lithuania, who had lived at the motherhouse; on an extended stay several years ago, Cyril had taught one of them English. She writes in Lithuanian, occasionally adding a phrase or two in English.

It is difficult to determine to what extent the early writing experiences of these women influenced their future vocations as nuns and teachers (as well as their avocation as letter- writers). They were probably predisposed by several factors to engage in work that played such a significant role in the education of Lithuanian American children and the maintenance of Lithuanian identity, as well as to achieve levels of education much higher than those of their compatriots. However, it is likely that their role as family scribes had at least some influence on their future decisions.

In addition to benefiting the young women, collaborative writing may have functioned to help parents feel a closer bond with their children, one based on the intimacy of a shared language. The maintenance of close family ties, difficult under ideal circumstances, can be especially problematic in immigrant families where parents are faced with children influenced by an alien culture, who are beginning to speak a language foreign to their elders. Jane Addams, in her 1910 autobiography, *Twenty Years at Hull-House*, writes of immigrant parents who relied on their often-wayward children for monetary support as well as for help in interpreting the mores and customs of American life. Addams put it aptly as "the premature dependence of the older and wiser upon the young and foolish."[31] For the parents of the participants in this study, having their children forget their native tongue, having them become too Americanized too quickly, was seen as a threat to family stability.

Final Thoughts

As immigration to the United States decreased and, after the First World War, eventually came to a standstill, collaborative literacy practices among Lithuanian immigrants declined. The second generation, those individuals born and educated in the United States, had no need to rely on intermediaries to fill out forms or help write letters.

The Soviet invasion of Lithuania in 1945, however, brought about a second wave of Lithuanian emigration. Although these individuals were more highly educated than those from the first wave, there were many with limited reading and writing skills. Irene Guilford's grandmother, for example, who emigrated to Canada in 1948, was raised on a farm and had never gone to school. As a young woman, Irene read aloud to her grandmother from Lithuanian newspapers and, at a somewhat later age, filled out her income taxes.

As with the earlier immigrants, Guilford's grandmother's lack of literacy skills did not prevent her from leading a productive life. She acquired a reputation for being a wonderful cook whose specialty was bakery goods, and ran a small but profitable business among Lithuanians in Toronto. In order to keep track of basic recipes, she learned to read numbers and distinguish several letters, those used to begin the words for the most common ingredients in her cakes, such as K for "kiausinis," or egg. Irene was ten when her grandmother asked her to rewrite an old recipe booklet that had grown worn from use: "She dictated. I wrote. She asked me to use a big, round script. This way, while she couldn't necessarily make sense of the script, she could pick out the K, P, S, M."[32]

After the Second World War, collaboration between Lithuanian parents and their children took on a new guise. A dramatically different social context, characterized by growing bureaucracy and increased industrialization, necessitated more writing in English on the part of the new wave of Lithuanian immigrants. Job applications, work permits, requests for medical services—many of these had to be completed in writing. Parents increasingly turned to their English-speaking children for help. Violeta Kelertas, who emigrated to Canada with her family as a young girl, remembers being a scribe for her mother, helping her fill out forms in English and writing letters to government agencies. Kelertas, like the women of the earlier generation, felt she had no say in the matter.[33]

While I have chosen Lithuanians as the focus of my research, similar collaborative practices were common throughout much of Central and Eastern Europe during the period of mass migration to the United States. Many of these involved the *reading* of letters. Stoyan Christowe, in his 1938 autobiography, *This Is My Country*, writes about how individuals in his native Celo, Bulgaria, who were able to read, helped those who could not. A letter from the United States would be passed from hand to hand until most of the letter-writer's friends and relatives were acquainted with its contents. Letters were public property; they belonged to the village or the boarding house, as opposed to the individual.[34]

Collaborative writing practices are found in many immigrant groups today. Marcia Farr has observed the phenomenon of informal, communal learning in her work with Chicago Mexicanos. While most members of the social network she has studied had learned to read and write as part of formal schooling, many, especially adult males over 35, learned without the presence of a traditional teacher, but with the help of family and friends. The primary motivation for learning to write for the Chicago Mexicanos was a desire to maintain connection with their relatives and friends back in Mexico. One might argue that it was more than a desire, rather, a responsibility, what one man in the network called a "personal obligation." While some families used the more expensive telephone to communicate, many others relied on letters. For these men, then, literacy was a social phenomenon in more ways than one. They learned to read and write through the support, example, and advice of others; this then allowed them to maintain important ties through letters.[35]

Notes

1. William Wolkovich-Valkavicius, Personal interview, Baltimore, March 23, 1999.
2. Antanas Kaztauskis. "From Lithuania to the Chicago Stockyards—An Autobiography," *The Independent*, August 1904, pp. 241–248.
3. Shirly Brice Heath, "Towards an Ethnohistory of Writing in American Education," in *Writing: The Nature, Development, and Teaching of Written Communication*, vol. 1, ed. Marcia Farr Whiteman (Hillside, NJ: Lawrence Erlbaum, 1981), pp. 25–55.
4. William Thomas and Florian Znaniecki, *The Polish Peasant in Europe and America*, vol. 1, 2nd edn. (New York: Dover, 1958).
5. Marcia Farr, "En Los Dos Idiomas: Literacy Practices Among Chicago Mexicanos," in *Literacy Across Communities*, ed. Beverly Moss (Creskill, NJ: Hampton Press, 1994), pp. 29–47. Amy Shuman, "Collaborative Writing: Appropriating Power or Reproducing Authority?" in *Cross Cultural Approaches to Literacy*, ed. Brian Street (Cambridge, UK: Cambridge University Press, 1993), pp. 247–271.
6. In addition to the historical and social circumstances that made letter-writing a more difficult undertaking for a Lithuanian immigrant than, for example, a Swedish one, there are several other possible explanations for the absence of Lithuanian letters in archival collections. One is that there have been no major campaigns, either on an individual, community, or government level, to gather immigrant letters, which is how many of the primary collections of other immigrant groups got their start. Another is that during the years of Soviet occupation, from 1945 to 1991, any documents professing a favorable or even a neutral view of the United States were repressed, including those written in the 1900s.
7. Interviews took place on March 18 and 19, 1998, unless otherwise noted, and were tape-recorded. Because much of this essay is based on interviews with the sisters, I will not repeat interview information after each reference. All translations of material from Lithuanian to English have been my own. Parts of this essay have previously appeared in the April 2003 issue of the journal *Written Communication* under the title " 'Talking Through Letters': Collaborative Writing in Early Lithuanian Immigrant Life."
8. Fainhauz. *Lithuanians in Multi-ethnic Chicago* (Chicago: Lithuanian Library Press. 1977), p. 42. Fainhauz. *Lithuanians in the USA: Aspects of Ethnic Identity* (Chicago Lithuanian Press: 1991), pp. 16–17.
9. A.S. Strazas. "Lithuania 1863–1893: Tsarist Russification and the Beginnings of the Modern Lithuanian National Movement," *Lituanus* 42, no. 3: (Fall 1996) 36–75. About 20 percent of Lithuanian immigrants were Jewish. Solomonas Atamukas, *Lietuvos zydu kelias [The Path of the Lithuanian Jews]* (Vilnius, Lithuania: Alma Littera, 1998), p. 147.
10. Fainhauz, *Lithuanians in the USA*, pp. 36–37. Two-way migration was widespread among immigrants of the time, with some groups having remigration rates of over 50 percent, as Mark Wyman points out in *Round-Trip to America: The Immigrant Returns to Europe, 1880–1930* (Ithaca: Cornell University Press, 1993), pp. 17–18. Wyman cites statistics provided by the Eleventh Annual Report of the U.S. Secretary of Labor (1923) that show that the return migration rate for Lithuanians of the time was 25 percent. I believe that it is also likely that Lithuanians would have had previous experience with emigration of a more local kind—looking for seasonal employment

in other parts of Europe, given the pervasiveness of this way of life among neighboring Russians and Poles.

11. Fainhauz, *Lithuanians in Chicago*, p. 21.

12. C.F. Kaestle, *Literacy in the United States: Readers and Reading Since 1880* (New Haven, CT: Yale University Press, 1991), p. 117.

13. Masha Greenbaum, *The Jews of Lithuania: A History of a Remarkable Community, 1316–1945* (Jerusalem: Geffen 1995), p. 88. Examples of scribal relationships exist in the literature of the time. In the Jewish-Lithuanian writer Abraham Cahan's classic immigrant novel *The Rise of David Levinsky*, the talented David, one of the star pupils at his yeshiva, earns his pay by writing letters for others in the local synagogue. (New York: Harper Torchbooks, 1960.) In *Memories of My Life* (Malibu, CA: Pangloss Press, 1991), Bella Lown talks about how her accomplished mother, Dvoireh Reisl, the daughter of a wealthy landowner in Lithuania, would write letters for villagers to local officials or to relatives who had emigrated to the United States. A.S. Johnson, in her 1908 short story, "A Ticket for Ona," set in the anthracite region of Pennsylvania, has her hero write to his sister living in Lithuania. The illiterate Ona hires a Jewish marketman to write letters back in Lithuanian. *The Atlantic Monthly*, January, 1908: 106–113.

14. See Ruth Gay, *Unfinished People* (New York: Norton, 1996); Irving Cutler, "The Jews of Chicago: From Shtetl to Suburb," in *Ethnic Chicago: A Multicultural Portrait*, ed. Melvin G. Holli and Peter D'A. Jones (Grand Rapids, MI: Wm. B. Eerdmans Publishing, 1995), pp. 122–172.

15. Fainhauz, *Lithuanians in the USA*, p. 13.

16. Tadas Kublickis. "Lithuanian Immigrant's Diary—A Rarity," *Lituanus* 27, no. 1 (Spring 1981): 39–48.

17. Christine Konstant, personal interview, Chicago, February 24, 1998.

18. Thomas and Znaniecki, *Polish Peasant*, p. 303.

19. David A. Gerber, "Epistolary Ethics," *Journal of American Ethnic History* 19, no. 4. (Summer 2000): 3–23.

20. Thomas and Znaniecki, *Polish Peasant*, p. 303.

21. Mikhail Bakhtin, *Speech Genres and Other Late Essays*, trans. Vern McGee (Austin: University of Texas Press, 1986), pp. 78–79.

22. Tamara Thornton. *Handwriting in America: A Cultural History* (New Haven: Yale University Press, 1996).

23. Fainhauz, *Lithuanians in Chicago*, pp. 6–9.

24. *Lietuva* [Lithuania], Chicago Foreign Language Press survey, Reel II, sec. A., University of Illinois at Chicago Library, microfiche department.

25. Advertisement, *Keleivis* [The Traveler], April 20, 1905.

26. E.J. Strong, *Standard Up-to-Date Practical Letter-Writer* (Charles C. Thompson: Chicago, 1902).

27. Mary Crowther, *The Book of Letters* (Garden City, New York: Doubleday, 1922), p. 6; Alfred B. Chambers, *The New Century Standard Letter-Writer* (Chicago: Laird and Lee, 1900), p. 29.

28. Strong, *Standard Up-to-Date Practical Letter-Writer*, pp. 26, 27.

29. Quoted in Algirdas Margeris, *Amerikos Lietuviai ir Angliskuju Skoliniu Zodynas* [The Lithuanians of America and a Dictionary of English Loan Words: 1872–1949] (Chicago: Naujienos, 1956), p. 66.

30. Fainhauz, *Lithuanians in the USA*, p. 32.

31. Jane Addams, *Twenty Years at Hull-House* (New York: Signet, 1961), p. 182.

32. Irene Guildford, personal e-mail, October 17, 2000.

33. Violeta Kelertas, conversation, November 2000.

34. Stoyan Christowe, *This is My Country* (Philadelphia: Lippincott, 1938).

35. Farr, *En Los Dos Idiomas*, p. 25.

6

Epistolary Communication between Migrant Workers and their Families

Miguel Angel Vargas

In historical and cultural studies there is growing interest in the process of writing and its products. Historian of writing Roger Chartier underscored this, pointing out that civilization exists, above all, in written culture.[1] In this study I seek to explore written culture for a community not normally associated with written communication: Mexican migrant families. This study analyzes writing on two levels. On the one hand, it describes epistolary communication, one of the most significant forms of writing. On the other hand, it contributes to the study of social phenomena such as labor migration through the analysis of practices of reading and writing.

With regard to epistolary communication, I define two principle ingredients for analysis: 1) those who use the letters (readers and writers—in this case people connected to an international labor migration dynamic) and 2) the texts themselves. The corpus I analyzed consisted of 91 private letters of a familial nature, all of them received between 1981 and 1991 in a small rural community located in the state of Zacatecas, Mexico. This community of 1,920 inhabitants, 375 families, had a strong tradition of temporary labor migration. Median size of the families in this study was between five and six persons, but included groups of up to fourteen (see table 6.1). At the time of the study 82 percent of the families claimed either a current or past international migrant among their members (see table 6.2). These international migrant workers—natives of Zacatecas living

Table 6.1 Distribution of the Community by Families according to the Number of Constituent Members

Families	Number of Members in Family	Population
73	2	146
54	3	162
57	4	228
49	5	245
46	6	276
20	7	140
35	8	280
21	9	189
11	10	110
5	11	55
3	12	36
—	13	—
1	14	14
375	Subtotal	1920

Source: Zacatecas. XI Censo General de Población y Vivienda, 1990. Resultados definitivos. Datos por localidad. Instituto Nacional de Estadística, Geografía e Informática, México, 1991; Encuesta de migración del estado de Zacatecas. Resultados definitivos 1992, Instituto Nacional de Estadística, Geografía e Informática, Gobierno del Estado de Zacatecas y Universidad Autónoma de Zacatecas, Zacatecas, 1992.

Table 6.2 Distribution of Families by Experience with International Labor Migration 1992

Families	Frequency	%
A. Migrant/s now in United States	184	49.1
B. Migrant/s in the United States in past	123	32.8
C. No migration record	68	18.1
Total	375	100

Note: A = Families with at least one member in the United States; B = Families with at least one member with a migratory record; C = Families without members in the United States and without members with migratory records.

Source: Survey by the author, undertaken with the assistance of school teachers in town.

in the United States—sent the 91 letters. I investigate the texts (e.g. their structure; the topics treated in them; the background information; and the instrument used for writing; the paper; the length), and the conditions of their production and reading (who writes to whom; where it is written; when and with what frequency it is done) as a means of access not only to describe the social practices of writing, but also to understand the social phenomena of which they are a part.

The Epistolary Text

Only in recent years has there been sufficient interest to dedicate a special section to the physical characteristics of letters. Previously there would have been little to say, and that would have been banal. On the one hand, scholars did not find it important to explore the phenomenon of communication through letters, and, on the other hand, they found it irrelevant to talk about the process of writing itself. Nevertheless, current scholarship allows for an expanded field of observation, including the supporting materials and the instruments of writing.

The 91 letters in the study represent an enormously homogeneous body of texts. Not only are the majority of the textual elements present in the bulk of the letters, they also are present in exactly the same form. This homogeneity runs from the graphic distribution of the text on the sheet of paper, to the general structure of the text, including the use of certain forms of politeness in the salutation as well as in the closing, the characteristics of background information, the instrument used to write, the frequency with which they are written, the quantity of text that is produced, and the type of location where it is written. A basic quantification of the elements that are present in these letters appears in table 6.3. In terms of physical characteristics, most letters were two pages long, written on letter-sized paper with lines (see tables 6.4, 6.5, and 6.6).

In addition to the content elements and physical characteristics, I need to consider the graphic quality of the texts. This reflects institutional practices of literacy—how people learn to write.[2] These texts utilize forms of writing that conflict with standard language as professionally defined, and the departure from graphic and textual standards is the norm more than the exception (see figure 6.1).

Transcribing a text with these characteristics implies, by nature, making a series of interpretations, all of them with serious theoretical and methodological consequences. For example, an erroneous or absent punctuation

Miercoles 1 de Febrero 1989
el Ruca miremamá Tomo la pluma para es
cribirle unos cuantos ringlones y para darle a
saber que estamos bien y esperando que ustedes
tanbien y que no les pase nada grasias aDios
mama lloquierosaber por queno mecontestan me
des es pere y lees cribi otrabes mas dermiñicale
es cribi della y me contesta odigame sileles lle
gan las cartas mamá lloquiero saber sibesesitan
algo por aca manuel llo es muy bisionte agarrael
cheque y diaquí a ocho dias llano Trainada y medijo
que piensa irpara en mayo pues llodoy grasias aDios
quesa balla porque biene apedirme dinero primero de
abeinte y ahorade acien y esos siselos boy apedir porque
armando sipiensa behir y boy aJuhtar para elcollote a
horita Tengo tresientos libres y boy agarar cheque llaba
naser quinientos libres siña sebiene delos wanpasar
alla pronto ay leplatico que andrea llano esta agosto
que se quiere irlla y llole platique deltolis y medijo que
se esperara aber que podiemos aser el tolis ledise a
manuel que agarremos undepar Tamento entrelos
Tros yel dis que el nose mete en eso pereso nopodemos
estar juntos pueandrea nadie la bisita nomoislo por
alla cada quisedias cuando puedo poreso siseba manue llo
dijo el Tolis quellano leyba apagar el collote porque Tam
bien ael lepide y manuel ganabuen dinero mas que nosotros
pereno cuida pues el sabra llotambien mestaba bolando ya
y baalbarle aseñar y poreso apenas yba pe medijo el tolis
que elme alía alludado para que meallidato llo siñaciena
da puesllo sabria mime mama abeses sí sueno pues Jaalla
y dispierto y nada abeses piensos irme peradigo aque siaqui
aymuchas dibersiones a idigame quepaso con carmela yaho
diJonada meda Risa porque siso mucho cvento simser sierto
aplatiqueme sitodabia nose muere migallo que meacor

de el y platiqueme cuantos pollitos secria
Ron y si estan bonitos que quiero que me los chiden
o digame si le batarron cosecha si ono y si an estado
batallando con los animales si llano ay agua si los lle
ban asta el Rio quiero que mi papa llano salga porque
llano puede y que ho le pase nada y si los niños llase cabu
rrieron que aguanten por que lo que pensamos es comprar
mas animales para que rindan ns ya que se llene el
corral para i llano benir para ca que al cabo es lomis
ma chas tapeor Porque aca diario trabaja uno y allano
Poreso que no sedes esperen y batallen con esos los
muchaschos y digame si la beserra negra lla se alboroto
para que la cuiden y digame delas niñas de ondia si no es
tan aburridas y si estan que se aguanten Platiqueme que
apasado por alla si no antenido problemas por que asta hora
me vi cuenta que les Robaron Un burro i me dieron ganas de llore nomas
para saber quien fue i no belba saludeme a mi aguelita a mi tio Jesus
y a martin a chirviana a collas al pabo a Jose a elias al
murlilla i algo Tone go yo que me acuerdo de ellos i meda gusto
que a quien encuentro solo a beses boy con el macho alli conchan
onde bibe manuel y para alo cantina puro bisio poreso no boy para
alla a y tabien llamiro a luis de lencha Traian carro y me saca para
un lado y para el otro y platiqueme de ex mimicia i do para alla
o no si se encuentra bien o y tabien miro a Juan de mi tia la salgo
a beses con el y el llase ba a fines de este mes y si no se biene a y mando
con el le mando lo que pueda pese ba mandar una grabadora pero me
dijo que salia mas cara por que cobran tambien en latinia poreso mejor
el dinero de aqui en delante boy en pesar aguardar sino no agonada
bueno se de pide el Ruca esperado que la resiban llenos de
salud y gusto mi mamá mi papá marsela ale Jandra
Jusina aurelia Paula y nena que desian que llano bolbiera
ahora me acuerdo bueno resiban saludes Todos del Ruca y
adios y asta la presente contesteme pronto
que me da pediente de ustedes y a mi papá no lo dejen
solir lejos cuidenlo y llano salgan a la leña obidense
de eso

Table 6.3 Structural Elements Present in the Texts/Letters and their Frequency

Number of Elements	Date/Place	Heading	Opening	Body	Closing	Signature	Post-script	Totals
Two	X			X				1
								1
Three	X			X		X		1
								1
Four			X	X	X	X		2
		X	X	X				1
	X		X	X	X			2
	X	X	X	X				4
								9
Five			X	X	X	X	X	1
		X	X	X	X		X	1
		X	X	X	X	X		2
	X		X	X	X		X	3
	X		X	X	X	X		3
	X	X		X		X	X	2
	X	X		X	X	X		3
	X	X	X	X			X	2
	X	X	X	X	X			14
								31
Six		X	X	X	X	X	X	3
	X		X	X	X	X	X	1
	X	X		X	X	X	X	1
	X	X	X	X		X	X	1
	X	X	X	X	X		X	8
	X	X	X	X	X	X		14
								28
Seven	X	X	X	X	X	X	X	21
								21
Totals	81	77	83	91	80	55	44	91
	89%	84.6%	91.2%	100% %	87.9%	60.4%	48.3% %	100%

Table 6.4 Paper size of the Texts/Letters

Size of the Paper	Totals
Letter	68 (74.7%)
Other	23 (25.3%)
Total	91

Table 6.5   Paper type of the Texts/Letters

Type of Paper	Totals (%)
Lined with margins	70 (76.9)
Lined without margins	16 (17.6)
Unlined with margins	1 (1.1)
Unlined without margins	3 (3.3)
Unlined with drawing/without margins	1 (1.1)
Total	91

Table 6.6   Length of the Texts/Letters

Letters	Frequency	%
One page	11	12.1
One page with additions	10	11.0
Two pages	57	62.6
Two pages with additions	2	2.2
Three pages	2	2.2
Three pages with additions	1	1.1
Four pages	6	6.6
Four pages with additions	1	1.1
Six pages	1	1.1
Total	9	100%

mark obligates us to fill the "holes" left by the scribe in order to interpret the text. Consider the following fragment:

65: dijo que salia mas cara por que cobran tambien en lalinia poreso major
66: el dinero de aquiendelante boy enpesar aguardar sino no ago nada
67: bueno se de pide el Ruca esperado que la resiban llenos de

Two possible transcriptions—or even, interpretations—of lines 66 and 67 exist, that depend on the potential "punctuation":

el dinero	the money
de aquí en adelante voy a empezar a guardar	from now on I am going to start to save
si no	if not

no hago nada bueno	I won't be doing anything good
se despide el Ruca	Ruca says goodbye
esperando que la reciban llenos de	Hoping that you'll receive it full of
el dinero	the money
de aquí en adelante voy a empezar	from now on I am going to start to save
a guardar	
si no	if not
no hago nada bueno	I won't do anything well
se despide el Ruca	Ruca says good-bye
esperando que la reciban llenos de	Hoping that you'll receive it full of

It is clear that the reader or transcriber must make a decision establishing the boundaries between two phrases. In many cases this decision can determine the very structural classification of a text. In the transcription/interpretation I employ the technique of skipping a line to establish communicative units. In the preceding example, I opted for the second transcription.

According to the standards of institutional literacy taught in school, these texts transgress the majority of conventional norms—orthography, punctuation, separation of words. Despite the reproach that these letters seem to merit from the scholastic point of view, an enormous amount of text is produced. This suggests that those who write are not necessarily concerned about respecting conventionality, rather, they are concerned with something more important: communicating. For those of us interested in pedagogy, this is particularly noteworthy. The conception of writing we teach formally does not reflect the social practices in which writing is used. If schools want to assume their role as exclusive repositories for teaching writing, they will have to eliminate this divergence, or, in other words, reconstruct the concept of literacy.

Writing as a Social Practice

In analyzing this research I assumed two principles: 1) epistolary communication in familial situations represents a valuable vantage point from which to study writing as a social practice; and 2) writing is a socially constructed and executed object. On the former point, studies of writing have tended to focus on texts not associated with family, with priority given to religious, political, and scholastic domains.[3]

What data supports the utility of letters as a means to uncover the social dimension of popular writing? First, the scale: our study population of 375 families (307 with current or past migrant members) generated an epistolary exchange of between 2000 and 4000 letters per month (see table 6.7).

The corpus of 91 letters I studied, collected from five families, was just a small sample of this exchange. Second, the gender dynamics: a large majority of these texts (70 percent) were produced and read by female subjects (see table 6.8).

The data also suggest a number of hypotheses. One: written language, in the mode of epistolary communication, occupies a niche in the communication between family members that cannot be supplanted by oral communication (face to face or long distance). In the study location, even though there are at least four alternatives to writing (telephone, radio, video, and tape recordings), the text production was enormous. Of the

Table 6.7 Monthly Letter Exchange between November 1990 and July 1991

Month	Received	Sent	Total
November	1,158	1,150	2,308
December	1,813	1,754	3,567
January	1,148	1,470	2,618
February	1,111	1,124	2,235
March	1,246	1,118	2,364
April	1,483	1,648	3,131
May	2,118	1,836	3,954
June	1,647	1,353	3,000
July	1,792	1,381	3,173
Total	13,516	12,834	26,350

Source: Records of the post office.

Table 6.8 Distribution of the Corpus by Familial Relation between Correspondents

Familial Relation	Female to Female	Male to Female	Male to Male	Total
Mother to daughter	3	—	—	3
Child to mother	19	29		48
Child to father	—	—	1	1
Sibling to sibling	7	2	1	10
Grandchild to grandmother	2	2	—	4
Cousin to cousin	—	1	—	1
Niece to aunt	5	—	—	5
Daughter-in-law to mother-in-law	4	—	—	4
Son-in-law to father-in-law	—	—	1	1
Friend to friend	—	14	—	14
Total	40	48	3	91

alternatives, only telephone was used frequently. My purpose was not to investigate the function (or functions) that epistolary communication serves; however, I have consistent indications that lead me to believe that epistolary communication is closely linked to the affective sphere.

A second hypothesis relates to the economic role of letters. At one time, I had the idea that the letters served an important economic function since the enclosure of remittances, often endorsed to the bearer of the text, was frequent. In 52 of the 91 letters there are references to such enclosures. Yet, in the majority of the cases, the relatively small amounts and the affective references to its potential uses lead me to believe that these monetary enclosures have a strong emotional value. In contrast, significant transfers of money (money orders, bank drafts) are handled directly by financial institutions.

The fact that women, as grandmothers, mothers, aunts, or sisters, are the privileged interlocutors of epistolary communication has caused me to rethink some of the ideas that have dominated the sphere of cultural products and processes, for example, the idea of writing being a cultural object dominated by men, or the idea that women do not participate in migratory processes.[4] Women are not only active participants in migratory processes by means of writing, they are the privileged users of written language in this social practice. Yet in our data wives of male migrants were absent as correspondents. I can only hypothesize that family structure made it more likely that mothers would be recipients of letters.

By the same token, the analysis of specific writing practices permits us to give new meaning or to re-conceptualize ideas regarding literate culture. That a community of 375 families produces and reads nearly 3000 letters in one month—enough to fill 30 100-page notebooks, averaging one notebook per day—causes me to rethink education. To wit, evaluations of social groups cannot continue to be based merely on indirect indicators such as the reading of commercial volumes of literature, political commentary, or memoirs.[5] In other words, the learned of a society cannot be measured by the consumption of only certain types of printed paper.

The community that I studied does not read contemporary novels or best sellers, nor do they read political commentaries or memoirs. Yet it is a community with a strong tradition of writing and reading. I believe that the simplistic affirmations that this social group "reads little and writes even less" ought to be seriously revised. What do they read and what do they write? Who reads and writes, when and how? These are obligatory questions when dealing with written culture.

In this study I demonstrate how epistolary communication is not only a fundamental part of a social phenomenon—that of labor migration—but I also demonstrate the community's enormous ability to describe that phenomenon. Analyses of the texts/letters allow us to identify how the writers, without being explicit, realize the different phases through which all who wish to cross illegally into the United States must pass:

1) Obtaining the funds necessary for the trip, including the money to pay the "coyote" [person who takes people across the border illegally];

14: Armando sipiensa benir y boy ajuntar para el collote a
15: horita tengo tresientos libres y boy agarrar cheque lla ba
16: naser quinientos libres sino se biene selos man para
17: alla pronto ay le platico que andrea lla no esta agusto

Armando sí piensa venir	Armando is planning on coming
y voy a juntar para el coyote	And I am going to save for the coyote
ahorita tengo trescientos libres	right now I have 300 saved
y voy agarrar cheque	And I'm going to cash my check
ya van a ser quinientos libres	It will soon be 500 saved
si no se viene	If he doesn't come
se los mando para allá pronto	I'll send them to you soon

2) Evading the risks that a trip like this implies;

05: Juán y para decirles que no ten-
06: gan pendiente (me) tubimos mu-
07: cha suerte por que (nin) ni una
08: Ves nos agarraron y llegé bién.
09: Lo Unico que si ciento es que
10: tardamos como 7 Horas arriba de
11: Una Camioneta y como con
12: 40 pleaos apilaos y yo entre
13: ellos. patas aquí, brasos por
14: ayá, Nalgas a un lado, etc. en
15: Fin. Lo Bueno fué, que
16: llegamos a Nuestros domicilios.

Juan	John
y para decirles que no tengan pendiente	And to tell you not to worry
tuvimos mucha suerte	We were very lucky
porque ni una ves nos agarraron	Because not even once did they nab us
y llegué bien	And I arrived ok
lo único que sí siento es que tardamos como	The only bad thing is that we spent
7 horas arriba de una camioneta	like 7 hours in the back of a truck
y como con cuarenta pelados (individuos) apilados	And with a mound of like 40 guys

y yo	And me
entre ellos	Among them
patas aquí	Feet here
brazos por allá	Arms there
nalgas a un lado	Butts on one side
etc.	Etcetera
en fin	Anyway
lo bueno fue que llegamos a	The good thing is that we arrived at
nuestros domicilios	our homes

3) Obtaining living quarters;
>   17: Mira Andre primero quiero decirte
>   18: que quiero con seguir donde vivir
>   19: para que puedas llegár porque
>   20: tu sabes que no pueden vivir muchos
>   21: en un apartamento.

Mira Andrea	Look Andrea
Primero quiero decirte que quiero conseguir	First I want to tell you that I want to
donde vivir para que puedas llegar	find somewhere to live so you can come here
Porque tu sabes que no pueden vivir muchos	Because you know that not many people can live in an
en un apartamento	apartment

4) Finding someone who can offer employment;
>   19: quedo hay Nada Mas aNdrea
>   20: No ha podido hallar Nada
>   21: le heMos buscado y No le heMos
>   22: podido eNcoNtrar trabajo y he

quedó ahí nada más	she stayed there, nothing more
Andrea no ha podido hallar nada	Andrea hasn't been able to find any thing
le hemos buscado y no le hemos podido	We've looked for him and haven't been able
encontrar trabajo.	find work for him.

5) Dealing with the unfavorable labor conditions;
>   15: angeles mire mama biera que lla me
>   16: aburre por que esta bien legos el
>   17: trabajo ipor que pagan bien poquito
>   18: poreso toi abuRido porque gano poco

Mire mamá	Look Mama
Viera que ya me aburre	You ought to see that I'm bored

porque está bien lejos el trabajo	Because work is so far away
y porque pagan bien poquito	And they pay so little
por eso estoy aburrido	And that's why I'm bored
porque gano poco	Because I earn so little

Thus, the written text provides an excellent way to study the social phenomena that give rise to writing, directly and indirectly documenting migration.

In historical studies the interest in the study of written culture is becoming more and more evident. This motivation to reconstruct and understand culture through one of its aspects, writing, has been the impetus of numerous historical studies on reading and writing practices. Here I must ask a question. Can studies like this one, which shed light on contemporary practices of writing, provide pertinent information for the analysis of practices rendered inaccessible by the passage of time? I believe this contribution is important. If I assume that the social practices of writing are products of diachronic processes, the documentation of the characteristics of current practices permits the discovery of common elements of practices of the past; or, in the very least, reorients the study of it. In other words, the results of contemporary data allow us to make projections on practices employed in the past.

Various indications found in this study allow us to speculate about the past. Let us note, for example, that the homogeneity of the corpus of letters in structure, constituent parts, graphic distribution, and perhaps content, reflects an extraordinary similarity with the letters written by migrant workers more than 450 years ago.[6] What are the reasons for the epistolary genre to be so resistant to transformation? Where can the origin of this resistance and the mechanisms that sustain it be found?

Epistolary manuals could provide a clue. Recent editions of the "modern" epistolary manuals that can be found in bookstores today show that even these have not changed much throughout the centuries. The techniques employed by their authors, the structure that privileges the appearance of "models" to imitate, the classification of subgenres, and so on are practically the same as those that were employed almost 500 years ago, as documented by Chartier.[7] Yet I have evidence that neither the writers who produced the corpus I analyzed nor the generations that preceded them ever had an epistolary manual in their hands. Thus, I tend to believe that the letter, as its use grew, became independent of such manuals and followed its own path; a path conforming to particular practices of writing and reading. Becoming familiar with this path would give us the answers we seek.

I believe that finding the closest extremity of this path is relatively easy: analyses like this essay are one possibility. But how do we trace back in time to find the other extreme? What data should be considered in addition to the manuals reported by Chartier and letters found in historical archives? I am convinced that the reading (and writing) practices of texts that can be documented with current "live" data could provide information and perspective in order to establish the characteristics of preceding practices from which they originated.

Notes

This essay was translated by Travis J. Hyer.

1. Roger Chartier, "Los secretarios. Modelos y prácticas espitolares," in *Libros, lecturas y lectores en la Edad Moderna* (Madrid: Alianza Editorial, 1993), pp. 285–316; *Lecturas y lectores en la Francia del Antiguo Régimen* (México: Instituto Mora, 1994); "Del códice a la pantalla: las trayectorias de lo escrito," *Sociedad y escritura en la Edad Moderna* (México: Instituto Mora, 1995), pp. 249–263.
2. E. Ferreiro, "Los límites del discurso: puntuación y organización textual" in *Caperucita Roja aprende a escribir*, ed. E. Ferreiro, C. Pontecorvo, N. Riveiro, and I. García Hidalgo (Barcelona: Gedisa, 1996), pp. 128–162.
3. See Alvarez del Castillo, *Cómo escribir cartas privadas*, 4th ed. (México: Editores Mexicanos Unidos, 1986); A. Lamar, *Correspondencia familiar y social*, 2nd edn. (México: Editorial Olimpo, 1972).
4. G.R. Cardona, *Antropología de la escritura* (Barcelona: Gedisa, 1994); M. Morokvsic, "La mujer es una emigrante," *Los emigrantes. Parte I, Suplemento Mundial de La Jornada* (de Junio 21, 1991): 12–13.
5. R. Rovelo, "75% de hogares mexicanos tiene menos de 30 libros," *La Jornada* (México) (de octubre 19, 1996): 25.
6. E. Otte, *Cartas privadas de emigrantes a Indias, 1540–1616* (México: Fondo de Cultura Económica, 1993).
7. Chartier, "Los secretarios," pp. 285–316.

Bibliography

Álvarez del Castillo, J. 1986. *Cómo escribir cartas privadas*. México: Editores Mexicanos Unidos.
Álvarez del Real, M.E. 1988. *Cómo escribir cartas de amor*. Panamá: Editorial América.
Bollème, G. 1986. El pueblo por escrito: Significados culturales de lo popular. *Colección los Noventa*, no. 47. México: Grijalbo y Consejo Nacional para la Cultura y Artes.
Branca-Rosoff, S. 1990. "Des Grilles pour l'Histoire du Français ecrit?" *Recherches sur le Français Parlé* 10.
Cardona, G.R. 1994a. *Antropología de la escritura*. Barcelona: Gedisa.
———. 1994b. *Los lenguajes del saber*. Barcelona: Gedisa.
Chartier, R. 1995. "Del códice a la pantalla: las trayectorias de lo escrito." *Sociedad y escritura en la Edad Moderna*, 249–263. México: Instituto Mora.
———. 1994. *Lecturas y lectores en la Francia del Antiguo Régimen*. México: Instituto Mora.
———. 1993. "Los secretarios. Modelos y prácticas espitolares." In *Libros, lecturas y lectores en la Edad Moderna*, 285–316. Madrid: Alianza Editorial.
Company, C. 1994. *Documentos lingüísticos de la Nueva España. Altiplano-central*. México: Universidad Nacional Autónoma de México.

Consejo Superior de Investigaciones Científicas. 1944. *Normas de transcripción y edición de textos y documentos.* Madrid: Escuela de Estudios Medievales.

Durand, J. 1994. *Más allá de la linea: Patrones migratorios entre México y Estados Unidos.* México: Colección Regiones, Consejo Nacional para la Cultura y las Artes.

Ferreiro, E. 1989. *Los hijos del analfabetismo. Propuestas para la alfabetización en América Latina.* México: Siglo XXI.

Ferreiro, E. 1996. "Los límites del discurso: puntuación y organización textual." In *Caperucita Roja aprende a escribir,* ed. Ferreiro, E.C. Pontecorvo, N. Ribeiro, and García Hidalgo, 128–162. Barcelona: Gedisa, Colección LEA.

Foisil, M. 1992. "La escritura del ámbito privado." In *Historia de la vida privada: El proceso de cambio en la sociedad de los siglos XVI y XVIII,* ed. P. Ariés and G. Duby. Madrid: Taurus, pp. 348–369.

Lamar, A. 1972. *Correspondencia familiar y social.* 2a edición. México: Editorial Olimpo.

————. 1974. *Para escribir una carta,* 2a edición. México: Editorial Olimpo.

Lestage, A. 1981. "Analfabetismo y alfabetización." In *Estudios y documentos de educación* no. 42. Paris: Unesco.

Martínez, J.L. 1990. *Documentos cortesianos I, 1518–1528.* México: Universidad Nacional Autónoma de México.

Morokvsic, M. 1991. "La mujer es una emigrante." *Los emigrantes. Parte I, Suplemento Mundial de La Jornada* (de Junio 21): 12–13.

Otte, E. 1993. *Cartas privadas de emigrantes a Indias, 1540–1616.* México: Fondo de Cultura Económica.

Pimentel, E. 1990. *O português popular escrito.* Col. Repensando a língua portuguesa. São Paulo: Editoria Contexto.

Rovelo, R. 1996. "75% de hogares mexicanos tiene menos de 30 libros." *La Jornada* (México) (de octubre 19): 25.

Russinovich, Y. 1986. "Lenguas maternas de la población hispánica en los Estados Unidos." In *Actas de II Congreso Internacional sobre el Español de América,* 198–206. México: Universidad Nacional Autónoma de México.

Part III

Silences and Censorship

7

Epistolary Masquerades: Acts of Deceiving and Withholding in Immigrant Letters

David A. Gerber

Those of us who do analytical work with personal letters soon become aware of the problem of being tempted to take for granted that what is written in them is a true account of the author's condition or intentions. It is not only that in the individual case we become suspicious of a particular letter-writer's motives and accounts. A moment's reflection tells an experienced adult who reads other people's personal letters that there is more going on than appears on the surface of the text, precisely because this is true in our own lives.

In this essay, I would like to open up a discussion of what is at once a significant and a profoundly elusive (and, hence, underconceptualized) subject—what is not made explicit, and is hidden or held back in immigrant letters as well as the untruths that are told in personal correspondence. I will be using examples from my own research with nineteenth century British immigrant correspondence. What I will *not* be doing is examining the ethics of the situation, as if I were a moral philosopher. I go forward with the understanding that in the best of all worlds, we would always tell the truth and completely disclose everything that is pertinent to being properly understood and evaluated by others. But this is not always possible. Nor is it always even desirable, for there are certainly times when lying or being less than forthright are salutary, not simply for ourselves, but for the welfare of others. Nor do I want to engage in the time-consuming enterprise of creating a taxonomy of deceitfulness, though we all know we need to make fine distinctions to guide our language and analysis. Nor will I deal with pathological liars or blatantly self-interested manipulators, who are well-practiced at using others for their own material gain or for the purpose of fulfilling obligations that they themselves had incurred. Instead I intend to examine, for the more or less ordinary emigrant letter-writer, the real world of situations, and the choices made within it, that touch on the problem of lying and withholding, and to distinguish, as we shall soon see, between, on the one hand, faithfulness and narrative truth, and, on the other hand, absolute honesty and forthrightness.

Having narrowed the analytical field, the author nonetheless cannot promise any neat solutions to the problems this essay confronts. The problem of tracing absences—of looking for what is *not* in letters, whether because of silence or the telling of untruths—is only a part, though an especially self-evident part, of a larger problem in analyzing personal correspondence. Puzzling gaps, in fact, pervade all aspects of the analysis of immigrant personal correspondence. The artifactual problems alone are daunting. In most cases, we may never know whether these archived collections that historians investigate are complete or a fraction of the total exchange of correspondence between the parties, because letters that would prove embarrassing or reveal intimate and private matters have been removed. We may never know how many complete exchanges of correspondence have been lost or destroyed, or are still in private hands. Each letter collection is, therefore, a part of a universe of documents, the size and nature of which can never really be known.[1] Nor can we know with any precision the size of the cohort of immigrants that actually wrote and received letters, though we can begin to move in on a rough estimation by looking at data on the volume of transoceanic mail exchanged and by analyzing the diffusion of literacy, and the social variables affecting it, in the immigrant's homelands. Even then, illiterates might have letters written for them, and they might take part orally in the collective creation of group letters of the sort frequently done by families and groups of friends.

Thus, problems lurk everywhere in generalizing about what goes on in—or in fact, doesn't go on in—personal letters. The acknowledgment of such difficulties carries significant problems for those who engage in the frequent practice of using letters for social documentation. Usually they seek to prove further what we already think we know as the result of research in other historical sources, such as government records or newspapers, or simply to add the color and authenticity of experiential testimony to narratives constructed around the use of such sources. Letters have been used by historians to examine significant issues such as cultural assimilation, social integration, the structure of occupations and job markets, or gender relations. But rare are acknowledgments of the tentativeness of evidence derived from such illusive texts.[2]

Such uses of personal letters would seem to bend them in a direction in which their creators did not mean to take them, for immigrant letters are not principally about documenting the world, but instead about reconfiguring a personal relationship rendered vulnerable by long-distance, long-term separation. It is in the service of that goal that the letter develops its content, so that goal, profoundly illusive in its own ways because it springs from the most profound recesses of human needs and emotions, needs to be understood as the source of the aspirations of the parties involved. This is precisely the point at which we need to begin to consider the problem of silences and untruths, which is intimately connected with those needs and emotions of the immigrants and those with whom they corresponded in their homelands.

*　*　*

Whether implicit or explicit, the negotiation of the epistolary relationship resembles a type of ethical discourse by which, as in conversation, the parties work to achieve a mutually beneficial modus vivendi, and thus, it demonstrates, depending on the individuals and the circumstances, varying degrees of mutual respect.[3] Immigrant letters, like all personal letters, not only sustained a dialogue between individuals, but also were themselves a mutual creation conceived in dialogue. As Janet Gurkin Altman, a student of epistolary fiction has remarked, letters cannot be born "out of a desire to merely express oneself without regard to the eventual reader." Instead, at some level, they must be "the result of a union of writer and reader."[4]

However fixed the outer boundaries of the form of the personal letter, each set of correspondents was faced with ongoing choices in conceiving together the organization, rhythms, and content of their correspondence. While creating the basis for continuing bonds, these negotiations served specifically to narrow the gap between writers and readers, and to put a seal of faithfulness upon the correspondence. In personal correspondence, writers take a formal and explicit responsibility for what they have written when they sign their name to the letters they have written. This becomes literally evident when a salutation such as "sincerely yours," or "yours truly" precedes the signature. But, as in any type of writing, readers may nonetheless derive their own meanings from texts, no matter who claims ultimate responsibility for them, and so transform them in ways unintended by their author. Yet immigrant letters seldom were open texts, subject to widely diverse interpretations. The possibility of a common reading emerges, not only because the reader and writer almost always share a personal history from before the inception of their correspondence, but because they also had come to share, to one extent or another, common assumptions about the purposes, and hence the content, tone, and rhythms, of their correspondence. Out of this sharing comes a fusing of the writer and reader. That is to say, the writer is the first reader of a letter, and reads not only as "I," but also inevitably as "you."[5]

But the gap between writer and reader in making the meanings of the letter transparent and providing desirable content is never completely closed, and the negotiations never cease, though in the press of other needs and obligations, they may be suspended for a time and correspondence might then settle into routine, or even stop. Events such as childbirth, sickness, the death of parents or siblings, or the onset of material hardship due to injury or unemployment, or plans to be reunited, or disputes about the distribution of inherited legacies, or suddenly rekindled conflicts dating from the distant past may all serve to revitalize these negotiations, whether they are explicit or implicit. What abides is the commitment to remain in communication, and hence to continue a relationship that takes its form ultimately, in place of face-to-face interactions and conversation, in written contact sustained by personal correspondence. Letters are not narratives, but a collaborative process of interpersonal communication that resists the type of closure that provides the poetic satisfaction for the narrative form. What we narrate about them is the history of the relationship that forms and is continued by correspondence.[6]

To say that the gap between writer and reader is never closed is to raise a number of problems that are difficult to conceptualize, but nonetheless cannot be evaded, if we are serious about decoding personal letters. It is obvious that circumstances will arise in which, for example, writers misapprehend what readers desire and readers cannot make literal sense of the letters their correspondents send them. Many of the immigrants and their homeland correspondents were hardly well practiced in creating written texts. Under the circumstances, it is to be expected that occasionally they would succeed in confusing each other. A process of clarification, however, may ensue that serves to provide correction. But there are more complex circumstances, lying at the heart of the roles people play in relation to one another and the motives they bring to fulfilling the terms of those roles, which also need to be addressed in connection with the durability of this gap between writer and reader. To speak in terms of *negotiation* and of *ethical discourse* seems to imply openness, honesty, and forthright dealing. Yet it is self-evident that not everything that appears in letters is truthful, and that not everything that may be said is always committed to paper.

This common sense insight raises an important point in the interpretation of all epistolarity that needs to be made explicit: the necessity for a morally realistic stance in thinking about personal relationships. In a thought-provoking work on the pre-modern European family, which is heavily based on collections of family letters, Steven Ozment has justified his dependence on personal letters to document family dynamics by stating, "Particularly in correspondence between family members, colleagues, friends, and lovers, where clarity and truth have a premium and can be matters of life and death, 'live' personal reactions to people, experiences, and events have been preserved as reliably as can be done in historical sources."[7] Immigrants' letters reveal a very different perspective. Precisely because the psychological and practical stakes are highest of all in dealing with such significant others as Ozment specifies, it may well be the case that the costs of "clarity and truth" are sometimes deemed much too high.

We may begin to examine the telling of untruths by observing that the commitment to maintain personal correspondence, which is above all the commitment to preserve a bond between individuals, rather than truth telling as such, may be considered the mark of faithfulness between correspondents. There are a variety of obvious reasons, some of them emotionally compelling and circumstantially mitigating, why correspondents might not choose to tell the truth to protect the people with whom they correspond, while remaining faithful to the larger purpose of maintaining a relationship by responsibly sustaining the cycle of correspondence. Sickness, unemployment, poverty, marital discord, drunkenness, rebellious children, or abject failure might not only prove variously embarrassing, but also prompt worry and concern in one's readers. In consequence of such circumstances, the temptation to engage in the often parodied "I am well and doing well" formulation present in some immigrant letters, or go beyond it to claim accomplishments or security that did not exist in reality was probably great for many immigrant letter-writers. Moreover, emigrants took risks in leaving their homes, and were often discouraged by their families, who warned of disastrous consequences, if parental authority, traditional cultural ways, and home places were abandoned. In the context of the demography and interpersonal hierarchies of most nineteenth century European emigration, what transpired was conflict between fathers, who might be traditionalists sensitive about challenges to their authority, and sons who wanted to get out of the country and out from under the parental yoke.

One senses the weight of these interpersonal difficulties in letters-series, such as those of George Martin, a carpenter from Kent who came to Upper Canada in 1834, or John McLees, an Irish Protestant who resettled in New York City around 1828, which begin with apologies to fathers or to both parents for unspecified transgressions. McLees wrote his brother, in what is his first archived letter, that, though "nothing could induce me to be content in Ireland," he was nonetheless hopeful that he could eventually return to "visit my native land once more that I might embrace my father and ask forgiveness for all that is past . . ."[8]

The tendency to exaggerate the gains derived from their steadfast resolve to emigrate, or at least to underplay the hardships encountered in order to be proven correct in the resolve to emigrate, or alternatively—as was the strategy of both George Martin and John McLees—to emphasize the hardships to win sympathy and respect, is easily understood in these familial circumstances, though it is difficult to prove the precise motivation for exaggeration or outright fabrication, let alone the material gains claimed. In reading immigrant letters, one sometimes finds writers who were deft strategists of interpersonal relations. They were skillful at finding formulations, which were based on recitations—often, manipulations—of the narrative of their experience, that were likely to sway the emotions of their readers.

In his first letter after arriving in Upper Canada, George Martin spun out a web of guilt in which his parents might easily be trapped, writing, that while he did not know "whether you wish to hear or know anything about us," he hoped nonetheless that "if there is any bitterness of feeling on your side still existing pray let it be forgot in the dangers and troubles I have encountered since the morning we departed but let all this be forgot." Martin went on the describe in elaborate detail circumstances so difficult— the intense perils of the ocean voyage, a bout with cholera amidst a local epidemic in which a number of people perished, the exhausting of his savings, and the prospect of a winter of subemployment and want—that only the coldest heart could resist feeling sympathy for him. Since we seldom know about the histories and emotional qualities of these relationships prior to their embedding in letters, however, contemporary readers have little context for taking the measure of what inner logic derived from past experiences in interpersonal relations guide the writer in assuming a stance toward the reader. We might return to John McLees, who complained in his early correspondence of unemployment, poor working conditions, family illnesses, and mounting bills for medical expenses, and also seems to have been making a claim for sympathy from the family members to whom he wrote. He never explained, or perhaps felt he had to explain, what he had done that needed to be forgiven. The closest we come to a hint of what might have prompted his apparent apology was three years after the date of his first archived letter, when he wrote cryptically that he wished his family to know "that as a vision my mind traverses all the pleasures as well as the evils I was led into in Ireland but now blessed by God can lead a happy life." The details of what might perhaps have been a reckless, irresponsible youth were perhaps only too well known for McLees to have to spell them out in detail.[9]

What we may observe with confidence amidst the difficulties of determining facts and deciphering motives is that, as Jerome Bruner has observed, narrative truth, which assists in establishing continuity and stability amidst the inconsistencies and the frequent contradictions of life, is more important for individuals than literal truth when it comes to the ongoing work of constructing personal identities. A good, coherent story—one that is consistent with regard to the individual's self-understanding in the context of one's most significant interpersonal relationships, even if not completely or even partially true—may serve a variety of psychologically functional purposes, not to mention its benefits for sparing the feelings of others. Moreover, the larger identity narrative, of which such stories were but a part, had special significance for immigrants, because international migration was a challenge to the continuity of relationships to the people and the places in which personal identity is constituted.[10]

Contemporary readers sense how great a temptation lying and withholding, or simple exaggeration, might be for someone like Robert Bowles, who left Kent for the United States at the age of 30 in 1823, and settled on a small farm not far from Harrison, Ohio, near Cincinnati and close to the Ohio River. Bowles's trade was making and repairing muskets and guns. He had inherited a property in England, but was not able to maintain it, and certainly was bitter about the problems this had caused him, all of which he attributed to the inequities of the social system in England. From the first letter Bowles wrote to his younger brothers shortly after arriving and taking possession of his farm, he engaged in unrelenting and outspoken defense of everything American and criticism of nearly everything English—climate, taxes, newspapers, church, state, health, fruits, and vegetables. (Even the English themselves seemed for him to be better in America, at least to the extent that Bowles continued to crave their company, and sought out English friends.) Within the first year after his arrival, he was boasting of his crop yield and the quality and neatness of his fields, and the ease with which his credit had become established in his neighborhood and he and his wife had been admitted to local social circles.[11] Though in the form—"extracts" that Bowles had entered into a copybook—in which we have his letters it is difficult for the contemporary reader to know what might be the actual and complete text of his letters, there seems almost no personal content to the letters, such as inquiries after his brothers' affairs or relation of his own family life. While Bowles certainly wanted to encourage his brothers to come and join him, and this may have been a motive for his almost propagandistic writing, this one dimensional discourse was so pervasive, repetitive, and heavy-handed that it ultimately comes to seem defensive. The reader begins to suspect that Bowles's discourse is overdetermined by some past conflict, which is unspoken but lurking in the background, and which eventuates from his previous failure. Thus, he may go on as he does about the successes he claims as a way of dealing with, indirectly and implicitly, abandoning his obligations in England and leaving the country rather than because it is a strategy to bring about family unity. It may be a substitute, too, for venting his anger about having to leave the England he reviled. But none of this is ever alluded to directly. We detect it instead in comments such as, "Here [in Ohio] I sit down and bless myself in plenty, and if I am not the greatest of my family, I do flatter myself I am the happiest . . . I again repeat that I consider my Emigration as the most fortunate step of my whole life, and I assure you no act of mine ever gave such complete satisfaction."[12]

We cannot know the truth of Bowles' situation during his first year in Ohio. Furthermore, the collection of "extracts" goes no further than that one year, so we cannot know much from the parts of his letters to which we have access about what comes afterward, during the remaining course of his life, which might provide clarification. Did he achieve instant success and personal satisfaction? We do know from his will that Bowles died a reasonably wealthy man, but that was many years later, in 1862.[13] There is certainly some suggestion in his letters that his wife was quite unhappy in her new situation, and that this affected the quality of his own life. Invited to go hunting in nearby Indiana, he had to decline. He wrote his brothers, explaining that "My wife is so timid that my going is completely out of the question."[14] In commenting on her state of mind later in the same letter, he could only say, tentatively and briefly, that "I think" she is becoming more comfortable in North America.[15] To this extent, his defensiveness about emigrating may have been a product, too, of a semi-conscious awareness of his wife's complaining voice and of her fears in her new situation in North America, even as he wrote his brothers. If, on the other hand, he did experience instant prosperity and social acceptance and, from the moment he arrived, the best of health, as he claimed, he was certainly unusual. But suppose Bowles had been successful in inducing his brothers to emigrate and join him, and they found him to have greatly exaggerated, if not simply lied, about his good fortune? Then the game would have been up, and he would have been revealed to be no better at managing his life in North American than he was in England. It was a situation that lent itself to truth-telling, whatever the precise variety of truth-telling, if only because one might have to bear the embarrassment of being caught in a lie. Most immigrants probably understood how vulnerable exaggerated claims and rank falsehoods were to some sort of detection.

Furthermore, one did not need to achieve family reunion to be discovered to be telling untruths or withholding information in one's letters. With so many immigrants coming to North America, and settling amongst one another, and with international postal service constantly improving after the 1830s, gossip became transnationalized. Gossip, or perhaps to put a less judgmental face on it, social intelligence, circulated in the international mails with alarming rapidity. Those who gossiped or simply spoke negatively of other immigrants in their midst in their letters soon became sensitive to the possibility that their homeland correspondents, in sharing their letters with others around them, might well set in motion a flow of information that would come back to haunt them. Some of the demand for privacy that we see in immigrant letters was rooted in just this fear. It was such a sensitivity that led Richard Hails, a tailor from Northumberland, who settled in Massachusetts in 1842, to caution his brother against circulating his letter in their town. Hails's brother George had asked him for a relation of the circumstances of his emigration and resettlement, because he was himself considering coming to North America. In response, Hails sent his brother an account that included a relation of those hometown Englishmen residing in Massachusetts who had helped him in his resettlement project and those who had, ungenerously, not done so. There is no reason to think the account anything but truthful, but Hails nonetheless cautioned his brother against sharing one of his letters with any local people, in fear that the ensuing gossip would cause divisions and bad feeling. He wrote: " I do not wish every one to read my letters and I suppose that it is best for you to keep things to yourselfe . . . in respect to what I told you of my il[l] usage. I did not tell to make truble among friends but only to answer your inquiries, so I hope nothing will be said to their friends but forget and forgive . . ."[16] Even though he believed himself to have been wronged, Hails's sensitivity to the discord that might result from his simply reacting to those wrongs seems a mark of his decency, perhaps added to which was some element of timidity.

But imagine if under the same social and communicative circumstances facilitating the spread of gossip, one really did have something embarrassing and shameful to hide. We may take William Darnley, a carpenter who left Stockport near Liverpool for New York City in 1857 in search of work, as an example. He certainly discovered for himself the full force of such gossip. It was Darnley's declared intention either to return home, or, more insistently spoken of, to send for his wife and five children as soon as he could afford to do so. When weeks turned into months, and months into years, and Darnley had made no move to bring about this reunion or to return to England, gossip, which was based on the letters of other immigrants from Stockport in the working class British immigrant community in New York City, began circulating in Stockport that Darnley was living with another woman, and had been heard to declare that his family was too expensive to support. For his part, Darnley seemed outraged in his response to the letters from his wife that confronted him with the gossip circulating around Stockport about his conduct. He claimed that circumstances beyond his control were responsible for the situation. He wrote that the sharp contraction of business in 1857 that brought the construction industry to a standstill and then the Civil War, which caused a slowdown in building left him unemployed and underemployed for extended periods. Economic hardship was joined at the time, he wrote, by ill-health to force him continually to have to live off the savings that he had been intending to use to send for his wife and children. He continued to send her small sums of money, especially for the children's education and clothing. But, while protesting he was innocent of infidelity, Darnley probably did nothing to stem his wife's suspicions about his conduct when increasingly he provided her with fewer and fewer details about his living arrangements. Moreover, though he claimed that he had difficulty writing when he had "no good news to share," his wife must also have grown suspicious when his letters back to Stockport grew infrequent. He was still aggressively justifying his behavior in July 1863, at a time when his family was not yet united with him and rumors continued to circulate of his liaison with another woman. We are unable to learn the truth, for the archived collection of his letters to his wife ends with that letter of July 1863.[17] But if Darnley were attempting to keep the liaison secret and then, when caught in the midst of it, he lied, he had failed because of contingencies he had not factored into his calculations. The cause of his failure was that gossip transmitted through the international mails now allowed those in European villages far across the ocean to continue to attempt to exert a degree of moral control on those who had emigrated.[18]

Such gossip might thus be seen as an incentive for truth-telling, or at least for avoiding behaviors that were likely to get one caught, if only in virtual, postal space, in flagrante delicto. But, more likely, the circumstances in which a Bowles or a Darnley might be trapped in a lie also lent themselves to a strategy of *silence*. By its very nature, silence is a particularly complex problem for the conceptualization of the negotiations that comprised immigrant epistolarity. One need not lie, but simply refuse to address certain matters, while at the same time maintaining the commitment to correspond and to write about everything else, including much that pleased one's unknowing correspondent. In understanding silence, just as should be the case in understanding lying, we need to approach it not as something we must overcome, as if it were our task as historians of the immigrant letter to fill in the blanks—though admittedly it is difficult to escape the voyeuristic temptation to imagine whether, for example, William Darnley was lying about his life in New York City, and then to try to imagine the life he shared with his lover. Darnley unmasked is a better story than Darnley indeterminate. The assumption in seeking to fill in these blank spots, however, is that the contemporary analyst is omniscient, and knows what belongs in the letter. If text is not there, then it should be there—a way of thinking that leads to a guessing game that is a plausible, but ultimately limited, analytical strategy. It is more availing of insight not to overcome silence by filling in the blank spaces, but rather to explain how it is that intentional, strategic silence, where we might be fortunate enough to find traces of it, may have been integrated into the negotiations that comprise epistolarity. We must seek to understand silence, as Altman has rightly understood it in such circumstances, as in itself a type of communication.[19] Silence of this sort in letters was a powerful tool that simultaneously preserved one's ethical position—for silence, after all, is not the same as dishonesty—while protecting oneself against the full force of self-disclosure and one's reader against the painful understanding that all was not well with the writer.

Silence, for example, might allow an emigrant son or daughter greater power in dealing with parents, who tried to reach across the Atlantic to exert their moral authority through correspondence. Not only did the exchange of letters, in and of itself, allow relationships that had been parental monologues before emigration to be equalized, but, through silence, the emigrant child had greater power to shape the agenda of correspondence, while continuing to maintain the relationship and to display familial loyalty and respect for parents. One could, to take one guise in which silence might present itself, simply temporarily delay answering a letter until one had something positive to report, a tactic confessed to his parents on several occasions by Titus Crawshaw, an emigrant cloth finisher from Huddersfield, who settled in Philadelphia in 1853. Crawshaw revealed in his letters a suspicion that his father had a low opinion of him, and he revealed at times, no doubt relatedly, that he had a low opinion of himself. On one occasion, when he confessed to having too little money to send any home to help his elderly parents, which he had apparently promised to do when he emigrated, he said, in what certainly must have been a painful confession, "I ought to be able to help you having nothing but myself to keep, but you see I am no good either to your or to anyone else. I am a blank on the face of the earth." Because giving bad reports simply confirmed this sort of judgment and, he feared, might lead to his father's censure, Crawshaw often shrank from giving them, and simply failed to write. It was probably to avoid moral control and censure as well that Crawshaw, like numerous other male immigrants, gave little warning that he was courting with the intention of marrying, and simply seemed to announce suddenly in a letter he had been married. True to character, however, he made himself pay a bit psychologically for his method of eventual disclosure and for his very existence, as a somewhat less than successful journeyman. In commenting on the "likeness" of his wife that he enclosed with the letter in which he spoke of her, he said, "You will see she is not a regular beauty, but she is as good looking as me. I agreed with her because I thought we should agree and live midling comfortable together."[20]

Avoiding the embarrassment of having to account for bad decisions and failure and being the agent of the hurt others would feel in one's behalf might provide another context for silence. Such was the case, it appears, with Judith White Hale, a young Irish Protestant woman who left the Sligo area for the United States in 1804. Then unmarried, Judith White left Ireland shortly after the emigration of her sister Jane, in the midst of a legal difficulty that imperiled the family's residence on its rented farm, and hence its livelihood. Her parents were deeply pessimistic about the future of Ireland. The Whites seem to have been lower country gentry holding a tenuous grip on respectability, and unable to maintain a large household. These older sisters were superfluous in a declining domestic economy. Their separate leave-takings had about them an air of secrecy, as if the Whites either feared signaling to creditors they might be in financial trouble, or were reluctant to share their difficulties with gossiping neighbors. But there was no doubt of the deep regret for the situation of her daughters' exile expressed by Letitia White, the mother and the letter-writing parent. From the beginning, however, Judith appears to have been an indifferent correspondent. She quickly fell out of touch with Letitia, who felt that her daughter's silence represented "a great unkindness." Judith did write her sister Jane, who conveyed to their mother in tempered form general news about Judith. Eventually, however, though the sisters lived near each other (by North American standards), in New York State and in Maine respectively, they, too, fell out of touch for as long as four years at a time, neither exchanging letters nor visiting. Perhaps Judith began her silence toward her parents in bitterness at the misfortunes that led to her being pushed out of her home, though there is no evidence of this. What is clear instead is that Judith never had any good news to send to anyone. Almost from its beginning, her American life was a protracted struggle against poverty. She contracted a marriage with a Mr. Hale, a sickly older, maritime man, who was barely able to make a living as a ship captain working at fishing and the coastal trade. Hale would eventually die and leave her with little in the way of resources. She tried maintaining a school in order to supplement their often dire finances, and eventually to support herself, but wrote her sister that she lacked the self-confidence and business ability to succeed at keeping a school. In the midst of years of these difficulties, she had at least five children, only one of whom was in a position to assist her after Hale died. In the final letter in the archived collection, written to her sister in 1826, Judith made a reference for the first time to her Irish family. She noted their "dear mother's death," about which Jane had apparently written her, and which Judith said, in implicit reference to the fact that she had long been out of communication with Letitia, she had imagined had taken place many years before.[21]

Judith's silence may well have been more a strategy than procrastination, for it was a means for protecting her mother against knowledge that her daughter, whom she reluctantly sent into exile, had suffered there. Silence also protected Judith against having to admit a failed life. After the passage of years without communicating at all, however, breaking silence and resuming letter contact was a psychological hurdle in itself. There was so much that might be explained, for both the circumstances that led to silence and the resort to silence to deal with those circumstances seem, at least on the surface, to require some explanation. So, too, did the reasons for finally breaking silence. One needed to be sure, for example, that one's motives were not misconstrued, or perhaps properly construed as self-interested. Those breaking silence in order to claim legacies left by parents they might logically believe to be dead certainly risked being seen as mercenary and encountering resistance from other legatees. Moreover, the need for explanation seems to mount in proportion to the length of the silence maintained. Short-term neglect is bad enough, but long-term neglect prompts unending worry, and in these circumstances ultimately perhaps grieving is worse. Yet the obstacles to giving account were formidable. The psychological impediments to making multiple confessions had to be overcome. Moreover, such confessions taxed the writing abilities of correspondents whose grasp on literacy might be tenuous, for exculpatory explanations are complex writing assignments that must acknowledge fault and save face simultaneously.

That it was not easy either technically or psychologically to muster the language needed to break a long silence was evident in a letter written by Radcliffe Quine, a ship's carpenter from the Isle of Man, who wrote his brother and sister from British Columbia for the first time in 1861, over 16 years after he emigrated. Quine's case also illustrates the practical costs of a long silence. Quine was certainly articulate enough on the surface of his letter, but the details of the assignment seemed to elude him, though we cannot know the degree of intentionality with which they eluded him. Quine wrote, "I take his opertunity of addressing you for the first time . . ." "When I look back to the date of my leaving my native home, I feel the most poignant sensations of shame and regret. I will not aggravate the impropriety of my omission by amusing you with childish excuses of illness and buisiness, but confess that an unaccountable negligence and foolish habit of procrastination have made me so inattentive. I thrown myself on your kindness, to excuse my fault."

Sixteen years is a long time to procrastinate and live with a knowledge of one's negligence. That other reasons for his silence, such as a feeling of alienation from his family, might be involved are not alluded to, but may be suggested not only by his silence itself, but by the fact that his siblings would be engaged in the next decade in attempting to deny Quine a share of his inheritance. But then Quine had given them an excuse. Because he had been out of contact for so long and only wrote episodically after reestablishing it, they were able to claim in the law courts that their brother was actually dead, and the author of these letters to them was an imposter, wanting money to which he had no legitimate claim. If they privately believed that the individual writing to them was in reality their long lost brother, but continued publicly to deny his identity, greed alone might not completely account for their behavior, for they may also have felt a certain bitterness at being neglected for so many years. Well into the 1880s, now a resident in a Seattle hospital and suffering, he said, from severe epilepsy, Quine was still writing his estranged brother and asking for his inheritance.[22]

Adult children attempting to wrest psychological control of their lives away from their parents, too embarrassed by lives that have spun out of control to report the details of their existence, or alienated for whatever reason from their families were not the only correspondents who might utilize silence, and then face the necessity of having to explain themselves. Out of pride, or embarrassment, or the desire not to spread anxiety, those who seemed well established in their mature years might do the same. Hattie Reid, an immigrant from Ipswich who lived in New York City in the 1870s and 1880s with a husband and eight children, provides a sad example. Reid also suggests the difficulties of breaking silence after years of engaging in it strategically. Hers was not, however, the silence of loss of contact as had been Judith White Hale's silence. It was instead the unwillingness for many years, while maintaining letter contact, to tell her sister the truth about the disastrous circumstances of her marriage.

Only in retrospect—reading the letters in reverse chronological order—does it appear that Reid had dropped suggestions for sometime that she was learning especially bitter lessons about life. But so guarded were her comments, and so easily taken for general observations about the human condition, that readers might be forgiven for seeing no autobiographical commentary in them. Thus, she writes approvingly of the resolve of someone who, her sister has written, recently signed a total abstinence pledge: "I hope he will stick to his pledge of total abstinence as there is nothing like it, no safeguard without it. If the tempting cup is indulged in at all any one is liable to fall victim at any time. There is no safty in so called temperance." The contemporary reader is likely as not to say simply that Reid has strong opinions about alcohol consumption, and to leave it at that.[23] Or, when she writes, "I am glad Alice has not married so young. It spoils all their enjoyment and makes old women of them before their time," we might briefly reflect on her own *eight* children, but turn from that reflection, because there is no indication anywhere in her letters that she might be speaking on the question of the age at which girls married from the perspective of her own experience.[24] That is until we read her letter of July 5, 1882, which appears in the letter-series just after the two letters that contain these same quoted passages. Now she begins her letter with an extraordinary confession about her approximately two decade long marriage: "I am in great trouble. My life has been one long series of misfortunes since I have been a wife. I hid them from you as well as I could, knowing that it would only make you miserable without benefitting me; but now the climax has come and I have left him for ever."[25] She went on to describe years of a hellish existence with a violent, abusive husband whose episodes of binge drinking required police intervention and frequent incarceration. The most recent of these episodes had lasted for weeks, she wrote, and ultimately had been written up in the newspapers. Perhaps the prospect of that publicity finding its way to England as gossip, as much as the breakup of her marriage itself, forced Reid to break her silence, and admit these immense difficulties.[26]

Neither falsehood nor silence is necessarily evidence of faithlessness so much as of the limitations and points of danger and stress present in relationships. Ultimately, therefore, both falsehood and silence are evidence of the difficulties immigrants experienced in the sustaining of personal identities. Even if not as frequently in dramatic circumstances as the Darnley and Reid families experienced, many epistolary relationships found correspondents misleading one another through falsehood and silence. Yet most of the parties continued to negotiate their correspondence with those significant others who were sources of continuity in lives disrupted by emigration. Even Judith White Hale, in her own indirect way, had contact with her mother through her sister. The parties to most of these cycles of correspondence continued to write, read, and exchange letters, leaving out only what was too painful, or at the very least too inconvenient, to address truthfully or at all, and hoping they would be able to carry off their often well-intentioned masquerade for one more letter.

Notes

1. Donald Harmon Akenson, "Reading the Texts of Rural Immigrants: Letters from the Irish in Australia, New Zealand, and North America," *Canadian Papers in Rural History* VII (1990): 387.
2. For a history of the uses by historians and social scientists of immigrant letters, see, David A. Gerber, "The Immigrant Letter between Positivism and Populism: The Uses of Immigrant Personal Correspondence in Twentieth Century American Scholarship," *Journal of American Ethnic History* 16 (Summer 1997): 3–34.
3. Michael A. Forrester, *Psychology of Language: A Critical Introduction* (London: Sage, 1996), pp. 78–81, 95–114; Peter Burke, *The Art of Conversation* (Ithaca: Cornell

University Press, 1993), pp. 9–33. These remarks should not be taken to imply that either conversation or letter-writing are necessarily democratic, for both may show evidences of differentials in influence, authority, or power rooted in gender, age, and other significant social markers.

4. Janet Gurkin Altman, *Epistolarity: Approaches to a Form* (Columbus: Ohio State University Press, 1982), pp. 88 (quote), 117, 138–139.

5. Forrester, *Psychology of Language*, pp.182–183; Louise Weatherbee Phelps, "Audience and Authorship: The Disappearing Boundary," *A Sense of Audience in Written Communications*, ed. Gesa Kirsch and Duane H. Roen (Newbury Park: Sage, 1990), vol. 5, *Written Communication Annual*, pp. 159–176; Susan Kissell, "Writer Anxiety vs. The Need for Community in Botts Family Letters," *Women's Personal Narratives: Essays in Criticism and Pedagogy*, ed. Lenore Hoffman and Margo Culler (New York: Modern Languages Association, 1985), pp. 48–53.

6. Elizabeth MacArthur, *Extravagant Narratives: Closure and Dynamics in The Epistolary Form* (Princeton: Princeton University Press, 1990).

7. Steven Ozment, *Ancestors: The Loving Family in Old Europe* (Cambridge: Harvard University Press, 2000), pp. 105–106. Ozment's analysis of family letters in this book does largely proceed on the assumption that his correspondents are indeed truthful with one another, and that they possess no hidden agendas that led to withholding or deceiving.

8. George Martin to parents, Coburg, Upper Canada, September 30, 1834, George Martin Letters, Seven Oaks Public Library, Seven Oaks, Kent, United Kingdom (hereafter *SOK*); John McLees to Brother, New York, August 28, 1828, John and Catherine McLees Letters, D. 904, Public Record Office of Northern Ireland (hereafter, *PRONI*).

9. George Martin to parents, Coburg, Upper Canada, September 30, 1834, *SOK*; and John McLees to brother, New York, November 7, 1831, PRONI.

10. Jerome Bruner, *Acts of Meaning* (Cambridge: Harvard University Press, 1990), pp. 111–115.

11. Robert Bowles, *Extracts of Letters from America 1823, Book the Third, Written by Robert Bowles to His Brothers John and Richard*, vol. 538, Ohio Historical Society. These extracts *appear* to be whole letters that either were recopied drafts or first drafts.

12. Robert Bowles to brothers, Harrison, Ohio, April 20, 1823, Ohio Historical Society (hereafter, *OHS*).

13. Robert Bowles, *Will*, November 20, 1856, Book 17, p. 265 (1862), Probate Court, Hamilton County, Ohio. Bowles left a farm of 295 acres and livestock to his two sons, $5000 to his daughter, and $1000 and a $500 annuity to his second wife.

14. Robert Bowles to brothers, Harrison, Ohio, August 3, 1823, OHS.

15. Ibid.

16. R. Hails and A. Hails to George, Lincoln, Massachusetts, July 31, 1849, in Charlotte Erickson, *Invisible Immigrants: The Adaptation of English and Scottish Immigrants in Nineteenth Century America* (Coral Gables: University of Miami Press, 1972), p. 318, and on Hails, pp. 307–309.

17. William Darnley to wife, Liverpool England, June 3, 1857, New York City, October 25, 1857, March 16, April 13, May 17, July 20, November 11, 1858, May 23, 1859, March 18, April 24, July 27, September 4, 1860, February 18, April 9, 1861, May 21, 1862, and July 4, 1863, which contains a long, angry summary of all of the reversals of fortune he had encountered in Canada and the United States and of the rumors that he was living with another woman; Darnley Family Letters, 1843–1884, New York Public Library.

18. Among the immigration analysts who have recognized the assertion of moral control via the transatlantic mails are: Ewa Morawska, "Labor Migration of the Poles in the Atlantic World Economy, 1880–1914," *Comparative Studies in Society and*

History 31, no. 2 (1989): 237–270; R.A. Schermerhorn, *These Our People: Minorities in American Culture* (Boston: D.C. Heath, 1949), pp. 369–370; Mark Wyman, *Round–Trip to America: The Immigrants Return to Europe, 1880–1930* (Ithaca: Cornell University Press, 1993), p. 51; Suzanne M. Sinke, *Dutch Immigrant Women in the United States, 1880–1920* (Urbana: University of Illinois Press, 2002) p. 19.

19. Altman, *Epistolarity*, p. 207; Blake Poland and Ann Pederson, "Reading Between the Lines: Interpreting Silences in Qualitative Research," *Qualitative Inquiry* 4 (June 1998): 293–312.

20. Titus Crawshaw to father, Crescentville, Pennsylvania, August 11, 1860, September 18, 1861, Philadelphia, December 9, 1862, Hespeler, Canada, July 31, 1863, Germantown, Pennsylvania, July 19, 1863, September 19, 1864 (quote), June 18, 1866 (quote), in Erickson, *Invisible Immigrants*, pp. 347, 348, 353, 354–357, 358–359, and on Crawshaw, pp. 329–332.

21. Letitia White to Jane White [Jane White Nugent], Sligo, Ireland, March 21, August 24, 1804, January 1, 1805 (quote), August 15, 1815; Judith White Hale to Jane Nugent, Gloucester, Massachusetts, February 23, 1810, July 12, 1814, Portland, Maine, August 18, 1826, White Family Letters, VFM2323, OHS.

22. Radcliffe Quine to "Deare Brother and Sister," Victoria, Vancouver Island, April 22, 1861, in Erickson, *Invisible Immigrants*, pp. 469–471"; and for other letters in the Quine series and additional contextualization by Erickson, see, pp. 467–469, 471–478. Quine also may have been embarrassed to acknowledge that he had abandoned his son to the care of a friend years before. Only when he was confronted by his brother with an accusation about his conduct as a father in a letter years after Radcliffe's epistolary reappearance, would he allude to this matter. The facts, which are difficult to discern, may be that his wife had died, and he was attracted to the prospect of going out to California and making a fortune in the gold rush. The boy would have been an encumbrance in this adventure. Quine may well also have felt that, under any circumstance, the task of raising the boy was beyond his abilities; Radcliffe Quine to brother John and sister, Seattle, March 22, 1878, in Erickson, *Invisible Immigrants*, pp. 471–472. His alienation from his family is very briefly suggested in this same letter when he speaks defensively of the care his son had received from his guardian. "I know," Quine wrote, "that he was brought up better then [h]is father."

23. Hattie Reid to sister, Brooklyn, New York, n.d., Erickson, *Invisible Immigrants*, p. 480.

24. Hattie Reid to sister, Brooklyn, New York, March 28, 1882, Erickson, *Invisible Immigrants*, p. 480.

25. Hattie Reid to sister, n.p., July 5, 1882, Erickson, *Invisible Immigrants*, pp. 481–482.

26. I have been unable to locate any newspaper references in either New York City or Brooklyn newspapers to the incidents Reid described in her letter to her sister.

8

Reading and Writing across the Borders of Dictatorship: Self-Censorship and Emigrant Experience in Nazi and Stalinist Europe

Ann Goldberg

This essay examines emigrant letter-writing strategies in Europe during the political crisis of the 1930s, a time when fascist regimes were overtaking Central Europe (Germany 1933; Austria 1938; Czechoslovakia 1938–1939) and when the Soviet Union under Stalin was undergoing its worst period of terror. Countless letters survive of Jews and other persecuted people in flight, or seeking flight, from these regimes. Their letters tell the story of an unfolding catastrophe, as would-be emigrants seeking rescue scrambled to communicate their plights to family, friends, and other contacts in the West.

Clearly, writing and (consequently) reading letters across the borders of dictatorship were anything but straightforward acts, given the danger of police surveillance. That danger turned letter-writing into a cat and mouse game with the authorities, as persecuted people sought to elude detection while smuggling out urgent and forbidden messages. Their resulting letters were distorted and self-censored, containing intentionally false or misleading statements; on the surface, these letters seemed to be silent about the really important matters in their authors' lives.

Instead of treating this fact as a problem to circumvent, this essay puts the silences, falseness, and "inauthenticity" of such letters at the center of its anaylsis. As such, the essay will focus on the form of 1930s emigrant letter-writing as much as its content. Indeed, it is very hard to separate form and content in these letters. I will show how the form of writing and reading changed as those people caught in Central and Eastern Europe seized on strategies of duplicity and subterfuge to communicate with the West. The essay is thus about how both dictatorship and resistance against it were inscribed in the acts of writing and reading letters. Finally, I will briefly try to put all of this into a longer-term historical perspective that links letter-writing, the modern self, and politics.

My focus is the correspondence of two German-Jewish sisters, Anne Bernfeld-Schmückle (1892–1941) and Elisabeth (Elli) Gundolf (1893–1958), born Salomon, whose letters cover the period from the early 1920s through the late 1930s, and, due to the nature of their emigrations, span the continent, from London to Moscow.[1] Anne and Elli, together with their brother Fritz, were raised in a progressive and assimilated middle-class family from Silesia (eastern Germany). The Salomon sisters were emancipated "New Women." They were unusually well-educated: Elli had a PhD in economics and subsequently worked in public relations, as well as a journalist, translator, and private tutor in Vienna and Rome; Anne earned a medical degree and became a practicing physician in Vienna. Both sisters made spectacular marriages (and friends) that connected them with some of the key people and movements of the era. Elli married Friedrich Gundolf (1880–1931), a celebrated literary scholar, Heidelberg professor, and close disciple of the poet Stefan George.[2] Anne's first marriage, which produced two daughters, was to Siegfried Bernfeld (1892–1953), the Viennese psychoanalyst, author, and member of Sigmund Freud's inner circle.

While the sisters were very close, they took diametrically opposite political paths, with important effects on their respective emigrant experiences. Elli, who shared her husband's conservative German nationalism, remained in Germany after his death until the Nazi takeover forced her to flee to England in 1934. Anne's communist sympathies[3] contributed to her emigration in 1926 to the Soviet Union after her marriage to Bernfeld had broken up and her daughters were old enough to be placed in a German boarding school.[4] Anne planned to accompany to Moscow as his assistant the Austrian Lamarckian biologist Paul Kammerer, whom the Soviet government had offered a research institute and university chair.[5] Shortly before their scheduled departure, however, in the "greatest scientific scandal of the first half of [the twentieth] century," Kammerer committed suicide (he was facing the allegation that he had falsified his sensational laboratory data, which had purported to prove the inheritability of acquired characteristics).[6] Daringly, Anne went anyway, arriving in the fall of 1926.[7] It is the correspondence generated by Anne's experience in the Soviet Union that is the topic of this essay.

I was disappointed when I first examined the correspondence. Anne's Moscow letters seemed to be filled merely with everyday trivia: travel arrangements, financial and child-rearing issues, and interminable lists of consumer goods she needed from the West. Months later, I came back to the letters and, examining them more carefully, I ordered and read them chronologically, as well as in conjunction with Elli's responses to Anne and her (uncensored) correspondence *about* Anne with third parties in the West. I also found several of Anne's uncensored letters that she wrote during visits to the West before 1937. A dramatic story started to emerge of political persecution, financial crisis, and Anne's mounting desperation to get out of the Soviet Union. Anne and Elli's attempts to communicate about these issues through various codes and subterfuges was a big part of the story. Indeed, the events themselves could only be pieced together indirectly by paying close attention to the form of their writing.

One can trace Anne's plight under political repression through her elaboration of deceptive writing techniques. To be sure, her letters, which always assumed surveillance, were self-censored from the beginning. As she put it in early 1927, "there is so much [happening] here [in Moscow] that I don't know what to write about, especially because one can't write about the most interesting things."[8] Months later, while visiting her daughters in Germany, where she felt free to elaborate on this point, she counseled Elli to watch out about her own letters: "you know that you can't write to me across the [Soviet] border . . . anything critical or political."[9] Anne's Moscow letters, therefore, if they mentioned politics at all, did so very obliquely. But there was a degree of openness in the early letters in striking contrast to the later ones. She felt free enough to complain about daily hardships and the stepped-up work measures under the First Five Year Plan, as well as to acknowledge the self-censorship of her letters in the aforementioned quote.[10] In 1927, she wrote with amazing candor about police-state surveillance and its effect on her behavior:

> Government officials [at the foreign embassies] are not only not useful to me,[11] they are harmful. Don't forget that here everything has a reversed meaning and that . . . personal contacts with representatives of the [Western] bourgeois states must be kept track of [and viewed] with suspicion [by the Soviet government]. There is here an enormous amount of spying and one does not want to expose oneself to suspicion. Especially because spying and counterrevolutionary activities are punished with the death penalty . . . and it is believed that there is more behind many "harmless personal interactions." So I keep myself as much as possible away from the foreign embassies, although they include many interesting people.[12]

This relative ease of communication coincided in part with the era of the New Economic Program (NEP), and with a time when the Soviet border was still fairly porous and open. The latter element was crucial. For when Anne emigrated to the Soviet Union, she became transnational, assimilating into a new life but also retaining strong links to her country(ies) of origin. On the one hand, she had become part of Moscow's German émigré community, which dramatically expanded after 1933 with the repression and subsequent flight to the Soviet Union of Communist Party members from Nazi Germany. In the early years (1926–1931), she worked at a privileged job at the Marx-Engels Institute on the legendary first edition of Marx and Engels collected works.[13] She began a new family, marrying her coworker and fellow German émigré, the Marxist scholar, journalist, and publicist Karl Schmückle (1890–1938), with whom she bore a son. At the same time, she had left behind family and friends, above all, her two daughters, with whom she remained in close contact. The responsibilities of juggling both lives required constant contact and access between the Soviet Union, on the one hand, and Germany and Austria, on the other. There were perpetual arrangements to be made about vacation trips, transfers of money, getting presents to her daughters on birthdays and holidays, visits, or arranging lodging for her children during school vacations, as well as about her apartment in Vienna. Given the endemic food and consumer shortages of the Soviet economy, Anne was also heavily dependent upon goods from the West, either via postal package from Elli or personal delivery by an acquaintance traveling to Moscow. For a number of years, all of this was possible, albeit difficult.

Things began to change in 1931, when political repression directly entered Anne and Karl's lives. It was the era of the enormous upheavals and suffering associated with Stalin's First Five Year Plan, of mounting political persecution, and massive food shortages. Together with their boss, the Marx scholar David Rjazanoff, they were fired from their jobs in a purge of the Marx-Engels Institute. The couple spent the next years struggling to survive on literary and journalistic work: Anne scrabbled together temporary freelance work writing articles and book reviews, editing, and translating;[14] Karl remained active in the Communist Party, both as a journalist and as head of the German section of the International Association of Revolutionary Writers. Their situation drastically worsened in the late 1930s at the height of the Stalinist terror when millions of party officials faced arrest, summary show trials, and execution. With his high profile, Karl was vulnerable: purged from the party in 1935, he was arrested in August 1936 during the first Moscow show trials. He was subsequently released, it seems, before being rearrested and disappearing altogether in late 1937.[15] Anne and Elli feared he had been sent to a Siberian prison camp. We now know that he was killed in a mass execution outside Moscow in 1938.[16]

Karl's arrest put Anne and her son in dire peril. Wives and family members of arrestees faced blacklisting in employment and housing, exile from Moscow and other cities, and were themselves at risk of arrest.[17] By the late 1930s, Anne, living in "agonizing fear and bitter poverty,"[18] was desperate for financial help from the West and frantic to get out of the Soviet Union altogether. Both options, however, were slipping away. The borders to and from the Soviet Union and the West, and across Europe, were shutting down; there was no longer a home to return to in Germany or Austria after the Nazi takeovers; and Anne's primary lifeline, Elli, was, by this time, herself living insecurely as a political refugee in London.

The sisters eventually came up with two schemes to rescue Anne: book royalties and remarriage. Their short-term plan was as gutsy and creative as it was a long shot: to fix Anne up with an income source in rubles from the royalties generated by the translation of Western authors into Russian. The idea was not as far-fetched as it sounded, since the royalties for the vast majority of translations, paid out in unexportable rubles, lay unclaimed by their authors. Yet from outside the Soviet Union simply figuring out which authors had been translated was a difficult and time-consuming task.[19] Even the authors themselves were not always privy to this information;[20] and some left-wing authors—such as Brecht and Feuchtwanger—who were certain to be widely translated, Elli thought were out of the question because of their "antipathy to my [conservative] husband."[21] Other authors, like Silone in fascist Italy, had to be ruled out because of the political danger in which participation in such a scheme would have put them.[22] Still, there were numerous possibilities among important authors living in western democracies: Freud, Einstein, Thomas and Golo Mann, Stefan and Arnold Zweig, all of whom, among many other writers, she contacted either directly or through third parties.[23] Driven by the enormity of the situation, Elli was seemingly tireless in her attempts, documented in her correspondence, to mobilize contacts and friendships of a lifetime within German and European intellectual circles and a loose rescue network stretching from Europe to the United States. Thomas Mann had no Russian royalties to release, but he tried to help by sending Karl an "invitation to work together."[24] Early on, the author Wolfgang Langhoff donated some funds to Anne.[25] Later, she found Karl Tolnay, the author of a translated book on Michaelangelo, who was willing to release to Anne his Russian royalty rights. Whether she ever benefited from his kindness remains unclear in the sources.

The sisters' second and long-term plan was for Anne's escape from the Soviet Union. Emigration to the West, however, required extremely difficult to obtain travel and residency papers. They needed to find a man in the West willing to marry Anne. Who? How?

To directly communicate any of this in writing—both the catastrophic situation in the Soviet Union and her rescue schemes—would have put Anne in great danger. (It was even too risky for her to receive book royalties directly in her name; therefore the sisters had worked out a plan to use a front person, an old German émigré friend of Anne's in Moscow.[26]) This is where subterfuge and duplicity became integral to the Salomon sisters' correspondence.

Silence was one tactic the sisters used. Silences in the early letters were generally negative, that is, they involved the simple failure to write on certain dangerous subjects. In the months after the Nazis came to power, for example, when Elli was still living in Germany, Anne refrained from any direct references to the Third Reich and the peril Elli faced, evincing what, on the surface, seemed like a lack of caring and curiosity but was undoubtedly intended to protect Elli.[27]

By the late 1930s, silences in the letters seem to have taken on additional "positive" meaning as strategic communication. This can be seen in the sisters' attempts to communicate about Karl's arrests. Anne tried to signal indirectly his physical disappearance through his literary absence in her letters. Thus, for a time in 1936, at the time of his arrest, when she reported family news, Karl was noticeably missing. (Anne did not know that Elli and brother Fritz [living in exile in Prague] already knew about the arrest but, as Fritz wrote to Elli, were unable to communicate this: "Obviously, there can be no mention in a letter to Anne that we know anything . . . it could put [her] in grave danger to be accused by the Soviet authorities of giving foreigners news of the [political show] trials underway.")[28] Then, weeks later, Karl made a sudden reappearance in Anne's correspondence when she reported him sending his "greetings"[29]—a signal either that he had been released from custody or was physically unharmed—before he disappeared altogether from her letters in 1937. In spring 1939, Elli explained to a friend who had inquired about Karl's fate: "for a long time [Anne] has never again written about Karl. But I know from an English acquaintance . . . that he was sent to Siberia for 15 years [sic]."[30]

Meanwhile, Anne and Elli were fashioning an increasingly elaborate coded language. To protect people's identities (or the danger of association with them) they used false names or abbreviations, and changed their biographies. In late 1938, for example, their brother Fritz, a former Social Democratic functionary in Berlin, who had fled to Prague after the Nazi takeover, was facing peril once again (as a Jew and a leftist) as the Germans closed in on Czechoslovakia. At the same time, these were the years of fratricidal warfare on the left as a result of the ferocious communist line against social democracy. Thus, from Republican-controlled Spain to the Soviet Union, any association with Social Democratic parties could and did lead to persecution as a "social fascist" at the hands of communist governments and/or parties and insurgents. It was therefore essential that Elli, in sending Anne word in Moscow about Fritz's plight, refrain from a single utterance about Fritz's employment—in Berlin and now again in his part-time work for the Social Democratic party in Prague. Hence, Elli turned the party into a "scientific institute" (in a 1932 autobiographical statement to the Soviet government that was presumably part of political investigations against her and Karl, Anne took the tack that her brother "is employed in Berlin [but] I do not know anything more")[31]

> As a representative of a foreign scientific institute, [Fritz] seems so far not endangered, particularly because he has received new legitimation through this.[32] But naturally, he can't remain in Prague and for a long time has not been able to correspond freely. I am in contact with organizations in Paris, which hopefully will help him get out; and that his institute [i.e., the Social Democratic party] can hopefully employ him elsewhere.[33]

In general, the sisters' modus operandi for communicating large amounts of forbidden information, including the two aforementioned schemes, was to strip that information of its real narrative context, substituting instead a fabricated and politically harmless-sounding one. Thus, for example, Anne was able to explain the royalties idea and provide detailed information on both Russian royalty law and authors in the West to contact by pretending that Elli had requested this information for a research project she was working on: "It occurred to me that you once asked about [Russian] publications of foreign authors . . ."[34]

Mostly, the sisters communicated in disguise by using the fabricated context of Nazi Germany and Austria. They made up fake people and scenarios having to do with persecution under the Nazis and fascists when what they were really talking about was the situation in the Soviet Union. In August 1938, this is how, for example, Anne first signaled her desire to leave the Soviet Union and how she hoped to pull it off:

> 'For your *girlfriend* [i.e., Anne herself] the most sensible thing would be if any sort of a husband with a usable passport could be found, it could be anyone . . . he can be ancient . . . impotent, and gay. That would be the simplest way because, as you correctly said, the democratic countries are not generous with giving passports to victims of Nazism, but many have laws that guarantee passports to the wives of citizens.[35]

The story became increasingly elaborate. In search of a means of escape, Anne, with Elli's help, called upon a network of family, friends, and acquaintances, most in various states of emigration and exile across Europe, from France and Switzerland to Prague and (Republican-controlled) Barcelona. Many of these people were themselves living precariously, stateless and without residency papers, in countries such as Switzerland that rigorously restricted (especially Jewish) emigration as well as enforcing censorship of the mail. Thus, when appealing to the Austrian writer Albert Ehrenstein, a friend living in Switzerland as a political refugee with a Czech passport,[36] Anne added an additional layer of fictitious narrative, writing under several disguises—the pseudonyms Anita and Karla—in order (presumably) to protect both herself and the letters' recipient.[37] "Karla,"[38] a Dutch woman living in Moscow, began her June 1938 letter to Ehrenstein with an apology for her poor German (Anne intentionally mangling the letter's prose to sound like pidgin-German), then moved to the topic of rescuing a "journalist" and her son from "Austria, which has become barbaric," by arranging her marriage to a citizen of a democratic country.[39] In later letters to Ehrenstein, Anne wrote about Karla in the third person, signing her letters "Anita," continuing in this way for several months, undercover, to maintain her contact in Switzerland while passing on important information like whom Ehrenstein should contact for help in Switzerland.

When direct contact between Anne and Ehrenstein became too dangerous, Elli, who was herself in regular contact with Ehrenstein, passed this information on to Anne by turning him into a female relative and, with this cover story, using the opportunity as well to inquire how much royalty money Anne had yet to receive:

> How many Rubles did the *Ahnfrau* [female relative] actually receive for her furniture? Prices are so different in every country so I don't know how to reckon it by [the British] Pound. Please don't write her anymore. If you have something to tell her, I can pass the message on to her.[40]

Anne complied. The letters from "Anita" stopped, and the next time she needed to communicate with Ehrenstein about ways to get her out of the Soviet Union, she managed to do so via Elli:

> I want to write Albert [Ehrenstein] soon. For his female friend [i.e., Anne herself] hopefully there is a way out. As far as I can judge her quandary, it's a question above all not of her attaining an entrance permit into a country but . . . an exit permit from Vienna [read: Moscow] or Germany, respectively. She will never receive this permit based on her Austrian or German [read: Soviet] passport;[41] she and her children can only apply for emigration . . . when she is sure that she will be granted citizenship in another country . . .[42]

In these and other letters, in carefully coded language, Anne was also able to provide a partial window to the urgency of her plight and the disastrous situation under the Stalinist terror. It was terrible, Anne wrote, to think of "Yorricks Frau[43] and many many others living . . . under the Nazis . . . [who are classified as] 'state criminals', threatened and hounded, dependent upon the help of friends and miserable casual work, and selling their last belongings, if they haven't already been confiscated . . ."[44] In Vienna, "Karla," in particular, was living in "tormenting fear and bitter poverty."[45] There, under the "fascist" justice system, people were being subjected to "false and senseless accusations . . . [and] mass arrests . . ."[46] And now "a new wave of terror is coming [as a result of the Nazi takeover of a part of Czechoslovakia] . . . Czech [read: Soviet] citizens or those who want to become citizens are being classified as 'enemies of the state.'"[47]

At the same time, Anne was always careful to throw the Soviet censors the obligatory bone, surrounding all of her statements about the calamitous conditions under the "fascists" with, in the blackest humor, a contrasting view of "beautiful and sunny"[48] Russia, a place filled with happy people enjoying "democratic elections"[49] and "work according to their qualifications."[50] "Karla," for example, "succeeded in smuggling a letter through the strict censors of the Third Reich (did you know that here [in the Soviet Union] mail privacy is guaranteed by the constitution? What a contrast!)."[51] Elli wrote similar absurdities. In enumerating the fates of friends under the Nazis and attempts to rescue them, she did not fail to put in a good word for the Soviet Union while, mimicking the communist line, bashing the West:

The democratic countries are difficult in accepting the passports of victims of the Nazis, whose fate they nevertheless regret. But we are not giving up. With respect to my friends, of course they don't long to live in a bourgeois saturated country. They would rather go to the Soviet Union, but in Germany if they were to apply [for a Soviet visa], they might as well give themselves an entry ticket to a concentration camp.[52]

* * *

We, today, in Western liberal societies still, to a large extent, retain a conception of letter-writing that derives from the eighteenth century. Letters are seen as private expressions of an authentic, individualized self. The philosopher Jürgen Habermas has shown how the rise of this modern form of letter-writing in the eighteenth century (together with the rise of the novel and the diary) was a key factor in producing the modern experience of subjectivity and individuality. This modern self, with its ideas of human intimacy, dignity, and freedom, was in turn crucial to the development in the eighteenth and nineteenth centuries of a critically engaged "bourgeois public sphere" and, concomitantly, liberal political institutions.[53]

It is interesting to think of the Salomon correspondence in this context. On the one hand, the correspondence was produced by two classically bourgeois, educated European women—women who, despite their politics, were distinctly rooted in the liberal and Enlightenment tradition Habermas writes about. On the other hand, their writing in the 1930s took place within a political context in which, in totalitarian fashion, the separation of private and public—the very basis of the liberal state and the modern self/letter-writer—was under attack. In these conditions, on the surface, letter-writing in the Salomon sisters preserved its outward "normal" form for the state (censor). But because authentic feelings and thoughts mostly could not be communicated, that form had become hollowed out and transformed. Letter-writing thus became a kind of mimicry of authenticity and privacy, a performance in which real communication of real thoughts occurred only in oblique, coded, and disguised form.

Thus one finds "normal" elements in the letters, such as talk about "feelings" and the exchange of family news, but one senses something is off and wrong. The communication of feeling, for example, became stilted, stereotyped, or inappropriate to the circumstances. Or it articulated outright lies that contradicted the author's beliefs and feelings. Elli, a conservative, extolling the wonders of human dignity and freedom in the Soviet Union, provides one example. (Such statements and the mouthing of communist jargon become more insistent in the later letters.) With its inappropriate effect, laced with fake political support of the Soviet Union, the following excerpt typifies all of these qualities. It is a blithe and playful statement from one of Elli's letters to Anne in November 1938 at the height of the Stalinist terror:

> I have you to thank for two golden letters, I [on the other hand, am an] unpunctual filthy beast. I'm glad that things are going well for you; how many people can say that these days, when the few shrewd people like you already, years ago, moved to the only country [i.e., Soviet Union] where human dignity is fully respected . . .[54]

In reality, Elli, at this moment, was frenziedly trying to rescue Anne and writing letters to her contacts in the West that, sounding a despairing alarm, were of a radically different nature in tone and content. "While the Jews are being slaughtered in Germany," she wrote to a friend, "my sister, together with her child, is starving in Moscow."[55]

Ironically, the sisters' mimicry worked in eluding the censors because it played upon the censors' own liberal-bourgeois expectations about normal letter-writing—this, interestingly, in a land dedicated to battling "bourgeois democracy." The mimicry worked in another sense as well, allowing Anne and Elli, who were generally expert in interpreting each other's coded language, to communicate forbidden content. Elli was adamant that all communication from the West with Anne "must go through me because we [Anne and Elli] have our own code, and any false word could put her in mortal danger."[56] Their code was possible, of course, only because the sisters knew each other so well, in a certain intimate bourgeois way, and thus could successfully play off of the glaring disparities between truth/reality and the patently false statements of their letters. Anne's statement above about a "girlfriend" provides one example, this non sequitur out of nowhere signaling a code because both she and Elli knew that there was no such girlfriend.

It is interesting how improvisational all of this was. To read the Salomon letters for writing strategies is to watch the learning curve required of inexperienced "ordinary" people thrown into extraordinary times, groping their way toward new ways of communication and interpretation. This makes for compelling reading. Elli and Fritz in 1936 exchanged urgent letters puzzling how to interpret the confused signals coming out of Moscow:[57] on the one hand, news of Karl's arrest, on the other hand, the subsequent appearance of his article in a Soviet journal. Did this mean he had been rehabilitated, or was it a mere oversight by the journal? And what did it mean that Anne's last two letters were dictated to and sent by someone else? Had she also been arrested? In those letters, Anne spoke of suffering from a kidney illness; was this a covert reference to prison abuse? Fritz, a long-time activist in the Social Democratic party, passed on to Elli speculations and cautionary writing advice, which he himself was gleaning from several sources with connections to the Soviet Union.[58] Elli and Albert Ehrenstein also helped each other decode Anne's letters.[59] Anne experimented for a short time with using acrostics, openly explaining her method.[60] Elli, as she wrote Ehrenstein in Switzerland, was appalled by Anne's "risky" behavior: "any half-intelligent censor can decode" her acrostics, but Elli didn't know "how to warn her" against it.[61]

Indeed, there was, in general, a certain lack of sophistication in their codes, exactly what one would expect from two ordinary people. The use of allegory (the fake narrative of Nazi Austria) to elude police authorities went back at least to the eighteenth century. One thinks, for example, of *Persian Letters (1721)*, Baron de Montesquieu's critique of French Absolutism via a set of fictional letters about, among other things, the oppression of male slaves and harem women in Persia. The authorities in the 1930s were on to such tactics in published works and other media. That the Salomon sisters were never caught may owe less to their cunning than to the possibility that the authorities, swamped by more pressing needs, were not even monitoring their mail, or not carefully.

This essay has shown how letter-writing shifted form under the exigencies of the twentieth-century police state. Communication of urgent and forbidden information occurred through silence and other tactics in a coded language of deception. Dictatorship, in this sense, was both present and resisted in writing itself. Theorists, such as Pierre Bourdieu, argue that all writing takes place within institutional contexts and thus, by definition, involves the author (consciously or not) in forms of self-censorship or learning "the rules of the game" about acceptable, legitimizing speech.[62] By extension, letter-writing is never really a "true" expression of an "authentic" self. It is always a social construction. Letter-writing even in the era of romanticism in the early nineteenth century, when self-expression was a paramount value, involved performance and the articulation of emotions based on "epistolary conventions" for which a whole genre of how-to books existed.[63]

The Salomon correspondence, in this sense, appears as merely an extreme and self-consciously purposeful version of this more universal fact. Although true on one level, I think it is important to maintain broad historical distinctions between types of writing and the selves on which they are based in different eras and societies. Habermas's model, in particular, of a bourgeois self/writer of liberal society in the late eighteenth and nineteenth centuries, which can be distinguished from other kinds of selves/writers in post-liberal societies,[64] provides, I believe, a more interesting way to think about the Salomon correspondence in broad historical terms. Frantic for ways to communicate, the sisters appropriated and transformed earlier, bourgeois writing practices and, in the process, unintentionally developed a kind of hybrid, post-liberal letter. This letter "worked" as communication because it utilized, through mimicry, older bourgeois notions of authenticity and intimacy, but did so in the entirely altered, non-liberal, police-state conditions of Europe in the 1930s.

Postscript

Elli survived the war in England. She died of natural causes in her adopted home of Oxford in 1958. Anne was never able to escape the Soviet Union. After the German invasion of 1941, the Soviet government evacuated all German émigrés to its Central Asian territories. Anne ended up in Tashkent. There—homeless and starving—she committed suicide in 1941. Her son, Michael, survived in the Soviet Union; her two daughters, Ruth and Rosemie, emigrated to the United States before the war.

Notes

1. The correspondence is located in the possession of the author, who is the grand-daughter of Anne Bernfeld-Schmückle. It includes Anne's letters to Elli (many dozens of them dating from 1921 to 1939; those from 1934 to 1935 are missing); a few letters Anne wrote to Elli's husband, Friedrich Gundolf, and to a friend in Switzerland, Albert Ehrenstein (explained further below). None of Elli's letters to Anne survived but there are copies she made of her letters in the years 1938–1939. The collection also contains Elli's correspondence with her brother Fritz (in Prague), and with friends, acquaintances, and other contacts in the West regarding Anne's situation in the Soviet Union.

2. For more on this relationship, see Ann Goldberg, "The Black Jew with the Blonde Heart: Race and Gender in the Correspondence of Friedrich Gundolf and Elisabeth Salomon-Gundolf" (unpublished paper).

3. In Vienna in 1926, prior to her emigration, she wrote articles and reviews for several communist papers, but she never actually joined the party, either in Austria or the Soviet Union, as explained in Anne Bernfeld, "Autobiografie Anne Bernfeld-Schmückle" (Moscow, January 20, 1932), courtesy of Kyrill Anderson, *Russische Zentrum zur Aufbewahrung und Erforschung der Dokumente der Neuzeit*, Moscow. I thank Dr. Reinhard Müller for his help in securing a copy of this document. The information from it (a short, nine page unpublished manuscript) must be used very cautiously since it was written under political duress.

4. The progressive *Freie Schulgemeinde* at Wickersdorf, where Anne herself had been a pupil.

5. A passage from Anne's first extant Moscow letter, written to Gundolf and dated October 12, 1926, suggests that, in addition, she and Kammerer had been romantically involved.

6. Arthur Koestler, *The Case of the Midwife Toad* (New York: Hutchinson, 1971), pp. 13–14. Kammerer's motivations for taking his life were apparently multiple but certainly related in part to the scandal. Koestler, who is sympathetic to Kammerer, provides a fascinating narration of this case.

7. It is impossible to date precisely her arrival in Moscow, which may have been shortly before Kammerer's suicide.

8. Anne Bernfeld-Schmückle (hereafter: Anne) to Elisabeth Gundolf (hereafter: Elli), May 3, 1927.

9. Anne to Elli, Wickersdorf, August 13, 1927.

10. See, for example, Anne to Elli, October 12, 1929.

11. That is, as a means to obtain money, travel permits, and other matters.

12. Anne to Elli, May 21, 1927.

13. A colleague, the Austrian poet Hugo Huppert, long claimed responsibility for the Institute's edition of Marx's immensely influential "Paris Notebooks." Reinhard Müller, ed., *Die Säuberung: Moskau 1936: Stenogramm einer geschlossenen Parteiversammlung* (Reinbek bei Hamburg: Rowohlt, 1991), has since revealed the real identity of its editor/transcriber: Anne Bernfeld-Schmükle. Anne tried unsuccessfully to find a paid job at her profession in medicine, though she did do part-time volunteer medical work (e.g., Anne to Elli, November 4, 1927).

14. She had been doing journalistic work for extra money off and on since at least 1925, publishing articles on a wide range of cultural and medical topics (e.g. child-drearing and hygiene, theatre, books, museum exhibits) in the *Moskauer Rundschau, Der Tag* (Vienna), *Die Wiener Roten Fahne, and Die Frau*. Drafts of many of her articles from 1925, a year she spent in Paris working as a journalist, survive in this author's possession.

15. The version of David Pike, *Deutsche Schriftsteller im sowjetischen Exil* (Frankfurt am Main: Suhrkamp, 1981), pp. 420–421, has Schmückle arrested and disappearing forever sometime after August 15, 1936. Other versions place Karl's final arrest in 1937, which accords better with the Salomon letters.

16. An account of the purge of Karl and some information on Anne can be found in Müller, *Die Säuberung*; Pike, *Deutsche Schriftsteller*. Also on the persecution of German émigrés in the Soviet Union, see Sigfried Bahne, Richard Lorenz, Hermann Weber, eds., *Kommunisten verfolgen Kommunisten* (Berlin: Akademie-Verlag, 1993). I thank Dr. Barry McLoughlin for sharing his information from newly available sources on Schmückle's ultimate fate.

17. Pike, *Schriftsteller*, pp. 441–443.

18. Anne to Albert Ehrenstein ("Freund"), October 12, 1938.

19. This applied as well to Soviet regulations regarding foreign marriages and emigration papers.

20. See, e.g., the Norwegian writer Dina Lea to Elli, December 2, 1938.

21. Elli to Ehrenstein, London, September 21, 1938. This, at any rate, was Elli's theory.

22. Elli to Ehrenstein, September 21, 1938; Ehrenstein to Elli, November 7, 1938.

23. Albert Ehrenstein, in particular, played a crucial mediating role in this enterprise. Other friends who helped Elli contact authors included the psychoanalyst Heinz Hartmann, Walter Pagel, Robert Klopstock, among others.

24. Ehrenstein to Elli, September 17, 1938; Elli to Heinz Hartmann, November 16, 1938. Neither Mann nor anyone else, of course, knew at the time that Karl was already dead.

25. Elli to Ehrenstein ("Herr Doktor"), September 10, 1938.

26. The friend was Elfriede Cohn-Vossen, a family friend from Breslau. Anne to Elli, October 7, 1938.

27. Only once did Anne make an oblique reference to the political situation in a comment on the "*Spiesserumgebung*" of Heidelberg, the town in Germany where Elli lived. Anne to Elli, September 23, 1933.

28. Fritz Salomon to Elli Gundolf, Prague, November 7, 1936.

29. The letter is dated merely September 19, but reference in it to the Spanish Civil War helps to place it in 1936.

30. Elli to Frau Schütte-Lihotzky, April 15, 1939.

31. Bernfeld, "Autobiografie Anne Bernfeld-Schmückle."

32. The "new legitimation" referred to the fact that Fritz found employment, albeit only part-time, once again for the Social Democratic Party in Prague.

33. Elli to Anne, November 14, 1938.

34. Anne to Elli, September 3, 1938; Elli to Anne, September 27, 1938.

35. Anne to Elli, December 24, 1938. My emphasis.

36. And, during the course of their correspondence in 1938, as a result of the German takeover of the Sudentenland, Ehrenstein's passport became essentially worthless, because of the reluctance of Western countries to admit persecuted victims of the Nazis.

37. Anne's letters to Ehrenstein survived because he passed them on to Elli in London, who saved them with her other Anne-related correspondence.

38. Karl + A: Anne's husband's name + the first letter of her name.

39. "Karla" to Ehrenstein ("Lieber Freund"), June 23, 1938.

40. Elli to Anne, November 14, 1938. The word "Ahnfrau" actually means (female) ancestor.

41. Anne had become a Soviet citizen.

42. Anne to Elli, January 12, 1939.

43. Another code name for herself.

44. Anne to Ehrenstein, August 29, 1938.

45. Anne to Ehrenstein, October 12, 1938.
46. Anne to Ehrenstein, August 29, 1938.
47. Anne to Ehrenstein, October 12, 1938.
48. Anne to Ehrenstein, June 23, 1938.
49. Ibid.
50. Anne to Ehrenstein, August 29, 1938.
51. Anne to Ehrenstein, October 12, 1938.
52. Elli to Anne, November 14, 1938.
53. Jürgen Habermas, *The Structural Transformation of the Public Sphere*, trans. Thomas Burger (Cambridge, MA: MIT Press, 1992). Habermas's thesis has had enormous resonance, influencing a wide range of scholarship on modern politics, social institutions, and culture, as well as being subject to extensive debate and criticism. On the latter, see, e.g., Craig Calhoun, ed., *Habermas and the Public Sphere* (Cambridge, MA: MIT Press, 1992).
54. Elli to Anne, November 14, 1938.
55. Elli to Raymond, November 18, 1938. The slaughter she referred to was the *Kristalnacht* pogrom, which had taken place only days earlier.
56. Elli to Heinz Hartmann, November 16, 1938.
57. Only Fritz's part of the communication—two letters dated November 7 and December 7, 1936—survives.
58. His letters mention as sources Hans Jäger, Bessmertny, and a Dr. Klein.
59. Elli to Ehrenstein ("Herr Diktor"), September 10, 1938; Ehrenstein to Elli, September 17, 1938; Elli to Ehrenstein, January 7, 1939.
60. Anne to Elli, August 5, 1938. The code words appeared in intentionally-altered literary quotes or rhymes.
61. Elli to Ehrenstein, London, September 21, 1938.
62. Gregory S. Brown, "Reconsidering the Censorship of Writers in Eighteenth-Century France: Civility, State Power, and the Public Theater in the Enlightenment," *Journal of Modern History* 75, no. 2 (2003): 235–268, provides a good introductory discussion of censorship, theory, and Bourdieu, in particular.
63. See, e.g., Marion Kaplan's very interesting analysis of a German Jewish couple's correspondence: " 'Based on Love': The Courtship of Hendele and Jochanan, 1803–1804," (in progress, 2003); Cécile Dauphin, "Letter-Writing Manuals in the Nineteenth Century," in *Correspondence: Models of Letter-Writing from the Middle Ages to the Nineteenth Century*, ed. Roger Chartier et al. (Princeton: Princeton University Press, 1997), pp. 112–157.
64. Habermas did not himself investigate (or even posit) shifting writing selves in post-liberal societies, although it is a logical and, if my analysis is correct, empirically valid extension of his theories.

Part IV

Editorial Interventions

9

"Going into Print": Published Immigrant Letters, Webs of Personal Relations, and the Emergence of the Welsh Public Sphere

William D. Jones

Scholarly opinion on the value and use of immigrant letters that were later printed in published media has changed significantly over the years.[1] This can be discerned in the judgments of editors of collections of immigrant letters, the format which, as David Gerber has pointed out, "has dominated the historian's approach to these sources" throughout the twentieth century.[2] Some of the earlier collections, notably Theodore Blegen, *Land of Their Choice: The Immigrants Write Home* (1955) and Alan Conway, *The Welsh in America: Letters from the Immigrants* (1961), drew extensively on published letters for their material.[3] Most of those in Conway's volume, for example, are drawn from the columns of newspapers and periodicals published in Wales in the nineteenth century. Both Blegen and Conway favored published letters because they believed these media had greater influence on potential emigrants and public perceptions of the United States than manuscript letters, and because of the public interest the publication of these letters aroused.[4] Two more recent influential collections of original English-language immigrant letters, Charlotte Erickson, *Invisible Immigrants: The Adaptation of English and Scottish Immigrants in Nineteenth-Century America* (1972) and David Fitzpatrick, *Oceans of Consolation: Personal Accounts of Irish Migration to Australia* (1994),[5] however, excluded published letters for a variety of very germane reasons. These include the belief that the writers of published immigrant letters were not socially representative; the difficulty of getting biographical information on the writers and thus verifying the authenticity of the letters and offsetting the bias evident in their contents; the fact that published letters reflect public controversies about migration prevailing at the time they were written; and the certainty that the policies of newspapers influenced their choice of letters for publication.[6] That such letters rarely survive in sequences and that textual analysis is not feasible because of editorial interventions have also both been cited as major limitations of this form of immigrant correspondence.[7]

Given these strictures, it is not surprising, perhaps, that while a growing number of studies in various disciplines have with increasing sophistication explored manuscript correspondence between immigrants and their families and friends in the homeland, very little attention has been paid to the nature and significance of published immigrant letters. This essay acknowledges the very real problems and limitations that are associated with published letters. Nevertheless, it also suggests that this particular type of source has possibilities for expanding our understanding of immigrant correspondence and poses intriguing questions that might be fruitfully investigated.[8] Among these questions are why some immigrants chose this method of retaining contact with their homeland, and how published letters came to appear in the columns of the press, an issue that encompasses the policies and practices of editors and more generally the relationship between the letters and print culture. Fitzpatrick rightly points out that the function of published letters "was fundamentally changed by their removal to the public domain" and that they contributed to the marketing of migration and diffusion of information; but as a genre they are distinct from personal letters even when . . . they exhibit an intimate or personal tone."[9] In this respect, this form of epistolarity offers the opportunity to explore the connection between immigrant letter-writers and the public sphere. However, in just the same way as private letters were sometimes experienced communally through being read and passed around,[10] the printing of immigrant letters in the press complicates neat categorizations of immigrant letters into "private" and "public."[11] This division is further problematized by the knowledge that, as Blegen and others have noted and as was the case in the Welsh published letters examined here, the recipients or other individuals sent personal correspondence to newspapers and periodicals for publication.[12] These perspectives suggest that published letters may well have greater substance, variety, and significance than scholars have usually accorded them.

This essay explores some of these issues relating to the published immigrant letter in the context of the large number of personal letters from Welsh immigrants that appeared in Welsh- and English-language newspapers and periodicals in the homeland in the late nineteenth century. Such letters were a regular feature of the press in this period, although they were becoming rarer by the end of the century. The essay does not aim to provide a comprehensive, systematic study of these published letters. Rather it seeks to suggest additional ways in which we might interpret them by examining in detail the motives and processes involved in the various stages of their journey into print. By so doing it aims to make a contribution toward extending and deepening our understanding of this particular form of immigrant letter and encouraging greater analysis of the phenomenon as a whole.[13] The essay will examine the motives of immigrants who corresponded directly with the press and of individuals in Wales who sent personal letters to editors for consideration for publication. The attitudes and practices of editors and the issue of editorial mediation will also be discussed. As we shall see, Welsh published immigrant letters are problematic documents that reinforce many of the criticisms that have been leveled at this type of source. However, it also argued that though they possess certain limitations, these particular texts are complex and multidimensional. They blur and complicate some of the distinctions made between manuscript and published letters and the boundary between the private and public spheres.

A key concern of the essay is to probe the relationship between the published letters and the media in which they appeared. Like their manuscript counterparts, Welsh published immigrant letters contributed substantially to the appreciable increase in the circulation of information about destinations and working and living conditions overseas, and especially in the United States, from the mid-nineteenth century onwards. However, it is argued that the interaction between the letters and the periodical press was more complex. The publishing of immigrant letters and the concerns that generated them cannot be properly understood without reference to the rapid expansion of the newspaper and periodical press in both languages in Wales in the second half of the nineteenth century and the development of a Welsh public sphere. For most of the late nineteenth century editors, immigrants and readers in Wales regarded published letters as an integral feature of the press, and one that catered to not only prospective emigrants but also the Welsh public in general. It will be argued that the appearance of Welsh immigrant letters was fundamentally shaped by social, cultural, and religious considerations, a growing sense of Welsh transnationality, and increased interest in the wider world.

The Welsh Press and the Welsh Diaspora

Letters from Welsh immigrants were regularly published in Welsh and English-language newspapers and journals in Wales in the nineteenth century. This pattern was established early. As far as can be determined, the first occasion on which letters from Welsh immigrants were published in periodicals in Wales was in the Baptist monthly, *Seren Gomer* [The Star of Gomer] in February 1820.[14] As commentators have noted, in the late nineteenth century the appearance of letters from Welsh immigrants became even more of a characteristic of the columns of many, if not most, newspapers and periodicals in Wales.[15] In one newspaper alone, *Y Gwladgarwr* [The Patriot], which was published in Aberdare between 1859 and 1882 and was estimated as having 9,000 subscribers in 1865, there appeared around 500 letters from Welsh immigrants. Of these, around 350 were from North America, most of them from the United States, the most popular destination for Welsh immigrants during this period, and a further 52 from Welsh immigrants in Australia.[16] In addition, the same newspaper published scores of letters from *Y Wladfa* [The Welsh Colony], the Welsh paper in Patagonia, South America, established in 1865 to preserve the Welsh language, and a smaller number from other destinations. Letters were also regularly published in other newspapers in both languages all over Wales, such as *Aberdare Times*, *Yr Amserau* [The Times], *Baner ac Amserau Cymru* [The Banner and Times of Wales], *Cambrian*, *Carnarvon and Denbigh Herald*, *Cardiff and Merthyr Guardian*, *Y Cymro* [The Welshman], *Y Fellten* [Thunderbolt], *Y Gwladgarwr*, *Yr Herald Cymraeg* [The Welsh Herald], *Merthyr Express*, *Merthyr Telegraph*, *Seren Cymru* [The Star of Wales], *Star of Gwent* and *Tarian y Gweithiwr* [The Workers' Shield]. It is also clear from editorial comments in the notes for contributors' columns in various issues of late-nineteenth-century titles that many more immigrant letters were received than were actually printed, ones sent either directly by immigrants themselves or indirectly via recipients.[17] In March 1860, for example, *Y Gwron* [The Hero] noted it had several letters in hand including "some interesting ones from America and Australia."[18] Six years later *Seren Cymru* acknowledged receipt of (but did not publish) a letter from Morgan Lewis, Cariboo, British Columbia, and stated it was pleased to hear the news of the setting up of a new Welsh chapel "in that distant place."[19]

The appearance of Welsh immigrant letters in increasing numbers in the periodical press in Wales in the mid- and late-nineteenth century reflected and contributed to the interaction of two broad developments in the history of the country in this period. These are the increase in emigration and the rapid growth of the periodical press and its emergence as a powerfully influential force in Welsh life. Although emigration from Wales had been increasing from the 1790s onwards, the size of the movement overseas and the range of destinations expanded appreciably after the late 1840s and early 1850s. A central manifestation of that outward movement was the emergence of a significantly sized Welsh migrant presence overseas, and the formation of Welsh settler communities that, initially at least, supported a distinctive Welsh-language religious and cultural life. The lack of a separate and comprehensive official statistical record prevents the drawing of a precise picture of the size and direction of the outflow. However, by the end of the nineteenth century there were around 100,000 native-born Welsh residents in the United States and around 30,000 in Australia, Canada, South Africa, New Zealand, and Patagonia.[20] The other crucial development that enabled the widespread diffusion of published immigrant letters was the contemporaneous rapid expansion and influence of the newspaper and periodical press in both languages in Wales. The number of newspaper titles in circulation increased from ten in 1846 to 37 in 1861 and 101 in 1891. The size of the readership also grew: in 1886 an estimated 120,000 Welsh-language newspapers were being printed each week, and every title sold more than 1,500 copies a week.[21] The number and circulation of monthly and quarterly periodicals also expanded after the middle years of the century. Around 154 Welsh or bilingual periodicals were published under various titles between 1735 and 1850, and 577 between 1851 and 1901. In 1886 it was estimated that 150,000 copies of Welsh-language magazines were in circulation.[22] Most of these served the various religious Nonconformist denominations, but they were by no means solely religious publications. Like the newspapers, they also carried news and comment and provided platforms for discussion on national and international contemporary affairs, politics, literature, philosophy and, as we shall see shortly, emigration.[23]

As the work of Aled Jones has shown,[24] in Wales, as in other parts of the world, the expansion of the periodical press in both languages in the nineteenth century was strongly associated with industrialization, urbanization, population growth, increased literacy (in both Welsh and English), and the extension of faster and cheaper forms of transport. The population of Wales increased from around 587,245 in 1801 to 1,412,583 in 1871 and 2,420,921 in 1911.[25] The expansion of Welsh-language publishing in this period was also facilitated by the increase in absolute numbers of Welsh speakers to just under a million by 1911.[26] The press emerged during a turbulent period in which the Welsh economy and society as a whole were transformed, as an overwhelmingly rural population was being reconstituted as an increasingly urban one. To a great extent the expansion of the press was a product of the tremendous growth of heavy industry in Wales, particularly coal, iron, steel, and slate. But the press itself was also an agent of change and modernization in the nineteenth century Wales. Jones argues that "the sudden expansion, in particular of newspaper journalism, during the nineteenth century affected the ways in which Wales was perceived, both within and without." There was "a shift towards a definition of Wales as a place which had its own public sphere . . . that emphasized both Wales's territorial autonomy from, and its political and other connections with, England."[27] The profound and rapid changes in the Welsh economy and society, the growth of the press and the emergence of a democratic public sphere were inextricably entwined with contemporary ideas of modernity. Modernization created a much sharper distinction between the public and private worlds and brought a new emphasis on the citizenship rights of individuals; how society was to be run became more a matter of debate than ever before. The modern public sphere emerged as a forum for public debate in which it was believed individuals could come together as equals, whatever their status, to discuss issues of common concern, formulate opinions, and determine what was in the public interest. The growth of the mass media expanded these interactions far beyond face-to-face communication alone and allowed people to participate in events and communities over long distances.

This new Welsh public sphere blended local and international as well as national (in terms of both Wales and Britain) awareness. As recent work has emphasized, the Welsh press showed a keen concern for local matters and was closely associated with the constructions of local identities and the development of civic pride.[28] The activities and experiences of Welsh communities outside the homeland was also an integral feature of the Welsh press's domain. Newspapers carried advertisements for emigration agents and shipping companies whilst both newspapers and periodicals provided vivid descriptions of the life and employment opportunities on offer overseas. They fed Welsh immigrant experiences back to the public at home by printing not only letters but also items of news (often in regular columns devoted to this purpose), reports of cultural, religious, and social events, and obituaries from widely distributed centers of Welsh settlement.[29] Some newspapers were strongly transnational in content and tone, notably *Y Gwladgarwr*, *Tarian y Gweithiwr* (Aberdare, first published 1875), *Y Fellten* (Merthyr Tydfil, 1868–1876), and the short-lived *Awel Eryri* [Snowdonia Breeze], (Caernarfon, 1907–1908), which carried a "Brodorion ar Wasgar" [Natives in Dispersion] column.[30] To be fully effective, these relationships depended on Welsh immigrants having access to the press of the homeland, and there is evidence to suggest this was true of some migrants.[31] There existed exchange networks whereby immigrants were sent copies of their native locality's newspaper(s) or denominational magazines. In turn, Welsh immigrants reciprocated by sending copies of, or cuttings from, national, regional, or local newspapers published in the areas where they had settled to relatives, friends, and newspaper correspondents and editors in Wales, especially if those items contained news of

Welsh activities or people in their new homes. Recipients of such material in Wales regularly sent it on to the press to be considered for publication. Many newspapers in Wales had exchange agreements with Welsh equivalents in the United States.[32] In a striking example of transnationality, in July 1858 the *Merthyr Telegraph* reprinted a letter that a native of Merthyr who had emigrated to Melbourne a few years previously had initially sent to the *Workman's Advocate* in Minersville, Pennsylvania.[33] In several respects, therefore, the publishing of Welsh immigrant letters was facilitated and shaped not only by the growth of the Welsh press in general but also by specific features of that periodical press as it developed.

Immigrant Letters in the Welsh Press

The immigrant letters that were published in Wales found their way into the columns of the press by several means. Some immigrants wrote directly to newspapers and periodicals, sometimes in response to requests to do so by editors, relatives, or friends. There are also a large number of examples where what originally appear to have been manuscript personal letters were sent to the press by the recipients themselves or by other intermediaries, as we might call them, in Wales. These intermediaries appear to have been a diverse group: parents, siblings, other relatives, friends, neighbors, ministers of religion, trade union leaders, newspaper reporters, and former fellow workers. This additional layer of mediation further complicated the process of transition from the personal to the published. Approximately a third of the letters consulted for this study offer no background information on the writers or other contextual information and they were printed without comment.[34] In some cases not even the writers of the letters are identified. However, in the remainder of the letters consulted, a greater or lesser degree of basic information is provided, either in the letters themselves or prefatory or concluding notes by editors or intermediaries. As we shall later see, such commentaries also often include brief reasons why the letters were being printed and/or why they were being sent to the paper or journal concerned. Whilst the loss of the original letters makes it difficult to dissect editorial policies comprehensively, these explanations sometimes offer teasing glimpses of the processes involved in the journey into print.

As far as can be ascertained, the great majority of the writers of immigrant letters published in the press in Wales in this period were males. A much smaller proportion was written by women,[35] and jointly by husbands and wives and brothers or sisters. There are examples of letters originally sent to a wide range of recipients: one or both parents, husbands to wives and /or children, close family members, friends, and former fellow workers.[36]

The writers also appear diverse in terms of social class. Internal evidence in the letters themselves and identification information supplied to readers by editors and intermediaries shows that many of the male letter-writers were representatives of the skilled industrial working class—miners, quarrymen, iron, and steel workers—and small farmers and agricultural laborers. This is not surprising perhaps, as from the 1860s onwards the periodical press in Wales increasingly turned to a working-class market.[37] Walters argues that "the press was maintained throughout the century largely by common working people" while "a fair proportion of the editors of Welsh periodicals were of the same social background as their readers."[38] Whilst acknowledging that the issue of what constitutes literacy is a problematic and much debated one,[39] it is nonetheless worth recording that literacy rates in Wales were quite high in the mid-nineteenth century because of the influence of Anglican and Nonconformist Sunday Schools, and they increased further with the introduction of state education. Although there were great geographic variations, in 1846 it was estimated that two-thirds to three-quarters of the population of England and Wales could read, with a higher proportion in Wales.[40] Yet, in the transition of letters from manuscript to print, the issue of the level of literacy of the sender may not always have been a crucial factor. In the case of the Welsh, as of other groups, individuals occasionally wrote private letters on behalf of immigrants and their families and friends in the homeland. Such work was done either on a formal basis, involving payment, or an informal one, as a friendly service.[41] In rare cases this occurred in the case of published letters as well. A letter from a Welsh immigrant in Minersville, Pennsylvania to his parents, brothers, and sisters in Wales, that was published in Y Gwron [The Hero] in 1860, stated explicitly that it had been written on his behalf by the pseudonymous "Penfelin," who in a postscript wished to be remembered to all who knew him, and especially his brother Evan. "Penfelin" also requested that, if it were to be considered appropriate, the letter could be sent to Y Gwron.[42]

Surviving commentaries suggest that, as in the case of "Penfelin" above, some intermediaries were responding directly to the senders' requests that their letters be sent to a newspaper or periodical. Judging by the following rare and probably extreme, example, some immigrants' instructions regarding what to do with their letters were remarkably detailed and specific. In 1870 Morgan Bowen, New Russia, Crimea, told relatives and friends to whom he had addressed the letter:

> I want you to hand this letter to Joshua Evans, and that he reads it to George Wilkinson, Esq., and also to my friends in Middle Duffryn [a coal mine]. Be so kind as to hand it to George Jenkins, Cwmpennar, so he can read it to my

friends in Mountain Ash. If they see some merit in it, they are welcome to print it.[43]

With its combination of reading aloud and publishing as well as, one assumes, private consumption, this is revealing testimony to how complicated the interface between oral transmission and print culture could be. Other intermediaries, as far as can be detected, acted either at the request of recipients of letters or on their own initiative, and sometimes sent letters to the press without the original writers' permission. For example in 1886 a letter from John R. Lewis, Washington Territory, United States to an unnamed recipient in Wales was sent to, and published by, *Baner ac Amserau Cymru*. The anonymous intermediary informed readers that since there was so much interest in emigration and as that newspaper was in tune with the needs of the Welsh nation, "doubtless [the writer] . . . will forgive us sending his personal letter to its columns."[44]

Understanding the Published Immigrant Letter

The variety of Welsh immigrant letters, the diverse means by which they made the transition from manuscript to print, and the ways they occasionally blurred the division between private and public spheres suggest that these documents are more complex than scholarly opinion on this type of source might imply. Nevertheless, Welsh immigrant letters still have key problems and limitations that bear out many of the concerns that scholars have expressed and that were noted at the beginning of this essay. It has not been possible to locate the originals of any published letters examined in the course of this study and it is extremely unlikely that they have survived. This absence severely limits our understanding of the relationships among the published text, the letter as originally written, and its writer. Conclusions about the level of the writers' technical skills cannot be ascertained without sight of the original letter before it was mediated editorially. Another ambiguity is that it cannot automatically be taken for granted that letters published in Welsh were originally written in that language.[45] In rare cases, editors of Welsh-language newspapers and periodicals or individuals who submitted items for publication explicitly indicated that the letters concerned had been translated from English into Welsh.[46] This practice is an example of the complex ways the two languages interacted with each other in the nineteenth century and it also reflects long-term changes in the market for newspapers and periodicals. Some 600,000 people, 95 percent of the population, spoke Welsh in 1801 and of these around 70 percent were monolingual. By 1911 the number of Welsh speakers had risen to just under a million, but they were by now only 44.6 percent of the total population and only 8.7 percent were monolingual Welsh. The national figures, however, conceal massive regional and local variations and the proportions of Welsh speakers and monolingual Welsh were much higher in the rural than in the industrial areas. By the end of the nineteenth century many, if not most, Welsh speakers were bilingual in English.[47] It is impossible to estimate what percentage of published Welsh-language immigrant letters were translations. Intriguingly, no references to the reverse process, that is Welsh-language letters being translated for publication in English-language media in Wales, have so far been discovered.

The absence of the original artifact also means that we do not know to what extent published letters were edited or rewritten by not only editors but also those who sent original letters to the press. In the case of these Welsh letters it is difficult to reach firm conclusions regarding how much of the original was discarded and how far its grammar, syntax, or even meaning were changed. Walters has argued that there is evidence from editorial comments in *Y Gwladgarwr* to suggest that, at times, immigrant letters published in that paper were heavily edited.[48] Occasionally, the inclusion of ellipses in letters in various newspapers and periodicals shows that excisions have been made whilst sometimes it was stated that letters had been edited or that extracts from one or more letters were being printed.[49] A key issue that obviously also arises is what exactly was cut. The prefatory explanations of editors and intermediaries and clues in the letters themselves sometimes offer revealing, if fragmented glimpses, of the criteria (beyond the obvious one of space availability) that may have been applied. In the specific case of a letter from Ann Ellis, Utah, to "Sister Jane" published "in the writer's own words" in the *Cardiff and Merthyr Guardian* in February 1856, an indication of the nature of the discarded material was given: "The writer in the commencement of the letter condoles with her father and sister on the death of her mother."[50] Similarly a letter from an Aberdare immigrant to his brother in Wales in July 1863 began with: "Dear Brother: I received your letter yesterday which was the first from home since I left." This is followed by a parenthetical editorial insertion: "The writer then refers to some family matters of no public interest."[51]

The distinction made here between what was perceived to be in the public interest (and thus suitable to be printed) and what was not echoes strongly Conway's belief that published immigrant letters "have the added advantage of being free from much of the personal inquiries, condolences, salutations, and endearments which the editors very judiciously cut out and which form such a prominent part of immigrant manuscript letters."[52] Yet, an examination of the original published versions of many of the letters Conway selected for his collection *The Welsh in America* shows that in many cases it was he and not his nineteenth century predecessors who had excised this type of material, in the same way as he excluded prefatory notes by editors or intermediaries who sent letters to the papers. Conway's actions in this respect are no doubt a consequence of his attitude toward content of a personal nature and seemingly mundane subject-matter in general in immigrant letters, whether manuscript or published. Like other editors of collections of immigrant letters in the middle decades of the twentieth century, Conway regarded this material as being trivial and of no interest to readers and little historical value to scholars, and its inclusion was thus unwarranted. Such editorial stances also reflect the practical problems involved in preparing immigrant letters for publication in anthologies.[53]

Many of the contemporaneously published Welsh immigrant letters contain stock salutations and even endearments similar to those found in manuscript letters. The following opening to a letter from Rees Morgan, a puddler in the ironworks in Catausaqua, Pennsylvania, published in *Y Gwladgarwr* in June 1864, does not appear in the version in Conway's volume:

> Dear Wife and Children: Here I am writing to you in the hope that you are well, as I am at present, thank the Lord for his fatherly care. I am longing to see you, even though it is only six weeks since we left each other; let the days until we meet again go by quickly.[54]

Furthermore, intriguingly, the letters regularly contain examples of those features of personal correspondence that Gerber has described as "epistolary ethics," informal agreements by which immigrants explicitly sought to reconfigure the nature of their relationships with people who had stayed at home, following the disruption caused by emigration.[55] Published Welsh letters often contain apologies for not writing sooner and for imperfections in style, expression, and grammar, references to the failure to receive mail, and comments on postal arrangements.[56] In a letter to her brother and sisters in Wales, which appeared in *Yr Herald Cymraeg* in May 1863, Ellen Jones, East Newark, New Jersey, asks her siblings' forgiveness for having taken so long to write to them. She states that she did not have the heart to write to them when America was in such a desperate state in the middle of the Civil War.[57]

This is by no means to argue that published letters could have the same level of intimacy as manuscript ones. Nor, evidently, can they realistically form the basis of an intensive investigation of the personal and social transformations immigrants experienced over time and the ways in which personal immigrant letters were, as Fitzpatrick puts it, an "instrument for defining and modifying human relationships."[58] Nevertheless, it remains the case that the original *published* forms of the letters Conway selected and edited are often more varied in content than his versions and statements suggest. The fact that personal matters are occasionally present in the published Welsh letters suggests, first, that at least some of the letters sent to the press for publication may have been closer in style and content to manuscript letters than might be expected. This bears out Gerber's point that the lines between "familiar" letters and (in the American context) "America" letters, as they have been typified by scholars, "are not absolutely fixed, because the question of *private* and *public* . . . does not easily admit to being fixed, and because social intelligence and personal message both characterize most letters."[59] Second, some editors appear to have been more reluctant to embark on "judicious cutting" than were others. These editors thought it *was* of public interest to include content of a personal nature. They may have believed this for several reasons, but it is clear that one reason was because this type of content helped to establish the credibility of personal documents. It encouraged readers' acceptance that the letter-writers were real individuals in real situations, and as a result increased the likelihood that their letters would be considered authentic and trustworthy. It seems reasonable to argue, therefore, that editors and intermediaries had differing opinions regarding to what extent it was acceptable to reproduce personal and family matters in the public sphere. Such a divergence again complicates the division between public and private.

In the same way that Welsh immigrant letters are more varied and multidimensional than might be expected, the motives of the immigrants in sending letters to the press may also be more complex than scholars have acknowledged. We have already noted that many scholars believe published immigrant letters are untrustworthy.[60] According to E.R.R. Green: "At the best, they have been written by people who look forward to the pleasure of seeing themselves in print. At the worst, they may be forgeries, or drastically edited so as to provide propaganda either for or against emigration according to the policy of the journal."[61] My study of published Welsh immigrant letters has not sought to establish whether the letters are forgeries or not in those cases where there they contain sufficient contextual information— for example, names, addresses, family connections, dates of birth, and emigration—to make such an investigation feasible. Even then, confirming that the authorship of a letter is genuine does not establish the credibility of its content. It is of course possible that some of the published Welsh letters are fakes, deliberately written by editors or other parties to publicize a particular viewpoint. This essay accepts that authenticity is an important issue and it reminds us that many conclusions regarding published letters must remain speculative to some extent.[62] No doubt the urge to have their names and adventures published was a factor in the decision of most, perhaps all, Welsh immigrants who wrote directly to the press in the homeland.[63] Contemporaries occasionally lamented that this impulse was one of the undesirable aspects of writing for the press.[64]

Equally, it cannot be denied that having a particular axe to grind about the advantages and disadvantages of emigration and a compulsion to persuade their fellow countrymen either to emigrate or stay at home motivated many immigrant writers as well as editors and intermediaries in Wales. Traces of this can be found in many of the published letters even if some writers insisted that they only wished to convey information and let readers decide for themselves.[65] Throughout the nineteenth century some Welsh writers and editors exploited personal letters that were originally intended as private communications in order to promote Welsh settlement overseas and influence the immigrant decision-making process. Letter-writers from overseas were also voluble and persistent contributors to the fierce debate and controversy—regarding whether Welsh people should emigrate, and if so, the most advantageous destinations—that regularly raged in the columns of the Welsh press at home and overseas in this period.[66] Extensive use of personal correspondence was made by supporters and opponents of, for example, the campaigns to encourage Welsh people to settle in Nova Cambria in Rio Grande do Sul, Brazil, in the early 1850s and in Patagonia.[67]

Given the partisan motives that sometimes lie behind the publication of Welsh immigrant letters and the problems of interpretation the letters generally present, it is important to maintain a skeptical attitude toward the reasons why some Welsh immigrants decided to go into print. Nevertheless, a closer reading of the words of letter-writers, intermediaries, and editors, as represented in the columns of the press, reveals a richer and more complex understanding of how such letters came to be published. Internal evidence in the published Welsh letters suggests that those immigrants who wrote directly to the press in Wales were partly motivated by pragmatic considerations. These factors may alternatively be interpreted as labor-saving strategies or, more uncharitably perhaps, laziness. In a letter to the Welsh-language journal *Y Bedyddiwr* [The Baptist] in August 1844, Robert Williams, of New York, asked the editor to print his letter because it would save him the trouble of separate letters to a number of people, and at the same time please several of his fellow countrymen as he had promised he would send them news of his voyage. He also thought that sending his letter to the journal was the best and most convenient way for them to hear in a short time.[68] A common refrain is that letters were being sent to specific newspapers because all the writers' friends and acquaintances read that particular title. William Williams, writing from Warrnambool, Victoria, Australia to *Y Gwladgarwr* in May 1863 told the editor of the paper that "I would be grateful if you would allow this letter to appear in the Gwladgarwr as everyone who asked me to write receives this paper."[69] Henry Davies, of Big Rock, Illinois, made a similar point in a letter to *Yr Herald Cymraeg* in January 1871: "Before departing [in 1866], I promised that I would correspond with some of my old friends. I kept my word in the case of most of them, but failed in the case of all. As I know that the *Herald*'s circulation is more general in Lleyn than any other newspaper, I decided to write to it, as I can greet all of my friends in one letter."[70]

As these comments help to illustrate, the published letters invariably make reference to the writers' desires to reach and maintain contact with as many people in the homeland as possible. Some immigrant writers chose writing to newspapers in order to solicit return correspondence as they often included their addresses and stated explicitly that they wished to hear from friends, neighbors, and former colleagues.[71] Equally, commentaries suggest that many wrote to provide news of their own experiences because they wanted to be helpful to friends and relatives, and even Welsh people generally. A consideration of perceived needs of a wider audience appears to be a central consideration in the process by which immigrant letters went into print. As Conway rightly remarks, many Welsh immigrants "undoubtedly realized the limitations of letters written to individual person or families and wrote to their friends by way of newspaper editors. In this way they expected to benefit as many as possible from the wider publication of their experiences."[72]

In writing directly to the press, some Welsh immigrants were responding to other contemporary social and cultural concerns, as indeed were the editors and intermediaries who facilitated the publication of their letters. Immigrants were urged by their peers to send news of Welsh social, cultural, and religious gatherings overseas as much as to provide information on economic conditions, job opportunities, and the fates of other immigrants.[73] Requests by editors, editorials, and articles in the press encouraged immigrants to send material for their columns.[74] In an article entitled "*Ysgrifennu i'r Wasg*" [Writing to the Press] in the Welsh-American periodical *Y Cenhadwr Americanaidd* [The American Missionary] in January 1857, a writer named "Iwan Cincinnati" argued that it was essential that Welsh immigrants wrote for the media: "Our nation is scattered throughout this large country [i.e. the United States] and it is a special duty incumbent on one or some in every settlement to send news of events to the weeklies and monthlies."[75] Interesting testimony in this respect is the immigrants' own reflections on how they regarded published letters before they emigrated. One told *Baner ac Amserau Cymru* in a letter printed on November 20, 1869:

> When I was home, before leaving the "old country," I would be very glad to see letters from America in the newspapers, now and then; perhaps there are

several who still like the same thing, especially if they want to go to America. I think it is almost a duty on everyone who comes here to send some news of things they see and hear, as that will be a help to those who have yet to leave.[76]

The frequency with which references to writing in order to fulfill promises appears in the letters or prefatory notes indicates the extent of peer expectations and hints at informal agreements made among parties, either orally or in writing, before departing. Reports of speeches at farewell meetings for immigrants sometimes reveal requests to departing migrants to submit accounts and impressions to local newspapers and send news of other, especially earlier, immigrants. At one such meeting in July 1866 a Welsh immigrant stated he "would be sure to write back regularly to newspapers in Wales."[77] Another, Hopkin Hopkin, was urged by the *Gwladgarwr* correspondent present at his farewell meeting in October 1879 to send that paper word of his experiences in Texas. For some unknown reason, however, the series of letters Hopkin duly sent back to relatives and friends in Wales were sent to, and were eventually published in, the rival newspaper, *Tarian y Gweithiwr* rather than *Y Gwladgarwr*.[78]

It was widely believed that the content of published immigrant letters was not just solely the preserve of potential emigrants but had a wider appeal and interest.[79] In July 1871, a Welsh immigrant in Kansas maintained that letters from America published in the homeland press appealed to two categories of readers: those who planned to emigrate immediately or in the future, and the many people "who have relatives . . . and dear friends here; it is a joy to them to hear something about, or from, the land of the West."[80] Similar sentiments were expressed in the commentaries of editors and intermediaries who supplied them with hitherto unpublished letters. Commenting on a letter it had received from Oregon City in 1865, the *Merthyr Telegraph* remarked that "the subjoined letter was last week received from Mr Richard Evans, son of Mrs Chattely, Rising Sun Inn, Pond Street, and as he is known to many of our readers, it will doubtless be found interesting."[81]

Numerous commentators emphasized that those left behind in the homeland not only had need of news about individuals. They also required information of a general nature about the places overseas where the Welsh were settling and specific updates on the condition of the Welsh language and Welsh cultural activity and the strength of Welsh religious causes in those locations. In November 1852 D.W. Prothero of Maesteg told *Y Cylchgrawn* that he had translated a letter from W. Williams, a Welsh copper miner in Burra Burra, South Australia, at the request of many of the subscribers of the magazine. He also stated that Williams was very well known in Rhymney and Dowlais (two industrial towns in south Wales). The letter included details of local wages, living conditions, and prices of goods, descriptions of the landscape, aboriginal people and *flora* and *fauna* of the area, and news of Welsh religious services being held there.[82] In July 1890 J. Williams of Charters Towers, Queensland, Australia, wrote to *Tarian y Gweithiwr* readers and "everyone who knows him" to tell them that their countrymen and relatives and friends who had gone to that part of the world, "were holding on to the old language [i.e. Welsh], the old customs, and the religion of Lord God, their Father."[83] The supply of information about the Welsh overseas was interwoven with the provision of information about the outside world in general. As we have already noted, this was a general feature of the Welsh press as newspapers and periodicals in Wales carried a significant amount of coverage of foreign news and international events.[84] Reading the letters their fellow countrymen and women abroad sent back to the press at home was a significant means by which the people of late-nineteenth century Wales learned about the wider world.

Published Letters, Transnationality, and Identity

It would appear, then, that newspapers in Wales, to a greater or lesser extent, regarded immigrant letters as a significant feature of their columns whilst readers and letter-writers both wanted and expected such correspondence to be included. It may be speculated that a number of complex impulses and factors were interacting to shape this apparently mutual relationship. Letters were the medium by which immigrants and their homeland correspondents created a transnational social space in which to reformulate their relationships. The publication of immigrant letters in the press represents a significant public manifestation of the phenomenon of transnationality. Sharron Schwartz has maintained that one of the chief ways in which Cornish people experienced the transnational dimension of life was through migrants' letters published in newspapers in Cornwall.[85] It seems reasonable to argue that a similar process occurred in Wales. The acts of Welsh immigrants in sending letters to the press may well be a function of their desire to shape the developing public sphere in Wales by injecting into it a transnational dimension. It might of course be argued that Welsh immigrants did not consciously seek to shape the public sphere in the same way as editors wished to do so. The molding of such a sphere evolved out of immigrant actions that sought more personal ends, such as maintaining links with family and friends and acquiring greater information on the Welsh overseas. Nevertheless there seems to be sufficient evidence to entertain the possibility that immigrants did believe that their voice ought to be heard and overtly sought to put their stamp on the public sphere by attempting to shape debates on emigration and gain public exposure for their views and concerns. Such an interpretation gains weight when the participatory nature of the general practice of writing letters to late-nineteenth century newspapers in Wales is considered, as we shall see shortly.

At the same time as published letters helped develop Welsh transnationality, the formulating of notions of national identity was also involved. As we have already noted, the press played a structuring rather than a merely reflective role in the institutions and activities of public life. In our study of the Welsh American newspaper *Y Drych* [The Mirror], Aled Jones and this writer have argued that this long-running newspaper was a particular cultural project which sought to construct a specific sense of *Welshness* in an American environment.[86] By the same token, the publishing of Welsh immigrant letters, from numerous destinations overseas, and in however modified a form, played an important role in the construction of a transnational Welsh identity in the late nineteenth century.

The processes which led to the publication of Welsh immigrant letters may also be understood more fully when the important role that readers' letters as a whole played in newspapers in this period is taken into account. Public involvement in the press in Britain generally was encouraged by the open space offered in readers' letters columns.[87] The letters that were submitted and published are one of many indications of the high level of readers' involvement in the press. They also show the great variety of social and occupational backgrounds of the correspondents; Aled Jones has suggested that the nature of the readership in Wales "was overwhelmingly plebeian." He also argues that the readers' correspondence "provides the clearest indication that the reading of newspapers was a creative process that could add to or alter intended meanings, and in turn produce a vast amount of new, unsolicited writing."[88] By writing directly to the press ordinary Welsh immigrants, no less than the editors and intermediaries who facilitated publication, were participating in and, at least to an extent, shaping a developing Welsh public sphere. The preponderance of male published letter-writers, however, reveals the strongly gendered nature of that public sphere.

The interrelationship between the publishing of Welsh immigrant letters and the development of the newspaper and periodical press in both languages in Wales, however, is even more complex as by the end of the nineteenth century the number of published immigrant letters appears to have declined significantly. An impressionistic survey of various titles at the turn of the twentieth century reveals that although immigrant letters continued to be published, they appeared far less frequently. In the case of

Tarian y Gweithiwr, for example, whereas the paper might publish an average of at least two letters per issue in the late 1870s, there appeared around 25 letters in 1890 and less than a dozen in 1905. Precisely why this general trend occurred is unclear and a detailed investigation of the trend, including systematic measurement of newspaper columns, is needed before firm conclusions can be made. Nevertheless, undoubtedly one reason is that the press embraced new styles of journalism and presentational techniques, involving bylines, shorter items, and bolder headlines.[89] Immigrant letters, which earlier in the century were often allocated several broadsheet columns, were arguably not suited to this style of presentation.

A crucial factor in the emergence of this less personal style was that increasingly toward the end of the nineteenth century Welsh journalism was becoming professionalized, with full-time trained reporters being appointed. Formerly, news-gathering had largely been the preserve of local amateur correspondents. Indeed it might be argued that immigrant letter-writers were in some respects a part of this latter group and shared with them similar concerns and fulfilled comparable functions. But the adoption of the practices and techniques of "new journalism" was uneven, and was naturally dependent on editorial policy. It does not appear that the general level of coverage of the Welsh overseas diminished markedly as these changes occurred. However, many newspapers preferred more (and often shorter) news items and features on the Welsh overseas, rather than immigrant letters. It is impossible to calculate how far the change was due to Welsh immigrants themselves writing fewer letters to the press, although this also may be a factor. Intriguing questions thus remain to be answered in this context, although it is clear that the creation and publication of immigrant letters in the late nineteenth century represents a distinctive, discrete phase in the processes through which Welsh immigrants retained contact with their homeland.

Conclusions

To conclude, this essay has argued that immigrant letters published in the Welsh periodical press in the late nineteenth century are richer and more complex sources than general observations on these phenomena might allow. They are multilayered texts, shaped by social, cultural, and religious considerations and, crucially, by the development of print culture. Their journey into print adds another dimension to the relationship between immigrants and the homeland. Undoubtedly these letters reflect efforts on the part of writers and editors to influence potential immigrant decisions and they function as a means of social intelligence, which might trigger or deter people from emigrating. Yet through acquiring a public audience these published Welsh immigrant letters also represent the desire to maintain personal links and relationships with a wider circle of friends, former neighbors, and acquaintances, and the notion of an international Welsh cultural and religious community. More generally, the possibilities and limitations of the published immigrant letters examined here reinforce many of the concerns that scholars have usually expressed about these sources. Nevertheless, the complex motives, factors, and processes involved in going into print that this specific study reveals suggests that an analysis of the functions and significance of published letters in a variety of diverse local, regional, and national contexts, and in different types of published settings, would be well worth undertaking.

Notes

1. This publication was prepared during a period of research leave funded by the British Arts and Humanities Research Board and I gratefully acknowledge its support. I would also like to thank Huw Griffiths, Carolyn Jacob, Gethin Matthews, and Huw Walters for their assistance with identifying sources, and David A. Gerber for his valuable comments on drafts of this essay. All English translations of quotations from the original Welsh are by the author. In Welsh-language quotations the spelling, punctuation, and grammar of the originals have been retained.
2. David A. Gerber, "The Immigrant Letter between Positivism and Populism: The Uses of Immigrant Personal Correspondence in Twentieth-Century American Scholarship," *Journal of American Ethnic History* 16, no. 4 (Summer 1997): 3–34, 5–6, 18–20.
3. Theodore Blegen, ed., *Land of Their Choice: The Immigrants Write Home* (Minneapolis: University of Minnesota Press, 1955); Alan Conway, ed., *The Welsh in America: Letters from the Immigrants* (Cardiff: University of Wales Press, 1961).
4. Blegen, *Land of Their Choice*, pp. vii, 3–4; Conway, *The Welsh in America*, pp. v–vi. As Gerber has shown, both authors' utilization of manuscript and published immigrant letters was informed by their disciplinary, egalitarian, and pluralist approaches to writing history. "The Immigrant Letter between Positivism and Populism," 3–34.
5. Charlotte Erickson, *Invisible Immigrants: The Adaptation of English and Scottish Immigrants in Nineteenth-Century America* (Coral Gables, FL: University of Miami Press, 1972); David Fitzpatrick, *Oceans of Consolation: Personal Accounts of Irish Migration to Australia* (Ithaca: Cornell University Press, 1994).
6. See Erickson, *Invisible Immigrants*, pp. 3–4; E.R.R. Green, "Ulster Emigrants' Letters," in *Essays in Scotch-Irish History* (London: Routledge, 1969), pp. 87–103.
7. Fitzpatrick, *Oceans of Consolation*, pp. 26–27. Gerber, "The Immigrant Letter between Positivism and Populism," p. 22.
8. This essay deals solely with those letters that appeared in newspapers and periodicals in Wales. As is evident, however, there are different types of published immigrant letters, ranging from those published letters in books, tracts, guides, and other forms of emigrant literature through to those published in contemporary newspapers and periodicals. Although the issue is not examined here, it seems reasonable to hypothesize that all these documents may have been too readily interpreted together in an undifferentiated manner.
9. Fitzpatrick, *Oceans of Consolation*, pp. 26–27.

10. I discuss this in the context of Welsh immigrant letters in my "Writing Back: Welsh Emigrants and their Correspondence in the Nineteenth Century" *North American Journal of Welsh Studies* 5, no. 1 (Winter 2005): 23–46, *esp.* 29–30. http://spruce.flint.umich.edu/~ellisjs/Jones2.pdf

11. See David A. Gerber, "Epistolary Ethics: Personal Correspondence and the Culture of Emigration in the Nineteenth Century," *Journal of American Ethnic History* 19, no. 4 (Summer 2000): 3–23, 10, 12–14.

12. Blegen, *Land of Their Choice*, pp. 3–4, 6–7, 179. See also 83–88 for a letter that appeared in *Christianssandsposten* (Norway) in 1843 which asks the recipients to seek to get it published in a newspaper. In 1852 an Aberdeen migrant in Australia instructed the recipient of his letter to "show this letter to as many of our friends as possible . . . perhaps the best way would be to send it to the 'Aberdeen Journal.'" *Aberdeen Journal*, May 12, 1852, cited in Marjory Harper, *Adventurers and Exiles: The Great Scottish Exodus* (London: Profile, 2003), pp. 238–239.

13. See the discussion in Gerber, "The Immigrant Letter between Positivism and Populism."

14. "Untitled," *Seren Gomer* 3, no. 2 (February 1820): 46–49.

15. Aled Gruffydd Jones, *Press, Politics and Society: A History of Journalism in Wales* (Cardiff: University of Wales Press, 1993), p. 197; Huw Walters, "*Y Gwladgarwr a'i Ohebwyr*" in *Cynnwrf Canrif: Agweddau ar Ddiwylliant Gwerin* (Swansea: Barddas, 2004), pp. 100–183, 151–152.

16. Calculated from an unpublished list of letters from Welsh immigrants in the U.S., Australia, Russia, and South Africa published in *Y Gwladgarwr* that has been compiled by Dr Huw Walters of the National Library of Wales, Aberystwyth, and which the compiler kindly made available to the present writer. For a discussion of the content and some of the more well known writers of immigrant letters in this newspaper, see Walters, "*Y Gwladgarwr a'i Ohebwyr*," pp. 145–162.

17. "At Ein Gohebwyr [To Our Correspondents]," *Seren Cymru*, March 27, 1863, August 31, 1866.

18. "At Ein Gohebwyr [To Our Correspondents]," *Y Gwron*, March 17, 1860. ". . . rhai dyddorol o America ac Awstralia."

19. "Llythyr o'r America [Letter from America]," *Seren Cymru*, August 31, 1866. ". . . yn y lle pellenig hwnw."

20. See Aled Jones and Bill Jones, "The Welsh world and the British empire, *c.* 1851–1939: an exploration," *Journal of Imperial and Commonwealth History* 31, no. 2 (May 2003): 57–81, also in *The British World: Diaspora, Culture, Identity*, ed. Carl Bridge and Kent Fedorowich (London: Frank Cass, 2003), pp. 57–81; Bill Jones, "*Raising the Wind*": Emigrating from Wales to the USA in the Late Nineteenth and Early Twentieth Centuries (Cardiff: Cardiff University, 2004); William D. Jones, *Wales in America: Scranton and the Welsh, 1860–1920* (Cardiff and Scranton: University of Wales Press and University of Scranton Press, 1993); David Williams, "Some Figures Relating to Emigration from Wales," *Bulletin of the Board of Celtic Studies* 7, no. 4 (May 1935): 396–415, 8, no. 2 (May 1936): 160.

21. Jones, *Press, Politics and Society*, pp. 94–97.

22. Huw Walters, *Llyfryddiaeth Cylchgronau Cymreig, 1851–1900. A Bibliography of Welsh Periodicals 1851–1900* (Aberystwyth, Wales: National Library of Wales, 2003), lx–lxi; Jones, *Press, Politics and Society*, pp. 96–97.

23. Brynley F. Roberts, "Welsh Periodicals: A Survey," in *Investigating Victorian Journalism*, ed. Lionel Brake, Aled Jones, and Lionel Madden (London: Macmillan, 1990), pp. 71–84; Huw Walters, "The Periodical Press to 1914," in *A Nation and its Books: a History of the Book in Wales*, ed. Philip Henry Jones and Eiluned Rees (Aberystwyth: National Library of Wales and Aberystwyth Centre for the Book, 1998), pp. 197–208.

24. Jones, *Press, Politics and Society*, pp. 2–4, 90–94.
25. John Williams, *Digest of Welsh Historical Statistics*, 2 vols (Cardiff: Welsh Office, 1985), vol. 1, p. 7.
26. See Dot Jones, *Statstical Evidence Relating to the Welsh Language 1901–1911* (Cardiff: University of Wales Press, 1998).
27. Aled Jones, "The Nineteenth-Century Media and Welsh Identity," in *Nineteenth-Century Media and the Construction of Identities*, ed. Laurel Brake, Bill Bell, and David Finkelstein (Basingstoke: Palgrave, 2000), pp. 310–325, 313. See also Jones, *Press, Politics and Society*, pp. 2–4.
28. Aled Jones, "Local Journalism in Victorian Political Culture," in *Investigating Victorian Journalism*, ed. Laurel Brake, Aled Jones, and Lionel Madden (London: Macmillan, 1990), pp. 63–70, 64–65; Andy Croll, *Civilizing the Urban: Popular Culture and Public Space in Merthyr, c.1870–1914* (Cardiff: University of Wales Press, 2000); Croll, "Street Disorder, Surveillance and Shame: Regulating Behavior in the Public Spaces of the late Victorian British town," *Social History*, 24, no. 3 (1999): pp. 250–268.
29. For fuller discussion, see Aled Jones and Bill Jones, *Welsh Reflections: Y Drych and America, 1851–2001* (Llandysul: Gomer Press, 2001); Jones and Jones, "The Welsh World and the British Empire"; and Jones and Jones, "Empire and the Welsh Press," *Newspapers and Empire in Ireland and Britain, c. 1857–1921*, ed. Simon J. Potter (Dublin: Four Courts Press, 2004), pp. 75–91.
30. See, e.g., "Brodorion ar Wasgar," *Awel Eryri*, April 2, 1908.
31. "Nodion o Affrica [Notes from Africa]," *Tarian y Gweithiwr*, February 20, 1890, "Llythyr o America [Letter from America]," *Tarian y Gweithiwr*, April 3, 1890.
32. See, e.g., "At Ein Gohebwyr [To Our Correspondents]," *Seren Cymru*, November 29, 1867, in which the editor notes receipt of New York, Melbourne, Scranton, and Pennsylvania newspapers. See also Jones and Jones, *Welsh Reflections*, pp. 30, 46, 52–53.
33. "Letter from Australian," *Merthyr Telegraph*, July 10, 1858.
34. See, e.g., "Llythyr o Awstralia [Letter from Australia]," *Yr Amserau*, April 26, 1854; "Llythyr o Awstralia [Letter from Australia]," *Yr Herald Cymraeg*, July 28, 1855; "O Treherbert i Conemaugh, Pennsylvania, America [From Treherbert to Conemaugh, Pennsylvania, America]," *Tarian y Gweithiwr*, August 7, 1890.
35. "The Cardiff Mormonites," *Cardiff and Merthyr Guardian*, February 28, 1856; "Taith o Hirwaun i'r Coal Valley, America [Journey from Hirwaun to Coal Valley, America]," *Y Gwladgarwr*, December 6, 1862; "Llythyr o Awstralia [Letter from Australia]," *Y Gwron*, June 7, 1855; "Llythyr oddiwrth Gymraes yn America [Letter from a Welshwoman in America]," *Yr Herald Cymraeg*, May 2, 1863; "untitled," *Monmouthshire Gazette and Forest of Dean Circular*, March 1850.
36. "Llythr o Awstralia [Letter from Australia]," *Yr Amserau*, February 15, 1854; "Llythyr o'r America [Letter from America]," *Y Byd Cymreig*, August 31, 1865; "The Cardiff Mormonities," *Cardiff and Merthyr Guardian*, February 28, 1856; "Llythyr o Awstralia [Letter from Australia]," *y Cymro*, April 22, 1853 and April 18, 1855; "Llythyr o America [Letter from America]," *Y Gwladgarwr*, April 18, 1863; *Yr Herald Cymraeg*, October 13, 1855; "O Treherbert i Conemaugh, Pennsylvania, America [From Treherbert to Conemaugh, Pennsylvania, America]," *Tarian y Gweithiwr*, August 7, 1890.
37. Jones, *Press, Politics and Society*, pp. 91–92.
38. Huw Walters, "The Welsh Language and the Periodical Press," in Geraint H. Jenkins, ed. *The Welsh Language and its Social Domains 1801–1911*, (Cardiff: University of Wales Press, 2000), pp. 349–378, 374; pp. 374–375. See also Walters, "Y Gwladgarwr a'i Ohebwyr," pp. 100–101.
39. David Barton and Nigel Hall, "Introduction" in their edited collection, *Letter Writing as a Social Practice* (Amsterdam and Philadelphia: John Benjamins

Publishing, 2000), pp. 1–14; Frances Austin, "Letter Writing in a Cornish Community in the 1790s," in *Letter Writing as a Social Practice*, 43–61; David Vincent, *Literacy and Popular Culture: England, 1750–1914* (Cambridge: Cambridge University Press, 1989).

40. Ieuan Gwynedd Jones, "The Nineteenth Century" in Jones and Rees, eds., *A Nation and its Books*, pp. 157–171, 166–167. Jones, *Press, Politics and Society*, pp. 93–94.

41. The diaries of John Davies (Brychan), Tredegar, reveal that between the 1830s and 1850s he provided this service for family and friends in Wales wishing to write to Welsh immigrants. Unfortunately there are no references in the diaries to indicate whether he was paid for this work or not. Dyddiaduron Brychan, vol. 1, Cardiff MS 3.512, Cardiff Central Library. See also Jones, "Writing Back," pp. 37–38.

42. "Minersville, Schuylkill Co., Pennsylvania," *Y Gwron*, March 24, 1860.

43. "Llythyr o Rwsia [Letter from Russia]," *Y Gwladgarwr*, October 22, 1870. "*Dymunwyf i chwi estyn y llythyr hwn i Joshua Evans, ac iddo ef ei ddarllen i George Wilkinson, Ysw, ac hefyd ei ddarllen i'm cyfeillion yn Middle Dyffryn. Byddwch mor garedig a'i estyn i George Jenkins, Cwmpennar, fel y bydd iddo ei ddarllen i'm cyfeillion yn Mountain Ash. Os gwelant hwy rhyw deilyngdod ynddo, y mae at eu gwasanaeth i'w argraffu.*"

44. "Gwladfa Big Bend, Washington Territory [Big Bend Colony, Washington Territory]," *Baner ac Amserau Cymru*, March 17, 1886 .... See "Llythyrau o America [Letters from America]," *Y Fellten*, April 7, 1871, for another example.

45. Walters, "Y Gwladgarwr a'i Ohebwyr," pp. 162–163.

46. In 1853 R.F. Edwards, Llanychan, translated into Welsh a letter from Edward Rogers, Saw Pit Gully, Victoria, Australia, to his mother and father, and was later published in "Llythyr o Awstralia [Letter from Australia]," *Yr Amserau*, February 15, 1854. Edwards did so because he thought the content of the letter would be interesting and educational to some of the paper's readers. See also "Ymfudiaeth i Queensland [Emigration to Queensland]," *Baner ac Amserau Cymru*, July 6, 1864; "Llythyr o Awstralia [Letter from Australia]," *Y Gwron*, June 7, 1855; "Llef Rybuddiol o Awstralia [Warning Cry from Australia]," *Yr Herald Cymraeg*, September 7, November 23, 1861.

47. Jones, *Statistical Evidence Relating to the Welsh Language*, pp. 211–333; Jenkins, *The Welsh Language and its Social Domains*.

48. Walters, "Y Gwladgarwr a'i Ohebwyr," pp. 162–163. See also, "Taith Lewis Job, Dilledydd, Gynt Heol-Y-Felin, Aberdar, o Liverpool i New York [Journey of Lewis Job, Clothier, formerly of Heol-Y-Felin, Aberdar, from Liverpool to New York]," *Y Gwladgarwr*, November 15, 1862.

49. "Australia," *Cambrian*, June 25, 1852, "Another Peep at Life in Australia," *Cambrian*, September 9, 1853; "untitled," *Carnarvon and Denbigh Herald*, June 18, 1853; "Llthyr o America [Letter from America]," *Y Diwygiwr* [The Reformer] 9, no. 101 (December 1843): 370–371; "Taith Lewis Job, Dilledydd, Gynt Heol-Y-Felin, Aberdar, o Liverpool i New York [Journey of Lewis Job, Clothier, formerly of Heol-Y-Felin, Aberdar, from Liverpool to New York]," *Y Gwladgarwr*, November 15, 1862; "Letter from Australia," *Merthyr Telegraph*, July 10, 1858; "Llythyr o Galifffornia [Letter from California]," *Seren Cymru*, March 11, 1864; "Llythyr o America [Letter from America]," *Seren Gomer* 39, no. 491 (August 1856): 382; "Emigration Notes," *South Wales Press*, October 26, 1871.

50. "The Cardiff Mormonites," *Cardiff and Merthyr Guardian*, February 28, 1856.

51. "Aberdarians Abroad," *Aberdare Times*, July 11, 1863. For an example of the same statement in Welsh, see "Llythyr o America [Letter from America]," *Y Gwladgarwr*, March 19, 1864.

52. Conway, *The Welsh in America*, p. vi.

53. See the discussion in Gerber, "The Immigrant Letter between Positivism and Populism," pp. 16–20.

54. "Llythyr o America [Letter from America]," *Y Gwladgarwr*, June 25, 1864; Conway, *The Welsh in America*, 216–217. *"Anwyl Wraig a Phlant*. *Dyma fi yn ysgrifenu atoch, gan obeithio eich bod yn iach, fel ag yr wyf yn bresenol, diolch i'r Arglwydd am ei ofal tadol. Mae hiraeth mawr arnaf am eich gweled, er nad oes ond wyth wythnos er pan ymadawsom a'n gilydd i dirio yma; yn fuan byddo y dyddiau ar ben i ni gael bod gyda'n gilydd eto."* For another example, see "Llythyr o America [Letter from America]," *Seren Cymru*, August 30, 1861.
55. Gerber, "Epistolary Ethics," pp. 3–23.
56. "Llythyr o Awstralia [Letter from Australia]," *Yr Amserau*, February 15, 1854; "Llythyr o'r America [Letter from America]," *Y Gwladgarwr*, April 18, 1863 and August 6, 1882; "Minersville, Schuylkill Co., Pennsylvania," *Y Gwron*, March 24, 1860; "Llythyr oddiwrth Ymfudwr Cymreig yn America [Letter form a Welsh emigrant in America]," *Yr Herald Cymraeg*, June 23, 1855.
57. "Llythyr oddiwrth Gymraes yn America [Letter from a Welshwoman in America]," *Yr Herald Cymraeg*, May 2, 1863. *"Anwyl Frodyr a Chwiorydd. Yr wyf yn gobeithio y bydd i'r llinellau hyn eich cael oll mewn iechyd da. Yr wyf yn yn erfyn eich maddeuant oherwydd i mi fod mor hor yn ysgrifenu atoch; ond, i ddyweyd y gwir i chwi, nid oedd genyf galon i ysgrifenu atoch pan y mae y wlad hon yn y fath gyflwr alaethus yn nghanol y rhyfel ofnadwy hwn, sydd yn dyfetha ein gwlad er's amser hir, ac yn debyg o bara am bedair blynedd neu ychwaneg."* These remarks were not included in the version in Conway's volume. Conway, *The Welsh in America*, p. 302.
58. Fitzpatrick, *Oceans of Consolation*, p. 23. See also Gerber, "The Immigrant Letter between Positivism and Populism," p. 22.
59. Gerber, "Epistolary Ethics," p. 10. Italics in the original.
60. Angela McCarthy has recently suggested that "[as] most commentators recognize, published letters are untrustworthy for they were often manipulated for propaganda purposes to promote or dissuade emigration." " 'A Good Idea of Colonial Life': Personal Letters and Irish Migration to New Zealand," *New Zealand Journal of History* 35, no. 1 (2001): 1–21, 1.
61. Green, "Ulster Emigrants' Letters," p. 89.
62. Although Welsh "fake" immigrant letters have not been identified or studied, I know of at least one. In July 1864 a correspondent warned readers that the real address of the Samuel Evans who had written a letter praising America highly as a field of emigration was not somewhere in America but "Cell No 3, Gaol, Cardiff." "untitled," *Baner ac Amserau Cymru*, July 20, 1864.
63. Conway, *The Welsh in America*, p. vi.
64. "Ysgrifennu i'r Wasg [Writing to the Press]," *Y Cenhadwr Americanaidd* [The American Missionary] 18, no. 1 (January 1857): 16.
65. Thomas Phillips, coalminer, of Wadesville, St Clair, Pennsylvania, and formerly of Aberdare informed his former fellow workers at Gadlys coal mine that "I have put things down before you as best as I can, you judge for yourselves." ["*Dyma fi wedi gosod pethau ger eich bron goreu y medrwn, barnwch chwithau drosoch eich hunain*."] "Llythyr o America [Letter from America]," *Y Gwladgarwr*, April 18, 1863.
66. See Gareth Alban Davies, "Wales, Patagonia and the Printed Word: The Missionary Role of the Press," *Llafur* 6, no. 4 (1995): 44–59; Jones and Jones, *Welsh Reflections*, pp. 7, 25–26.
67. See, e.g., "At Ymfudwyr i'r America [To Emigrants to America]," *Yr Amserau*, April 9, 1851, "New Cambria, Brazil," *Yr Amserau*, May 28, 1851, January 7, 21, March 31, April 14, and May 5, 1852; "Patagonia Notes," *Baner ac Amserau Cymru*, May 13, 1868, "Patagonia," *Baner ac Amserau Cymru*, May 16, 1868; "Llythyr o Brazil [Letter form Brazil]," *Y Cylchgrawn* 3, no. 31 (October 1853): 307–308, and 4, no. 43 (October 1854): 310–311; "Llythyr o Brazil [Letter from Brazil]," *Y Diwygiwr* 15, no. 184 (November 1850): 150–151, 19, no. 299 (October 1853): 310–311;

"Llythyr o Batagonia [Letter from Patagonia]," *Llais y Wlad*, July 6, 1877. See also Davies, "Wales, Patagonia and the Printed Word." Private emigrant letters were also regularly published in travel books and emigrant guides. An early and celebrated example is John Davies (Brychan), *Newyddion Da o Wlad Bell* [Good News from a Faraway Country] (Merthyr Tydfil: the author, 1830). For a fuller discussion of this work, see Jones, "Writing Back," 31–32.

68. "Taith Robert Williams i'r America [Robert Williams's Journey to America]," *Y Bedyddiwr* 3, no. 32 (August 1844): 259–261. "*Os byddwch mor garedig a rhoddi lle i'r hanesyn canlynol yn y BEDYDDIWR, gwnewch arbed llawer o drafferth i mi, yn nghyda boddloni llawer o'm cydgenedl y Cymru, y rhai yr addewais anfon hanes fy nhaith forawl atynt; ac yr wyf fi yn barnu mai dyma y ffordd oreu a mwyaf didrafferth iddynt gael clywed mewn byr amser.*" For a similar case, see "Llythyr o America [Letter from America]," *Y Diwygiwr* 18, no. 216 (June 1853): 179–181.

69. "Taith i Awstralia [Journey to Australia]," *Y Gwladgarwr*, May 30, 1863. "*Diolchaf i chwi os gadewch i'r llythyr hwn gael ymddangos yn y GWLADGARWR, am fod pawb a ofynodd i mi am ysgrifenu yn derbyn eich newyddiadur.*"

70. "Llythyr o America [Letter from America]," *Yr Herald Cymraeg*, January 27, 1871. "*Cyn cychwyn addewais y buaswn un gohebu â rhai o'm hen gyfeillion. Cedwais fy ngair â'r rhan fwyaf ohonynt, ond methais wneyd â'r oll. Gan fy mod yn gwybod fod cylchrediad yr 'Herald' yn fwy cyffredinol trwy Lleyn na'r un newyddiadur arall, penderfynais anfon gair iddo, gan y gallaf gyfarch yr oll ag un llythyr.*" For similar sentiments, see *Y Gwladgarwr*, "Llythyr o America [Letter from America]," April 28, August 11, 1882; "Llythyr o Efrog Newydd [Letter from New York]," *Tarian y Gweithiwr*, May 15, 1890.

71. See, e.g., letter from John Davies, Trumbull County, Ohio, "Llythyr o Ohio, America [Letter from Ohio, America]," *Y Gwladgarwr*, April 25, 1868.

72. Conway, *The Welsh in America*, p. vi.

73. The same is true of at least one Norwegian immigrant. See Bergen, *Land of Their Choice*, p. 83.

74. See, e.g., "Llythyrau o America [Letters from America]," *Y Felten*, April 7, 1871; "Columbia Brydeinig [British Columbia]," *Seren Cymru*, January 23, 1863, "At Ein Gohebwyr [To Our Correspondents]," *Seren Cymru*, June 12, and September 25, 1863.

75. "Ysgrifennu i'r Wasg [Writing to the Press]," *Y Cenhadwr Americanaidd* 18, no.1 (January 1857): 16. "*Y mae ein cenedl ni yn wasgaredig yn mhob rhandir o'r wlad fawr hon, a dyledswydd arbenigol ydyw i ryw un neu rai yn mhob sefydliad I yru newyddion a dygwyddiadau i'r cyhoeddiadau wythnosol a misol.*"

76. "Llythyr o Minnesota [Letter from Minnesota]," *Baner ac Amserau Cymru*, November 20, 1869. "*Pan oeddwn yna, cyn gadael yr 'Hen Wlad', byddwn yn hoff iawn o weled llythyr o America yn y papurau newyddion,* now and then [in English and italics in original]; *hwyrach fod yna amryw etto yn caru yr un peth, yn enwedig os ydynt â'u bryd ar 'fyned i 'Merica'. Yr wyf yn meddwl ei bod agos yn ddyledswydd ar bawb ddaw yma yru tipyn bach o hanes y pethau a wêl ac a glyw, gan y bydd hyny yn gynnorthwy i'r rhai fydd heb gychwyn.*" See also "Llythyr o America [Letter from America]," *Yr Herald Cymreig*, July 14, 1871.

77. "Cyfarfod Ymadawol Mr E. Evans (Morddal), Llanfabon [Farewell Meeting of Mr E. Evans (Morddal), Llanfabon]," *Y Gwladgarwr*, July 7, 1866. "*Byddaf yn sicr o anfon i newyddiaduron Cymru yn fynych.*"

78. "Cyfaarfod Ymadawol [Farewell Meeting]," *Y Gwladgarwr*, October 24, 1879; "Llythyr o Texas [Letter from Texas]," *Tarian y Gweithiwr*, December 19, 1879 and January 9, 1880, "Llythyr o America [Letter from America]," *Tarian y Gweithiwr*, May 7, 1880.

79. I discuss this dimension at greater length in my *"Raising the Wind,"* pp. 36–41, and in my "Inspecting the 'Extraordinary Drain': Emigration and the Urban Experience in Merthyr Tydfil in the 1860s," *Urban History* 32, no. 1 (May 2005): 100–113.

80. "Llythyr o America [Letter from America]," *Yr Herald Cymraeg*, July 14, 1871. *"Y mae gan amryw berthynasau yma; ac ereill gyfeillion hoff; ac y mae clywed rhywbeth am, neu o wlad y Gorllewin yn hyfryd iddynt."* For similar sentiments, see "Taith o Fforest Fach i Awstralia [Journey from Fforest Fach to Australia]," *Tarian y Gweithiwr*, April 3, 1890.

81. "Letter from California," *Merthyr Telegraph*, February 23, 1856. For further examples in English-language newspapers see "Letter from Australia," *Merthyr Telegraph*, November 3, 1860; "The Cardiganshire Farmer in Australia," *The Welshman*, January 8, 1847.

82. "Llythyr o Mwnglawdd Burra Burra, Adelaide [Letter from Burra Burra Mines, Adelaide]," *Y Cylchgrawn* 2, no. 20 (November 1852): 340.

83. "Llythyr o Queensland [Letter from Queensland]," *Tarian y Gweithiwr*, July 31, 1890. *". . . yn dal at yr hen iaith, yr hen arferion, ac at grefydd Arglwydd Dduw eu tadau."*

84. Jones, *Press, Politics and Society*, pp. 54–55.

85. Sharron P. Schwartz, "Cornish Migration to Latin America: A Global and Transnational Perspective," unpublished PhD thesis, University of Exeter, Exeter, UK, 2003, p. 253.

86. Jones and Jones, *Welsh Reflections*, esp. pp. 55–76.

87. Jones, "Local Journalism," p. 67. See also Croll, "Street Disorder, Surveillance and Shame." He argues that through their correspondence columns "the late nineteenth century local newspapers augmented existing networks of communication and made them more efficient and far-reaching," Croll, "Street Disorder, Surveillance and Shame," p. 261.

88. Jones, *Press, Politics and Society*, pp. 197–198.

89. For discussion of these trends, see Jones, "Victorian Journalism," pp. 40–41, 67–68.

10

As if at a Public Meeting: Polish American Readers, Writers, and Editors of *Ameryka-Echo*, 1922–1969

Anna D. Jaroszyńska-Kirchmann

I would like to say thank you to all the authors sending their correspondence and articles to the "Corner for Everybody" (*"Kącik dla Wszystkich"*). For such plain people like myself, who can hardly read and barely know how to sign their names, the "Corner" is like food for souls and minds. The "Corner" is a school for us. Each week one can understand and learn something new.

Those who write to the "Corner" express various opinions on God. Because God knows about everything and, no doubt, reads *Ameryka-Echo*, I wonder what He really thinks about those "Corner" writers. I think that those religious and anti-religious letters put God into good mood. Surely He finds the writers to the "Corner" entertaining, and after they die He'll give them the best spots in Heavens, because they had courage to express their views.

This letter came to *Ameryka-Echo* in 1953 from Emmet, Idaho, from a Polish-American reader.[1] He belonged to the vast and devoted following of *Ameryka-Echo*, one of the most popular Polish language weeklies in the United States. The "Corner for Everybody," to which the letter referred, was a regular section of the newspaper, which printed letters from readers from 1922 until 1969. The "Corner" was the largest of the several sections featured in *Ameryka-Echo*, which promoted interaction between readers and editors and among readers themselves. Throughout the three decades of the greatest popularity of the "Corner," from the 1930s through the 1950s, the "Corner" published an average of 400 letters a year. The experiment of *Ameryka-Echo*, which gave such a considerable amount of space to its readers' letters, is unprecedented among the ethnic press of the same period. Almost all ethnic newspapers and journals did include, in one form or another, some correspondence from their readers, but their volume, character, and freedom can hardly be compared.[2]

Letters to the editor sections of any newspaper are the creation of three distinctive groups: readers of the newspaper, readers who write to the newspaper, and editors of the newspaper. All three groups remain in an intimate and complex relationship with each other, but most of the time it is impossible to re-create its nuances and intensity for lack of sources: the original correspondence with editors of ethnic newspapers is rarely preserved. Consequently, we are faced with a kind of Bermuda Triangle, which forever swallows information about the interactions among those who read, who wrote, and who edited immigrant letters published in the press. Only seldom and by sheer good luck are we faced with an opportunity to explore the depth of this Bermuda Triangle and to recover original letters, including those portions of the correspondence which never made it to print. Fortunately for us, the *Ameryka-Echo*'s original immigrant letters for the 1940s and 1950s remain preserved in the manuscript collection of the Paryski Publishing Company, housed at the Immigration History Research Center at the University of Minnesota, United States.

Ameryka-Echo was the sole creation of one man who was as much outstanding as controversial: Antoni Alfred Paryski.[3] Paryski, born in Poland in 1865, was the son of Polish farmers. In 1883, at the age of eighteen, he left Poland for America. He worked a string of jobs as a printer, an editor, and a reporter for several Polish-language and some American newspapers. In 1889, Paryski started his own newspaper, *Ameryka*, in Toledo, Ohio, and in 1902, combined it with an older one, *Echo*, to become *Ameryka-Echo*. By 1907, Paryski enlarged his enterprise through the purchase and merger of about 40 different publishing houses, creating his own press and publishing empire, and acquiring the reputation of being the "Polish Hearst."

Paryski's success was a result of his exceptional organizational abilities and business talents. He was the first to introduce modern commercial techniques into the Polish-American press, including American yellow press strategies. He established a prosperous publishing house that put out more than 2,000 titles, over 8 million copies in all by the mid-1930s. His specially trained agents moved around the country promoting his newspapers and books, selling products from the glove factory he owned, and offering banking services through his savings company.[4]

Paryski, who excelled at populist self-promotion, consciously built his reputation as a progressive champion of the Polish immigrant "masses." His goal, he claimed, was to bring education and enlightenment to oppressed people, and free them from exploitation and manipulation. Paryski secured *Ameryka-Echo*'s position as an independent newspaper, with a free thinking, strongly anticlerical, and pro-working class bent. *Ameryka-Echo*'s anticlericalism became one of its most characteristic features. The journal was so fervently vocal about its anti-Roman Catholic attitudes that many Roman Catholic priests openly fought *Ameryka-Echo* readership in their parishes and tried to limit its circulation.[5]

The first period of *Ameryka-Echo*'s existence coincided with the greatest development of the Polish language press in the United States. Between 1890 and 1916 the number of Polish American newspapers increased almost five times (from 15 to 71), and in 1929 it reached a peak of 92 Polish language titles.[6] At the beginning of 1915, *Ameryka-Echo* (with its daily edition since 1914) had over 100,000 copies printed, and in the 1920s surpassed most newspapers with a circulation of about 40,000 for the weekday and 120,000 for the weekend edition.[7] The character of Polish American journalism began to change in the 1930s, and the number of the Polish press titles also began to decline steadily. According to one scholar, "The economic consequences of the Great Depression, the effects of immigration restriction, the passing of a great number of immigrants into middle and old age, and the gradual loss of competent editors and publishers through death and retirement meant the beginning of the end of the Polish-language press as it had appeared during the heyday of immigration."[8] Despite problems, *Ameryka-Echo*'s circulation remained high; *Ayer's Directory* lists the circulation of the daily for the years 1931–1934 as close to 25,000, with the weekly reaching 95,000. In 1934, however, Paryski decided to discontinue the daily, and focused solely on the weekly.[9] In 1935, *Ameryka-Echo* printed 80,400 copies; 74,900 copies in 1936, and 68,900 copies in each of the years from 1937 to 1940.[10]

During World War II the Polish press continued to decline, but the influx of the Polish displaced persons and political refugees following the war gave it a much needed shot in the arm. The quality of language and sophistication of materials generally increased, as newly arrived Polish émigré journalists joined the editorial staffs, including that of *Ameryka-Echo*. These improvements could not, however, save the press from further deterioration in the number of subscriptions. Many Polish American publications were forced to develop schemes of "survival through adaptation," which included subsidies from large fraternals, mergers with other printing businesses, and the introduction of English language pages.[11]

There is no doubt that *Ameryka-Echo*'s survival depended first and foremost on the solid financial base of the entire publishing empire of Antoni Paryski. However, in 1956 the founder's son, Tadeusz Paryski, sold *Ameryka-Echo* to a group of private Polish-American investors, but continued to provide facilities and printing services for the newspaper. In 1961, *Ameryka-Echo* was again sold, moved out of Toledo, and merged with Chicago's *Dziennik Chicagoski*.[12] Till the end of its existence in 1971, *Ameryka-Echo* resisted any usage of the English language on its pages, and retained its general public orientation.

Ameryka-Echo owed its success also to its own original "survival technique," directing special attention to its readers and their need to speak for themselves in several different readers' sections, including *"Kącik dla Wszystkich"* (A Corner for Everybody). *"Kącik dla Wszystkich"* appeared for the first time on February 26, 1922. It evolved from earlier sections of *"Korespondencye"* (Correspondence) and *"Głosy czytelników"* (Readers' Voices), and a short-lived section *"Kącik Piorunkiewicza"* (Piorunkiewicz's Corner), which throughout 1921 featured mostly religious discussions between readers and editor Piorunkiewicz.[13] The "Corner" soon developed its own identity as a forum for lively polemics and gained a loyal following. The section appeared in almost each weekly edition, and contained several letters; many of them were on religious subjects, openly anticlerical and critical of the Roman Catholic Church. This religious focus became very characteristic for the early "Corner," as were the issues of class, labor, and social injustice. Throughout the decades of its greatest popularity the "Corner" readers and writers discussed everything from religion, class, ethnicity, and gender, to the world economy, the New Deal, rise of Fascism, war, Communism, arrival of Polish political refugees, history of East Central Europe and changes within Polish-American communities in Diaspora. The 1960s marked a slow demise of the *Ameryka-Echo* readers' sections. The "Corner" shrank from a full page to just a quarter, and by 1967 it was published intermittently, to finally vanish from the pages of *Ameryka-Echo* in August, 1969.

Other readers' sections included an irregular section *"Korespondencye"* (Correspondence), which appeared first in 1903, and contained letters from readers on events in the local Polish-American communities. From 1909 a new section, *"Głosy"* or *"Głosy czytelników"* (Voices or Readers' Voices) contained similar material, but allowed more religious discussions, some readers' poems, and occasional polemics. *"Korespondencye"* (later in a modernized spelling as *"Korespondencje"*) and *"Głosy"* coexisted through the 1920s, to be overshadowed and eventually replaced by *"Kącik dla Wszystkich."* *"Odpowiedzi Redakcji"* (The Editors' Responses) which appeared throughout the entire period of the newspaper's existence, included the editors' replies to letters from the readers on a variety of matters, such as legal advice, immigration laws, medical questions, family matters, and numerous other problems of everyday immigrant life. The section did not print readers' letters to which it responded. *"Nadesł ane"* (Sent Over) published the readers' information on and description of the events in the Polish American communities, such as meetings, elections, picnics, and cultural events. *"Poszukiwania"* (Searches), published letters from readers who were looking for lost relatives and friends. Readers' poems, which initially appeared in several different sections, found a permanent home in a separate *"Wiersze Czytelnikòw"* (Readers' Poems) section of the newspaper. *Ameryka-Echo* also published *"Listy z Polski"* (Letters from Poland), which printed personal letters from relatives in Poland, supplied by readers to the newspaper for publication. In 1929, journalist Czesł aw Łukaszkiewicz began his popular *"Pogadanki z Czytelnikami"* (Chats with the Readers), written in an easy, casual tone, and commenting on a variety of problems in the Polish-American communities and on current world events. *"Pogadanki"* utilized the readers' letters (quoted in full or in fragments) to provide examples and commentaries.[14]

From the first issues of *Ameryka* in 1889, Paryski encouraged readers' participation in the editing of his newspaper and looked for correspondents who could send in news from local Polish American communities.[15] The last issue of *Ameryka* from November 29, 1902 printed on the first page a direct appeal to readers under the title "Who can write to the newspaper?" The article began: "Every person should from time to time write to a newspaper. If you like some project, praise it; if you don't, condemn it. If something important had happened, which should be publicly known, write to *Ameryka* about it. Warn your neighbors against evil. If somebody has written lies, your duty is to set the facts straight."[16] The article further defined news as "everything which informs, evokes curiosity or brings enjoyment to the readers; the more people can be amused by something, entertained or educated—the better news it is."[17]

As the readers' sections developed, the editors outlined the rules for participation. "Corner's" early predecessor *"Gł osy"* included for example the following heading:

In this section everyone (even those who are not *Ameryka-Echo* subscribers) can express their opinion as if at a public meeting. The editors assure complete tolerance for all beliefs and opinions; but they do not allow personal attacks or agitations.

"He sins who allows sin." Let nobody remain indifferent to bad deeds. If we all fight against evil; if we all think about better and more just ways of life—the Polish nation will rise high, and will be apt to govern itself. Others will willingly give way to us and respect us, when we are wise, tolerant, understanding, and fair.

Dear Reader! If you have anything to say for the good of all or to defend those wronged—write to the editors of *Ameryka-Echo*, and your voice will be treated in good faith. Do not be shy, do not be afraid of anything. We want the whole nation to better itself. Away with hypocrisy, and on with the will of the people.[18]

"Corner" had appeared for three years, when in January 1925 it too received a heading proclaiming: "The publisher of *Ameryka-Echo* does not participate in religious disputes personally; however, he allows each reader to freely express his views on not only religious but any matters, without restrictions. It is understood by itself, that we do not allow personal insults and such things, which are forbidden by the law."[19] The heading continued with little alteration throughout the 1930s,[20] until February, 1940, when the section opened with a special statement addressed to the "Corner" writers, asking them to "take into consideration the on-going tragedy of the Polish nation and aim in their correspondence for the good of our Homeland (*Ojczyzna*) from beyond the sea and the achievement of unity." The statement further explained that due to the heavy volume of correspondence, "Corner" contributions should be as brief as possible, while the editors reserved the right to further summarize them in the interest of space.[21] Since May, 1940, the heading included an additional disclaimer: "Articles sent by the readers to the "Corner for Everybody" reflect their personal opinions and views, for which the publishers and editors of *Ameryka-Echo* are not responsible."[22] With only minor modifications, the heading remained in this form until the disappearance of the section.[23]

The editors rarely intervened in the "Corner" discussions directly on the pages of the newspaper. In the early stages of the "Corner's" existence, some of the readers' letters were followed by the editors' comments, referring the writers to specific books (published by Paryski, of course) that could expand or correct their knowledge on the subject matter. Only occasionally did the editors announce the closing of some debate, which continued for too long a time, overwhelmed other topics, or turned into a personal "shouting match" between two writers. Such instances, however, were uncommon, and the editors remained largely invisible to the readers, allowing them to freely share—or fight out—their opinions with other "Corner" readers.

The scholarship on immigrant letters published in the press has a long history, which began with Theodore C. Blegen's call to study "America letters" in 1928, carried on with the 1959 publication of Welsh letters by

Alan Conway, and still continues with the inclusion of published letters in various editions of immigrant correspondence.[24] However, it was the 1972 publication of Charlotte Erickson's collection of English and Scottish immigrant letters that firmly turned the tide of scholarly interest in the direction of unpublished personal correspondence. Erickson saw published letters as providing only limited value. According to her, such letters were biased since their primary goal was to either encourage or discourage emigration; their credibility could not be appraised; they were authored by "an educated, socially prominent elite who had access to newspaper columns and publishers in the countries of their birth"; and, finally, political controversies about emigration informed the editorial choices and decisions, which could further distort the information the letters carried.[25] Following the publication of Erickson's *Invisible Immigrants*, a multitude of historians undertook the editing of private immigrant letters representing different ethnic groups and different continents.[26] They summarily excluded published letters, often echoing Erickson's early charges. For example, in one of the most recent and well-received collections David Fitzpatrick questioned the credibility and authenticity of letters published in newspapers "since the function of these letters was fundamentally changed by their removal to the public domain, and editorial excisions render textual analysis unfeasible."[27] It is my firm conviction that the pendulum has swung too far away from the constructive analysis of published letters and it is time to restore a more balanced view of published and unpublished correspondence, especially since the division into public and private realm of immigrant letters has always posed a problem for scholars, who recognized a blurring between private and public spheres.[28]

The tradition of letter writing among Polish nineteenth century peasants is well documented.[29] In addition to the astonishingly large volume of private correspondence (defined broadly in terms of what David Gerber describes, using Stephen Fender's concept, as "vernacular publication"[30]), Polish peasants wrote prolifically to the Polish press of the late nineteenth and early twentieth centuries.[31] The blurring of borders between private and public is nowhere more visible than in the originals of letters to the editors, which combine elements of both, and reveal the very personal nature of the relationship between the editors and readers-writers to the "Corner."

As a rule, the letters include, borrowing Znaniecki's terminology, the "bowing section," which performed an important function of establishing and/or confirming the relationship between senders and addressees of correspondence.[32] The bowing section could be located either at the very beginning or at the very end of a letter, framing the text submitted for publication in the "Corner." A fully developed bowing section would include five distinctive parts: salutation, greetings, and praise; writer's self-identification; "loyalty statement"; and subscription and book order information.

Salutation usually included one of the following phrases: *Szanowna Redakcjo* (Dear/Esteemed Editors); *Szanowny Panie Redaktorze* (Dear/ Esteemed Mr. Editor); *Szanowni Panowie* (Dear/Esteemed Gentlemen). Less frequently, the writers addressed their letters directly to the editor-in-chief, writing to, for example, "Dear Mr. Rosinski," or "Dear Mr. Publisher W. Rosinski."[33] Salutation was then followed by special greetings, for example for Christmas, Easter, the New Year, and the like, and good wishes for the future. Most of the time, these were simple formulas, such as for example "For the New Year 1951 I am wishing all the publishers and editors and employees of *Ameryka-Echo* good health and all the best."[34] Sometimes, however, these special greetings could take on a more elaborate form and include very particular wishes, as for example those found in a letter from Chicopee, Massachusetts: "Esteemed Editors (*Szanowna Redakcjo*) of *Ameryka-Echo*. First of all thank you for publishing my correspondence; I am sending New Year's greetings and wishes for good health and prosperity and at the same time endurance in the work for the people (*lud*) and a free Poland."[35]

Even without a special occasion, many writers expressed thanks for a job well done to the editors and all *Ameryka-Echo* employees and profusely praised the newspaper. Jan Borkowski from Summit Hill, Pennsylvania, wrote: "I am also very grateful to the honest employees and editors of *Ameryka Echo* for sending me regularly every week this very interesting information *Am. Echo* (sic)! I confirm this to the Editors of Ameryka Echo as an old reader of this newspaper! Which gives most news from the entire world, and even about the Polish society. God bless you all (*szczęś ć wam Boże*) in your further work for Ameryka Echo, you, the workers for the enlightenment (*oś wiata*). . . ."[36] Some writers demonstrated their appreciation in similarly flowery terms, such as for example Marya Burda Krzyżowa from Carnegie, Pennsylvania, who wrote to the editor: "Blessed is the ground, which breeds such sons as you are . . ."[37] Another writer noted that *Ameryka-Echo* was "the only newspaper in America, not tied by 'censorship' and in which readers can openly express their thoughts and opinions."[38] Somewhat less eloquent writers simply passed on heartfelt greetings (*serdeczne pozdrowienia*), thanked for the hard work, and wished continued success.[39]

In the next part of the bowing section writers frequently identified themselves, including information about when they came to America, where they lived, worked, and how old they were. These self-identifications could be relatively brief, for example: "I have never yet written to '*Kącik*,' but I read *Ameryka-Echo* for 42 years, since 1905;"[40] "I am an *Ameryka*

Echo reader for 30 years, and in the past I used to be a [sales] agent for Mr. Paryski"[41] or more exhaustive, as in a letter from Alberta, Canada, which carefully detailed the writer's life of hard work on a farm since his immigration in 1927.[42]

An important part of the bowing section was what I term a "loyalty statement," which demonstrated a strong relationship between *Ameryka-Echo* and the readers. Here the writers recalled the first time they had a chance to read the newspaper, commented on the persecution that they allegedly endured for staying loyal to it, or described their efforts to co-opt new subscribers. For example, one writer recalled:

> I began to read *Ameryka Echo* since 1903, and what made me do it? . . . Here is how it happened: when people were leaving the church after mass, [news-paper] boys were loudly calling to buy their papers, I remember they were selling *Gazeta Chicagowska*, *Wielkopolanin*, and *Ameryka Echo*. One Sunday Reverend Mickiewicz in his sermon admonished all not to buy or read *Ameryka Echo*, because it is a newspaper excommunicated and banned by the church, and after the mass when the people left the church, Reverend Mickiewicz left with them through the side door and with a stick he expelled the [newspaper] boys, who were selling *Ameryka Echo*. The boys moved to other streets and still were calling to buy *Ameryka Echo*. That racket with the priest sparked my interest what kind of cursed newspaper that was, so I bought my first issue of *Ameryka Echo* and I read it till today.[43]

Another writer described his effort to introduce *Ameryka-Echo* to a friend, but was rebuffed that it was "a heretical newspaper, which hates priests" and a good Catholic must not read it. "There is no way to talk to such a stick-in-the-mud," the *Ameryka-Echo* subscriber concluded his story.[44] Perhaps the most dramatic loyalty statement came from a reader in Mechanicville, New York, who related a death threat from a local grocery store owner, upset that the reader "wrote badly about the Poles to the Polish paper." Worried, the reader cautiously tested the mood of the town in the "Polish saloon," but after encountering no more hostility, continued to write to the "Corner" on a regular basis.[45]

Although most of the time the bowing section was in its entirety omitted from print, in some instances the editors chose to publish all or fragments of the thanks and praise, self-identification, and loyalty statements, bridging the gap between private and public parts of the letter. The information on the subscription status and book orders, which was also a part of the bowing section was, however, as a rule left out of print. Information on the status of the subscription played an important role confirming the currency of relationship between *Ameryka-Echo* and its readers. The readers for example notified that a check for the subscription renewal was attached to the "Corner" letter, informed that the newspaper was arriving regularly, or included orders for purchase of new books.[46] Sometimes the readers included detailed explanations why the subscription could not be renewed or more books purchased at that time, mostly due to the extenuating personal circumstances, usually family emergencies, employment problems, and the like. These explanations were followed by sincere apologies and a promise to renew as soon as the situation improved.[47]

The "introduction of the submission section" followed the bowing section and carried its own complex ritual and structure. It never appeared in print, becoming the most personal part of the communication between the writers and editors. Although some introductions of the submission were short and simple, a fully developed introduction of the submission contained five characteristic elements: apologies and excuses; explanation of motivation to write; requests regarding identification; and requests and comments on the editing.

The writers presented apologies and excuses for the assumed poor quality of the submission, such as old age and poor health. A good example is Jan Mastalerz, who wrote: "I don't use a pen often, since I passed 70 plus, so the hand does not work well any more."[48] Another writer pleaded: "Please forgive my unruly handwriting, but my hand is shaking and I am nervous . . . and I can't do the letter right, the way it should be written to you, esteemed gentlemen."[49] A reader from Wisconsin simply noted: "More than 90 years old man writes the way he can."[50] The most frequent apology had to do with lack of education. One writer repeatedly referred to it in his letters. Once he explained: "You know I am self-taught (*samouk*), did not sit in schools for years, had to work since 7 years old for a piece of bread. . . ."[51] On a different occasion the same writer added: "If this [the submission] is not quite the way it should be, don't be surprised; while you attended schools, I tended to the cows and oxen, and they weren't even mine."[52]

Excuses and apologies continued with self-deprecating evaluation of the text for publication, clearly leaving the decision whether to publish it or not to the editors. A remark from John Bajer, who wrote from Canada, is representative of this attitude: "If this correspondence is too long, it does not have to be published all at once. If it is not interesting, you can throw it into trash."[53] With remarkable frequency other writers echoed this sentiment and their comments about unworthy *gryzmoł y* (scribbles) and the referrals to the metaphorical trash can abound in letters to the editor. Only on rare occasions more articulate and perhaps better educated readers asked to have their manuscripts returned if not approved for publication.[54]

And yet, despite qualms about the quality or validity of their writing the readers felt motivated to pick up their pens and write to the "Corner."

Conforming to the polemical character of the "Corner" writers referred to other pieces that appeared there and continued the debate, demanding further explanations, retractions, supporting or disagreeing with other discussants, and so on.[55] Others responded to articles on current events, or felt moved by the world situation, like for example a reader from Chicago, who on December 22, 1944, wrote a letter about feeling unable to joyfully celebrate Christmas while Poland suffered under the German occupation.[56] In 1948, a reader from Toronto revealed his motivation writing with pathos: "I urge you, Gentlemen, to stand up and fight with this Moscow scourge, since there [in Poland] our brothers, sisters and even children suffer terrible misery. . . ."[57] Other writers claimed that they simply wanted to share with others what was on their mind.[58]

The introduction of the submission also incorporated requests to disguise the writers' identity under pen names or initials. Rationale for such actions was diverse, including for example, efforts to avoid endangering relatives in Poland, if published texts were anti-Communist in tone.[59] The editors confirmed the writers' right to withhold their identity from the public, even in cases when an upset reader demanded a disclosure.[60] One writer, who sent in a brief piece about the war and a poem for publication, noted at the end of his letter: "Dear Editors, if possible, please publish this poem and these remarks without change, with only errors corrected; and if it is not suitable and needs change, do not put my name under it—I do not want fame if I am incompetent."[61]

His was not the only request for gentle editing. Numerous writers willingly accepted some degree of editing, perhaps recognizing their own limitations, particularly as far as grammar and spelling were concerned. They thanked the editors for "improving" their previous letters for the "Corner," and counted on them to do the same with new submissions. "I apologize for style and spelling errors; please correct them when needed," wrote, for example, Józef Stańczak.[62] Roman Fedorczuk justified his request by emphasizing that he and *Ameryka-Echo* shared common goals: "Please correct it the way you like it, it is mine but it is also yours, since the spirit knows no division."[63] Authors agreed to changes in titles, or division of their lengthier texts into installments, but generally did not want to see their correspondence cut and shortened. "If there is a need to correct some words, I count on you," Alfreda Borucka wrote to the editor, "But please print my manuscript in full, since one does not write such articles every day."[64]

Readers took seriously the policy statement that appeared in the heading of the "Corner." For example, a concerned reader from Newark, New Jersey, waiting for his correspondence to appear in the "Corner" wrote to the editors in a follow-up letter: "I would like to ask the Editor to kindly note whether it [the submission] might perhaps offend anybody, [perhaps] there are a few incompetent words in it, [which] maybe harmful. Let the editors clarify it, since it has not been printed yet."[65] When the editors sent out a note to a different reader rejecting his correspondence and suggesting that he write in a more temperate manner, he wrote them back on the reverse side of their note: "I am a reader and subscriber of *Am. Echo* (sic) for over 46 years. *Kącik* printed several dozen of my letters (sic). Each of them has been more or less corrected. I never had anything against it, and I even appreciated it. And I will appreciate when the editors do the same with this article." He further stated that he did not mean to stir up trouble, so if the editors deemed it necessary, they should feel free to "tone down my remarks in the article and include it in the *Kącik Dla Wszystkich.*"[66]

Not everybody, however, was happy with the editorial changes and some readers challenged the editors in their letters to *Ameryka-Echo.* A reader from Minneapolis protested cuts and changes introduced in his submission despite his efforts to respect the policy statement: "The Esteemed Editor of our *Kącik*—like an unconscientious surgeon— operated on it [the submission] so mercilessly, that almost all that was the healthiest and what I cared about the most—he cut out, leaving only a skeleton, which makes no sense."[67] A different reader sternly warned against too much of editorial eagerness: "Just don't use your scissors."[68]

Readers responded with equal protest and emotion to the additions that the editors introduced to their texts. Two readers sent letters objecting to the explanatory sentence, which the editors injected into the correspondence about the Jehovah Witnesses, and demanded its retraction, as inaccurate.[69] An upset reader from Toronto, after his letter had appeared in the "Corner," later wrote to the editors: "I agree that the editors have the right to cross out certain words or even full sentences in an article accepted for publication, but it is absolutely unlawful for the editors to add some words, which disfigure and change the sense [of the text] and the author's [original] thought." The reader was so appalled by this incident that he vowed to write for *Ameryka-Echo* no more in order to avoid seeing his remarks "castrated from thoughts and ideas."[70]

The existing records seem to indicate that the editors of the "Corner" hardly ever communicated directly about editorial issues and decisions with the authors of submissions. They sent out short notifications about rejection of submissions, which sometimes suggested ways of improvement: toned down rhetoric, friendlier style, or a more constructive rather than critical approach.[71] Although occasionally readers did complain about the lack of communication, the majority apparently accepted this practice.[72] The records rarely allow us a closer look into the inner world of the editors than in the case of correspondence from a frequent "Corner" writer from Minneapolis, Minnesota. Correspondence from him had a handwritten note attached, asking whether his letter merited a response and if contact with him should be terminated. Another note, typed, and signed with initials S.J., stated: "I think it best to leave his letters as usual without answer. As far as contact—I think about "status quo"—in time he will send correspondence, which either will go or not, depending on the contents." In a different note enclosed with two more letters from the same reader, S.J. explained his decision to reject them, as they contained too many accusations and complaints and would require too much "cleaning up."[73]

After *Ameryka-Echo* had been bought out by a group of postwar exiles in 1956, some of the editorial policies changed. The new management aspired to raise the intellectual level of the weekly and abandoned the traditionally anticlerical and anti-Roman Catholic orientation of the newspaper.[74] Files marked with "AA" (*ad acta*) grew in size, gathering letters rejected by the editors.[75] There were among them letters that according to the new higher standards were not suitable for the "Corner" (although reading them one is under a distinct impression that they would have been "improved" and published in the earlier decades), as well as letters openly criticizing a changing profile of *Ameryka-Echo* and a new direction and character of the "Corner."

The existence of the original letters provides a unique opportunity to explore the scope and content of editorial intervention in the correspondence published in the "Corner" between 1944 and 1958. The analysis of the letters might lead one to the conclusion that most of the submissions for the "Corner" were barely touched by the editor's pen. In the preserved "Editorial Materials" portion of the archival collection I found originals of the letters simply stapled to the bundle of materials marked for the "Corner." Some of them had few handwritten (more rarely typed) editorial marks right on them. Only those letters which were too hard to read because of the writer's poor handwriting were re-typed.

However, a closer comparison between other portions of the collection containing original letters and the correspondence that was actually published in the "Corner" suggests that sometimes significant changes were made without leaving any mark on the original submission. Editorial intervention was the most radical during World War II, when even the heading of the "Corner" clearly indicated a rationale for the more invasive editorial policy. When after Marie Paryski-Rosiński's death in 1945, her husband, Dr. Victor Rosiński became an editor-in-chief, the editorial intervention dramatically decreased, although it still responded to the political climate of the Cold War. In the 1950s, this trend continued and the editors more often saw fit to publicly justify their intervention. For example in 1953, a letter from Montreal, Canada, which took sides in Polish government-in-exile's political party squabbles, had those fragments crossed out and an attached note explained: "From the Editors: For the good of the Polish Cause (*Sprawa Polska*) and the need to unite rather than divide the [Polish] society into groups and parties . . . the Editors regarded as necessary to remove some of the remarks made by the author of this correspondence."[76]

In general, in addition to the exclusion of the bowing section and the introduction of the submission section, the editors improved grammatical errors, corrected spelling, divided text into paragraphs, added capital letters, punctuation, and added or changed titles. They also followed the requests to change names and/or disguise identity of the authors. But they also intervened in the original text in several other ways.

The editors either removed or toned down personal attacks in more aggressive polemics and deleted generally offensive terms. For example, in a letter from Rhode Island about some Polonia celebration those fragments that derided a community activist whom the author called a Communist were removed.[77] Similarly, in an aggressive polemical response to a published letter of another "Corner" writer the editors cut out direct personal attacks ridiculing the author, his knowledge, and sources.[78] As a rule, the editors also cut out lengthy anecdotal evidence, some sweeping generalizations, as well as more transparent efforts at self-promotion. For example, a letter from a Polish American from Florida, which praised Florida's landscape, climate and possibilities of social life for retirees, originally included also an address of an agency that could offer advice to those interested in the prices of the real estate and help them in their transactions. That not-so-veiled effort at advertising was deleted.[79]

The editors excluded more vicious attacks against other ethnic groups, especially Jews and Ukrainians. Some letters to the "Corner" were representative of ethnic hostility, stemming from experiences and attitudes learned in the Old Country, and expressed by *Ameryka-Echo*'s readers of different ethnic and religious backgrounds. While the editors allowed a remarkably open debate, particularly if we accept today's standards for what we consider offensive, they did reject the most virulent cases of prejudice.[80]

Since religion and church were particularly popular topics of discussion, the "Corner" writers pursued criticism of both Roman Catholicism and, to a lesser degree, the Polish National Catholic Church (PNCC), an independent church that broke away from the Roman Catholic structure in 1904. Some degree of such criticism was admissible, but the editors, following Paryski's and Łukaszkiewicz's lead, steered away from too much praise for the Roman Catholic Church and too harsh a view of the PNCC. When in the late 1950s, *Ameryka-Echo*'s traditional anticlericalism and a supportive attitude toward the PNCC were abandoned by new editors who courted newer Polish immigrants, in their majority loyal to the Roman Catholic Church, the editors received numerous letters from readers commenting on the change. One of them read: "Your newspaper is sliding promptly to the right . . . Criticism of all obscurantism has disappeared, and specifically of the clergy, who more and more is running the show . . ."[81]

The role of the ethnic press as a tool of assimilation is by now well documented. *Ameryka-Echo*, especially in the times of World War II and the Cold War, played the same role, eagerly stressing anti-Communist attitudes within the Polish-American community, loyalty to American ideals as well as policies, and bringing Polonia closer to the cultural and political mainstream. For example, the editors of *Ameryka-Echo* disallowed any criticism of western style democracy, the American Constitution, or, in the 1940s, President Roosevelt. When a Polish immigrant to Canada described how after weather related crop failures his farm was foreclosed on and in 1938 he found himself without means to support his wife and nine children, he blamed the Canadian government for lack of concern. "And this is supposed to be democracy, about which one reads so much in all newspapers," he stormed. "This is tyranny, despotism, and robbery, same under the Prussian, under the English, and under the Mongols."[82] The sentence was promptly crossed out and did not appear in print. Another example comes from a letter on pensions for the elderly, originally entitled "Mr. President Truman and In-Justice," whose first two sentences were "Constitution tells us that people govern this country. This is only on paper and in theory, but not in practice." In the "Corner" the letter's title was: "For Justice for the Elderly," and the first two sentences did not appear at all.[83] The editors purged also any remarks that could put Communism or Soviet Russia in a better light. For example, a letter, which discussed the Marshall Plan and the economy argued that in order to counteract Soviet influence, western democracies should give their societies more than the Soviets gave theirs, which included free education, health care, and common access to national culture. The fragment about positive achievements of the Soviets was cut out in its entirety.[84]

On the other hand, the editors of the 1940s used the pages of the "Corner" to spread a pro-American message, even if it was done through substantial change and manipulation of the readers' original texts, including insertion of additional paragraphs. It seems that the practice was limited to the war years and the immediate post war period and did not carry over to the late 1940s or the 1950s. For example, in 1945, a reader from Pennsylvania sent in a letter describing his love of books and learning, which he could not pursue because of life of poverty he lived in America. He concluded his letter by writing with bitterness: "I wonder about and am jealous of those who are so well educated and have high positions, but for poor people they have no goodness or heart or love, and only look to exploit and make them docile and never make them equal or [like] brothers. [T]hat is how it was in the past, is now and I think will be in the future. . . ."[85] The published version paraphrased the above remark, emphasizing that "An uneducated person must be always dependent on others and must be docile towards them and can't ever be equal or like brothers to the people in high positions," and added the following three sentences: "It is because they are separated by the world of education, to which a worker failed to gain access for himself. But I think it always has to be this way, because one person's mind is unequal to another's. In a free country, such as the United States everybody, however, can climb upwards, can get education and everybody receives equal support for education—a poor or a rich person alike."[86] The editors took a similar opportunity to champion the cause of Poland. For example, a reader's original sentence stating that public opinion demands that "America speaks with a different voice, clearer and more confident . . . about the politics of united nations struggling for a better future and freedom," was "improved" to read as follows: "Nowadays not only American Poles, but the entire American nation expect and await that the United States government speaks clearly and openly on the issue of Poland as well as entire Europe. The whole world waits now for this voice of American government."[87]

As the reader quoted at the beginning of this essay implied, all the writers to the "Corner for Everybody" probably do deserve a comfortable place in Heaven for their courage, curiosity, passion, and honesty. The continuous existence and popularity of the letters to the editor section in *Ameryka-Echo* for five decades created an unprecedented community of readers and reader-writers, who established strong relationships with each other and the editors of the "Corner." Their correspondence highlights creativity in bending and re-inventing the rules of formal letter writing practices to suit the special needs of their communication, often negotiating and blending elements of public and private spheres. In the case of the original letters to the "Corner," the metaphorical Bermuda Triangle of letters to the editor ever so slightly parts the waters and allows us to catch a rare glimpse of the intricacies of the editorial decision making process and their impact on the relationship between ethnic writers and editors of *Ameryka-Echo*.

Notes

1. *Ameryka-Echo*, July 19, 1953, p. 14. All translations by the author.
2. See for example Carl Wittke, *The German-Language Press in America* (University of Kentucky Press, 1957), pp. 217–234; Doris Meyer, *Speaking for Themselves: Neomexicano Cultural Identity and the Spanish-Language Press, 1880–1920*

(Albuquerque: University of New Mexico Press, 1996); John W. Briggs, *An Italian Passage: Immigrants to Three American Cities, 1890–1930* (New Haven: Yale University Press, 1978), pp. 177–187; Sally M. Miller, ed., *The Ethnic Press in the United States: A Historical Analysis and Handbook* (New York: Greenwood Press, 1987); Ruth Seifert, "Women's Pages in the German-American Radical Press, 1900–1914: The Debate on Socialism, Emancipation, and the Suffrage," in *The German-American Radical Press: The Shaping of a Left Political Culture, 1850–1940*, ed. Elliott Shore, Ken Fones-Wolf, James P. Danky (Urbana: University of Illinois Press, 1992), pp. 122–143. Perhaps the longest lasting section of letters to the editor existed in the *Forward*, a Yiddish daily newspaper, established in New York in 1897. Isaac Metzker, ed., *A Bintel Brief: Sixty Years of Letters from Lower East Side to the Jewish Daily Forward* (New York: Schocken Books, 1990); Isaac Metzker, ed., *A Bintel Brief, Volume II: Letters to the Jewish Daily Forward, 1950–1980* (New York: Viking Press, 1981).
3. "Antoni A. Paryski," *Ameryka-Echo*, December 27, 1902, p. 9; "Czterdzieści Lat Pracy Oświatowej Antoniego A. Paryskiego, Wydawcy i Naczelnego Redaktora "Ameryki-Echa," *Ameryka-Echo*, March 11, 1928, pp.11–12; Czesław Łukaszkiewicz, *Nauczyciel wychodźtwa: Antoni A. Paryski (1865–1935)* (Paryski Publishing Company: Toledo, n.d.); Wiktor Rosiński, *Antoni A. Paryski: życie, prace i czyny, 1865–1935* (Toledo: *Ameryka-Echo*, [1945]); David Gwidon Chełmiński, "From *Gwiazda* to the *Ameryka-Echo*: Antoni Alfred Panek/"Paryski" and His Publications," *Polish Heritage* 35, no. 1 (Spring 1984): 4–5.
4. A.J. Kuzniewski, "The Polish-American Press," in Miller, *Ethnic Press*, 285–286; Wacław Kruszka, *A History of the Poles in America to 1908*, Part I, trans. Krystyna Jankowski, ed. James S. Pula (Washington, DC: Catholic University of America Press, 1993), p. 83; Stanisław Osada, *Prasa i Publicystyka Polska w Ameryce* (Pittsburgh, PA: "Pittsurczanin," 1930), pp. 54–55; Karol Wachtl, *Polonja w Ameryce: Dzieje i Dorobek* (Philadelphia: Polish Star Publication, 1944), p. 227; Chełmiński, "From *Gwiazda*," pp. 4–5.
5. Kuzniewski, "The Polish-America Press," p. 279; Rosiński, *Antoni A. Paryski*, pp. 28–31.
6. Eugene Obidinski, "The Polish American Press: Survival through Adaptation," *Polish American Studies* 34, no. 2 (1977): 39. Robert E. Park, who in 1922 compounded statistics of foreign press titles for the period 1884–1920, noted 89 titles of Polish press in existence for the period 1884–1892; 229 titles for 1893–1900; 459 for 1901–1910; and 676 for the decade of 1911–1920. In the overall statistics of the foreign language press titles for 1920, Poles, according to him, were in the fifth place, following Germans, a combined Spanish and Portuguese speaking group, a combined Scandinavian group, and Italians. Robert E. Park, *The Immigrant Press and Its Control* (Westport, CT: Greenwood Press, 1970), Table XVIII, 319; Table XVI, 313.
7. Joseph A. Wytrwal, *America's Polish Heritage: A Social History of the Poles in America* (Detroit: Endurance Press, 1961), p. 328; *Ayer's Directory* for the years 1920–1929.
8. Kuzniewski, "The Polish-American Press," p. 281; Obidinski, "The Polish American Press," p. 39.
9. Łukaszkiewicz, *Nauczyciel*, pp. 59–61.
10. *Ayer's Directory* for the years 1931–1940. *Ameryka-Echo*'s postal subscription records for the years 1932–1942 give lower numbers: 75,562 copies for 1932; 20,780 for 1933; 51,734 for each year between 1934 and 1937; 14,147 for 1938; 15,511 for 1939; 16,434 for 1940; 16,592 for 1941; 15,434 for 1942. The numbers showed the number of copies to be mailed to subscribers outside the county of publication. Immigration History Research Center (IHRC) 117, Box 27, F. 2.
11. Bernard Pacyniak, "An Historical Outline of the Polish Press in America," in *Poles in America: Bicentennial Essays*, ed. Frank Mocha (Stevens Point, WI: Worzalla

Publishing, 1978), p. 525; Kuzniewski, "The Polish-American Press," 281; Obidinski, "The Polish American Press," pp. 46–47.

12. Marian Wojciechowski, phone interviews, March 22, 23, 24, 2004. In the 1940s circulation of *Ameryka-Echo* remained between 20,000 and 22,000, but by 1956 it dropped to 16,263, beginning a steady downright trend for the rest of the decade. *Ayer's Directory* for the years 1941–1956.

13. Piorunkiewicz's first name was never given and his last name was likely a pseudonym; *piorun* in Polish means thunderbolt.

14. In mainstream American journalism readers' sections became popularized through the concept of "service journalism," developed and promoted by James Keely, the managing editor and editor of Chicago's *Tribune* between 1898 and 1914, and editor of the *Herald* since 1914. David Paul Nord, "Reading the Newspaper: Strategies and Politics of Reader Response, Chicago, 1912–1917," *Journal of Communication* 45, no. 3 (Summer 1995): 66–93.

15. In 1889, *Ameryka* appealed to the readers to send in news about Poles in Polish communities around the United States. Articles on "scholarly matters, stimulating people for education" were also encouraged. Authors of both types of submissions were to be paid. "Who has a good thought to communicate publicly, let him write to *Ameryka*. No worker should be embarrassed of errors, since we have a sharp pen to cut out all bad things," the editors cheered on the readers. *Ameryka*, October 12, 1889, p. 2.

16. "Kto może pisać do gazety?" *Ameryka*, November 29, 1902, p. 1.

17. Ibid.

18. *Ameryka-Echo*, January 7, 1917, p. 15.

19. *Ameryka-Echo*, January 18, 1925, p. 12.

20. Beginning in 1934, the sentence about religious disputes was modified to read: "The editors of '*Ameryka-Echo*' allow each Reader to express himself freely." The heading was changed from February 18, 1934.

21. The statement appeared first on February 25, 1940, and ran for several weeks.

22. *Ameryka-Echo*, May 19, 1940, p. 19.

23. In 1953, the heading added a requirement to use only one side of the paper while typing and double space between the lines. *Ameryka-Echo*, January 25, 1953, p. 14. The heading was again revised a few months later and read: "Correspondence from the readers published in the "Corner" reflects their personal opinions and views. Editors of *Ameryka-Echo* allow every reader to express himself freely in the matters aiming at general good (*dobro ogólne*). Obviously, we do not allow tactless personal attacks and insults. We do not print accusations, rumors, and gossip." *Ameryka-Echo*, April 9, 1953, p. 14.

24. Blegen defined "America letters" as "letters written by immigrants in America to friends and relatives in the old world, primary sources of value for the history of emigration and immigration, human documents of interest for the social history of the nineteenth century." Theodore C. Blegen, *America Letters* (Oslo: I Kommisjon Hos Jacob Dybwad, 1928), p. 4. See also Theodore C. Blegen, *Norwegian Migration to America, 1825–1860* (Northfield, Minnesota: The Norwegian-American Historical Association, 1931); Theodore C. Blegen, ed., *Land of Their Choice: The Immigrants Write Home* (Minneapolis: University of Minnesota Press, 1955); George Stephenson, "When America Was the Land of Canaan," *Minnesota History* 10 (September 1929): 237–260; Walker D. Wyman, ed., *California Emigrant Letters* (New York: Bookman Associates, Publishers, 1952); Alan Conway, ed. *The Welsh in America: Letters from the Immigrants* (Minneapolis: University of Minnesota Press, 1959); H. Arnold Barton, ed., *Letters from the Promised Land: Swedes in America, 1840–1914* (Minneapolis: University of Minnesota Press, 1975). See also David A. Gerber, "The Immigrant Letter between Positivism and Populism: The Uses of

Immigrant Personal Correspondence in Twentieth-Century American Scholarship," *Journal of American Ethnic History* 16, no. 4 (Summer 1997): 4–34.

25. Charlotte Erickson, *Invisible Immigrants: The Adaptation of English and Scottish Immigrants in Nineteenth-Century America* (London: Leicester University Press, 1972), pp. 3–4.

26. Examples of such collections include: Frederick Hale, ed., *Danes in North America* (Seattle: University of Washington Press, 1984); Walter D. Kamphoefner, Wolfgang Helbich, and Ulrike Sommer, eds., *News from the Land of Freedom: German Immigrants Write Home*, trans. Susan Carter Vogel (Ithaca: Cornell University Press, 1988); Solveig Zempel, ed. and trans., *In Their Own Words: Letters from Norwegian Immigrants* (Minneapolis: University of Minnesota Press, 1991); Samuel L. Baily and Franco Ramella, eds., *One Family, Two Worlds: An Italian Family's Correspondence across the Atlantic, 1901–1922*, trans. John Lenaghan (New Brunswick: Rutgers University Press, 1988); David Fitzpatrick, *Oceans of Consolation: Personal Accounts of Irish Migration to Australia* (Ithaca: Cornell University Press, 1994); Herbert J. Brinks, ed., *Dutch American Voices: Letters from the United States, 1850–1930* (Ithaca: Cornell University Press, 1995); Wendy Cameron, Sheila Haines, and Mary McDougall Maude, eds., *English Immigrant Voices: Labourers' Letters from Upper Canada in the 1830s* (Montreal, Canada: McGill-Queen's University Press, 2000); Kerby A. Miller, Arnold Schrier, Bruce D. Boling, David N. Doyle, eds., *Irish Immigrants in the Land of Canaan: Letters and Memoirs from Colonial and Revolutionary America, 1675–1815* (New York: Oxford University Press, 2003).

27. David Fitzpatrick, *Oceans of Consolation: Personal Accounts of Irish Migration to Australia* (Ithaca: Cornell University Press, 1994), p. 26. See also Gerber, "The Immigrant Letter," p. 4.

28. Miller, *Irish Immigrants*, p. 9; William I. Thomas and Florian Znaniecki, *The Polish Peasant in Europe and America*, vol. 2 (New York: Dover Publications, 1958), pp. 303–305; David A.Gerber, "Epistolary Ethics: Personal Correspondence and the Culture of Emigration in the Nineteenth Century," *Journal of American Ethnic History* 19, no. 4 (Summer 2000): 10.

29. Thomas and Znaniecki, *The Polish Peasant in Europe and America*; Witold Kula, Nina Assorodobraj-Kula, Marcin Kula, eds., *Listy Emigrantów z Brazylii i Stanów Zjednoczonych, 1890–1891* (Warszawa: Ludowa Spół dzielnia Wydawnicza, 1973), and its American edition in translation, Josephine Wtulich, ed. and trans., *Writing Home: Immigrants in Brazil and the United States, 1890–1891* (East European Monographs, Boulder; New York: Columbia University Press, 1986).

30. David A. Gerber uses the term *vernacular publication* to denote "the acts of sharing the familiar letter through oral communication, which not only served to make the private letter public, but elevated it within the status of its own lifetime from a private writing to a document." Gerber, "Epistolary Ethics," pp. 12–13. See also Stephen Fender, *Sea Changes: British Emigration and American Literature* (Cambridge, England: Cambridge University Press, 1992). Gerber also notices that the specific request for privacy in immigrant letters was designed to ensure that the details of correspondence remain confidential. Gerber, "Epistolary Ethics," pp. 12–14. Editors of Polish immigrant letters from the last decade of the nineteenth century also point to the custom of collective reading (and sometimes writing) of letters, particularly common among illiterate peasants. Their analysis of letters demonstrates that private communication has often been affected by the presence of a hired writer/ reader of letters, the so-called *pisennik*, or a literate person. Kula, *Listy*, pp. 30–33.

31. Danuta Piątkowska, ed., *Korespondencja z Ameryki w prasie polskiej na Śląsku (1868–1900)*, with an introduction by Andrzej Brożek (Wrocław: Zakład

Narodowy Imienia Ossolińskich, Wydawnictwo Polskiej Akademii Nauk, 1980); Krzysztof Groniowski, "Korespondenci 'Przyjaciela Ludu' w Stanach Zjednoczonych (1896–1932), *Przegląd Polonijny* 13, no. 2 (1987): 5–21. Thomas and Znaniecki quote from close to two hundred letters, which were published in the Polish press in Poland, *The Polish Peasant*, vol. 2, Part II: "Disorganization and Reorganization in Poland."

32. Thomas and Znaniecki, *The Polish Peasant*, vol. I, pp. 303–307. The importance of the bowing section has been recently reiterated by other scholars; see Fitzpatrick, *Oceans of Consolation*, pp. 485–495; Gerber, "The Immigrant Letter," p. 20.

33. For example A. Kowalewski, Hollywood, California, January 31, 1951, Immigration History Research Center (IHRC), 117, Box 430, F. 8; Leona Karaś New Britain, Connecticut, January 18, 1955, B. 433, F. 11. Examples of all other letters also come from the same collection, IHRC 117.

34. Stanisł aw Rapciak, Chicago, Illinois, December 23, 1950, B. 430, F. 8.

35. Fr. Liguda, Chicopee, Massachussetts, December 29, 1947, B. 427, F. 1.

36. Jan Borkowski, Summit Hill, Pennsylvania, June 1954, B. 433, F. 4.

37. Marya Burda Krzyżowa, Carnegie, Pennsylvania, January 25, 1948, B. 427, F. 3.

38. Stanisł aw Smietana, New Bedford, Massachussetts, May 20, 1956 B. 435, F. 1.

39. See for example Michael Piatkowski, Philadelphia, Pennsylvania, December 17, 1947, B. 427, F. 1; Karol Wojciechowski, Madison, Wisconsin, January 4, 1949, B. 428, F. 1.

40. Steve Setlak, February 15, 1948, B. 427, F. 3.

41. J.A. Wolniewicz, E. Springfield, Massachussetts, 1945, B. 422, F. 4.

42. Signature illegible, Mannville, Alberta, Canada, December 23, 1947 B. 427, F. 1.

43. Teofil Bastecki, Natrona, Pennsylvania, August 8, 1959, B. 419, F. 5.

44. Julian Bierdoń, Bulford [?], May 8, 1956, B. 435, F. 1.

45. Józef M. Koper, Mechanicville, New York, May 22, 1954, B. 433, F. 4.

46. Julian Kruczek, Newark, New Jersey, May 10, 1956, B. 435, F. 1; Joseph Gortych, Syracuse, New York, [probably 1951], B. 431, F. 3; A. Kowalewski, North Hollywood, California, January 31, 1951.

47. See for example Julian Kruczek, Newark, New Jersey, May 10, 1956, B. 435, F. 1.

48. Jan Mastalerz, New Bedford, Massachussetts, April 2, 1950, B. 429, F. 8.

49. Julian Biedroń, Bulford [?], May 8, 1956, B. 435, F. 1.

50. F. Plucinski, Madison, Wisconsin, March 14, 1946, B. 422, F. 1.

51. Roman Fedorczuk, June 3, 1951, B. 431, F. 3.

52. Roman Fedorczuk, Coatesville, August 5, 1956, B. 435, F. 2.

53. John Bajer, Canada, February 8, 1948, B. 427, F. 3.

54. For example W. Gajewski, May 12, 1948, B. 427, F. 10; Stanisł aw J. Rapciak, Chicago, Illinois, December 23, 1950.

55. For example Apolonia Jamróz, Wisconsin, December 3, 1954, B. 432, F. 8; W. Kozakiewicz, Minneapolis, Minnesota, October 29, 1953, B. 432, F. 5.

56. Weronika Wierzgacz, Chicago, Illinois, December 22, 1944, B. 421, F. 3.

57. Jan Babiarz, Toronto, Canada, February 2, 1948, B. 427, F. 3.

58. I. Jasionowski, December 12, 1948, B. 427, F. 13.

59. Signature ineligible, Canada, May 20, 1951, B. 431, F. 3; Signature ineligible, New Britain, Connecticut, January 20, 1947, B. 352, F. 4.

60. B. 401, F. 1, includes correspondence from a Ukrainian reader who demanded to know who was hiding under the initials A.T., since, as the reader believed, A.T.'s letters were defaming the Ukrainian minority in prewar Poland. The editors attached a typed response, which reaffirmed an author's choice not to reveal his name in public. Zenon Stefaniw, April 28, 1957.

61. Joseph M. Romanowski, New York Mills, New York, February 1941, B. 438, F. 3.

62. Józef Stanczak, February 13, 1949, B. 428, F. 1.

63. Roman Fedorczuk, Coatesville, August 5, 1956, B. 435, F. 2.
64. Alfreda Borucka, Mokena(?), Illinois, December 12, 1948, B. 428, F. 1.
65. Julian Kruczek, Newark, New Jersey, May 10, 1956, B. 435, F. 1.
66. St. Kowalewski, 1957, B. 436, F. 2.
67. W. Kozakiewicz, Minneapolis, Minnesota, January 23, 1953, B. 431, F. 7. This author, whose correspondence appeared in the "Corner" frequently, wrote also long letters to the editors protesting any changes, and accusing the editors of "hiding the light" of truth from the readers. See for example W. Kozakiewicz, Minneapolis, Minnesota, October 29, 1953, B. 432, F. 5.
68. Rudolf Krawiec, May 12, 1957, B. 401, F. 2.
69. Stanisł aw J. Rapciak, Chicago, Illinois, January 18, 1951, B. 430, F. 8; A. Kowalewski, North Hollywood, California, January 31, 1951, B. 430, F. 8.
70. M. Górczewski, Toronto, Canada, November 5, 1956, B. 435, F. 1.
71. See, for example, a note with no addressee or date in B. 436, F. 4; a note to St. Kowalewski, January 8, 1957, B. 436, F. 2.
72. For an example of complaint see Stanisław Rapciak, Chicago, Illinois, May 25, 1951, B. 431, F. 3.
73. B. 436, F. 2. The second note is dated January 8, 1957.
74. Wojciechowski, phone interview.
75. See for example B. 446, F. 7 (letters from 1954–57); B. 435, F. 9; B. 436, F. 1(most letters dated 1957).
76. A. Pytlak, Montreal, Canada, [1953], B. 386, F. 2.
77. Michał (last name illegible), Providence, Rhode Island, December 17, 1947, B. 427, F. 1.
78. W. Doleżuchowicz, Baldwinsville, New York, May 12, 1957, B. 401, F. 2.
79. Antoni Bentley, May 1, 1955, B. 392, F. 4.
80. For example, anti-Semitic remarks were deleted from the letter from Wł adysł aw Furmański, Chicago, Illinois, January 4, 1948, B. 427, F. 1.
81. A. Wardzał a, Easthampton, Massachussetts, January 10, 1957, B. 436, F. 1. The same box contains more letters on this topic.
82. Signature illegible, Mannville, Alberta, Canada, December 23, 1947, B. 427, F. 1.
83. Wł adysł aw Furmański, Chicago, Illinois, no date, B. 424, F. 1. The letter appeared in Kącik on April 7, 1946, p. 14.
84. W. Gajewski, May 12, 1948, B. 427, F. 13.
85. Michał Skibicki, McKeesport, Pennsylvania, May 12, 1945, B. 422, F. 5.
86. Michał Skibicki, McKeesport, Pennsylvania, "Ze Wspomnień Starego Czytelnika," Ameryka-Echo, July 8, 1945, p.14.
87. W.J. Trzuski, Lonsdale, Rhode Island, December 27, 1944, B. 421, F. 3; Czytelnik, Rhode Island, "Budzi się Opinia Narodu," Ameryka-Echo, January 14, 1945, p. 14.

Part V

Negotiations of Identity

11

Negotiating Space, Time, and Identity: The Hutton-Pellett Letters and a British Child's Wartime Evacuation to Canada

Helen Brown

Seven-year-old John Hutton was an unlikely emigrant who was unexpectedly evacuated to Canada in 1940. He traveled under the British government's Children's Overseas Reception Board Scheme (CORB) that sent approximately 1,500 children to Canada in the summer of 1940. John's placement with the Pellett family in May 1941 led to an extensive and richly detailed correspondence. Of the three main correspondents, neither Kathleen Pellett nor H.F. (Fred) Hutton had any extensive pre-war experience of letter-writing and John Hutton, a young boy, was just learning to write.[1] Yet their letters are emotionally engaging and tell a compelling story. They draw modern readers back into the heart of wartime and illuminate the multiple ways the home fronts in Canada and Britain were woven into the war effort.[2] But this was not why they came to be written. Rather, these were family letters and it is with that aspect of them that this paper is primarily concerned. In the Second World War these letters negotiated space, time, and identity for the Hutton and Pellett families and they continue to do so now for a broader audience in ever more complex ways.

The Huttons, the Pelletts, and CORB

With any family letters it makes sense to begin by situating them in their historical and familial contexts. To provide some opportunity for children of parents without private means or connections to be evacuated from Britain, the British War Cabinet approved CORB on June 17, 1940.[3] Geoffrey Bilson argues that "the coincidence of the announcement of CORB with the fall of France produced a response no one had anticipated."[4] Within a few weeks over 200,000 applications had been received.[5] The first ship carrying CORB evacuees left England July 21, 1940 and the last just two months later.[6] CORB was only a small part of massive wartime evacuations of British children, most of which removed children from London to the British countryside.[7] The total number of children and families involved in the in-Britain evacuations was staggering both in terms of physical logistics and emotional ramifications.[8] In his popular history of the evacuation, Mike Brown characterizes it as "an event unlike any other in modern history. A large part of a generation [would be] separated from their families during a part of their formative years."[9] The space and time of that separation would be greatly exacerbated for the children who were sent overseas.

Estimates of the numbers of British children evacuated to overseas destinations vary from source to source. Some were moved on the basis of private family arrangements and some with their schools.[10] Others emigrated as part of privately run programs by groups such as the University of Toronto Women's War Service Committee and the American Committee for the Evacuation of Children.[11] CORB, however, was the sole government program for overseas evacuation. Canadian historian Jeffrey A. Keshen notes that 5,954 British children came to Canada during the war, including 1,532 who were part of the CORB scheme.[12] John Hutton was one of them.

John's situation as a child was a complicated one. He was born in 1933 and, as Fred Hutton explained to Kathleen Pellett, "His early life was disturbed on more than one occasion. When two years old he broke his thigh and spent some months in hospital. The following year he had another long spell away from home when he contracted typhoid."[13] In November 1938, John's mother, Grace Hutton, "died of septicemia . . . following on the death of [his] infant sister Mary at birth."[14] His paternal grandmother, who then helped his father to care for John, died in July 1940. John's father, Fred Hutton, a department manager for Kent Blaxill Limited of Colchester, a builders' merchants firm, was unsure whether or when he would be called up for active duty. By the spring of 1940 there was widespread concern that if the Germans attacked, England's east coast would be on the invasion route.[15] As Mike Brown argues, "With the fall of France, the south and east coasts became potential invasion areas and so were quickly evacuated."[16]

It was in these circumstances that Fred Hutton applied to CORB for assistance.[17] John was accepted for the program and sent to Canada where his initial placement with the Bourne family in Toronto lasted less than a year as Mr. Bourne was called up and Mrs. Bourne and their daughter Betty Ann moved away to live with relatives.[18] From the Bournes, he was moved in May 1941 to the Pellett family.[19] Thirty-one year old Kathleen Pellett was a homemaker and her 36-year old husband William (Bill) Pellett, a mechanical engineer, was assistant superintendent at Link Belt manufacturing in Toronto.[20] William and Kathleen had two young children, Bobbie, almost six, and Doris who was four (figure 11.1).[21] John stayed in his new home until 1945 and for four long years the Huttons and the Pelletts collaborated to make a success of a situation none of them could have imagined.[22] The letters they exchanged were at the heart of their joint endeavor.

Provenance of the Letters

The provenance of the Hutton-Pellett letters requires clarification, but opens up new interpretive opportunities. Fred Hutton typed his letters and in May 1943 he explained why:

> Letter Number 100! There should be some quality about this letter to distinguish it from its predecessors but the Muses have not granted me any inspiration at the moment and this letter must follow the lines of the others. I have always thought that personal messages should be in one's own hand-writing and my earlier Canadian letters were written with a pen but I wanted to keep copies and the process of keeping a precis of each proved too waste-ful of time. Glancing back I find that nearly all the letters, if not all, sent to Agincourt have been typewritten. They make interesting reading now and may gain something in the years to come. I have never aspired to writing a book but circumstances have compelled me to perform something approaching such a task the professional writer would need to write more quickly than I if he was to earn his bread and butter.[23]

Fred Hutton's decision to type his letters so that he could keep carbons was fortuitous. He also kept the letters he received from Kathleen, John, Bobbie, and Doris.[24] From 1943, if not earlier, he appears to have sensed the potential of the letters for allowing future readers to bridge barriers of space and time to access the experience of the two families in wartime.[25]

In the mid-1970s, Fred Hutton retyped the letters as a manuscript for a book he entitled *Ere Their Story Die*. John, then in his forties, wrote a foreword.[26] Fred gave copies of this manuscript to John, Kathleen, and the Essex County Record Office in England. He was unsuccessful, though, in his efforts to find a publisher and both the manuscript and letters lay dormant for some time. There is a multifaceted relationship between the

Figure 11.1 Photograph of John Hutton with Doris and Bobbie Pellett. John Hutton, a wartime evacuee from England, was welcomed into the Canadian family of Kathleen and William Pellett and lived with them from 1941 to 1945. Here Doris Pellett (7), Bobbie Pellett (9), and John Hutton (11) are visiting the farm garden of friends of the Carrs, the Pellett children's maternal grandparents: May 14, 1944, Oakridges, Ontario.

Credit: John Hutton.

original letters and Fred Hutton's 1970s manuscript. For one thing, the manuscript aids historians in several ways. It includes letters that were sent and received, but for some reason are missing from the collection of originals. An example is Fred's letter 100 cited above.[27] Also, in some instances the photocopies I used of the carbon copies of Fred's letters are extremely difficult to read and having the 1970s manuscript for comparison actually makes it possible to decipher these letters.

On the other hand, there are some aspects of Fred Hutton's manuscript that require caution on the part of modern readers. For example, *Ere Their Story Die* includes letters that were lost in transit and never received. More importantly, the edited manuscript is just that—an edited version of the originals. Comparisons show that the editing was extensive. For example, Fred deleted five paragraphs from Kathleen's letter of May 20, 1943. In one of the deleted paragraphs, she had written in very critical terms of the Agincourt school. "[John's] teacher is absolutely hopeless and I just feel sick over it. The trustees have been told by many parents but still they keep her on and I guess there is nothing we can do until we can get new trustees and any man who is capable or qualified in the community is either away in the army or working long hours on defense work so it seems to be a hopeless mess just now."[28] In the four other deleted paragraphs, Kathleen said she thought things at school would get better, described John's bout of mumps, and talked of finishing a dress she was making for her mother. While the sheer volume of the letters meant that some kind of distillation was necessary, it is impossible to know for certain why Fred Hutton left out particular paragraphs.[29] In this case he may have wanted to avoid any public criticism of the Canadian school system. For those interested in family life in wartime, though, that information is significant as are details of daily life such as mumps and dressmaking.

Also missing from the edited version of the letters are the many drawings that are part of the original letters. The children constantly used pictures to communicate with Fred Hutton. This was particularly important in cases where he might not know what something looked like. The British did not eat corn on the cob so John carefully drew three pictures of himself picking the corn, stripping the corn, and eating the corn (figure 11.2).[30] He used drawings so that his father could understand baseball and also so he could visualize the scene when John and Bobbie were playing and a fire engine raced past to put out a near-by brush fire.[31] John continued to include drawings in his letters throughout the time he was in Canada although they became smaller and carried less of the message relative to the text.[32] When Doris finally got her chance to write to "John's daddy," Kathleen added a note: "Doris has been so anxious to write to you that at last I've consented to send her letter. Of course it is copied but she told me what she

Figure 11.2 John Hutton Drawing: Eating Corn-on-the-Cob. John Hutton and Bobbie and Doris Pellett used drawings in their letters to John's father, H.F. (Fred) Hutton, to communicate what they could not say with words. John, 8 years old, drew these pictures to tell his father about eating corn on the cob, one of the many new and exciting experiences he had in Canada: John Hutton to H.F. Hutton, August 12, 1941.

Credit: The Canadian Letters and Images Project.

wanted to say. She has drawn a picture of her shoes, her bed, dolls bed, herself dressing and the boys on Halloween."[33] A few months later Kathleen added a postscript to one of her letters saying, "I have to enclose this little bit from Doris. She is standing right beside me to make sure I put it in. She draws you a picture every time I write a letter but I generally manage not to put it in and she has found me out."[34] Four-year-old Doris made sure that Fred Hutton knew what her possessions, activities, and siblings looked like. Drawing pictures served a double function: images made things clear and they communicated at a level of complexity the children could not achieve with words.

Ere Their Story Die differs significantly from the letters written in the 1940s. Fred Hutton's editing was not simply limited to deletions. He also revised and rewrote many of the original letters to greater or lesser degrees. Therefore, the original letters and *Ere Their Story Die* each contain things missing from the other. The 1970s manuscript version is important in terms of its interplay with the original letters and is valuable in its own right. Through the editing process Fred Hutton was, in effect, renegotiating space and time with the perspective of hindsight, at a different stage in his own life, and in the context of a later era. In doing so he constructed both opportunities and limitations for new readers.

The story of the provenance of the letters did not end when they were written in the 1940s or when *Ere Their Story Die* was compiled in the 1970s. Recently, Doris (Pellett) Stephens retyped Fred Hutton's 1970 manuscript on a word processor, bringing the letters into the computer age. Then in 2001, the families generously offered a copy of this voluminous collection to the Canadian Letters and Images Project, a digitalized archive of war letters created and directed by historian Stephen Davies.[35] As a result, 60 years after the correspondence began the letters were on the move again. This time they traveled west from Warsaw, Ontario, and Henley-on-Thames in England to Malaspina University College in Nanaimo, British Columbia. Because of my interest in the history of childhood, Stephen Davies suggested I read them and that led to a paper at the "Reading the Emigrant Letter Conference" in Ottawa in August 2003.[36] Doris Stephens and her daughter, Linda Millar, attended the session, John Hutton and Robert (Bob) Pellett read the paper, and all of them were able to comment on it. Letters, in this sense, are living organisms that can take on new lives. As this happens more stories attach to them and they reach new audiences. The Hutton-Pellett letters, and readings of them, continue to travel and to negotiate space and time in ever more complex ways. In the process they acquire new meanings and are transmitted in new forms.

The evolution of letters' meaning and the importance of their material nature have been subjects of interest to conservator Ala Rekrut of the

Archives of Manitoba. Discussing a letter from Louis Riel to his wife Marguerite, she notes that "The personal communication . . . became a family treasure, then a commodity—we know it sold through auction at least twice. It later became a cultural and political symbol for the Métis community and its 'repatriation' became a priority for the Government of Manitoba, whereupon the Archives used it as a publicity tool . . . . The meaning of this item shifts and changes because of the mainly intangible creative acts of its custodians, communicating their messages without changing a word of Riel's text."[37] Riel, of course, is a unique and important historical figure because of his role in the 1870 and 1885 uprisings in western Canada. Nevertheless the insight that letters have profoundly shifting meanings and contexts over time is equally applicable to those written by ordinary individuals. Letters have a provenance and exploring it—not just taking it for granted—opens doors to a deeper understanding of the ongoing life of historical correspondence. In the case of the Hutton-Pellett letters, an examination of their complex provenance reveals that the letters have assumed multiple forms and that their function of negotiating the space and time of wartime lives continues to the present day.

The Nature of the Letters

This section of the paper turns to a consideration of four elements that characterize the Hutton-Pellett letters. These include the fact that the adults involved did not know one another, the three-sided nature of the correspondence, the complexity of establishing a chronology and sequence for the letters, and the relationship of the letters to other forms of communication between the two families. The section concludes with an examination of the historical significance of the letters.

An important aspect of the Hutton-Pellett letters is that Kathleen Pellett and Fred Hutton were complete strangers who were catapulted into the intimacies of a long distance cooperative parenting relationship. Through John they shared a common present, but they did not have a common past. Basic information about their families had to be shared in a concise and timely fashion. The implications of this for modern readers of the letters are considerable. It means that we, also strangers to the two families, are privy to information that would not normally have been detailed in letters between people who knew one another. The result is that the letters offer particularly rich and textured insights into the daily life of two families in wartime.

Another important aspect of the Hutton-Pellett letters is the three-sided nature of the correspondence. The collection includes two primary sets of letters, those between Kathleen Pellett and Fred Hutton, and those between

John and his father. However, at the outset Kathleen was very involved in the production of John's letters. She discussed his letters with him, often helped him decide what to write about, and regularly proofread for grammar and neatness. This resulted in an unusual level of observation, commentary, and introspection on her part. A typical interaction between Kathleen and John is evident in a letter she sent Fred in September 1941:

> John has written part of his letter to you but he is describing in his letter the arithmetic he is taking at school and there was one type of sum he was showing you that didn't seem to be quite correct so he is bringing his book home tomorrow so that we may look over it together and see just what the trouble is and then he will finish his letter off. He wants particularly to have this sum in the letter. To describe all his school work to you is quite a task for him at one time so I have suggested that he take one subject each week and tell you all about it and give you a sample of what work he is doing.[38]

The Hutton-Pellett letters thus involved a three-sided correspondence among John, Kathleen, and Fred. That this was so was partly a function of the fact that John was a young child and partly because Kathleen had an organic approach to schoolwork. She viewed John's letters as another opportunity for him to practice the skills he was learning at school. As John got older the process changed in some ways. In June 1943 Kathleen told Fred, "As [John] is now 10 years [old] I have given him full responsibility in writing you. I am not reading or correcting his letters . . . . I have done so much teaching and correcting this school year that we are both tired of it . . . ."[39] Kathleen was referring to the fact that she reviewed the children's schoolwork and homework with them every evening after supper. A month later she wrote again to Fred saying, "I didn't write you last week . . . but John sent [a letter] to you alone and also sent some snaps."[40] John's ability to use letters to negotiate the wartime separation from his father at first required adult assistance, but as John grew up and as his writing skills developed, Kathleen became less directly involved in supervising his letters.[41]

Issues of chronology are important to our understanding of this correspondence. The sequencing of the Hutton-Pellett letters is complicated. There was a lapse time of about a month and a half from first writing to the arrival of a reply. By the time the response to a letter was received several others would often have been written. This complicates any attempt to establish a chronology for the letters that accurately recaptures the way they were actually experienced. Not until Kathleen Pellett's seventh letter did she report getting her first letter from Fred Hutton.[42] He noted on her letters the date he received them and the date he replied. For example,

Kathleen's letter of May 13, 1941 arrived June 9 and he answered on June 11. That letter reached Agincourt shortly before June 28.[43] What might be expected to be the normal order of arrival was often disrupted and some letters never completed their journey. In July 1941 Kathleen wrote, "Well mail seems to be coming along a little more frequently thanks to the British Navy and Air Force I guess. We received your letter #3 a week later than we received #4 and #5. [Number] 3 was mailed on the 9th or 11th of June, I'm not sure which but I had noticed in our paper that all mail posted on these dates had been lost by enemy action so I guess the fishes must have brought your letter across. I guess letter #2 has gone to Davy Jones."[44] Fred Hutton replied saying, "Your letters arrive but the sequence gets muddled up and I learn of John's, or Bobbie's, or Doris's complete recovery long before the complaint has been diagnosed."[45] Historian Luisa Passerini found the same discussions in a wartime correspondence she examined. She argued that the constant listing of letters "indicate[s] the great importance attached to each letter, the symbolic value it had as an object."[46] She also concluded that when letters arrived in the wrong order it "required a readjustment of the internal scansion between the rhythms of life and those of letter-writing."[47] Certainly, the complications of sequence indicate some of the difficulties involved in negotiating time in the context of the war.

Two distinct sequencings of the Hutton-Pellett letters exist today. The original letters from Canada and Fred Hutton's carbon copies of his letters are in two groups each in chronological order. Reading the Canadian and British letters this way, as two separate collections, loosens the connection between the family in Agincourt and the family in Colchester as their lives appear to unfold quite independently of each other. On the other hand, in his 1970s manuscript, *Ere Their Story Die*, Fred Hutton integrated his letters with Kathleen's and John's, sequencing them by date. Reading them in this order conveys an entirely different impression of the lives of the Huttons and Pelletts. This arrangement of the letters emphasizes the close connection and continual interaction between them. The two different orderings of the letters may serve as a key to the lived experience of the two families. Both led double lives: they lived in different countries and in quite different circumstances over several years, but at the same time their lives intersected and overlapped through the letters. Luisa Passerini seeks to capture a sense of this when she refers to the world shared by correspondents as "a world different from actual life."[48] Yet, it might be more accurate to say that both worlds were "actual life" and that the letters functioned then and now as the essential medium in bridging the space and time between them.

The Hutton-Pellett letters were intimately related to other forms of communication by those who wrote and read them. For example, CORB children could send a free monthly cable to their families.[49] Copies of many of these cables are included with the Hutton-Pellett correspondence, but they contain only a single formal sentence and are strikingly uninformative compared to the letters. Two weeks after John moved to the Pelletts, Kathleen wrote to Fred, "I am wondering if you have yet heard about John changing homes. We sent the cable for May last week so hope now that you know. When choosing the cable to send to you John was going to send [one?] about liking his new home then he got to thinking about it and said, 'I don't think I'll send that one. If Daddy hasn't got our letters saying I have moved it will give him a shock.' I thought it was very thoughtful of him."[50] Letters, then, made the cables intelligible and situated them in context. The stark nature of the cables emphasizes the central role of the letters as the main forum of communication between John's two families.[51]

John listened to his father speaking to him from England on the radio in June 1941 first on short wave and then on CBC. Kathleen described John's reaction. "John was a very brave little boy when he heard you. When the announcer gave your name out my it was wonderful to see the beautiful expression and lovely smile break out on John's face and then when you finished speaking he quite filled up with tears but he wouldn't let himself cry. It was all I could do to keep from crying myself. He was pretty blue for a while afterwards but the children and he got out to play and he was soon alright again."[52] Two months later John wrote, "in the letter that you sent me you asked if I recognise[d] your voice. Well I did recognise your voice very well."[53] Kathleen used her letters to convey a sense of the scene when the broadcast was heard. Fred and John, through their letters, added a further layer of meaning to the broadcast.

John received gifts from his father at Christmas and birthdays and at other times as well. He also regularly got mail and parcels, often books, from his extended family.[54] Kathleen and Fred exchanged photographs and parcels as well as letters.[55] When John received a picture of his father he wrote saying, "and do you no where I put it, over my bed."[56] He also told his father, "I keep all your letters in one box and all the other letters in another box."[57] Fred Hutton, in his turn, gave a vivid and detailed description of the arrival of a package containing tea, tobacco, chocolate, toffee, and a pail of honey at the home of the Rev. and Mrs. King with whom he boarded. "Mrs. King said the lunch was getting cold but there was still the honey to come so I dipped down again and pulled out the tin . . . . Let's have a look at the contents. Mrs. King, still anxious about the lunch, found an opener and we managed to get the lid off. Then we found a knife, dipped it into the honey and tried a sample each. Jolly good!"[58] For John and the Pelletts there could be little doubt that their parcel had been received with joy and excitement. Over and over again, the letters contextualized and enhanced the cables, radio broadcasts, photographs, and gifts. They provided enriching detail about the difficulties and hopes involved in the things that were sent and touching, often amusing, images of how things were received.

Today the letters still perform that function. When John Hutton and his wife Rosemary visited Malaspina in May 2002, he brought a number of postcards of Colchester that his father had sent to him, Bobbie, and Doris during the war. They were interesting to look at, but their significance only became clear to me when I later read a letter from Fred Hutton explaining that he intended the postcards to anchor the image of home in John's mind (figure 11.3). He sent a first set early in October 1941 and another set at the end of the month. With the second ones he wrote, "Enclosed are some postcards for the children; the stocks of local views are very limited but I will risk the chance of repetition to keep John's home town firmly fixed in his mind."[59] No doubt the picture postcards helped to do that, but more importantly the explanation in the letter must have carried a subtext for John that his father wanted to keep him connected to his home until he could return. Fred Hutton's letter makes clear why the postcards were sent, but perhaps it also explains why they were important enough to John that he would bring them back to Canada 60 years later. By giving meaning to the other forms of communication, the letters were intricately connected to them and multiplied the messages they carried. In the process, the letters negotiated space and time in a way that other forms of communication alone could not do.

The significance of the Hutton-Pellett letters rests in part on the historical value of the experiences of ordinary people. One way to approach this issue is to consider the argument of the British historian David Vincent who, in writing about nineteenth century autobiographies, reminds us of the importance of individual lives. "Family experience has the effect of differentiating otherwise homogenous social, economic, and occupational sections of the population . . . . This point is obvious enough to anyone who has considered family experience at all, but it is proper to stress that the huge variety of family experience that we find in these autobiographies should not be regarded merely as an obstacle to the pursuit of historical generalization but is rather an essential historical reality."[60] Vincent's point is an important one. The diversity of individual experience, which is so readily accessible through personal letters like those of the Huttons and Pelletts, is "an essential historical reality." The Canadian war historian Jeffrey A. Keshen makes this point in a different way. In his recent seminal work *Saints, Sinners, and Soldiers: Canada's Second World War*, Keshen argues that in every aspect of Canada's war effort the single defining characteristic was full spectrum diversity. In his discussion of the CORB

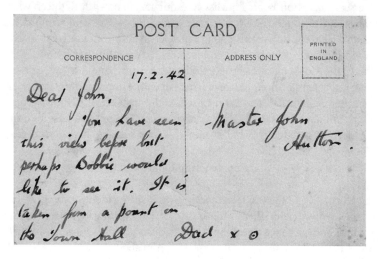

Figure 11.3 Postcard of Colchester from Fred Hutton to John Hutton. High Street Looking East, Colchester: one of many postcards Fred Hutton included in his letters to his son John in Canada to ensure he remembered his home in England and to show Doris and Bobbie Pellett where John's family lived.

Credit: John Hutton.

children, for example, he demonstrates this by discussing the very different experiences of particular children and families. The Hutton and Pellett letters provide empirical information about the unique experiences of two families in wartime and thus document the essential historical reality of diversity.

The Hutton-Pellett letters can also be used to assess historical generalizations. For example, in addition to arguing diversity, Keshen also makes some general claims. He argues that "follow-up investigations [on foster homes] were at best haphazard. Unless a problem was reported, the CORB children were typically left on their own."[61] This did not happen in John's case. His social worker, Miss Chesnut, was with him from the beginning, moved him from the Bournes to the Pelletts, and visited him regularly throughout his time in Canada.[62] Kathleen described one visit in September 1941. "Miss [Chesnut] from the Children's Aid called in last Wednesday morning. John was at school so she didn't see him but I had a nice visit with her. She told me that she had written to you after her last visit to us. She seemed to be quite well satisfied with everything here. She was so pleased over John's report that she took down all his marks and was going to send them into someone at the parliament buildings connected with the Overseas Reception Board."[63] Miss Chesnut consulted with Kathleen when John was ill, brought him home after a stay in hospital, and wrote to his father.[64] Her reports were also sent to the CORB authorities in London who provided brief reports on John to his father.[65] Was John's experience of the Children's Aid Society really atypical and if so, why? As a test case for historical generalizations personal letters open the door to important questions that might not otherwise be raised. In this instance, the Hutton-Pellett letters enhance the ability of historians and general readers to more effectively negotiate between now and then and between here and there.

Constructing Identity

The Hutton-Pellett letters were an important site of identity construction for all involved with them. A number of key factors in John Hutton's evacuation experience eased the traumas dislocation could so easily have inflicted, and the letters helped to create in him an identity acceptable to all parties.

For all the difficult experiences John had in his early years, he was fortunate in a number of ways. The age at which he was evacuated was critical.[66] A recent study on the long-term psychological effects of the evacuation cites the age of the child as one of the factors "that would moderate the possible impact of evacuation on attachment style."[67] Although he was a child when he came to Canada at seven, John was old enough to understand who he was, where he was, and where his future lay. Thirty-five years later he wrote:

> My earliest recollection of Canada is of my father arriving home one day in July 1940 and telling me I would be going off to Canada in a few days. I was a self-reliant little boy and do not remember being put out by the idea. I asked where Canada was and whether I should be able to speak the language. My uncle Leslie, being a scholar, soon produced an atlas showing Toronto, Ontario, where I would be living. He told me that the people in that part of Canada spoke English . . . . As the train sped over the viaduct at Lexden we looked down across the Hilly Fields and over to the town . . . . The vision of my home town receding in the distance stayed with me throughout my five years in Canada.[68]

As discussed earlier, John could read and write when he came to the Pelletts and his ability to do so naturally improved as he got older. In her second letter to Fred Hutton, Kathleen addressed this issue, indicating that she recognized how important it was. "I hope you will be able to understand John's letter to you. He was writing it when I was up bathing and putting Doris to bed so he had no help whatever with grammar or spelling. I thought you would enjoy however getting it exactly as he composed and spelled it." She added, "John does quite a little reading himself."[69] Therefore, by the time John reached the Pelletts he could write to his father and extended family at home and read the letters and books he received from them.[70]

Other critical factors in John's experience were, quite simply, the characters and values of those involved. The Pellett family welcomed him and in a myriad of ways Fred Hutton supported John's integration with his Canadian family. In very difficult circumstances, and in spite of some health problems, John had the chance of a safe and happy childhood in part because of the responsible and committed attitudes of those who parented him. Their values are conveyed in the letters by the articulation of a shared vision for John's future return to England, in the efforts they made to connect the diverse elements of his young life, in their development of a sibling relationship for John, Bobbie, and Doris, and in their support of the naming language John chose for his several parents. In this way, the Hutton-Pellett letters served as the medium for the construction of a stable identity for a child caught up in the vagaries of war.

The letters provide insight into the complex emotional situation that John's evacuation created for both families. From the beginning, Kathleen Pellett was cognizant of some of the implications involved in caring for a child who was not her own. In her first letter to Fred Hutton, Kathleen made the Pelletts' position clear. "May I say right at the beginning that we are very happy to give John a place in our home for the duration of the war . . . as long as John is in our home he will be given the same care and treatment exactly as our children."[71] She then went on to say, "I'm sure we will be heartbroken when it comes time for him to leave us and that is the way we want to feel about it."[72] This was a sentiment she reiterated on several occasions.[73] She was negotiating a difficult balance. John was part of the Pellett family, but his relationship with his father, family, and home in England needed to be nurtured. There was never a question but that John would, and should, go home when the war ended. Many families of CORB children in Canada sought to adopt them.[74] That never happened in John's case. In spite of the enormous commitment they made to John through the years from 1941 to 1945, the Pelletts always created a future for him of going home to his father in Colchester when the war was over. In 1947 Kathleen articulated how clear her vision had been. "I wanted John to want to go back to England and I wanted him to like it when he got there. I felt that with you settled in a good position there, that was where John belonged and I tried so hard not to alienate his affections from England."[75]

For his part Fred Hutton was equally concerned about connecting John to England. The postcards he sent and his reasons for doing so have been discussed earlier. On another occasion he sent a full account of each Christmas card and gift he received in 1941. He ended by saying, "Mrs. Rose, the old lady from next door in Military Road, stopped me in the street and asked how you were and told me to say that she often thinks of you."[76] This letter would serve as a reminder to John of all the relatives, friends, and neighbors who were part of his Colchester world. Kathleen recognized the efforts Fred had made when she wrote to him in December 1943: "The time has been so long since your separation but no one could have done more than you to keep him close and I think you have succeeded."[77] The letters the Huttons and Pelletts exchanged created an identity for John as a child who was away from home only for the duration of the war.

The letters forged other connections for John as well. He had initially spent a year with the Bourne family in Toronto and this relationship was nourished. Kathleen wrote to Fred saying, "I had a letter from Mrs. Bourne this week . . . . We will try to let John meet Mrs. Bourne from time to time . . . . I have invited her to call and see John here if she ever has the opportunity and I sincerely hope she will do so."[78] Several months later, describing a trip into Toronto, she reported, "then we went up to see Mrs. Bourne until it was time to go over to the stadium where the circus was held. We enjoyed our visit with Mrs. Bourne very much . . . . She seemed quite pleased to see John."[79] At about the same time, Fred closed a letter to Betty Bourne adding, "Do go along to see John when you can and write and tell me all about him."[80] John also used letters to maintain connections that mattered to him. This was particularly evident with regard to his cousin and friend, David Churchman. On one occasion he wrote, "Give David the piece of paper that says David on it" and later he told his father, "In this letter you will find a letter for David. Please send it to David I want David to get it so badly."[81] A month later Kathleen mentioned to Fred that John was writing a letter to David.[82] When John joined Cubs he asked his father whether David, also in Cubs, had similar experiences.[83] The veritable web of letters that surrounded John functioned to create an integrated identity for him in the fractured circumstances of his life.

The letters show that Kathleen believed John's relationship with Bobbie and Doris Pellett was important in making him part of the family. Her letters to Fred Hutton often emphasize that Bobbie and Doris accepted John as a sibling when he arrived in their home. For his part, Fred sent letters to Bobbie and Doris as well as to John.[84] In large part, too, John's self-reliance and his ability to construct himself as a member of the Pellett family were crucial. "John is so good with Bobbie and Doris. He and Bobbie get along very well together. They have a wagon and they have great times with it. It is everything from a moving van to an Army tank. John is just lovely with our little girl Doris too and he seems to think the world of her. He and Doris played all morning with some building bricks that they make little houses with."[85] A month later Kathleen mused, "I'm not sure what John thinks of having a younger brother and sister . . . . He seems to be very fond of both Bobby and Doris but sometimes I think he feels Doris especially is a dreadful nuisance . . . . However they have a grand time together and he seems to be living a normal child's life by having a sister to tease and a brother to scrap with. I must say though that the scraps are few and far between and of very little importance."[86] John muted his assessment slightly allowing that, "Doris is a fairly good girl."[87] A few months later Kathleen reaffirmed that John "and Bobbie get along beautifully. Their relationship couldn't be better. Then too, [John] is very good. He has conformed, without any urging, to our customs such as the children's daily routine and behavior and is of great assistance to Bobbie in *his* development."[88] At the end of the year she wrote:

> [John] and Bobbie are at present playing out on the kitchen table with an airplane that John has built with Meccano and an airport that Bobbie has built with building bricks. They are having quite a time. They play so nicely together. Really John has fitted in so splendidly with our children. They all seem to like the same things and are all interested in the same things. I don't think any other child could have fitted in to our home as well. It has certainly made having John a pleasure to us. Naturally it isn't all harmony but no two brothers could get along any better.[89]

The excerpts quoted here show how Kathleen gave John a "normal" identity by depicting him doing what children do—playing for hours with his siblings, Bobbie and Doris, and joining with them in the routines of family life.

The letters also illuminate another component of John's family identity. Kathleen's letters indicate that from the beginning John, like Bobbie and Doris, called her Mommy. "John said to me today, 'Don't be surprised Mummy if we have fifteen boys up after school today. We are going to have a parade on Saturday and we want to get ready for it.' "[90] She added a hand-written note to explain that "John has taken Doris's name for me which is 'Mummy'. He was undecided for a time what to call me. I suggested Auntie, but that just didn't suit him."[91] A month later Kathleen replied to Fred, "You asked me by what term John spoke of me. He mostly calls me 'Mother'. He started off with 'Mummy' but I notice it is always 'Mother' now."[92] John also called Bill Pellett "daddy". In April 1943, he wrote excitedly to his father in England to tell him that, "Next [Saturday] . . . Mummy, Daddy, Bobby and I are going to the city to the pictures."[93]

When Fred Hutton wrote a joint letter to Kathleen and the children, he supported their naming system, addressing the letter to, "Dear Mommy and Doris, Bobbie and John."[94] On another occasion he wrote to John saying, "Mummy tells me you may start reading 'Alice in Wonderland[.]' "[95] As well as referring to Kathleen as "mummy," Fred referred to Bill Pellett as "dad" when he wrote to John.[96] The children sorted out other naming issues quickly. Mr. Hutton became "John's daddy" to Bobbie and Doris and "my daddy" to John, while Bill Pellett was "our daddy" to the three of them.[97] John's early decision to call Kathleen "mommy" and Bill "daddy" created an identity for him as one of the Pelletts, a brother to Bobbie and Doris. Calling his father "my daddy" indicates that although he was highly integrated into the Pellett family he simultaneously remained his father's son. John's use of "mommy" and "mother" for Kathleen continued as is evident in letters he wrote to his father at the time of his tenth birthday in June 1943: "I have played baseball all week, with the baseball and bat mommy gave me."[98] A week later he happily reported, "Mother said that if we work two hours a day we get ten cents, fivepence in English money . . ."[99] John created a double identity for himself. Kathleen was "mummy," but John, like money, fitted in and had value in both Canadian and English contexts.

Through the letters, John was defined as a child temporarily away from home, but connected to family and friends in England and to those who first cared for him in Canada. Most importantly he was part of the Pellett family. At the same time his home and his father were in Colchester. In the circumstances, there was nothing simple about constructing John's identity.

The same was true for the other members of the two families, all of whom found themselves in a significantly different family structure following John's arrival in Agincourt. The letters were a necessary part of the process of identity construction for both the children and parents in the Hutton and Pellett families.

Conclusion

John Hutton was repatriated when he was 12. Kathleen, Bill, Bobbie, and Doris Pellett said goodbye to him at Union Station in Toronto on a summer evening in July 1945. Kathleen anticipated their feelings when she told Fred, "there is going to be quite an empty place in our home here and in our hearts . . . ."[100] John picked up the story in England: "From Liverpool on a misty summer morning we traveled by train to London, through soft green country full of patchwork fields and little houses . . . . Arriving at Euston station in mid-afternoon, I stepped out of the carriage to find my father at the carriage door . . . ."[101] Fred described the scene to Kathleen: "Uncle Cecil, young [cousin] David and myself met at Euston station to await the arrival of the boat train from Liverpool. There was a last minute scramble from the indicator board as we learned the platform to which the train would arrive . . . [and] by good fortune [we] were within a few yards of the door from which John emerged. We recognized each other immediately. I shall never forget his first, 'Oh, Dad.' I knew in that moment that John had always remembered."[102]

In the years that followed the Huttons and Pelletts continued to write to one another and the Pelletts visited England on several occasions. Bill Pellett died in 1978 at 74, Fred Hutton in 1982 at 79, and Kathleen Pellett in 1983 at 74.[103] John Hutton, Bob Pellett, and Doris Stephens continue a friendship that has extended across the six decades since John went home.

The Hutton-Pellett letters remain as tangible evidence of an uncertain time when the lives of two families intersected in an unexpected way. The letters are not fixed, but fluid. They have assumed multiple forms as the time and space they bridge evolves. They were authored by an unlikely triangle of two adults who were strangers and a child who was learning to write. Their transit was never secure and their chronology complex, yet they collapsed distance and functioned as the critical site of shared experience. Through them the identities of a young boy and two families an ocean apart could be normalized and stabilized in the midst of a world war. They continue to be engaging to read and historically significant. As the historian Martha Hanna reminds us, "letter-writers knew in ways that historians have forgotten that the letter itself was a physical artifact that could cultivate intimacy by making the absent correspondent seem almost palpably present."[104] For the Huttons and Pelletts, their Second World War letters negotiated space, time, and identity and made possible the intimacy of family.

Notes

John Hutton, Doris Stephens, and Robert (Bob) Pellett have extended unfailing goodwill and support in the preparation of this essay and I would like to express my deep appreciation to them. I would also like to thank Stephen Davies who encouraged me to work on the Hutton-Pellett letters when he first received them for the Canadian Letters and Images Project and acknowledge his good-natured assistance in everything to do with the digital world. Bruce Elliott organized the "Reading the Emigrant Letter Conference" in Ottawa in August 2003 and provided those interested in letters a unique opportunity to share questions and insights. I am further indebted to him for his astute editorial insights.

Abbreviations
KP = Kathleen Pellett
HFH = H. F. (Fred) Hutton
JH = John Hutton.

Note
In quotations, the spelling and grammar of the original letters has been reproduced. All references are to the original letters except those shown as being from H.F. Hutton, ed., *Ere Their Story Die* (*ETSD*), with a foreword by John Hutton, unpublished typescript of the Hutton-Pellett letters, n.d. (ca. 1970s). John Hutton wrote and Doris Stephens typed a revised introduction to *ETSD* in 2004.

1. For an examination of wartime correspondence that was steeped in and shaped by a letter writing tradition see Martha Hanna, "A Republic of Letters: The Epistolary Tradition in France during World War I," *The American Historical Review* 108, no. 5 (December 2003), 1336–1361; http://www.historycooperative.org/journals/ahr/108.5/hanna.html (August 18, 2004).
2. For a brief comment on this aspect of the letters see John Hutton, foreword to *Ere Their Story Die* (*ETSD*), p. 6.
3. For accounts of CORB children in Canada see Geoffrey Bilson, *The Guest Children: The Story of the British Child Evacuees Sent to Canada during World War II* (Saskatoon: Fifth House, 1988); Jeffrey A. Keshen, *Saints, Sinners, and Soldiers: Canada's Second World War* (Vancouver: UBC Press, 2004), pp. 194–201; and Penny Wheelwright, Starry Night Productions, *A Rough Crossing*, video recording, National Film Board of Canada, 1995.
4. Bilson, *The Guest Children*, p. 21.
5. Keshen, *Saints, Sinners, and Soldiers*, p. 195. CORB had received 211,548 applications by July 4, 1940 and no further applications were accepted after that date. Parents could indicate the Dominion to which they wanted their children sent. Martin Parsons and Penny Starns, *The Evacuation: The True Story* (Denton, Cambs: DSM, 1999), pp. 128 and 130; and Bilson, *The Guest Children*, p. 21.
6. Parsons and Starns, *The Evacuation*, p. 136 and pp. 141–142. The sinking of the *SS City of Benares* with the loss of 77 CORB evacuees brought an end to CORB evacuations. Forty-six of the *Benares's* children were rescued after eight days in open lifeboats. Parsons and Starns, *The Evacuation*, p. 146.

7. For an overview of the British evacuations the following are useful: Mike Brown, *Evacuees: Evacuation in Wartime Britain* (Phoenix Mill, Gloucestershire: Sutton, 2000); Ruth Inglis, *The Children's War: Evacuation 1939–1945* (London: Collins, 1989); Martin L. Parsons, *"I'll Take That One": Dispelling the Myths of Civilian Evacuation 1939–45* (Denton, Cambs: Beckett Karson, 1998); Parsons and Starns, *The Evacuation*; and Ben Wicks, *No Time to Wave Goodbye* (New York: St. Martin's Press, 1988). For a recent study of the long-term effects of the evacuation see D. Foster, S. Davies, and H. Steele, "The Evacuation of British Children during World War II: A Preliminary Investigation into the Long-term Psychological Effects," *Aging & Mental Health* 7, no. 5 (September 2003): 398–408.

8. For a discussion of the numbers involved in the massive in-Britain evacuations, and the difficulties of being precise about them, see Inglis, *The Children's War*, xi and pp. 1–2. There were three major government evacuations. They occurred in September 1939, the summer and fall of 1940, and the summer and fall of 1944. Inglis argues that far more than the 7,736 children who were killed in bombing in Britain during the war would have died had the evacuations not occurred. Inglis, *The Children's War*, p. 5. Parsons and Starns indicate that the initial evacuation, code-named "Operation Pied Piper," saw one and a half million children moved from their homes in three days. Elsewhere Parsons states that 1,500,000 were officially evacuated by the end of September. Approximately 900,000 of these evacuees returned home during the "phony war" period. Inglis, *The Children's War*, pp. xi and 5; Parsons and Starns, *The Evacuation*, pp. 55 and 64; Parsons, *"I'll Take That One,"* pp. 68 and 143.

9. Brown, *Evacuees*, p. 116.

10. Alistair Horne, *A Bundle from Britain* (London: Macmillan, 1994) is a memoir by a historian of his experience as a child privately evacuated to the United States.

11. For a discussion of activities of the many groups in Canada who supported evacuation of British children to Canada, the reluctance of the government to allow the children to come, and the complicated politics that ensued see Bilson, *The Guest Children*, pp. 2–30. The Eugenics Society of Canada in concert with the British Eugenics Society was one of the groups that considered sponsoring the evacuation of selected British children, but their plans did not materialize. Parsons and Starns. *The Evacuation*, pp. 161–163.

12. Keshen, *Saints, Sinners, and Soldiers*, p. 198. Other accounts give different numbers for children evacuated overseas. For example, Martin L. Parsons indicates that a total of 13,000 British children were evacuated to North America. In one instance he seems to indicates that there were 3,119 CORB evacuees and in another 2,664. Like Keshen, Parsons states that 1,532 CORB children came to Canada. Ruth Inglis claims that CORB evacuated 3,500 children to four British dominions. She agrees that 1,532 of these came to Canada. She claims the total number of mothers and children and unaccompanied children evacuated overseas did not exceed 20,000 and that there were no overseas evacuations after mid-1941. Martin Parsons and Penny Starns say that 17,000 private evacuations occurred after June 1940. This number would be in addition to all private evacuations before June 1940 and the CORB evacuation. This suggests the total overseas evacuation was greater than 20,000. Nevertheless, it is clear that the overseas evacuation was completely dwarfed by the in-Britain evacuations. Parsons, *"I'll Take That One,"* pp. 167, 170, 171; Inglis, *The Children's War*, pp. 105, 111, and 117; and Parsons and Starns, *The Evacuation*, p. 161.

13. HFH to KP, *ETSD*, December 13, 1941; and Hutton, foreword to *ETSD*, pp. 1–8.

14. John Hutton, introduction to *ETSD*, p. 4.

15. Hutton, foreword to *ETSD*, p. 3; and Hutton, introduction to *ETSD*, p. 2. The second major government evacuation of children within Britain occurred as a

result of German air attacks following the surrender of France. Ironically in the first evacuation, many children were sent to the east coast including Colchester. Ruth Inglis says of one group of children, "they ended up at Colchester station . . . for many young East Enders, it was the start of a lifelong love affair with Essex." Inglis, *The Children's War*, p. 14.

16. Brown, *Evacuees*, p. 46; and also Parsons and Starns, *The Evacuation*, p. 76. For a discussion of the evacuation of children from Colchester in September 1940 see Brown, *Evacuees*, p. 47.

17. Hutton, foreword to *ETSD*, p. 1. Ruth Inglis points out that "whether children were to be evacuated or not was a decision left to parents and it was a nerve-wracking one." In 1940 the government, for a variety of reasons, actively encouraged parents to evacuate their children from the danger areas. CORB employed a variety of criteria such as race, religion, health, and conduct for accepting a child for the program. Inglis, *The Children's War*, p. 35; Parsons and Starns, *The Evacuation*, p. 82; and Bilson, *The Guest Children*, pp. 22–23.

18. John was very much a part of the Bourne family as he subsequently was of the Pellett family. Hutton, foreword to *ETSD*, pp. 4–5. Approximately 30 percent of CORB evacuees were moved from their initial placements. Parsons and Starns, *The Evacuation*, p. 28.

19. Hutton, foreword to *ETSD*, pp. 5–6.

20. KP to HFH, May 6, 1941; KP to HFH, May 21, 1941; and KP to HFH, May [23? 25?], 1941. John Hutton and Doris Stephens describe W.H. (Bill) Pellett as "a mechanical engineer . . . employed as a plant manager and professional engineer with companies engaged in war work in the Toronto area, with a short period in California on aircraft production." Hutton, introduction to *ETSD*, p. 2.

21. Kathleen Pellett consistently referred to her son as Bobbie and I have followed her practice. In his letters to "John's daddy" he signed himself Bobbie once and then used Bobby. John always referred to him as Bobby. Bobbie Pellett to HFH, ca. October 30, 1941; Bobby Pellett to HFH, ca. December 30, 1941; and JH to HFH, July 8, 1941.

22. Jeffrey A. Keshen notes that repatriation of the CORB emigrants began in late 1943 and by early 1945 only 205 remained in Canada. If this is correct, John was one of the last CORB children to return home. Martin Parsons and Penny Starns paint a different picture. They note that communications regarding the repatriation of CORB children began "as early as February 1944," but that overseas evacuees normally stayed till 1945 with the last not repatriated till 1947. Keshen, *Saints, Sinners, and Soldiers*, p. 201; and Parsons and Starns, *The Evacuation*, pp. 124 and 159.

23. HFH to KP, *ETSD*, May 9, 1943. Kathleen Pellett's letters are almost always typed and John Hutton's letters are printed at first and later written.

24. Today the original letters are in the care of John Hutton.

25. In a thoughtful analysis of a wartime correspondence, Luisa Passerini suggests that "both men and women save letters but it is the latter that reorganizes, orders and binds them together." This observation does not apply in the case of the Hutton-Pellett letters. Luisa Passerini, *Europe in Love, Love in Europe: Imagination and Politics between the Wars* (New York: New York University Press, 1999), p. 302.

26. Hutton, *ETSD*; and Hutton, foreword to *ETSD*, pp. 1–8.

27. It is clear from Kathleen's letters that this letter did reach her as she comments on it. Fred Hutton's letter explaining something of John's early years, cited earlier in the essay, is another example of a letter that appears in the edited version, but not the originals. Again, Kathleen comments on the letter so it is clear she received it as well.

28. KP to HFH, May 20, 1943.

29. Fred Hutton died in 1982. John Hutton, introduction to *ETSD*, p. 2.

30. JH to HFH, August 12, 1941.

31. JH to HFH, September 19, 1941.
32. JH to HFH, September 18, 1944.
33. Doris Pellett and KP to HFH, ca. November 19, 1941.
34. KP to HFH, January 8, 1942.
35. http://www.mala.bc.ca/history/letters
36. I am indebted to Gordon Hak for drawing my attention to the call for papers for the Emigrant Letters Conference.
37. Ala Rekrut, "Material Literacy: Reading Records as Material Culture," *Archivaria* 60 (Fall, 2005), forthcoming.
38. KP to HFH, September 10, 1941.
39. KP to HFH, June 9, 1943.
40. KP to HFH, July 2, 1943.
41. In a more limited way, the Hutton-Pellett letters were even more multisided since Fred Hutton wrote some letters to Bobbie and Doris Pellett and they wrote some to him. For example, Kathleen wrote to Fred, "Thank you for sending the comics to the boys and the card to Doris. Doris loves her cards you send her. She is busy now writing a letter to John's Daddy in fact she is always scribbling on a piece of paper and says she is going to send it to 'John's Daddy.' " KP to HFH, September 10, 1941. Kathleen also read Fred's letters aloud and discussed them with the three children. John Hutton, phone conversation with Helen Brown, May 27, 2003. In addition, John's social worker, Miss Chesnut, wrote about John to his father, as did officials from CORB. Effie Chesnut, Social Worker, Children's Aid Society of York County, to Mr. Hutton, June 1, 1942; June 8, 1942; and October 17, 1942. Elspeth Davies, Children's Overseas Reception Board, to Mr. Hutton, May 6, 1942; December 10, 1942; and July 10, 1944. Nevertheless, Fred, Kathleen and John wrote most of the extant Hutton-Pellett letters.
42. KP to HFH, June [23? 25?], 1941. Kathleen Pellett's first letter to Fred Hutton was dated May 6, 1941. She addressed her letters "Dear Mr. Hutton" until late in the war when she changed to "Dear Fred." KP to HFH, October 12, 1944. Fred Hutton addressed his letters to "Dear Kathleen." Kathleen's letters are dated from the beginning and John Hutton's from June 16, 1941.
43. In another example, Kathleen Pellett's letter of June 19, 1941 arrived on July 12 and Fred Hutton replied on July 14. Note written on letter from KP to HFH, June 19, 1941.
44. KP to HFH, July [23?], 1941.
45. HFH to KP, August 18, 1941.
46. Passerini, *Europe in Love*, p. 303.
47. Ibid.
48. Ibid., p. 295.
49. KP to HFH, May 21, 1941; and KP to HFH, June 19, 1941.
50. KP to HFH, May 21,1941. The full wording of the cable the following month read, "Very happy in new home and settling down fine." JH cable to HFH, June 25, 1941.
51. On at least one occasion this process was reversed and the cable created the context for the letters when John sent his father a cable saying, "Delighted to receive your cable but no letters received for long time. All well." JH cable to HFH, [handwritten notation "received 17.11.41."]
52. KP to HFH, June 3, 1941. John also heard his father via short wave and on CBC in January 1943. JH to HFH, January 14, 1943; and KP to HFH, January 22, 1943.
53. JH to HFH, August 12, 1941.
54. KP to HFH, May 21, 1941; and KP to HFH, June 18, 1943.
55. KP TO HFH, June 3, 1941; and KP TO HFH, June 19, 1941.
56. JH to HFH, ca. May 21, 1941.
57. JH to HFH, August 19, 1941.
58. HFH to JH, November 24, 1941.

59. HFH to JH, October 3, 1941; and HFH to KP, October 24, 1941.

60. David Vincent, *Bread, Knowledge and Freedom: A Study of Nineteenth-Century Working Class Autobiography* (London: Europa Publications, 1981), p. 59.

61. Keshen, *Saints, Sinners, and Soldiers*, p. 197.

62. Hutton, foreword to *ETSD*, p. 5.

63. KP to HFH, September 10, 1941.

64. KP to HFH, May 29, 1942; Effie Chesnut, Social Worker, Children's Aid Society of York County, to Mr. Hutton, June 1, 1942; June 8, 1942; and October 17, 1942.

65. For example, Elspeth Davies, Children's Overseas Reception Board, to Mr. Hutton, May 6, 1942; December 10, 1942; and July 10, 1944.

66. For a discussion of the way age affected children's experience of World War II see William M. Tuttle, Jr., *"Daddy's Gone to War": The Second World War in the Lives of America's Children* (New York: Oxford University Press, 1993), pp. 16–29.

67. Foster, Davies, and Steele, "The Evacuation of British Children," p. 400.

68. Hutton, foreword to *ETSD*, p. 3. John's question about language was one that does not seem to have concerned British planners who sent thousands of children to Wales. This caused problems for many of them. Some who became fluent in Welsh encountered further difficulties when they returned to their homes in Liverpool. Parsons and Starns, *The Evacuation*, p. 96.

69. KP to HFH, May 13, 1941.

70. John Hutton and his father lived in a flat in the home of his paternal grandmother until her death in 1940. John was part of a close extended family that included three paternal uncles all of whom came home to their mother's "frequently especially at weekends." All the uncles spent time with John and one of them, Cecil, John recalled, "wrote frequently to me in Canada but alas, none of his graphic and inter-esting letters of life in England in wartime have survived." John's maternal Aunt Alice, her husband, and their son David Churchman, who was three months younger than John, also lived in Colchester. As well, his maternal uncle, Harold, his wife Tilly, and their children, Joan and Sonny, were also part of John's life. Hutton, foreword to *ETSD*, pp. 1–3. John's maternal grandfather also wrote to him while he was in Canada.

71. KP to HFH, May 6, 1941.

72. KP TO HFH, May 6, 1941.

73. KP TO HFH, May 28, 1941; and KP to HFH, September 10, 1941.

74. Kathleen indicated her awareness of this in a letter written after John returned to England. "So many of the guests leaving were quite resentful and were determined to come straight back as soon as they were able that we felt rather sorry for their parents. Their foster parents didn't seem to be discouraging them any either in their attitude. It seemed unfair that their affections should be so alienated." KP to HFH August 23, 1945.

75. KP to HFH, June 12, 1947.

76. HFH to JH, December 28, 1941.

77. KP to HFH, December 28, 1943.

78. KP to HFH, June [23? 25?], 1941. Mrs. Bourne sent John a birthday card a month after he had moved to the Pelletts and listened to Fred Hutton's radio broadcast in June 1941 and again in January 1943. KP to HFH, June 19, 1941; JH to HFH, *ETSD*, June 28, 1941; and Betty Bourne to HFH, January 21, 1943.

79. KP to HFH, October 29, 1941.

80. HFH to Betty Bourne, October 28, 1941.

81. JH to HFH, ca. May 28, 1941; and JH to HFH, July 8, 1941.

82. KP to HFH, August 12, 1941.

83. JH to HFH, ca. February 23, 1943; and JH to HFH, February 3, 1945.

84. KP to HFH, July 14, 1942.

85. KP TO HFH, May 13, 1941; and KP to HFH, May 21, 1941.
86. KP to HFH, June [23? 25?], 1941.
87. JH to HFH, *ETSD*, June 28, 1941. The wording is the same as in the undated original.
88. KP to HFH, August 20,1941.
89. KP to HFH, December 12, 1941. John had brought the Meccano set with him from England. A year after John's arrival Kathleen wrote, "Bobbie, John and Doris are still having lots of fun together. They sure do get along well. It is going to be simply dreadful when John goes home." KP to HFH, May 13, 1942.
90. KP to HFH, May 21, 1941.
91. KP to HFH, May 21, 1941. The end of the postscript is missing from the photocopy of Kathleen Pellett's original letter. The complete version can be found in KP to HFH, *ETSD*, p. 21 May 1941.
92. KP to HFH, June [23? 25?], 1941.
93. JH to HFH, April 26, 1943. See also, April 10, 1942, October 8, 1942, September 1, 1944.
94. JH to HFH, May 2, 1943. Not all British parents allowed their children to call the Canadian parents by any variant of mother or father. Bilson, *The Guest Children*, p. 179.
95. HFH to JH, September 29, 1941.
96. HFH to JH, October 3, 1941.
97. KP to HFH, June [23? 25?], 1941. John also referred to Kathleen Pellett's mother, Mrs. Carr, as "Grandma." JH to HFH, July 16, 1941.
98. JH to HFH, June 18, 1943.
99. JH to HFH, June 30, 1943.
100. KP to HFH, July 19, 1945.
101. John Hutton, introduction to *ETSD*, p. 11.
102. HFH to KP, August 12, 1945.
103. JH, introduction to *ETSD*, p. 2.
104. Hanna, "A Republic of Letters," par. 21.

12

The Ukrainian Government-in-Exile's Postal Network and the Construction of National Identity

Karen Lemiski

Recent treatments of the history of nationalism and nation-building have rightly emphasized the important role of modern communications in forging national identity. Effective communications, the printed word especially, allows individuals to comprehend in a general way the existence of multitudes of other people just like themselves. This type of unification takes on an added significance in modern states that have been created during revolutionary circumstances, when ancient allegiances are destroyed in favor of newer concepts and when positions of authority must continually be used to maintain and propagate a particular image of the world. By uniting the population, the mail carried through the post office serves to reinforce the bonds of union, therefore acting as an agent of national integration.

Within this context, the introduction of postage stamps is significant. With their depictions of national history, culture, and political subjects, stamps are an effective means of reaching and educating the population. In the case of the Ukrainian community, its post–World War II government-in-exile exploited the post to construct and propagate a distinctive set of national ideals. Moreover, the appearance on stamps of national symbols, whether traditional or newly created, became a critical design element. The emblems united the far-flung exile community by presenting the political leaders' notions of shared historical and cultural bonds. In accomplishing this task, the Ukrainian government-in-exile's motivation was the same as that associated with official postal authorities around the world.

Historical Background and Precedents

The outbreak of World War I in August 1914 ushered in a period that had a profound impact on the territories that, in various formations, came to be considered as Ukrainian lands. In the course of only five years, these regions witnessed the military conflicts of World War I, the breakup of two long-standing empires, and attempts to establish Ukrainian statehood, both as an independent non-Soviet state and as a republic in close alliance with the new Soviet Russia. Moreover, all of these developments took place in an extremely complex environment that was marked by struggles between competing Ukrainian governments, peasant uprisings, foreign invasions, and civil war.

With the overthrow of the Russian monarchy and the collapse of the imperial system in 1917, leaders in the Dnieper region of Ukraine formed a council under the leadership of Mikhailo Hrushevsky (1866–1934), who returned from exile to assume the presidency. Democratic and strongly socialist in its ideology, the Central Rada (Tsentralna Rada) was the creation of the leftist intellectual groups that had dominated the Ukrainian national movement before World War I. In November 1917 and January 1918, it proclaimed the existence of an autonomous and then independent Ukrainian National Republic (Ukrainska Narodnia Respublika/UNR). To strengthen its foundations, Kiev was chosen as the new capital, thus instilling a sense of continuity with the center of the medieval state of Rus. While the Soviet authorities initially recognized the new republic, in February 1918 the Red Army overthrew the UNR. Soviet rule, in turn, was overthrown by the advancing German army. Beginning in April 1918, Germany gave its support to a new government known as the Hetmanate. This quasi-monarchial, pro-German government was led by Pavlo Skoropadsky (1873–1945), who was a member of the landowning aristocracy and a descendant of a Zaporozhian Cossack leader. Skoropadsky remained in power until the end of 1918, when he was deposed by the Directory of the UNR (Dyrektoriia UNR), under the leadership of Volodymyr Vynnychenko (1880–1951) and Symon Petliura (1879–1926). This restored regime included the former organs of the Western Ukrainian National Republic (Zakhidno-Ukrainska Narodnia Respublika/ZUNR), which had functioned as an independent state ruled by Ievhen Petrushevych (1863–1940) that had been centered in Lviv for eight months, beginning in November 1918. The Directory itself was driven out by General Anthony Denikin's White forces. With Denikin's subsequent withdrawal in the autumn of 1919, Soviet troops restored Soviet authority while the Polish army simultaneously occupied several regions of Ukraine. In April 1920, Ukrainian emissaries in Warsaw accepted the terms of a peace treaty, which led to the formal surrender of western Ukrainian territories to Poland. In the summer of 1920, Viacheslav Prokopovych (1881–1942) formed the last UNR government for the remaining Ukrainian provinces. The final blow to Ukrainian independence came with the Polish-Soviet armistice, reaffirmed by the Treaty of Riga in March 1921, by which Ukraine's territories were divided between Soviet Russia and Poland.

In their struggles between nation and empire, the various Ukrainian governments actively promoted a distinct Ukrainian identity, unique in terms of culture and history, and the necessity of the population bonding together in support of their new state. Despite their ultimately unsuccessful tenures, the Ukrainian leaders actively campaigned for international political recognition on behalf of a nation that perceived itself as having suffered centuries of oppression, including distortions of its own history. The Ukrainian nation was conceived as a horizontal comradeship that lacked claims to ancient noble families of its own. The image that was propagated was of Ukrainians as the European descendants of good peasant people, of multiethnic pioneers, and of an ancient multiethnic state. The implied bonds to the land translated as ties to a Ukrainian land. This image reinforced Ukraine's aspirations to democracy and freedom, underlined its multiethnic character, and suggested that Ukraine was distinct from its neighbor to the north, Russia. Overall, the resulting sense of patriotism, along with such putative peasant values as honesty and hard work, were just what a new nation and new state needed.

As with any other established government, the leaders of the autonomous Ukrainian states used the postal network to reach both their domestic citizens as well as the wider international community. In this regard, two factors relating to the nationalist objectives of the Ukrainian governments are crucial for this study. The first concerns the establishment of a distinctly Ukrainian postal system. It simply did not happen. Rather, the various twentieth-century Ukrainian states inherited from both the Russian and Austrian empires well-organized postal administrations that were maintained intact with only changes to the directing personnel. But given the instability of their regimes and the ongoing civil unrest in the region, the Ukrainian governments could neither derive a substantial income from the post nor claim that great improvements had been made to the services it offered, which are two basic fundamentals behind postal operations. Instead, the postal administration became a weapon in the ongoing domestic and international political struggles.

The second element is that throughout each phase of Ukrainian statehood, specific visible signs repeatedly emerged as banners around which to rally the nation. Along with legitimizing the relations of authority, the new national flag and national coat of arms helped Ukraine to proclaim its identity and sovereignty, therefore commanding respect and loyalty. Whereas Soviet stamps from this period reflect the tenets of socialist realism which were enforced by the central authorities as part of larger political goals, Ukrainian stamps never achieved this degree of sophistication. The stamps' iconography was built around the coat of arms of the Ukrainian National Republic. The designs combined the tryzub or trident—which, having been the emblem of the Kievan Grand Prince Volodymyr (956–1015), symbolically linked the states of the twentieth century with a medieval one—with elements of folk life and several notable figures from history to support specific characterizations of the Ukrainian nation. Perhaps most obvious are the images derived from the cossack Hetmanate of the sixteenth and seventeenth centuries, which as an example of self-government became a key component of Ukrainian national history and the nation-building myth.

The earliest instance in which the novice governments appropriated and "Ukrainianized" existing postage stamps occurred in August 1918, when the minister of postal and telegraphic services for the Ukrainian National Republic ordered all postage stamps of Russian origin that were being used for postage "in the territory of Ukraine be overprinted with the national emblem of the Ukrainian state."[1] This meant that the trident was to be printed on top of the imperial Romanov coat of arms. In a parallel occurrence in November 1918, the deputy director of the post office in the Western Ukrainian National Republic ordered that denominations from the now obsolete 1916–1918 Austrian issue, which featured the Austrian coat of arms, be overprinted with the coat of arms for the province of Galicia (where the capital city of Lviv was located) and the inscription "Zakhidno Ukr[ainska] Narodnia Respublika."[2] Building on such official precedents, nationalist organizations would later take spontaneous advantage of other opportunities to "Ukrainianize" the postage stamps that were circulating on Ukrainian territory. One notable occasion came during the joint Polish-Ukrainian offensive against Soviet-occupied Ukraine, when the Ukrainian army overprinted the stamps it was consigned with the phrase "Vil'na Ukraïna" (Free Ukraine).

This practice continued throughout the interwar period as pro-Ukrainian groups circulated private labels. In part this reflected a growing worldwide phenomenon. While North Americans became familiar with applying Christmas Seals to letters as complements to the required postage, in the Soviet Union, by contrast, private labels were often applied instead of postage stamps. In total 58 issues were prepared in the Soviet Union on Ukrainian territory and in nine other countries between 1918 and 1939.[3] These stamps were never used for postage nor were they sanctioned for payment for any type of postal charges; instead, the nationalist movement counted on inattentive postal employees overlooking or ignoring the labels.[4] Yet their role in spreading Ukrainian ideas should not be underestimated. Of more significance, perhaps, is that from this point until modern Ukraine's declaration of sovereignty in 1990, the medium of postage stamps was increasingly adopted as a means of spreading nationalistic messages.

Circumstances at the end of World War II provided Ukrainian leaders with unexpected forums from where new campaigns for national recognition could be launched. At the beginning of 1946, there were still some 220,000 Ukrainian emigrants who had escaped forced repatriation to the Soviet Union living in West Germany, Austria, and Italy. Most of these people had been sent to these countries as labor conscripts during the war, but there were also forced evacuees, former prisoners of German concentration camps, prisoners of war, refugees from Ukraine, and political émigrés from the 1920s. All of them refused to return to the Ukrainian S.S.R., claiming they would be subject to religious, national, or political persecution. Instead, they were resettled in more than 100 displaced persons (DP) camps, 80 of which were either predominantly or completely Ukrainian.[5]

With the approval of the U.S. authorities, who were assigned control over the largest Ukrainian settlements,[6] some camps organized their own postal services that were responsible for the acceptance of incoming mail delivered by the German post office and its distribution within the camps, the collection of all mail from within the camps and its transfer to the German postal system, and the transmittal of all internal camp correspondence. Among the historical precedents for these systems were the mail services created in 1919 by Belgian prisoners of war in the Dutch camp Nymwegen, by English prisoners in the German camp Ruhleben, by German prisoners in the Japanese camp of Bando, as well as in 1946 by Ukrainian prisoners of war at Rimini, Italy.[7]

To obtain funds for administering the DP postal systems, the U.S. Military Government granted permission for the establishment of postal rates and the production of postage stamps.[8] For internal correspondence, only camp stamps were needed. For mail sent to addresses within the settlements from other places, it was necessary to affix camp stamps to pay for the services provided by the local camp post. Finally, because the German postal system did not recognize the camp stamps as payment for the services it offered, German postage was required in addition to the camp stamps for all mail destined beyond the camp.[9] The postage stamps that were produced for use within the network of Ukrainian settlements combined three key elements: the designation, or a variation of, "Ukrainska Taborova Poshta" (Ukrainian Camp Post) as the authority for which they were issued, a number specifying the face value of the stamp, and one of several emblems to represent the stamps' national origin.

Postage stamps were issued at four of the Ukrainian DP camps in Germany: Camp Ganghofersiedlung (Regensburg), Camp Leopoldkaserne (Bayreuth), Camp Ludendorfkaserne (Neu-Ulm), and Camp Sedankaserne (Ulm/Donau); one additional settlement at Ellwangen-Jagst was also authorized to issue a cancel reading "Ukrainian DP Camp Post." In general, these postal designs, as well as those from the earlier prisoner-of-war camps, united the trident emblem with strong ethnographic and cultural themes, and understandably, depictions of the military quest for independence. For example, a set of stamps released in 1947 at Camp Ganghofersiedlung featured the trident along with specific dates from Ukrainian history: the declaration of Ukraine's independence by the Organization of Ukrainian Nationalists (June 30, 1941), the formation of the Western Ukrainian National Republic (November 1, 1918), the declaration of the Fourth Universal (January 22, 1918), which established the Ukrainian National Republic, the unification of the Western Ukrainian National Republic with the Ukrainian National Republic (January 22, 1919), and the proclamation of Carpatho-Ukraine's independence (March 15, 1919).

Ultimately, it was through the establishment of the camp-based postal services that the Ukrainian national movement took a marked step toward achieving one of its long-sought goals. While Italy and Germany (the host countries of the POW and DP camps) were independent states, Ukraine was not. By receiving the authorization to issue postage stamps to pay for the delivery of mail through its own postal system, the Ukrainian community was approximating the functions of a sovereign state. However, for nationalist Ukrainians, the stamps fell short of the ultimate goal because only the first design from the prisoner-of-war camp was released with "Ukrainian" denominations; all subsequent values were prepared with amounts given in Italian lire and, then at the DP camps, in German pfennings and marks.

The Ukrainian Government-in-Exile

As Bolshevik troops occupied Ukrainian territories in the early 1920s, the government of the short-lived Ukrainian National Republic was evacuated, first to Poland, and later in 1939–1940 to Paris and Prague. Taking on various forms during the interwar period, the government-in-exile continued the ideological and legal traditions of the independent Ukrainian state even after the creation of the Ukrainian Soviet Socialist Republic. Its foundation was based in part on the thousands of Ukrainians who were either caught in wartime combat or who otherwise could not reconcile themselves to the lack of cultural freedom and independence in the Soviet republic. In other words, the political émigrés, having no desire to abrogate their struggle to establish an independent Ukraine, viewed the creation of the Soviet Union not as a signal to disband but merely as the prologue to a new era. Given this perspective, a new purpose for the government-in-exile arose, namely continued opposition to the Moscow regime on behalf of Ukrainians both in and outside the state's boundaries. Until the creation of a newly independent Ukraine, the government-in-exile would work to keep alive the spirit of an independent and democratic nation-state.

The Ukrainian government-in-exile was the first such government to issue postage stamps. As part of its ongoing diplomatic activities, it prepared stamps, especially in early 1923 when it seemed possible that a return to Ukraine was imminent. In subsequent years, in order to raise funds for the continuation of its international activities, the government-in-exile occasionally issued stamps carrying the Ukrainian denomination of hryven for use on correspondence sent within the Ukrainian community. For instance, 65,000 stamps were released in 1935; one design mourned the tenth anniversary of Symon Petliura's death, while the other two commemorated the 950th anniversary of Christianity in Ukraine.

Having been forced by the conditions of World War II to defer its activities, the political base for the government-in-exile was undoubtedly strengthened after 1945 by the large number of Ukrainians who were living in Europe. Munich, as the principal center for displaced persons, also became the nucleus for most Ukrainian émigré political organizations. It was in this context that the Ukrainian National Council (Ukrainska Natsionalna Rada/UNC) emerged in 1947 as the parliamentary body of the government-in-exile and the ideological and legal successor of the Ukrainian National Republic. The UNC was established as the result of a pact between the émigré Ukrainian political parties that had survived the collapse of the Ukrainian bid for independence but that remained divided operationally. By consolidating the independentist parties and organizations, the UNC successfully renewed itself as the axis for long-held goals of a sovereign Ukrainian state.

Overtures toward the establishment of a postal network were among the first ideas advanced by the UNC. According to Directive No. 3 of the Executive Branch, postal rates were set for correspondence between Ukrainians living in exile.[10] The rate schedule from December 1948 was relatively simple: in addition to the regular postage required by the countries of residence of the Ukrainian populations, postal cards sent between Ukrainians were to carry an additional five shahiv in "Ukrainian" postage, and an additional ten shahiv were required for letters and packages weighing up to five kilograms.[11] Because numerically these amounts matched the rates prescribed by the German postal administration, it meant that those Ukrainians who chose to participate in the program were consciously doubling the amount of postage that was required to send an item. Through these statutes, the UNC effectively maintained an international postal presence and also established the connections among the Ukrainian emigrant communities and between the Ukrainian diaspora and its center. Further, the use of the monetary designation shahiv effectively tied the exile government's postage to the 1917 Ukrainian National Republic, which had itself adopted this currency value from the medieval state of Rus. The use of the denomination was additionally significant because it meant that symbols associated with an independent Ukrainian government circulated openly to a potentially widespread audience, even though the government structure itself was based in exile.

Corresponding to its rate schedule, the UNC began to produce postal stationery and postage stamps. These were then distributed to the postal stations the UNC organized in areas where large Ukrainian emigrant populations resided—including, but not limited to, the DP camps—and in the 17 countries where it had agents.[12] The offices in Argentina, Belgium, Canada, England, Germany, and the United States also had available the UNC postal cancels that carried both the name of the city or event for which they were prepared and the appellation Poshtova Stantsiia Ukrains'koï Natsional'noï Rady (Postal Station UNR). In addition to the official Ukrainian National Council outlets, some postal products were also sold through various Ukrainian exile organizations such as the Association of Ukrainian Democratic Youth (Obiednannia Demokraychnoï Ukrainskoï Molodi/ODUM) in Canada and the Society of Friends of the UNC in the United States, as well as through businesses associated with the UNC. News releases concerning postal rates and new postal issues were reproduced in the bulletins of the UNC as well as in the Ukrainian-language press.

The Ukrainian postal stamps—all secondary to the official postage of the host countries—were to be affixed on the addressed side of the envelopes or packages, to the left of the recipient's address. In practice, though, many of the stamps were simply applied to the left of the host country's postage (figure 12.1). In countries which forbade the practice of affixing stamps other than their own to the address side, the Ukrainian labels were to be affixed on the reverse side of the card, envelope, or package. Finally, in those places where this also was forbidden, the stamps were then to be applied to the first page of the letter, or in the case of postal cards and packages, on the separate receipts of a Ukrainian postal station.[13]

Because of the proximity of the UNC center to the main Ukrainian DP camps, especially those in Munich, Regensburg, and Berchtesgaden, there

Figure 12.1   Ukrainian National Council Postal Usage. This registered cover sent from Munich to Bremerhaven, Germany, in November, 1953 bears, to the left of the required German postage, two stamps issued by the Ukrainian National Council, the parliamentary body of the Ukrainian government-in-exile. To emphasize the UNC's claim to national status, the stamps carry the legend "Ukrainian Post." The design on the left Commemorates the 700th anniversary of the founding of Lviv; the semi-postal issue on the right includes a surcharge to benefit Ukrainian war invalids.

Credit: Karen Lemiski.

was some overlap in the two authorities' postal networks. The UNC stamps were used on par with the camp stamps to deliver mail. In practice, this also meant that letters might be cancelled at one of the DP settlements with a UNC postmark instead of the camp's own cancel (figure 12.2). It is difficult to say whether or not such occurrences reflected an intentional decision or the convenience of one canceling device compared to the other. It may have been simple oversight by the postal personnel, facilitated by the corresponding numerical values between the DP and UNC stamps. No matter the case, the mismatching of stamps and cancellation marks proves that both the UNC and DP postal networks indeed were operational.

The Regensburg DP and the UNC postal systems shared resources in at least two additional areas. At least four of the first six UNC stamp designs were printed by Friedrich Pushtet, who also produced the majority of the Regensburg DP camp stamps. Secondly, after having designed

Figure 12.2   Displaced Persons Camp Cover. Airmail cover sent in April 1948 from the Soviet Union to a resident in the Regensburg, Germany, Displaced Persons Camp. As forerunners to the postal network of the Ukrainian National Council, the DP camps were authorized to organize their own postal services and to produce postage stamps for delivery within the camps. The stamp at lower left, issued by the Regensburg camp, is cancelled by a UNC postmark, showing the overlap in the DP and UNC postal networks.

Credit: Karen Lemiski.

two issues (1947 and 1948) for the Regensburg settlement, the artist Myron Bilynsky created three sets of stamps (1949 and 1950) for the UNC.

Some general observations can be made concerning the UNC's production of stamps. In total, the UNC printed and distributed more than 1.2 million stamps over a span of ten years; new designs were released on 12 occasions. Not surprisingly, the UNC prepared the largest number of stamps during the first two years of its postal program, when the greatest number of Ukrainians were still living in Germany. In 1948, the UNC issued its first set of stamps (six images) with a sum quantity of 850,000 copies, followed the next year by four additional designs with a total count of 205,385 stamps. Yet, as many refugees emigrated from Germany, fewer designs and smaller issues were generated. There were no new designs in either 1951 or 1952. And while 58,128 stamps were printed in 1954 (three motifs), in both 1955 and 1956 only one new design was released, each time with only 20,000 copies. By the time the final regular design was released in 1957, less than 10,000 stamps were prepared.

The money collected from the sale of the UNC postage stamps was deposited into the Ukrainian National Fund. Because of the rate schedule that was adopted and the large quantities of stamps that were initially printed, there was the potential for significant income. In 1951, ten shahiv equaled one U.S. dollar so that, for example, if all copies of the first ten-shahiv stamp had been sold, it would have meant revenues of U.S. $240,000.

An indication of how many stamps were actually needed is suggested by the appearance of several overprinted designs. Most likely this was done to use up the remaining stocks of earlier values that had been printed in large quantities. In 1953, for example, 23,600 stamps from the 1938 ten-shahiv issue and 17,200 stamps from the 1949 25-shahiv issue were overprinted to commemorate the 700th anniversary (1253–1953) of the founding of the city of Lviv and the coronation of Danylo as ruler of the Halych-Volhynian state.[14] At the same time, the ten-shahiv stamps were surcharged to 20 shahiv to reflect an increase in the UNC's basic postal rates.

In addition to the actual stamps, the UNC postal department also prepared five sets of postal cards and three commemorative envelopes for general correspondence. The first pieces were produced in 1954 and 1956, when the designs of new stamps were simultaneously reproduced on the postal stationery with only changes in color and, in one case, a change in denomination. The last stationery designs were released as late as 1973 and 1976, long after the UNC had issued its final stamps. As can be expected, though, the quantities of these items were held at several thousand copies each.

To some extent, there is a correlation between the release date of new stamp designs and the schedule of the UNC's initial parliamentary congresses.[15] In its early years when the UNC was holding sessions on a somewhat regular basis in Munich—in 1948, 1949, 1954, and 1957—new stamps were prepared. Most obviously, the UNC's first set of stamps was issued on December 1, 1948 to commemorate its first parliamentary session. Similarly, when the UNC met in London in 1972, another set of stamps was prepared.

Finally, the transient nature of the Ukrainian population in the postwar period also had an impact on the UNC's postal system. The permanent resettlement of refugees began in 1947, and by August 1948, more than 33,000 Ukrainians had emigrated from Germany. During the 14 years during which the UNC was actively producing postal stamps and stationery, only two artists created more than one design and seven other individuals each prepared one issue. In terms of style, this means that the 26 motifs have little in common.

Moreover, the UNC in its later years recycled stamp designs from earlier Ukrainian postal authorities on three occasions. First, to celebrate the 25th anniversary of the UNC in 1973, three postal cards adopted the images from the first values of stamps that the Ukrainian National Republic had prepared in 1918. This series, in fact, would be among the strongest influences for later stamp issues. The set was prepared by the prominent graphic artists Heorhiy Narbut[16] and Antin Sereda,[17] and released in 1918 as both paper currency tokens (to counteract the shortages of silver and copper that was needed for the minting of coins) and postage stamps. The designs of the five values were: a trident against a stylized background of the sun shining on the earth, a farm worker with a scythe, the head of a young girl who presumably symbolized the new Ukrainian state,[18] the trident emblem, and post-horns against an ornamental background.

Similarly, a 1973 UNC postcard marking the centenary of the founding of the Taras Shevchenko Society reused a design from a series of 14 stamps printed in Vienna at the end of 1920, by which time the forces of the Ukrainian National Republic had been defeated. Designed by the artist Mykola Ivasiuk,[19] this set is probably the best representation of the Ukrainian national character ever produced, with portraits of the poet/author Taras Shevchenko, Symon Petliura, the hetmen leaders Bohdan Khmelnytsky, Pavlo Polobotok, and Ivan Mazepa, a personification of independent Ukraine in the form of a young maiden, the monument in Kiev to Grand Prince Volodymyr, and several images of cossacks.

And as the third instance, the image of Symon Petliura that was used in 1976 for two pieces of postal stationery reused a 1935 stamp that the then Warsaw-based government-in-exile had issued to commemorate the tenth anniversary of Petliura's death. The motif was created by Petro Kholodny, Jr.,[20] who prepared all three designs that were released by the government-in-exile in Warsaw as well as five designs for the UNC.

The UNC's Postal Designs

Three goals associated with the UNC's production of stamps are reflected in the composition of their designs: preserving a claim to national status, propagating symbols of national identity, and generating income.[21]

To preserve a claim to national status, all of the stamps carried a legend reading either "Ukrainian Post," "Ukrainian National Council," or "Ukrainian National Council Post." This title was written unilingually in Ukrainian on approximately two-thirds of the designs. On the remaining one-third, the inscription was written in a combination of Ukrainian and

English, possibly to catch the attention of a wider audience and one that included non-Ukrainian individuals. For later issues, which were printed with eight or nine stamps in a complete pane, the inscription "Ukrainian National Council" was written around the border in English, French, and German. Writing the word "Ukrainian" in English not only deciphered the Cyrillic letters but also distinguished the national origin of the stamps from being classified as Russian. On half of the postal cards, the word "postcard" was written in Ukrainian, German, and English; French was added to these languages for the other half of the designs. The use of these languages followed the regulations set forth by the Universal Postal Union.

Symbols of authority appeared on three designs: a reproduction of the document that had established the UNC, a cossack wreath and scepter, and the coat of arms of Carpatho-Ukraine. Although the trident emblem was not included in the majority of designs for the regular postage stamps, it was obvious on both souvenir sheets as well as on eight of the nine revenue stamps. Related to political aspirations was the use of one slogan that was repeated on three issues: "An independent Ukraine secures the peace for Eastern Europe."

To propagate symbols of national identity, the UNC endorsed specific historical events and cultural figures. Within this pantheon of easily recognizable images, several themes can be catalogued. Landmarks and buildings formed the basis for five designs from the first set of six stamps that the UNC sponsored. The Monastery of the Caves in Kiev and St. George's Cathedral in Lviv were chosen to emphasize the leading role these two cities assumed in the history of Ukraine as well as the bond between the Ukrainian nation and its faiths (in contrast to the officially atheistic Soviet Union). Based on the postal rate schedule that was adopted by the UNC, placing these images respectively on the five- and ten-shahiv stamps guaranteed they would receive the widest circulation. The next three stamps carried images of the Central Rada and Workers' Congress buildings in Kiev and the seat of the short-lived Carpatho-Ukrainian government in Khust,[22] bearing witness to the development of a Ukrainian parliamentary tradition and the Ukrainian nation's goal of freedom. In total, Lviv was the focus of four designs, including two stamps that were modified by overprinted slogans. Kiev was highlighted on five stamps, two of which reused the same image of the Central Rada building.

Specific events from Ukraine's history were celebrated on 13 postal issues while 11 designs included a set of commemorate dates. Included in this category are stamps marking the 900th anniversary of the death of Prince Yaroslav the Wise (1054–1954), the 300th anniversary of hetman Bohdan Khmelnytsky's rebellion (1648–1948) against Polish domination over the cossack territories, the 40th anniversary of the Ukrainian National

Council in Kiev (1917–1957), the 30th anniversaries of the November 1918 uprising in Lviv and the unification of Ukraine (January 22, 1919), and the tenth anniversary of the declaration of independence in Carpatho-Ukraine (March 15, 1939).

By contrast, certain episodes from Ukrainian history were depicted on Soviet postal designs, but from the Soviet point of view. Thus, several issues commemorated the Red Army's liberation of Ukraine from Nazi Germany as well as anniversary dates of Ukraine as a union republic. But no stamps marked the anniversaries associated with the Ukrainian National Republic, the Western Ukrainian National Republic, or Carpatho-Ukraine, suggesting that the official Soviet version of history did not recognize these dates. Designs prepared in 1967 and 1977, however, featured the building where the First All-Ukrainian Communist Congress was held in Kharkov (1917) and the monument to the proclamation of Soviet government in Ukraine. Along this line, perhaps the most controversial series appeared in 1954 on the 300th anniversary of the Treaty of Pereiaslavl, a document used repeatedly by the Russians and Soviets to legitimize their hegemony over Ukraine.

Prominent Ukrainian figures were also featured on UNC issues. Of the eight stamps that included a person's portrait, six were of twentieth-century Ukrainian political figures; the other two were the medieval prince Yaroslav and the poet/author Taras Shevchenko, who was the only cultural figure to be honored. No women were specifically honored, although one stamp carried the generic image of a female nurse.

Among the politicians were three members of the Ukrainian exile government: Stepan Baran (1879–1953), chairman of the UNC's Executive Branch (1951–1953); Borys Ivanytsky (1878–1953), chairman of the UNC presidium (1948–1953); and Isaak Mazepa (1884–1952), one of the founders of the UNC and first chairman of its Executive Branch (1948–1952). Ivanytsky and Mazepa had also both served the original UNR government, respectively as director of the forestry department and as minister of internal affairs, later prime minister and minister of land affairs. Baran had also been the secretary of agriculture in the Western Ukrainian National Republic.

Symon Petliura, president of the UNR's Directory and commander-in-chief of its armed forces, was the most frequent to appear among the other politicians the UNC honored; his image appeared on one stamp, one envelope, three postal cards, and a commemorative sheet issued in 1976 to celebrate the "Petliura Year," the 50th anniversary of his death. The design combined a portrait of Petliura with his statement, "The gaining of Ukrainian statehood is a matter of the Ukrainian nation and not of class or party." Mikhailo Hrushevsky, first president of the UNR, and Andriy Livytsky (1879–1954), president of the government-in-exile, each appeared on one stamp and one envelope.

The only military motifs appeared on three stamps produced in 1950, with the images of a nurse with a wounded soldier, the branches of service, and two insurgents in action. Religious themes were on two stamps, one to mark the Marian Year in 1954 and the other depicting St. George slaying the dragon.

Finally, to generate income, several tokens were created as receipts for the voluntary donations made directly to the Ukrainian National Fund. These so-called revenue stamps generally displayed only a number against a background of wavy lines. The first set, prepared in 1949 in the denominations of 5, 10, 20, 50, 100, 200, 300 shahiv, was given in exchange for monthly payments to the fund. Two later issues of revenue stamps were created in 1954 without nominal values; one stamp was to be exchanged for five shahiv, while for the second, the payment of one day's wages was expected. These donations were to be made annually on January 22, the anniversary date of the declaration of the Fourth Universal (1918), which had established the Ukrainian National Republic. As late as 1972, specific

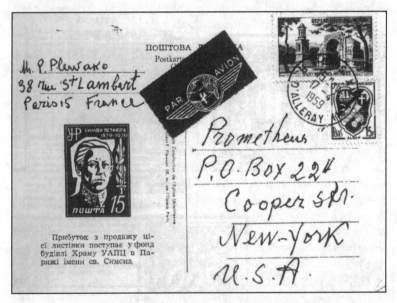

Figure 12.3   Ukrainian National Council Postcard. Ukrainian National Council postcard mailed from Paris to the United States in 1959. Under the UNC stamp in the lower left corner is the text "Profit from the sale of this card goes into the building fund of the Ukrainian Autocephalous Orthodox Church of St. Symon in Paris." Issued for both propaganda and fund-raising purposes, the use of UNC stamps in addition to national Postage was a voluntary act of support for the Ukrainian government-in-exile.

Credit: Borys Fessak.

revenue stamps were also issued to support the seventh congress of the government-in-exile. The revenue stamps were meant to be stored in one of two special folders that were prepared by the Ukrainian Financial Committee, in 1951 in the United States and in 1954 in London, England.

To appeal to stamp collectors—whether inside the Ukrainian community or not—printing varieties and color variations from most issues were also made available. And as was mentioned earlier, two stamp designs were modified and issued as souvenir sheets as a means of encouraging additional sales.

Within this category of revenue stamps I will also mention the two charity issues that the UNC prepared. In May 1950, four stamps (the only ones with military themes) were released with their surcharged amounts intended for the benefit of Ukrainian war invalids. Then in 1956, the UNC prepared a postal card that carried the notation "Profit from the sale of this card goes into the building fund of the Ukrainian Autocephalic Orthodox Church of St. Symon in Paris" (figure 12.3).

The Government-in-Exile's Legacy

The UNC government-in-exile never established itself as the sole political center for displaced Ukrainians, and it was often treated as just another political party. More significantly, though, as the Ukrainians moved to other countries to establish their new lives, the UNC lost at least some of the foundation for its postal network. Unquestionably, there is a distinct correlation between the decrease of stamps produced by the government-in-exile and the increase in the private labels issued by Ukrainian community organizations outside Europe, mostly in Canada and the United States.

In this regard, the images that were selected for the UNC's postage stamps became the foundational designs for the impressions produced in the Ukrainian diaspora by individuals and cultural organizations, ranging from the Plast boy scouts to the Organization of Ukrainian Nationalists, the Sich Riflemen, and the Ukrainian Bandurist Chorus. In practice, the mail that Ukrainians sent amongst themselves that also conveyed these decorative designs constituted the "Ukrainian Underground Post" (Pidpilna Poshta Ukraini). The role of this network in spreading nationalistic Ukrainian messages cannot be overestimated. According to one Ukrainian living in Canada, the private issues "expressed the yearnings Ukrainians felt for the freedom denied them in their native land."[23]

Myriad private designs were created on an equally wide variety of topics, ranging from simple "poster-type" stamps that were illustrated with ethnographic designs and portraits of historical Ukrainian personalities to those spreading militantly nationalist messages. The majority of motifs with blatant political statements were prepared in the United States in reflection of the settlement there of the more politicized post-1945 emigration as well as the more politicized U.S. population in general (in contrast to the situation in Canada where the emigrants were focused more on cultural and community affairs). The messages on these political labels were written in English as a means of reaching a broad audience as well as the younger generations of Ukrainians who may not have been fluent in their parents' language. While the inscriptions may not have encouraged many people to act, their effectiveness would have been derived from the obtrusiveness of the slogans, which should have held the readers' attention long enough for the messages to be registered mentally.

Clearly, the UNC's postal program was meaningful. However, given that the Ukrainian state formed a republic within the Soviet Union for almost 70 years—the same time during which the majority of these stamps were produced—the government-in-exile promoted itself as an independent state-in-waiting. The UNC's system helped to educate the emigrants and possibly even a wider audience—at least those individuals who paid attention to postage stamps—about Ukrainian politics, history, and culture. While the majority of people who were exposed to the UNC's stamps may themselves have been ethnically Ukrainian and therefore possibly already aware of the images portrayed, this does not lessen the impact of the designs. Instead, the stamps maintained this knowledge of national and historical events among members of the displaced nation, preparing them for eventual statehood.

This is not to say that nations must be on their own sovereign territory in order to set up postal services. As countries were overrun during World War II and their governments were transferred to other countries, their rights as members of the Universal Postal Convention were maintained. Poland, Norway, and Yugoslavia were each allowed to issue stamps for use on their naval vessels as expatriated posts. The Czech government-in-exile was also granted the use of a postmark to commemorate the 23rd anniversary of the foundation of the Czechoslovak Republic, for use on letters posted from Czech forces in Great Britain.

In none of these examples, however, did the displaced governments establish such extensive postal programs or exploit the potential opportunity of postage stamps to advance their ethnicity as did the Ukrainians. According to my research, in this aspect the Ukrainian experience is unique. No other ethnic community has produced this number of stamps and over such an extended period of time. The closest parallel is Poland's Solidarity movement. Yet in Poland's case, the production and circulation of private postal stamps and stationery by the civil society was only a means of internal opposition, and letters displaying the Solidarity stamps were neither allowed beyond Poland's borders nor openly circulated within Poland. Another similar case involves the labels produced by Northern Ireland's Sinn Fein movement. But here again, letters carrying these labels were sent back to senders because the political leadership did not enter into agreements with modern postal authorities to allow their stamps to circulate on international mail. Finally, while other ethnic immigrant communities in the United States and Canada, including the Poles and Slovaks, did issue private labels, they were neither as numerous as the Ukrainian issues nor motivated by such strong political aspirations, and they were not associated with a governmental authority, but rather were produced sporadically by private organizations.

There are several reasons that can account for the Ukrainian system. First, the size and diversity of the Ukrainian nation-in-exile allowed for the development of such an administration. Unquestionably, in addition to the intelligentsia that found itself outside of Ukraine's borders following the formation of the Soviet Union, leaders from the independent governments were active in the government-in-exile while the large displaced community also included graphic artists who could design the ephemeral pieces. Second, given that Ukraine did experience several periods of independence, however brief, there was some understanding of the obligation of new governments to release postage stamps. Because the UNC viewed itself as the successor to the Ukrainian National Republic, its postal administration continued to fulfill this task. Finally, philately itself was historically important and had a foundation in the Ukrainian community. The government-in-exile merely capitalized on this interest while promoting the messages of Ukrainian nationalism.

As a final comment, the postal program of the Ukrainian government-in-exile did have significance for modern Ukraine: the emigrant experience itself served as a period of preparation. With the breakup of the Soviet Union and the founding of an independent Ukraine, Mykola Plaviuk, then president of the government-in-exile, dissolved the UNC and transferred its powers to the newly elected president, Leonid Kravchuk. As at other times in Ukrainian history, the move was intended to form a link between the youngest Ukrainian state and earlier autonomous ones.

In terms of postage stamps, the majority of modern Ukraine's first issues were produced in Canada and often designed in keeping with the trends established by the diaspora's postage. Ukraine resumed issuing stamps in March 1992 with the release of a pair of 15-kopiok stamps. The first commemorated the 500th anniversary of the Ukrainian cossack state (1490–1990) and the second stamp honored the centennial of Ukrainian emigration to Canada (1891–1991). These two stamps carried great significance: they were the first regular stamps released by a Kiev-based, Ukrainian government since 1919. According to Vasyl Boyarchuk, Deputy Chairman of the Ukrainian State Committee on Communications, "the issuance of our own stamps is yet another affirmation of Ukraine's statehood."[24] Yet even before the release of these first official stamps of Ukraine, the trident emblem was used as an overprint and placed on the stamps of the former Soviet Union, just as had been done in 1918 on imperial Russian stamps. Thus, the postal traditions established by the UNR and government-in-exile were returned to Ukraine as a practical program.

Moreover, when the designs produced in the newly independent Ukraine strayed too far from the canons established in the diaspora, the loudest criticisms came from the Ukrainian communities in Canada and the United States, which argued that the stamps were "too Soviet" and not "Ukrainian" enough in appearance. In the context of modern Ukraine, then, where the notion of "Soviet" has been overturned, the earlier emigrants continued to work toward building a strong Ukrainian nation that is united behind the ideas and symbols it promoted publicly for 40 years on its own stamps.

The exile stamps and postal stationery are thus important historical artifacts, telling the wider international community about the existence of the government-in-exile, and more importantly, spreading strong nationalistic and cultural messages among Ukrainians themselves during the period in which no independent Ukrainian state existed. The messages carried on the stamps played key roles in defining and perpetuating the notions associated with the Ukrainian national identity. In the context of the Cold War, the stamps further created a sense of solidarity among Ukrainians by contrasting the "evil" Soviet Union with the "good" government-in-exile. The impact of the émigrés' postal system was in part brought to light by the official protests made by the Soviet Union and its efforts to halt mail from Canada carrying the exile stamps that was posted to Ukrainians still living within its borders. For better or worse, though, the Soviet efforts only further encouraged the Ukrainian community—as maintained and continued by second and third generations of Ukrainians in exile—to circulate nationalist stamps as conscious political weapons in its wider anti-Soviet campaign.

Finally, the UNC postal network may partially account for the eventual success of Ukraine in gaining its independence. That the modern state has performed more cohesively as a unit—albeit still faced with numerous political, economic, and social problems—than many other parts of the former Soviet Union may be based on the strong nationalistic ties that were encouraged by the Ukrainian government-in-exile and then maintained in the diaspora, especially since many high-ranking officials in Ukraine are exiles returned to the now-independent homeland. In the words of one individual, "Millions of letters with Ukrainian stamps, as they travel throughout the world, carry a much wider message about our country than the hundreds of ardent speeches in the Verkhovna Rada [Ukrainian Parliament]."[25]

Notes

1. As minister of postal and telegraph services, V. Kuliabko-Koretsky issued the order on August 20, 1918. The document is translated in Val Zabijaka, "The Trident Overprints of 1918," *Introductory Handbook of Ukrainian Philately/Ukrainian Philatelist* 40, no. 1/2 63/64 (1993): 14.
2. Volodymyr Holovatsky (1875–1963) was the deputy director of the post office for the Western Ukrainian National Republic.
3. The private stamps appeared in Czechoslovakia, Poland, France, Austria, Belgium, China, the United States, Canada, and Argentina.
4. The situation was also made easier by the sheer number of new stamps that were released by the Soviet government. This meant that postal clerks did not always recognize the designs, which was especially possible as some Soviet stamps carried regional and ethnically non-Russian motifs.
5. Ihor Stebelsky, "Ukrainian Population Migration after World War II," in *The Refugee Experience: Ukrainian Displaced Persons after World War II*, ed. Wsevolod Isajiw, Yury Boshyk, and Roman Senkus (Edmonton: Canadian Institute of Ukrainian Studies, 1992), pp. 27–28.
6. The largest Ukrainian camps (2,000 to 5,000 people) in the U.S. zone were located near Munich (Warner Kaserne), Augsburg (Somme Kaserne), Mittenwald (Jäger Kaserne), Regensburg (Ganghofersiedlung), Aschaffenburg, Berchtesgaden (Orlyk), Bayreuth (Leopold Kaserne), Neu Ulm (Ludendorf Kaserne), Leipheim, and Dillingen (Luitpold Kaserne).
7. Julian Maksymczuk, *Ukraïns'i poshtovi marky* (n.p.: Financovoho Resortu Vykonoho Orhanu Ukraïns'koi Natsional'noi Rady, 1949), p. 25.
8. H.F. Stich, *Postwar Years of Germany 1945–47* (Vancouver: the author, 1994), p. 234. Displaced Persons did not fall under the jurisdiction of the German authorities but rather under a special legal system that granted them almost extraterritorial rights to set up, conduct, and administer their own internal affairs, security, and matters of everyday life. The DP camps were initially supervised by the United Nations Relief and Rehabilitation Administration (UNRRA) and later by the International Refugee Organization (IRO).
9. Stich, *Postwar Years of Germany*, p. 234; Maksymczuk, *Ukraïns'i poshtovi marky*, pp. 23–24.
10. Directive No. 3 was based on the UNC's Resolution No. 1, dated August 8, 1948, which established the Ukrainian National Fund as the treasury to support the government-in-exile's activities. The money collected from the sale of the Ukrainian postage stamps was therefore deposited into this fund.
11. Directive No. 3 of the Executive Branch of the Ukrainian National Council, dated December 2, 1948; cited in *Visti: Poshchtovoho viddily resorty finansiv vo Ukrains'koi natsional'noi rady* (Munich), no. 2/3 (1954). Other postal rates established by the UNC were five shahiv for printed matter weighing up to fifty grams and ten shahiv for registration.
12. Argentina, Australia, Austria, Belgium, Brazil, Canada, England, France, Germany, Italy, The Netherlands, Spain, Sweden, Switzerland, Tunisia, the United States, and Uruguay.
13. *Visti: Poshchtovoho viddily resorty finansiv vo Ukrains'koi natsional'noi rady* (Munich), no. 2/3 (1954). The receipts indicated the recipient's address and, in the case of packages, their contents.

14. Both of these stamps featured images from the city of Lviv, thus explaining their selection as the base stamps for the overprinted slogans. It is possible that there were similar numbers of unused stamps from the other values in this series.

15. The council convened for ten sessions: July 1948 in Augsburg; June 1949 in Leipheim; March 1954, March 1957, November 1961, and March 1967 in Munich; December 1972 in London; June 1979 in Munich; July 1984 in Toronto; and June 1989 in South Bound Brook, New Jersey.

16. A member of the Ukrainian Commission on Heraldry, Narbut (1886–1920) also helped design the currency and state seals during Mikhailo Hrushevsky's presidency as well as the flags and various insignia that Pavlo Skoropadsky (1873–1945) later requested for the Hetmanate.

17. Sereda (1890–1961) was a prominent designer of commercial logos. He taught at the Kiev Architectural Institute (1920–1924), the Kiev State Art Institute (1924–1929, 1934–1941, 1944–1950), and at the Ukrainian Printing Institute in Kharkov (1929–1934).

18. In traditional iconography, freedom is generally represented as a young maiden in classical dress.

19. Ivasiuk (1865–1930?) agreed to undertake the project without pay in return for a percentage of the finished stamps. He disappeared after being arrested by the Soviet secret police in Kiev in 1930.

20. Petro Kholodny, Jr. (born in Kiev in 1902) left Ukraine in 1920, following his father who worked with the UNR's Secretariat of Public Education and Ministry of Education. He studied art at the Ukrainian Studio of Plastic Arts in Prague (1926–1927) and the Warsaw Academy of Arts (1928–1934), and exhibited in many European cities.

21. The designs of the Ukrainian National Council stamps are best described by Borys Fessak, *Ukrainian DP Camp, POW Camp, Government in Exile, and National Council Issues*, 2nd edn. (Washington, DC: Ukrainian Philatelic and Numismatic Society, 2003), and by Wolodemer Klisch, *Ukrainian National Post 1948–1993: Philadelphia Exhibition October 23–October 30, 1993* (Philadelphia, 1993). I thank both authors for providing me with accurate descriptions and details of these stamps, and Mr. Fessak for his further details on the operations of the UNC postal system.

22. As a result of an agreement concluded in November 1918 with the leaders of Czechoslovakia, Ukrainian emigrants from the Transcarpathia region accepted the incorporation of their homeland into the new Czech state on the condition of Transcarpathian autonomy. Then, following the Munich Pact of September 1938, Czechoslovakia was transformed into a federal republic that granted its easternmost province a special autonomous status. On March 15, 1939, a national assembly meeting in Khust proclaimed independence for Carpatho-Ukraine. To mark the opening of its First National Assembly, a stamp design consisting of the inscription "Karpatska Ukraina" (Carpatho-Ukraine) against the silhouette of a church was released. By late March 1939, however, the Hungarian occupation of Carpatho-Ukraine was complete; the territory would be administered by Hungary until September 1944, when it was occupied by Soviet troops.

23. Alexander Malycky, "Ukrainian Non-Postal (Private or Cinderella) Stamps, 1900–1945," *Introductory Handbook of Ukrainian Philately/Ukrainian Philatelist* 40, no. 1/2, 63/64 (1993): 57.

24. Cited in "The First Postage Stamps of a Reestablished Ukraine," *Ukrainian Philatelist* 39, no. 2, 62 (1992): 57.

25. Cited in "The Stamps Will Tell About the Country," *Trident-Visnyk* (October–November 1995): 120.

Part VI

Letters and the State

13

Immigrant Petition Letters in Early Modern Saxony

Alexander Schunka

Introduction

The early modern world was to a large extent manufactured and shaped through migration. The dissemination of goods, ideas, and knowledge accompanied or followed people on the move.[1] In many cases, these exchanges of experience and transfers of goods and people were neither purposely planned by the migrants nor based on rulers' decisions, but forced by the decision of ordinary Europeans to make their living and secure subsistence or betterment elsewhere.[2] In order to find the best possible circumstances for religious, economic, or social security, migration in the early modern period was not an exception but a rule, for individuals as well as for specific social groups.[3]

The following remarks are intended to provide a glimpse at one specific feature of migration. For a long time, the phenomenon of intra-European migration in sixteenth- to early eighteenth-century Europe has been characterized as "religious" or "confessional" migration.[4] This was due to the fact that the Protestants of specific areas were affected by attempts at confessional homogenization by the ruling Catholic elites, particularly in France and the Habsburg territories. Apart from some exceptions, for example, in Ireland or Sweden, the larger emigrant groups such as Dutch, Austrians, and Huguenots were Protestants leaving Catholic countries.[5] Significantly, the historians who dominated the study of these groups from contemporary times onwards were likely to be descendants of these particular groups of migrants or, later on, at least influenced by concepts of Protestant historiography. Thus conceptions of religious migration and exile still found in the research literature often derive from the self-images of the Protestant migrants and therefore tend to be rather one-sided views of persecution and martyrdom. In this essay, however, I try to contrast this view through examining the letters of one large group of European migrants, the so-called "Bohemian Exiles": Protestants leaving the recatholizised Bohemian (Habsburg) states in the seventeenth century. Contrary to the largely substantialist view of older, Protestant-based historiography, my approach will be more functionalist, looking at the arguments, the *topoi* (repeated and expected stereotypes in letter-writing), and the stories. I suggest that analyzing only the macro structures and the historical data can sometimes give a misleading picture of migration patterns. It is equally important to show which stories were told by the migrants, how the migrants told them, under which circumstances, and for what reason.

My arguments will be based on petition letters written by Bohemian emigrants to the government of neighboring Protestant Saxony. In general, petition letters are abundant in European archives and are not restricted to contents related to immigration; they can address any topics where a subject asked the ruling authority for assistance, in legal, economic, or even social matters. Yet in the field of early modern German history, petition letters have long been neglected. They have occasionally been analyzed, though mainly from the perspectives of legal or administrative history.[6] One striking feature of petitions is how the stories are presented by the supplicants. In this respect, internationally renowned works, such as Natalie Zemon Davis's *Fiction in the Archives*, have highlighted the innovative potential of stories, (in Davis's case in pardon tales in early modern France), and have illuminated the narrative strategies employed by their tellers.[7] It has also been stressed that it is not only worthwhile but also necessary to look at these narrations in order to gain better insight into early modern society and the possibilities of "self-fashioning" within it.[8] A functionalist way of analyzing the individuals' use of stories in documents such as petition letters can contribute substantially to our understanding of the early modern fashioning and self-fashioning of immigrants. In our case, looking at the narrative strategies of migrant petition letters allows us to analyze the migrants' motives regarding how and where to settle, how to integrate with or segregate from the locals, the intellectual horizon of a mobile society, and many more issues of this kind.

The migrant petition letters are not completely unknown to researchers dealing with Bohemians in Saxony, although they have been analyzed with a rather narrow focus. On the one hand, they have long served as proof of personal religious loyalty and individual fate; on the other, they have been used to demonstrate the dramatic Catholic persecution of the non-Catholic population of Bohemia.[9] I would argue, however, that the immigrants themselves knew when and how to select special, topical arguments in order to succeed in their requests. They used these *topoi* either intentionally, or unintentionally, according to their own social knowledge.[10]

The volume of immigrant petition letters is rather large. There are a few thousand such letters. Unfortunately, it is almost impossible to analyze them statistically, as they are widely spread among the archives in Saxony, and there are hardly any consistent bodies of petition letters within these archives. Instead of attempts at quantification, the following approach will have a different goal. So far nobody has examined the narrative strategies these Bohemian immigrants used to explain their individual situations, their migrational experiences, and their expectations of the receiving society. This essay therefore aims to look at the *topoi* and arguments in immigrant letters, the way the migrants reproduced or even constructed their own history of persecution and migration, their mental maps between home and exile, and, furthermore, the role of the hosting ruler, the Elector of Saxony, as a presumed protector of the oppressed. The main features in the strategies of the petitioners show their desire for and expectations of order,[11] and document their wish to adjust their lives to their new surroundings. Ultimately, it can be shown that these petitioners used their pasts to argue for a better and more secure future status, sometimes employing religious means to do so.

The essay will first give an overview of the historical setting of the migrations, followed by an analysis and contextualization of the form and content of immigrant petition letters. Finally, the case study of a petitioning migrant woman will serve as an example to illustrate the aims and needs of petitioners.

Migration and Faith

From the early 1620s, the German state of Saxony became the refuge of supposedly steadfast Protestants from neighboring countries. These people were seeking shelter with the government of one of the most influential Lutheran rulers in Germany: the Elector *(Kurfuerst)* of Saxony. The migrations continued throughout the seventeenth century but are usually connected with the Thirty Years' War. Accepting, welcoming, and hosting the immigrants have been primarily attributed to the reign of Elector Johann Georg I (1611–1656). Later in the century, the Saxon Elector and his territories attracted not only Lutherans, but also a few Catholics, some of them converting to Protestantism, and many more formerly un-free laborers in the Habsburg empire.

By far the greatest number of immigrants came from the neighboring states south and east of Saxony, which were then part of the lands of the Habsburg Monarchy: Bohemia, Moravia, Silesia, and in the later seventeenth century, Upper Hungary (known today as Slovakia). They fled either the cruelties of the Thirty Years' War or the ongoing, more or less forcefully applied efforts of the Habsburg administration to recatholizise their Protestant population. Many of these people came to Saxony hoping to stay for just a few years, but a significant number of them settled permanently.

The number of people who left the Habsburg states and settled in Saxony and elsewhere is supposed to be somewhere between 100,000 and 1,000,000. Eduard Winter has highlighted the waves of emigration from Bohemia during the seventeenth century with its peak period during and shortly after the Thirty Years' War.[12] A significant number of immigrants settled close to the Bohemian-Saxon border; many others went to the bigger cities like Dresden, Pirna, or Zittau. Some of them kept their Bohemian-Czech traditions in church rites and daily life, but the German-speaking majority of the immigrants melted into the local population after only a few generations.[13]

The immigrants left their traces in the archives as writers of petition letters. In these letters, they usually stressed their status as exiles and their true belief in the Lutheran faith, as this was a necessary precondition to receiving permission to settle and become a Saxon subject and burgher.[14] Thus the migrants' expressions of Lutheran faith were not unbiased, as the letter-writers expected the Saxonian ruler to support them. Immigrants writing petition letters ranged from members of the nobility to clerics, craftsmen, and ordinary working people. Their letters were sent to the Saxonian ruler and his administration, who then decided whether to grant or refuse the immigrants' requests.

In their petition letters, the authors tried to present themselves to their best advantage. According to their own words, their Lutheran faith had been a key factor in the decision to leave all their belongings, their homes, their families, and most importantly, their native countries. They had chosen to keep their faith and leave all their material things behind, the immigrants explained. A few centuries later, Protestant and even nonreligious historians who addressed the topic argued in a very similar way.

However, the arguments of the petition writers were, to a great extent, part of a game between authors and recipients. The game involved the interplay of mutual expectations on the recipients' as well as on the senders' side, concerning individual subsistence and security as well as social order in the post-migrational situation: for the immigrants, as they needed to settle and start a new life, and for the administration, as they expected the newcomers to become Saxonian subjects and taxpayers. Therefore, it was necessary for the petition writers to express their belief in the ways expected by the authorities in the receiving country. The immigrants themselves knew well when and how to select special, topical arguments in order to succeed in their requests. So these petition letters are not only an expression of Lutheran persecution and faith, but also a very pragmatic way to deal with religious arguments, and these religious arguments do not necessarily show what the immigrants truly believed. This view runs counter to the paradigm of "confessionalization" which gave the confessional and religious factor a primary role in the emergence of the (early) modern state and society, and which dominated the history of early modern Europe for quite a long time.[15] This paradigm, moreover, made historians look more at the institutionalized, modernizing forms of faith and less at the role religion truly played for ordinary people in their daily lives.[16]

There is still little knowledge of non-confessional factors within the early modern confessionally influenced migrations, that is, how people placed themselves in their new surroundings, what kinds of arguments they considered successful, and which strategies they pursued in order to receive the support they needed. The almost institutionalized system of petitions illustrates how immigrants developed ties to their new home, as well as how they established means of communication which helped them adapt their new life circumstances for settlement, material subsistence, and integration. In this respect, it also shows that in daily life religion was a phenomenon that could be handled very pragmatically.

Immigrant Petition Letters

The phenomenon of handling petition letters was not at all unique to Saxony. For most chancelleries of almost any early modern European court, dealing with petition letters was a major issue if not the main occupation. The practice was even satirized in famous theater plays, such as in the introductory scene of Lessing's *Emilia Galotti*. Even if the recipient usually were the ruler, for practical reasons functionaries dealt with them on his behalf.

The archives of upper Saxony boast a significant number of petition letters written mainly by seventeenth-century immigrants from Bohemia. The letter-writers usually personally addressed the Elector of the state of Saxony. Most wrote seeking permission to settle in Saxony, requesting financial help, or asking for particular administrative assistance. In many cases, they tried to use quite sophisticated or at least very touching explanations to convince the Saxonian administration to grant what they wanted.

The petition letters are, at first glance, emotionally moving documents. The writers tell of their lives and hardships in Catholic Bohemia, the trials of escape and migration, and sometimes they relate their expectations of the ruler and of life in their new Lutheran surroundings. Read in quantity, they come to seem quite stereotypical, sometimes even boring, and redundant. Still, there is a considerable amount of detail worth looking at. Let us examine the typical structure of the letters Bohemian immigrants wrote to the Elector of Saxony in the seventeenth century.

The petition letters follow a strict and well-ordered formula, as described in contemporary manuals concerning the *ars dictandi* and following the styles of letter-writing common since antiquity, in accordance with Ciceronian rhetoric. In late-medieval and early modern Europe, these manuals for letter-writing increased in number and size. Their influence extended beyond early modern Europe. As David Fitzpatrick has shown, even the letters of Irish migrants to Australia in the nineteenth century followed rules based on the antique and medieval *ars dictandi*.[17]

An ideal letter consisted of seven different and clearly distinguishable parts. These parts were the *salutatio, exordium* (or *captatio benevolentiae*), *narratio, petitio, conclusio, subscriptio* and *inscriptio/suprascriptio*.

In practice, a typical petition letter looked as follows:

First, the petitioner had to humbly greet his addressee, in our case the Elector of Saxony (*salutatio*). He then appealed to the ruler's position as the most important Lutheran ruler in Germany (*captatio benevolentiae*). This proved to be crucial in order to arrange a common basis of communication between the sender and the receiver, the immigrant and the ruler or his administration. Later in the seventeenth century, especially when the social and confessional make-up of the immigrants changed, a petitioner would most likely stress not the Lutheran faith of the Elector, but his ideal, faithful, and just rulership over his subjects. This becomes explicitly evident in petitions of Lutherans recently converted from Catholicism, or Catholics.

After this introduction, the writer would usually refer to the many others who, like him- or herself, had had to endure the hardships of war and religious persecution, and who had also decided to emigrate to Saxony instead of converting to Catholicism in Bohemia (*narratio*). The writer would stress the urge to migration for the sake of God (similar to the medieval concept of *peregrinatio*) and also his and his fellow Lutherans' constancy, thus using a term highly popular in contemporary sixteenth- and seventeenth-century political theory, as well as in the writings of Protestant emigrant clerics and ideologists such as Jan Amos Comenius. These writers derived their usage of constancy from Iustus Lipsius's famous dialogue *De constantia* (on constancy), which was in its time extremely successful as a manual for comforting oppressed and doubtful individuals, people who were deeply shaken by their political and religious circumstances.[18]

This part of a typical petition letter was followed by the main cause of the petition, the request (*petitio*). At this point, the writer usually switched from plural to singular, depicting his own fate between former home and current exile. Depending on his reason for writing and on what he actually needed, he used certain topical elements to emphasize his request. People asking for a passport in order to travel back to Bohemia and trade their former belongings stressed their mobility; others, in need of a permit to beg for money in Saxon communities, said they were exceptionally poor due to their age or to having many children. People trying to settle in a certain place in Saxony argued that they were predestined to serve the community according to their particular skills. If they, for instance, had claimed poverty, the cities in early modern Saxony would most likely not have let them settle, as towns were already full of poor people.

In the petition letters, the stories leading to the request are normally where we can catch a glimpse of the geographic dimension, and of the mental maps the writers had. When people wrote about their old homes and their new surroundings, it is noteworthy that they mentioned the persecutions in Bohemia, but usually did not refer to the journey to Saxony itself. If we take the issues in the petition letters seriously, it is sometimes tempting to think of the Bohemian capital of Prague as a suburb of Dresden in Saxony. This leads to the assumption that the mental maps of the immigrants, as well as their whole petition letters, are largely centered on their new surroundings, looking forward into Saxony rather than back to their former homes.

Some petitioners, especially in the 1620s, considered it necessary to stress the fact that they were not even born in Bohemia or other Habsburg countries, but in Saxony (the word they use is *Landkind*, i.e. "child of this country" or native-born).[19] This is because of a circumstance widely neglected in research on Bohemian emigration: many German-speaking Bohemian immigrants into Saxony were not native Bohemians, but had migrated into Bohemia at an earlier stage. These people are to be found particularly among clerics, craftsmen, and traders, highly mobile social groups. Nevertheless, when they re-migrated into Saxony, they all felt the need to emphasize that they were persecuted Lutherans who had lost their beloved homeland when they left Bohemia, even if it was not their native country. Therefore Habsburg or Bohemian immigration into Saxony proves not to be a singular phenomenon but part of larger early-modern migration patterns. We might go so far as to talk about a Habsburg-Central German Migration System.[20] On the other hand, it is obvious that the receiving country expected to receive persecuted Lutherans only, using such means of administration as petition letters. What these petitioners had in common was that they belonged to the category of religious "exiles" (*Exulanten*). It was one of the main requirements of Saxon policy toward Bohemian immigrants to accept only truly persecuted victims and steadfast Lutherans: illegal immigrants such as serfs or criminals were not to be accepted, but, in principle, had to be sent back into Bohemia. The term "exile" more and more became a stereotypical signifier of group coherence regardless of other social distinctions. It served to integrate anybody, from nobles to beggars. These exiles therefore soon made up a social group of their own in the receiving country. Here, the Saxon administration contributed to the shaping of this group through administrative demands such as immigration lists and the petition letters. So the expectations in the receiving country largely contributed to shaping a distinct social group—the religious "Bohemian Emigrant," or, in contemporary German, the *Exulant*.[21]

As mentioned earlier, the typical petition letter closely corresponded to the acquired formula of early-modern letter-writing. This can be inferred from numerous contemporary manuals on how to write letters and which style to employ.[22] However, the petition letters show a couple of peculiarities. One of them is the very request itself. Usually the petitioner wrote that if the Elector treated his request favorably, he in turn would promise to pray for the Elector and his family. This looks like a form of a religious contract, and it might be seen as running counter to the Lutheran theology of justification *sola fide* (only through faith). Thus, it could be interpreted as a way of giving and taking, as recent publications on the social dimension of gifts in the early modern era have shown.[23] This is striking because, for quite a long time, research on poor relief in early modern Europe has emphasized the differences between Catholic and Protestant areas. Whereas in Catholic territories it was said to be common for the recipient of alms to pray or do pilgrimages in favor of the giver, Protestants were expected *not* to connect good deeds directly with rewards. In the Protestant case, only God would be expected to decide autonomously whether to grant the giver a reward or not. The petition letters, however, show that Lutherans apparently had no problem arguing in a slightly Catholic direction sometimes, if it empowered the petitioners' position and therefore seemed necessary or proved successful to them.[24] The use of *topoi* such as this was not limited by confessional borders, but followed pragmatic concerns.

But who wrote these petition letters?

This is a difficult question, as it is not always clear whether the letter was written by the petitioner himself or by a professional letter-writer. There is a wide range of possibilities: In some cases, the petitioner told his story to the writer, who would write the letter accordingly. Sometimes the scribe signed the letter with his own name instead of the petitioner's, sometimes he wrote down the petitioner's signature, and sometimes the petitioner himself signed the letter, or was able to write the whole letter himself.

One might suspect the letters written by professionals to be less personal or autobiographical than the ones written by petitioners. We might even expect that private people, not as well-trained or experienced in letter-writing as scribes, would stick to the formula more closely than professional writers. These professionals might have felt more free to leave the structures of the *ars dictandi*. This assumption proves to be untrue, however. There is usually as much or as little personal information in both types of letters, and it is difficult to ascertain from the contents whether a letter derives from the petitioner himself or not. From its appearance, however, the producer is easier to trace, although a whole variety of possibilities occurs. Some petitions' authors can be identified by the quality and grade of experience in spelling and hand-writing, some by signature, some others by the sign "*manu proprie*" (by my own hand) or "*mppr*," some even by the scribe's signature.

The structure of most petition letters is very close to that advocated in the early modern manuals on letter-writing. And the fact that the petitioners used certain *topoi*, like poverty, illness, age, or a large number of children to emphasize their neediness, does not make it particularly easy to trace the "individual" or the "ego" in this material.[25] Still, it can be shown that these petition letters, whether written by the petitioners themselves or by professional writers, tell us a lot about the "self," especially since the petitioners individually adapted these *topoi* according to their own needs. For example, in the early 1620s, one Bohemian translator sought permission to live in the Saxonian capital of Dresden. When he wrote to the town council, he stressed the fact of being a persecuted Lutheran and omitted detailed information concerning his profession. When he wrote to the Elector the same day, he instead argued that people of his profession were strongly needed in the Saxonian capital.[26]

This example and the variety of arguments prove how well-informed the letter-writers were. The translator obviously knew that the Elector had recently decided to let the municipal council of Dresden decide whether somebody was a true victim of religious persecution or not, and if the immigrants proved themselves in view of the town council to be persecuted Lutherans, then and only then would the Electoral administration decide whether a person was to be accepted or not.

We might also cite the regular petitioning of a group of some 10 to 20 Hungarian (i.e. Slovak) immigrants in the late seventeenth century who, for almost 20 years in a row and at average intervals of 6 months, regularly asked for monetary subsistence, which they just as regularly received. With the help of the usual terminology of religious exiles, they argued that their current petition letter for monetary subsistence was likely to be the final one, as many group members were already very old and about to die soon. In reality, the group did not die out at all but even grew slightly in number, and their members eventually did not even consist of the Hungarians/Slovaks they had claimed to be. But for about 20 years nobody really bothered. Both the Hungarians and the municipal and church authorities seemed to have taken enough benefit from the stability and order of the relationship between administration and supplicants to justify the petitions.[27]

The Case of Anna Wodianskin and the
Pragmatic Dimensions of Faith

It needs to be taken into consideration that the petition business was not restricted to male petitioners. In the course of the Bohemian migrations, many single women arrived in Saxony as well. Some of them had refused to obey their husbands and thus did not convert from Lutheran belief to Catholicism but decided to emigrate; some others had husbands who served in the armies of Saxony, Sweden, or the Habsburg Empire. Others had to make their living in Saxonian cities like Dresden on their own because their husbands were abroad to work or beg. Some were simply widowed. In the petition letters and in other related sources such as immigrants' lists, most of the single female migrants claimed to be widows, although in a strict sense they were not, either because their husbands were still alive, or because the women had not been married at all. Single women traveling were seen by the society as a threat to order, whereas widows in the early modern era were considered legal successors of their late husbands and thus enjoyed a better status. This is why the proportion of widows looks extremely high in some immigrants' lists, totaling one third of all immigrants. Still, petition letters written or signed by women amount to only a very small percentage compared to the large number written by men.

However, it is fascinating to see that women possessed their own structures of communication, quite independent from male petitioners. They wrote not to the Elector but to his wife, and they had different personal ties to the court to facilitate getting their petition letters through to the higher-ranking officials. Most importantly, women expressed different needs, and they seemed to stick less carefully to the forms of letter-writing than men did. The case of the Bohemian Anna Wodianskin illustrates these peculiarities lucidly. Furthermore, the example shows that it is not only the use of *topoi* that gives these letters such insight into the self and the self-fashioning of the writers. Sometimes the petitions become very personal documents. This may justify a closer look at Anna's story.

When she decided to write her petition letter in the year 1647, at the end of the Thirty Years' War, Anna Wodianskin was the owner of a small food stall in the Saxonian capital of Dresden.[28] She wrote to the wife of the ruler a long and moving story. She had left her native city of Prague in Bohemia in 1628, having been thrown out of her husband's house because she had refused to convert to Catholicism. With only her two children and what belongings she could carry on her body, she made her way to Saxony, troubled by the fact that she had disobeyed her husband. One of her children died soon after the "poor deserted exile" (*arme verlassene Exulantin*) arrived in the Saxonian capital. Anna spent her life selling pickled cucumbers and salads, sometimes earning a little extra money by roasting and selling a suckling pig or a goose. Her business, however, failed to prosper because she experienced envy and hatred from the citizens of Dresden, particularly from the competing local market women who sabotaged her attempts to buy meat and other ingredients. Therefore Anna had written a petition to Abraham von Sebottendorf, the Saxonian Elector's powerful counselor. He had intervened on her behalf with the municipality of Dresden, but still her female rivals managed to influence the officials so as to exacerbate Anna's economic and social difficulties even more. Anna, fed up with these circumstances, had then decided to go one step further. Now she wrote directly to the Elector's wife. She told the whole story of her immigration, her difficult life as a Bohemian exile in the Saxonian capital, and the envy she faced from the locals. She also told the Electress that other people in the same situation were not hindered from roasting geese and pork, and therefore asked her to intervene with the municipality again. If she did, the Lord would reward the intervention a thousandfold, Anna concluded, at the same time wishing her and her husband and children health and good fortune.

We do not know how the Electress responded, nor do we know anything more about Anna's fate. Her petition letter only gives us a glimpse of the life of a female immigrant in early modern Saxony. Still, her petition letter, moving as it is, reveals a couple of characteristic details and stereotypes common in letters of this kind.

It is highly likely that Anna's petition was not written by her own hand. The handwriting, as well as the signature, suggests that it was written by a professional scribe, although this scribe did not leave any signature on the letter himself. Furthermore, Anna's story as well as her social and economic background, and even her age (she must have been at least in her 40s) lead to the assumption that her education had probably been rather basic. It is therefore unlikely that she knew how to address high advocates. Instead, she resorted to a professional letter-writer, who was skilled in using the appropriate style and *topoi*. On the other hand, she and/or her scribe seemed to know very well *whom* to address. Significantly, Anna approached the wife of the Elector and not the Elector himself. It is a very typical feature in immigrants' letters that women possessed their own communication structures, addressing the Electress whereas men would write to the Elector. Young petitioners even wrote to the sons of the Elector.

The selection of addressees therefore reflects the composition of society, based on the Lutheran idea of family and the early modern notion of the household.[29] It was ideally depicted in the ruler's family and consisted of the father (Elector), the mother (his wife) and the children (princes). Each of them was to fulfill certain roles in the society of their subjects. Not surprisingly, when the succeeding Saxonian Elector Frederick Augustus I ("the Strong") converted to Catholicism some 50 years later, it was his still-Lutheran wife who championed the Lutheran belief of the Saxonians.[30]

A crucial point for a petitioner was the means of delivery of the letter to the recipient. Petitioners had to know to whom at court to give their letter, in order to have it forwarded to the higher authorities. For this the services of a professional scribe were also helpful. However, this did not in itself secure the acceptance of the letter by the ruler. There were cases when a ruler refused to accept a petition letter because it was felt to be inappropriate or even offensive to his status. Approaching the ruler too directly could be interpreted as questioning the social order.[31] Once the letter was accepted, the supplicant would have to wait for the answer. Normally this was a matter of a few days only; sometimes the answer arrived the next or even the same day.[32] If the answer was favorable, the petitioner was advised to keep in touch with these authorities and to write a letter expressing his gratitude, so that he might approach the same addressee again for future requests. If the answer turned out not to be favorable or if no answer arrived at all, the petitioner wrote again, referring to his first petition in the *narratio* of the second, and using an equally polite, though slightly different style than before. Even the early modern manuals of letter-writing provided the reader with examples for a second petition letter.[33]

On top of this, success was usually not merely dependent on a grant letter following the petition, but on other authorities to whom the grant letter had to be shown. If, as in the case of Anna Wodianskin and the municipality of Dresden, the latter did not act in favor of the migrant petitioner, one more petition, preferably to an even higher authority, could be necessary. This is exactly what Anna Wodianskin did. First she gave her letter to the councillor Sebottendorf, and when his answer proved worthless to secure her needs, she resorted to the typical channels of communication, addressing the wife of the ruler directly.

For the Bohemian immigrants, petition letters were one of the most important channels to express their needs. Due to this fact, it appears as if there existed some kind of a semi-professional petition market in the Saxonian capital with scribes waiting for their customers. In some cases petitioners from far away would travel to Dresden just to get their petition written and delivered there. On the other hand, there were people who wrote a request for settlement in Saxony even before they decided to emigrate, the most famous being the Rudolfine astronomer Johannes Kepler, who eventually decided not to move to Saxony but to settle in the Silesian duchy of Sagan.[34]

As we know from other petitions, the letter derived from an oral communication between the petitioner and the scribe.[35] The petitioner would tell his or her fate to the writer, who then shaped the story, using the style and *topoi* expected by the receiver. In the case of Czech-speaking Bohemians who neither used the Latin language, nor were fluent and skilled enough to write a letter in German, the scribe could also serve as a translator, and this is one reason why there are hardly any Czech petitions to the Saxonian Elector, but some Latin and mainly German letters.

It must be stressed, though, that the use of scribes left much space for individual expressions and differences in approach, depending on the request as well as on the personal situation of the applicant, his migrational experiences, or simply his temperament. Anna Wodianskin is a picturesque example, though not an exceptional case. It may be that women tended to express their needs in much more extensive, refined, and even more emotional terms than men, although this point deserves further research, as there are far fewer petitions from women.

By looking at the text of Anna Wodianskin's request, we can clearly distinguish between the single parts of the formula as handed down by and compliant to the ancient and medieval *ars dictandi*. The *intitulatio*[36] is followed by the *exordium*, with Anna's promise to always include the Electress in her prayers. After this, the *narratio*, depicting the story of her attempts to make a living in Dresden and being hindered by the locals, follows immediately. This is striking and rather exceptional, as it would have been expected from other petitions that the petitioner would first summarize the hardships of his/her fellow Bohemians, using terms like *Exulant* or *Vertriebener*, and using the grammatical plural instead of the singular. Anna however, calls herself a "poor, deserted, exile." She refers extensively to her personal problems and hardships before posing the request in the *petitio*. Anna closes her lengthy petition with the promise to pray for the Saxonian ruler's family for any given grant, and at the same time stresses

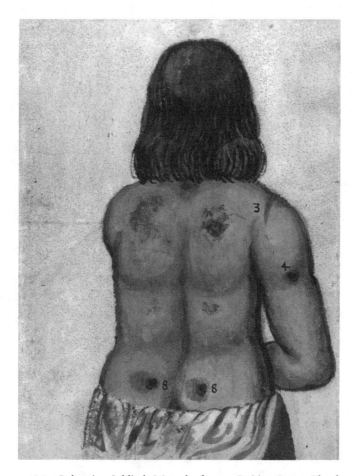

Figure 13.1 Bohemian Soldier's Wounds, from a Petition Letter. The former Bohemian soldier Daniel Hubatka added this remarkable image to his petition letter to the Elector of Saxony. By showing the scars he received while fighting for Saxony and the Holy Roman Empire in the Thirty Years' War, the Catholic Hubatka tried to justify his expected financial aid from the Lutheran Elector.

Courtesy of Sächsisches Hauptstaatsarchiv Dresden. (Sächsisches Hauptstaatsarchiv Dresden, Geheimer Rat, Loc. 8754, Intercessiones 1654–1657, Bl. 58a.)

the reward the Electress would be due to receive from God for her kindness. The letter ends with Anna's signature.

Mentioning the inclusion of a benefactor in somebody's prayers and the reward being given by the Lord is very common in migrants' petition letters. The connection of earthly generosity with heavenly support sets a connection, or even a means of religious pressure on the patron. This proves to be a pragmatic use of elements of the Christian faith, not always in strict accordance with Lutheranism. During the seventeenth century cases even seemed to increase where a petitioner used arguments of his own position as a religious exile or of his or the Elector's Lutheran faith in order to achieve his request, thus dealing with religious matters in a rather pragmatic manner. At the same time, even members of bi-confessional families or Catholics immigrated into Saxony, sometimes adopting parts of the discourse of the Protestant exiles, sometimes arguing in more ecumenical terms.

One of the most striking examples is the petition of the Catholic Daniel Hubatka. His letter dates from the early 1650s, only a few years after the end of the Thirty Years' War. He had started working as a tax collector in Bohemia, but due to his own carelessness he lost a lot of the money he was supposed to collect. The officials put him into prison, and now he asked the Saxonian Elector for help by recalling not his "lutheran faith" but his "christian clemency." Moreover, he impressively showed what dangers he, as a Catholic, had endured for Saxony and the Holy Roman Empire in earlier days, by adding a finely drawn portrait picture to his petition (figure 13.1). The image depicts his body bearing eight scars. Wounds 2, 4, 5, 6, and 8 he received at the battle of Wittstock in 1636; 1, 3, and 7 he received at Magdeburg in 1631. Hubatka therefore concluded that his hardships in the war would give him the right to address the Saxonian Elector and ask for support.[37]

It is remarkable that the Elector became increasingly accessible to non-Lutherans, who addressed him in a non-confessional way. All this underlines the openness of confessional boundaries and the flexibility and interchangeability of confessional identities. In some cases the supplicants apparently switched between confessional loyalties and even inverted the exiles' arguments in order to try putting the Elector under religious pressure. A couple of petitions forward the argument of Jacob Schmidt, who bluntly wrote that were he not given citizenship in Saxony, the Elector would have to accept responsibility for the fact that he, together with his Catholic wife and little children, would have to go back into Bohemia, and be forced to convert to Catholicism, thus being lost forever to the true Lutheran faith.[38] This way of arguing usually worked well.

Conclusion

The above examples have shown that we must be careful in accepting the letters as proof of the religious belief or the Lutheran loyalty of the petitioners. Even though we do not know the true motives behind Anna Wodianskin's emigration, it is obvious that even she utilized confessional arguments at the point of immigration in order to receive what she wanted, just as so many other people before and after her. Still we should not consider the petitions as mere instruments. The way Anna Wodianskin arranged her story into a coherent tale of persecution and hardships shows not only inventiveness, but also the ability to mix her experiences of the past with her goals and expectations for the (immediate) future. In her stunning book on British captivity narratives, Linda Colley wrote: "It is important to get away from the notion that these . . . narratives can usefully be characterized as either truthful or crudely mendacious. We all of us convert life's crowded, untidy experiences into stories in our own minds, rearranging awkward facts into coherent patterns as we go along, and omitting episodes that seem in retrospect peripheral, discordant, or too embarrassing or painful to bear."[39] This is equally true of the Bohemian immigrants' stories. Early modern narratives, and especially the petition letters, considered not just as legal instruments but as narratives, reveal much of the self of the petition writers as well as of their self-fashioning, the way they wanted themselves to be seen, and of their expectations.

As petitioners, the seventeenth century Bohemian immigrants adapted, emphasized or perhaps even amended parts of their own biographies in order to present a coherent story that helped them to make their lives fit the circumstances in Saxony. They used elements of the Protestant discourse on faith and martyrdom in a non-dogmatic, often pragmatic way and contributed to the blurring of formerly distinctive confessional differences. It is noteworthy that the contents of the petition letters as well as the choice and order of arguments were more strongly influenced by the situation in the receiving country than by the places of origin. In this respect, even the notion of *Exulant* was literally derived from the post-migrational situation.

This is not to say that all these letters were completely fictional. But a major part of the elements used in these letters proved to be "fiction in the archives," as Natalie Zemon Davis has put it. If we do not look at the facts, but at the stories and the way they are being told, they give insight into the needs and thoughts of these people, otherwise unable to articulate themselves to us.

This is why it is necessary to consider the strategies and arguments in these Saxonian immigrant letters and the way the immigrants reproduced or even constructed their own histories of persecution and migration. In this respect, these letters and the often quadrangular communication system of petition-writing among the immigrant, the scribe, the ruler as their presumed protector, and those authorities deputized to read and answer the letters, constructed and stabilized the status of the immigrants in Saxony and their relationship to the Saxonian government. Petition practices and the whole communication system associated with them—from letter structures to bureaucratic procedures, from the Lutheran family ideal to the presentation of immigrants' stories—acknowledged social order, and the letters helped the petitioners to find a distinctive place in early modern Saxonian society. Thus, even if a considerable number of petition letters might not have been useful for their authors in practical terms because they did not result in a grant, letter-writing fostered integration through communication.

Notes

This essay is based on arguments derived from my doctoral dissertation at the University of Munich, Germany: Alexander Schunka, *Gäste, die bleiben. Zuwanderung in Kursachsen und der Oberlausitz im 17. und frühen 18. Jahrhundert* (Münster et al.: Lit, 2005). I am very grateful to Anna Larsson for corrections to the text.

1. On recent discussions about the German-French concept of cultural transfers/ *transferts culturels* see Wolfgang Schmale, ed., *Kulturtransfer im 16. Jahrhundert* (Innsbruck: Studienverlag, 2003). On the dissemination of goods in Renaissance Europe see Lisa Jardine, *Worldly Goods. A new History of the Renaissance* (New York: Norton, 1996).
2. Dirk Hoerder, *Cultures in Contact. World Migrations in the Second Millennium* (Durham-London: Duke University Press, 2002).
3. Klaus J. Bade, *Europa in Bewegung. Migration vom späten 18. Jahrhundert bis zur Gegenwart* (München: Beck, 2000); Leslie Page Moch, *Moving Europeans. Migration in Western Europe since 1650* (Bloomington-Indianapolis: Indiana University Press 1992); Klaus J. Bade, Pieter C. Emmer, Leo Lucassen, and Jochen Oltmer, eds., *Migration, Integration, and Minorities since the 17th Century. A European Encyclopedia* (Cambridge: Cambridge University Press, 2005).
4. Heinz Schilling, *Niederländische Exulanten im 16. Jahrhundert. Ihre Stellung im Sozialgefüge und im religiösen Leben deutscher und englischer Städte* (Gütersloh: Mohn, 1972); Schilling, "Confessional Migration as a Distinct Type of Old European Long distance Migration," in *Le migrazioni in Europa Secc. XIII–XVIII*, ed. Simonetta Cavaciocchi (Firenze: Le Monnier, 1994), pp. 175–189.
5. Heinz Schilling, "Die frühneuzeitliche Konfessionsmigration," in *Migration in der europäischen Geschichte seit dem späten Mittelalter*, ed. Klaus J. Bade (Osnabrück: Rasch, 2002), pp. 67–89; Alexander Schunka, "Glaubensflucht als Migrationsoption. Konfessionell motivierte Migrationen in der Frühen Neuzeit," *Geschichte in Wissenschaft und Unterricht* 56 (2005).
6. Helmut Neuhaus, "Supplikationen als landesgeschichtliche Quellen. Das Beispiel der Landgrafschaft Hessen im 16. Jahrhundert," *Hessisches Jahrbuch für Landesgeschichte* 28 (1978): 110–190; 29 (1979): 63–97; Paola Repetti, "Scrivere ai potenti. Suppliche e memoriali a Parma (secoli XVI–XVIII)," in *Lesen und Schreiben in Europa 1500–1900; Vergleichende Perspektiven*, ed. Roger Chartier and Alfred Messerli

(Basel: Schwabe, 2000), pp. 401–428; Cecilia Nubola and Andreas Würgler, eds., *Suppliche e "gravamina." Politica, amministrazione, giustizia in Europa (secoli XIV–XVIII)* (Bologna: Il Mulino, 2002).

7. Natalie Zemon Davis, *Fiction in the Archives* (Cambridge: Polity Press, 1987).

8. On issues of "self-fashioning" see Stephen J. Greenblatt, *Renaissance Self Fashioning. From More to Shakespeare* (Chicago: University of Chicago Press, 1980); Peter Burke, *The Fabrication of Louis XIV* (New Haven: Yale University Press, 1992).

9. Christian Adolph Pescheck, *Die böhmischen Exulanten in Sachsen. Zur Beantwortung der von der Fürstlich Jablonowskischen Gesellschaft gestellten historischen Preisfrage* (Leipzig: Hirzel, 1857); Georg Loesche, *Die böhmischen Exulanten in Sachsen* (Wien and Leipzig: Klinkhardt, 1923).

10. Alexander Schunka, *Soziales Wissen und dörfliche Welt. Herrschaft, Jagd und Naturwahrnehmung in Zeugenaussagen des Reichskammergerichts aus Nordschwaben (16.-17. Jahrhundert)* (Frankfurt/Main et al.: Lang, 2000).

11. Alexander Schunka, "Autoritätserwartung in Zeiten der Unordnung. Zuwandererbittschriften in Sachsen im 17. Jahrhundert," in *Autorität der Form—Autorisierung—Institutionelle Autoritä*, Wulf Oesterreicher, ed. Gerhard Regn and Winfried Schulze (Münster et al.: Lit, 2003), pp. 323–337.

12. Eduard Winter, *Die tschechische und slowakische Emigration in Deutschland im 17. und 18. Jahrhundert. Beiträge zur Geschichte der hussitischen Tradition*, (Berlin [Ost]: Akademie-Verlag, 1955).

13. See Schunka, *Gäste*.

14. Among others: Staatsfilialarchiv Bautzen, Oberamt 4278, fol. 35v (1650).

15. For a concise summary in English see, for instance, Heinz Schilling, "Confessional Europe," in *Handbook of European History, 1400–1600*, ed. Thomas A. Brady, Heiko A. Oberman, and James D. Tracy (Grand Rapids: Eerdman, 1996), pp. 641–681.

16. On questions of religion and belief in daily life see Thomas Luckmann, *The Invisible Religion* (New York: Macmillan, 1967); Jens Ivo Engels and Hillard von Thiessen, "Glauben. Begriffliche Annäherungen anhand von Beispielen aus der Frühen Neuzeit," *Zeitschrift für Historische Forschung* 28 (2001): 333–357.

17. David Fitzpatrick, *Oceans of Consolation. Personal Accounts of Irish Migration to Australia* (Ithaca-London: Cornell University Press, 1994), and see Fitzpatrick's contribution in the present volume. On the *Ars dictandi* see Franz-Joseph Worstbrock, "Ars dictaminis, Ars dictandi," in *Reallexikon der deutschen Literaturwissenschaft*, vol. 1, 3rd edn., ed. Klaus Weimar (Berlin et al.: de Gruyter, 1997), pp. 138–141.

18. Justus Lipsius, *De Constantia. Von der Standhaftigkeit*, trans. Florian Neumann (Mainz: Dieterich, 1998). On the notion *peregrinatio* see Juergen Hahn, *The Origins of the Baroque Concept of Peregrinatio* (Chapel Hill: University of North Carolina Press, 1973), pp. 114–173.

19. Many of these can be found in Stadtarchiv Dresden, Ratsarchiv, G XXV 17b.

20. On the concept of a migration system see Hoerder, *Cultures*, pp. 16–19.

21. Franz Eppert, "Exulant und Emigrant bis etwa 1750," *Zeitschrift für deutsche Sprache* 26 (1970): 188–192. Schunka, *Gäste*, chapter 2.

22. See, among others, Joachim Knape and Bernhard Roll, eds., *Rhetorica deutsch. Rhetorikschriften des 15. Jahrhunderts* (Wiesbaden: Harrassowitz, 2002).

23. Natalie Zemon Davis, *The Gift in Sixteenth Century France* (Madison: University of Wisconsin Press, 2000).

24. On this aspect see Alexander Schunka, "Exulanten, Konvertiten, Arme und Fremde. Zuwanderer aus der Habsburgermonarchie in Kursachsen im 17. Jahrhundert," *Frühneuzeit-Info* 14 (2003): 66–78.

25. On the discussion around ego-documents see Rudolf Dekker, ed., *Egodocuments and History. Autobiographical Writing in its Social Context since the Middle Ages*

(Hilversum: Verloren, 2002); Winfried Schulze, ed., *Ego-Dokumente. Annäherung an den Menschen in der Geschichte* (Berlin: Akademie-Verlag, 1996).

26. Stadtarchiv Dresden, Ratsarchiv G XXV 17b, 91r, 92r.
27. Stadtarchiv Dresden, Ratsarchiv B XIII 14a, 2 vols., 1674–1700.
28. Stadtarchiv Dresden, Ratsarchiv B I 10, 3r–4r, Dresden, November 6, 1647.
29. Otto Brunner, "Das 'ganze Haus' und die alteuropäische', Ökonomik', " in *Neue Wege der Verfassungs- und Sozialgeschichte*, 2nd edn. (Göttingen: Vandenhoeck und Ruprecht, 1968), pp. 103–127. On the implications of Brunner's concept see Valentin Groebner, "Außer Haus. Otto Brunner und die 'alteuropäische Ökonomik', " *Geschichte in Wissenschaft und Unterricht* 46 (1995): 69–80.
30. Helen Watanabe-O'Kelly, *Court Culture in Dresden. From Renaissance to Baroque* (Houndmills et al.: Palgrave, 2002), p. 196; Jochen Vötsch, *Kursachsen, das Reich und der mitteldeutsche Raum zu Beginn des 18. Jahrhunderts*, (Frankfurt/Main et al.: Lang, 2003), pp. 33–34.
31. Maria Theresia refused to accept one petition at all: Hauptstaatsarchiv Dresden, Geheimer Rat, Loc. 10330/7 (final pages, no page-numbers).
32. For instance Stadtarchiv Dresden, Ratsarchiv B XIII 14a, vol. 1, 48r (1686).
33. Alexander Huge, *Rhetorica Und Formularium Teutsch, beynach alle Schreibereyen betreffend, von vilerley Epistlen, under und Oberschrifften, an allerley Geistliche unnd Weltliche personen, auch vilerley Supplicationes . . .* [1529] (Basel: Henricpetri, 1572), pp. lii–lxi.
34. Hauptstaatsarchiv Dresden, Geheimer Rat, Loc. 10331/13, 85r–86r, 19 (29) February, 1628.
35. Stadtarchiv Dresden, Ratsarchiv, B I 10, 19r: oral dictation of a petition letter (1709).
36. "Durchlauchtigste Hochgeborene Fürstin."
37. Sächsisches Hauptstaatsarchiv Dresden, Geheimer Rat, Loc. 8754, Intercessiones 1654–1657, 56r–58v, Daniel Hubatka's petition letter; illustration on 58a.
38. Hauptstaatsarchiv Dresden, Oberkonsistorium, Loc. 5838, 14r–16v; on a similar case see Alexander Schunka, " 'St. Johanngeorgenstadt zu kurfürstlicher Durchlaucht unsterblichem Nachruhm'. Stadtgründung und städtische Traditionsbildung in der Frühen Neuzeit," *Neues Archiv für Sächsische Geschichte* 75 (2004).
39. Linda Colley, *Captives. Britain, Empire and the World, 1600–1850* (London: Pimlico, 2003), p. 92.

14

"To His Excellency the Sovereign of all Russian Subjects in Canada": Emigrant Correspondence with Russian Consulates in Montreal, Vancouver, and Halifax, 1899–1922

Vadim Kukushkin

Consular officials form an important element in the institutional frameworks that historically have supported transnational human relationships.[1] But probably because functions performed by consulates tend to be considered too mundane, they seldom appear in the foreground of migration history. When consuls do receive a mention, it is most often as monitors of emigrants' political orientations and promoters of the official ideologies of the governments they serve. What usually remains out of the picture is the fact that the initiative in contacting consular officials often came from emigrants themselves. Most authors who have written on emigration from Europe, and from the Russian Empire in particular, seem to take it for granted that moving overseas effectively cuts off the emigrants' ties to the state of birth and its overseas agencies. While Russian political exiles or religious dissenters may indeed have preferred to keep an arm's length distance from the czarist government and its representatives, the relationship of the ordinary labor emigrant with the home state was different. Long after leaving the country of their birth, many peasants and artisans who ventured out to America in pursuit of the dollar rather than freedom continued to stay tied not only to Old World family and kin networks, but to the institutions of the Russian imperial state as well. Having for the most part remained Russian subjects, they were not only liable to be taxed or called up to the army, but also entitled to the services and protection of the imperial government, despite the fact that about 75 percent of the emigrants left Russia in a clandestine way without taking out a passport.[2] As public officials responsible for the supervision of Russian subjects abroad, the consuls often became the medium that allowed emigrants to maintain contact with the home state and turn it to their advantage.

Based on the analysis of a large volume of correspondence between Russian-subject emigrants in Canada and three czarist consulates that operated in that country between 1899 and 1922, this essay explores emigrant attitudes to and perceptions of their home state.[3] It argues that, contrary to the conventional views of Russian emigration as driven mostly by political and religious oppression, the reality of these attitudes, as demonstrated by emigrant letters to the consuls, was more complex. Rather than eschewing the consular officials, many emigrants, particularly (but not only) those of eastern Slav origin and Orthodox faith, attempted to use the paternalist character of the Russian monarchy, which posed as supreme protector of its Slavic Orthodox subjects, known as *korennye russkie* or "indigenous Russians," to meet their own needs and deal with a variety of problems encountered in the New World or needing attention in the homeland.

As a British dominion, Canada could not have direct diplomatic relations with foreign states, but it was allowed to host their consular representatives. By the end of the nineteenth century, most large European states had established consular missions in Canada. The first Russian consulate, later raised to the status of consulate general, was opened in Montreal in 1899, followed 16 years later by the establishment of a second consulate in Vancouver, which was made responsible for serving Russian emigrants west of Saskatchewan. The Russian government also employed Halifax businessman Henry Mathers to serve as honorary consul in that city, although his prerogative in immigration matters was limited (he could not, for instance, issue Russian passports or identity papers).[4] The consulates survived the two Russian revolutions of 1917 but, having refused to serve Russia's new Bolshevik government, eventually became a political anachronism and were forced to close down in 1922.

Analyzed chronologically, the consular correspondence with the emigrants reflects the changing sources and character of early twentieth-century Russian migration to Canada. While the early writers were primarily persons of Jewish or German origin with a smattering of Poles and Finns, most letters dated 1910 or later came from Ukrainians and Belarusans, who began to dominate the migration stream by the early 1910s. Random sampling of more than 11,000 personal emigrant files that constitute part of the Russian consular records showed that the bulk of the Ukrainians hailed from the empire's southwest—the provinces of Podillia (Podolia), Kiev, Bessarabia and Volyn (Wolhynia), while Belarusans came primarily from Hrodna (Grodno) Province. The majority of the emigrants were peasant men who arrived in Canada as industrial laborers rather than land seekers. Most of them intended to return to their families, left behind in the Old Country, after earning enough money to fulfill the trip's purpose, be it purchasing a plot of land, building a new house, or providing a daughter with a dowry. Thousands of "Russians" (the usual label affixed to eastern Slav immigrants from the Romanov empire) were found in railway construction and lumber camps scattered across Canada's resource frontier and in the mining towns of northern Ontario and the Crow's Nest Pass. Others gravitated to urban areas, primarily Montreal, Windsor, and Toronto, filling the increasing demand of Canadian industries for unskilled labor.[5]

Of about 200,000 emigrants from Russia recorded between 1900 and 1915 by Canadian statistics,[6] perhaps no more than 10 to 15 percent made contact with the czarist consulates. The propensity of emigrants to seek consular assistance was related to a variety of factors, of which literacy in the Russian language was one of the most important. It would be safe to say that for the majority of the czar's subjects, contact with state officialdom was much more a matter of being able to communicate in the official language than a question of political attitude toward the czarist monarchy. By the early twentieth century, Russia's improving educational system made elementary education available to most of its population, resulting in increased literacy rates among the younger peasant generation.[7] A comparison of data from Russian passports, appended to 671 emigrant personal files, with 1897 census statistics shows that the emigrants on average possessed an even higher degree of literacy than the general peasant population in the places of origin.[8] As part of its Russification policy, the government had achieved a reasonable degree of success in spreading the knowledge of written Russian among the empire's Ukrainians and Belarusans, whose own tongues were considered vernacular dialects. To the extent that the emigrant letters can be viewed as an indicator of the writers' literacy, emigrants from Ukraine and Belarus were hardly inferior to ethnic Russian correspondents in their command of the language, although Ukrainian and Belarusan words did occasionally creep into their writing.

Some emigrants, illiterate at the time of arrival in Canada, evidently acquired basic writing skills during their Canadian sojourn, as illustrated by a letter sent to the consul in August 1918 by Adam Shpiruk from Volyn, who apologized for his poor grammar "because [it is only] here [that] I have learned a little writing."[9] Those who found writing hard to master contacted the consulate by engaging someone they knew, often a Jewish fellow countryman, to write a letter on their behalf. Applications for Russian passports or citizenship certificates were also commonly filled out at large labor and steamship agencies owned by Jewish proprietors—Louis Gurofsky in Toronto, George Rabinovitch in Montreal, or J. Goodman in Hamilton. By 1900, good knowledge of Russian was common among the younger, better-educated and more assimilated generation of Russian Jews, who quickly assumed the middleman's role in Slavic emigrant communities. Russian-German emigrants usually also had a good or passable command of Russian, as did many Poles, especially from the Ukrainian and Belarusan territories subject to Russification policies.[10]

Literacy no doubt played a key role in determining the likelihood of contact between emigrants and the consuls, but factors related to individual migration strategies and goals were just as important. The typical seeker of consular aid was a temporary labor emigrant, who had not spent enough time in Canada to lose any connections with the czarist state or need for its assistance. The availability of community support networks also mattered a great deal. In contrast to the more stable and gender-balanced Jewish, German, and Finnish settlements, Slavic worker communities, scattered across Canada's cities and resource frontier, were predominantly male and had little in the way of organized social life. Ruthenian community organizations, which began to appear by 1914 in many urban centers of western and central Canada, held little appeal for Russian-born Ukrainians, for they were usually dominated by Greek Catholic leaders from Galicia, hostile to Russia and Russian Orthodoxy. For many Russian peasants-turned-workers, unschooled in organized class protest, appealing to the consul was one of the few avenues of obtaining a satisfactory resolution of a dispute with an employer, a labor agent, or contesting unlawful action by Canadian police. Writing to the consulate held out at least a slight promise that real or supposed injustice would be remedied. While many emigrants must have had unpleasant memories of dealing with a cumbersome czarist bureaucracy, the consulate was nevertheless an island of the familiar universe in the ocean of foreign speech and strange customs. The extent of return migration—and hence the need for travel papers, which could only be obtained from the consulates—was also higher among eastern Slavs than it was among non-Slavic nationalities.[11]

Due to its volume and diversity, the incoming consular correspondence defies easy categorization. However, most of it can be placed in one of two broad categories: 1) letters related to the maintenance of ties with the homeland and 2) those dealing with problems arising from maladjustment or discrimination in the host country. The first category comprises, among other types of correspondence, thousands of inquiries about and applications for

Russian travel papers (so-called *prokhodnye svidetelstva* or "entry permits," which allowed illegal emigrants or those with expired or lost passports to return to Russia). The onset of World War I brought an avalanche of applications for Russian nationality certificates, which gave their holders a measure of protection from being interned as "enemy aliens" or conscripted into Canadian military forces as naturalized British subjects. Although applications of both types had to be made on special forms, obtained from the consulates, they were often accompanied by less formal correspondence, explaining the person's situation and the reason for applying. The help of the consul was also sought in financing a return trip, sending money or correspondence, or locating emigrants' families in Russia, displaced by World War I. The most common subjects in the second category of letters were disputes with Canadian employers (unpaid wages, abuse by foremen, work injuries, swindling by labor agents, etc.) and conflicts with Canadian law enforcement and military authorities over the possession of identification papers or conscription issues during World War I. On occasion, the consuls were asked to arbitrate in conflicts that erupted between Russian Orthodox priests and their congregations, usually over the control of parish money.[12]

Needless to say, emigrant letters to consular officials differ from the personal (familial) letter in function, structure, and linguistic expression. While the purpose of emigrant family correspondence was to maintain and negotiate personal relationships,[13] here the writers negotiated their status and rights as subjects of the state to which they still had both mental and legal ties. The style and structure of the letters reflect their function. Most begin with a deferential salutation (often chosen without any regard for the official hierarchy of titles), followed by the narration of the writer's problem and, finally, a request for help. Many writers, as we shall see, adopted a supplicatory tone or deliberately fashioned their requests as petitions, which, as historian Sheila Fitzpatrick pointed out, constitute "almost the archetypal expression of the relation between subject and ruler in a paternalist state."[14]

The reading of the letters leaves no doubt that their authors had a clear sense of entitlement to consular service and protection. This sense, however, stemmed not so much from the concept of legal right, alien to the political system of Imperial Russia and even less characteristic of peasant thinking, as from the belief in the ultimate moral law, which required the state official to care about the subjects of the tsar as a father would care about his children. Most writers, especially before the fall of monarchy in 1917, seem to have taken paternalism for granted as a "natural" form of relations between the state and its subjects. An emigrant fresh from his native village saw the consuls in much the same terms as he had viewed state officials at home. Regarding the state (especially when it presented itself in the form of tax collectors or recruitment officers) with deep-seated mistrust, the peasants were at the same time accustomed to rely on it as a source of protection, particularly against forces beyond the control of the peasant commune, and as an arbiter in village disputes or conflicts with the landlord. In a classic analysis of Polish peasant attitudes to the state, Thomas and Znaniecki wrote that the latter appeared to the peasants as akin to the natural order—"absolutely mysterious, whose manifestations can possibly be foreseen but whose nature and laws cannot be changed by human interference." Yet in peasant thinking the political system also had another side, which resembled the divine world—"more comprehensible but more unforeseen, with some moral character, that is, capable of being just or unjust and of being influenced . . . The bearers of political power whom the peasant meets are men, and their executive activity can be directed within certain limits by gifts or supplication, or they can be moved to intercede before those higher ones whom the peasant seldom meets. . . ."[15] Such attitudes, typical of Eastern European peasantry, were transplanted onto Canadian soil as part of the emigrants' cultural baggage. It should also not be forgotten that the privileged status that "indigenous Russians" enjoyed in the czarist empire avowedly entitled them to priority treatment by the state. Apparently aware of this, many emigrants invoked the rhetoric of Russian nationalism, addressing the consuls as protectors of "*Russian people*" in Canada—something that seldom, if ever, appears in letters written by Jews, Germans, or Poles.

Historian Emily Pyle, who studied Russian peasant petitions for government allowances during World War I, has demonstrated that in their attempts to secure financial assistance from the state, the peasants usually followed certain strategies, which involved posing as a "beggar," a "victim," a "flatterer," a "monarchist/patriot," or some combination of the above.[16] The purpose of these strategies was to convince the state official of the supplicant's trustworthiness and eligibility for assistance. The analysis of the consular correspondence shows that Russian emigrants in Canada, recruited by and large from the peasant class, employed essentially the same techniques, and adopted similar roles, to obtain consular aid (financial or other). The similarity is further increased by the fact that, due to the lack of rules laying down precise criteria of assistance, the final decision in both cases rested with the state official who dealt with the petition.

Begging the authorities for relief on the grounds of poverty or inability to support the family was a survival strategy that Russian peasants practiced for centuries. In the peasant moral code, to plead with a state official for help was not considered degrading if destitution resulted from circumstances beyond the supplicant's control. Emigrants who adopted the role of "beggars" utilized the same methods as their fellow villagers at home, making an appeal to the official's conscience. To put themselves in a position of moral power, they tried to muster all their eloquence with the goal of dramatizing their condition and presenting it in the most pathetic tones. Most requests for relief were written during the economic recession of 1913–1915, which put thousands of immigrants out of work and forced them to rely on occasional day jobs, charity, or begging. Adam Kostiuk wrote to the consul from Vancouver that he had remained without a job for weeks and humbly asked for an allowance: "I beg Your Honor: please, send my perishing and starving soul at least five dollars. Please do me a favor, Your Excellency, and may God give you happiness and good health. I will never allow myself to pay for good with evil. If I stay alive and go back to Russia [through Montreal], I will visit Your Excellency and will kiss your hands and your feet for such relief. Do not ignore my plea, Your Excellency, support me in some way . . ."[17] Married writers made references to their indigent families, obviously reasoning that should the consul remain untouched by descriptions of their own suffering, he would certainly be moved by an image of starving children back in the Old Country. Dmitry Burdiuzhan, a native of Bessarabia, wrote that he had arrived in Canada in early 1914, leaving a wife and six children to mind the house and hoping to return in two years. While he was struggling to find steady employment, his wife suddenly died and his oldest son, who was left in charge of the household, was mobilized to the army in August 1914. Burdiuzhan asked the consul, Sergey Likhachev, for a loan to help him buy a steamship ticket, which he promised to pay back on arrival in Russia.[18] Pavel Kozak used similar images when he pleaded for help in locating the current whereabouts of his family, who had fled eastward after the German takeover of his native village in 1915: "My heart bleeds, because I hear that people in Russia are famished, and I cannot sleep at night, thinking that my poor children may already have died of starvation."[19]

As a strategy for obtaining aid, begging was often combined with self-presentation as a victim of some form of mistreatment, such as agent swindling, or an industrial accident. The combination was a sensible one, for it was important for a "beggar" to show that his indigence resulted from no fault of his own. Harsh working and living conditions in which many recently arrived labor emigrants found themselves gave the letter-writers plenty of opportunities to use the discourse of victimization in seeking consular assistance, not to mention the fact that railway construction, mining, and lumbering, which employed most immigrant workers from Russia, were also the three most hazardous occupations in the country. The papers of the Montreal and Vancouver consulates contain more than a hundred individual and collective cases involving denial of compensation for work injuries sustained by Russian-subject emigrants. By 1913–1914, the number of complaints against employers and agents was growing so fast that the consulate general thought it best to refer them to the reputable Montreal law firm of Dessaulles, Garneau, and Vanier, which investigated the case and provided the plaintiff with legal counsel. After frustrating and often fruitless encounters with Canadian lawyers and courts, the injured workers regarded the consuls as their only remaining hope for justice. In a typical letter of this kind, Ivan Bespalko, a native of Kiev Province, described the circumstances of his injury and asked for help in obtaining an indemnity from his employer:

> Your Excellency, I beg for your help in an accident.... I worked for the Canadian Copper Company at Creighton Mine and I was injured by a dynamite explosion so badly that I have been disabled for 6 months—my whole right side was injured, my right eye was completely blown out and I also lost two teeth. My right cheek is all black from gunpowder. Therefore I want some aid from the company. Let it pay me for the lost eye and give a good job, because now I cannot do any hard work. So I have to suffer now, for I cannot get a job at another company. I have become a cripple for my whole life, and therefore I ask that I be given some allowance.[20]

Old-world experience taught Russian peasant emigrants that if they wanted to achieve any success with the unwieldy czarist bureaucracy, they often had to become a thorn in the official's flesh, pestering him with repeated pleas and inquiries without dropping a perfectly respectful or even obsequious tone. Such tactics seemed to work with the consuls as well. Petr Dudchenko, injured when working for the Canadian Pacific Railway (CPR), sent thirteen letters to the consulate during a period of one year while his case was being investigated by Dessaulles, Garneau, and Vanier. The court ruled that the company must provide Dudchenko with compensation of $225—less than he had claimed, but more than the CPR had been prepared to pay.[21]

Other letter-writers presented themselves as victims of Canadian state officials. Such complaints became especially common during World War I, when Canadian police began to practice round-ups of immigrant men looking for "enemy aliens" or (after the introduction of conscription in 1917) for draft evaders. Panteley Vakulchik, arrested by the police for failure to provide identity papers, resorted to the use of metaphor to describe the treatment he had received. "Canadian gentlemen catch us like dogs, lock us up in stables and keep under watch worse than inmates and [then] tell us that we are in a free land," he wrote to the consul in June 1918.[22] Many emigrants, whose notions of permissible behavior and standards of morality often differed from those set by Canadian law, deemed criminal sentences handed out by Canadian courts to be unjust and discriminatory. The letter from Paraskeva Shumovich of Sault Ste Marie, Ontario, dated January 1918, is notable for being one of the few petitions in the consular records written by a woman. She complained that her husband Andrey had been sentenced to a year in prison, allegedly for striking a police officer who had attempted to arrest him for disorderly conduct. The incident happened when the couple was returning from the neighboring state of Michigan, where they had allegedly gone to track several men who boarded at their house and owed them rent. Having admitted that her husband had "had a few drinks" during their trip, Paraskeva nonetheless claimed his innocence and accused the police and the Jewish court interpreter of fabricating the case. "They have jailed my husband for a year and I don't know what to do now. But since we are from Russia and don't know the language, they treat us as they want. And I ask Your Excellency to help me in my misery or give an advice what to do," she concluded her entreaty.[23] An inquiry made by Consul Likhachev with the Chief Constable of Sault Ste Marie revealed that not only was the man indeed sentenced for obstructing a police officer, but also that the couple had already had several conflicts with the law, including assaulting the police, drunkenness, selling liquor without government license, and, bizarrely, cutting off a cow's tail. Unsurprisingly, in this case as in several similar ones, consular help was refused.

Often used in combination with other strategies, flattery was another common way of currying favor with the consul and drawing attention to the supplicant's case. In the deliberately self-effacing and often awkwardly obsequious manner typical of peasant petitions, the "flatterers" praised the consul as "the father of all Russian people in Canada," "our only protector," and the like. Anton Syvak, who asked for Likhachev's help in obtaining indemnity for a work injury, addressed him as "the sovereign of all Russian subjects living in the United States, in Canada and in America [sic], and especially of those people who get into accidents, who receive blows and mutilations from [Canadian] companies and whose wives and children become orphans for their whole life . . ."[24] Some correspondents went even further, ending their letters with phrases like "I am waiting for your reply like a bird awaits the spring" or even "I kiss your sweet lips." The obvious purpose of such language was to personalize the relationship between the supplicant and the consul in the hope that such effusive expressions of trust would make any refusal of help on the consul's part look like a breach of familial obligations.

Perhaps sensing that begging or flattery alone might not bring quick results, occasionally the correspondents tried to appeal to the consuls' self-interest by offering them pecuniary rewards, sometimes openly but usually by way of hinting. While in most cases such propositions were simply ignored, repeated offers of money coming from the same individual elicited an angry reaction. Bribery may have flourished at the lower levels of the Russian administration, but high-salaried senior officials deemed it below their dignity to accept petty monies offered by the lowly supplicants. After receiving several money-offering letters from Pavel Babichuk, who asked the consul to track a missing money order he had sent to his family in Russia, an irritated Likhachev ordered his secretary to "tell the bastard to stop writing nonsense about giving rewards to the consulate." Babichuk was informed that the consulate was "not a ticket or labor bureau and [did] not charge money for its services."[25]

The outbreak of World War I saw the appearance of a new type of petitioner—the "patriot" or "loyalist." In most cases, patriotism was used as a lever to obtain a travel allowance to return to Russia. Hundreds of emigrant reservists assured the consuls that if they only had the money to buy a return ticket, they would immediately volunteer to fight for "the Faith, the Tsar and the Fatherland" (it should be noted here that most Russian reservists were not called up until 1915–1916). A group of workers from Le Pas, Manitoba, wrote a collective petition to the consulate general, asking to be shipped to Russia:

> Mr. Consul, I have the honor to report to Your Excellency that here in Manitoba, in a small town of Le Pas, there are very many Russian emigrants, and also a large number of reservists, and besides these reservists, there are many recruits due to perform military service in 1912, 1913 and 1914. But since they could not report to service in time, we are now writing to you all together that we wish to serve His Imperial Majesty Our Sovereign and Emperor Nikolai Aleksandrovich and our Holy Russian land, and we wish to go and fight at your first call. But we ask you to send us from Canada to Russia at government expense, and [we also ask] that each of us be given several dollars as a travel allowance. And we beg you to honor us with your response.[26]

In some cases, emigrants invoked popular images borrowed from the extreme right-wing version of Russian nationalism with its distinct mix of anti-Semitism and anti-socialism. The writers evidently hoped that the use of such rhetoric would strike a sympathetic chord with the czarist official and thus increase their chances of receiving aid. The author of an unsigned letter, who described himself as a peasant from the village of Fridrovtsi in Podillia and a former private in an artillery battalion, asked the consul to do him a favor and "give instruction and advice" on how to contribute to the war effort because he had no means to return home: "If I was [in Russia], I would know what I am suffering for, but here I am surrounded by the most wicked socialists, who were swineherds at home but in Canada [pose as] socialists. And these other bastards—the Jews—wish they could see our people dead. They are all for the Germans. I cannot take this, and I have already turned many of them in to the police . . ."[27] The flow of loyalist correspondence subsided by 1916, when the ineptitude of the czarist government became painfully obvious, but patriotic letters continued to arrive occasionally even after the fall of the monarchy so long as Russia remained at war. "I would rather kill myself than be forcibly drafted to the Canadian army," wrote Timofey Fedyk, a naturalized farmer in Alberta, who asked to be provided with travel papers for passage to Russia, because "it is better to die in the homeland than to suffer and die for Canada, a country I do not love."[28] He tried to convince Likhachev that his earlier decision to renounce Russian citizenship and become a British subject was dictated solely by a practical consideration: a desire to obtain legal title to his farmland. Presenting Canada in an unfavorable light as an inhospitable and individualist nation often went hand in hand in the loyalist letters with the praise of Russia as a morally superior society. A group of unemployed Russian workers in Brantford, Ontario, who, similar to hundreds of their compatriots, asked for financial assistance in returning to Russia, wrote that in Canada they felt "like beggars in Russia or even worse, because in Russia anyone will let a beggar in [to their home] for a night, whereas in Canada, unless you have ten cents, nobody will ever let you in even for a single night."[29]

A petition received in 1915 by the Montreal consulate from a group of Russian workers employed in railway construction in northern Ontario provides another good illustration of the ways in which emigrants put patriotism and popular nationalism stirred by the war to practical uses. The laborers complained that their section of the railway had a large number of Austrian navvies, who taunted their Russian coworkers and mocked the Russian government. "You must have this Austrian scum removed from this railway section," the petitioners insisted.[30] A similar appeal came from 47 miners in Sudbury, who blamed high unemployment among local Russian emigrants on the fact that many jobs were held by "enemy alien" workers.[31] Protests and strikes against the employment of enemy aliens were not uncommon in wartime Canada, almost always having the goal of freeing up jobs for native-born workers and citizens of the Allied powers. City boardinghouses and streets also witnessed scenes of fighting between Russians and Austrians, usually fueled by excessive consumption of alcohol.

The fast-growing number of "indigenous Russian" emigrants in North and South America forced the czarist state to begin taking more seriously the dual role of its consular missions as protectors and monitors of the emigrant population. In a January 1912 circular from St. Petersburg, Russian consuls were reminded that "taking care of the interests of Russian subjects in foreign countries and giving [them] protection when necessary" was one of their primary responsibilities. As "head *(glava)* but by no means a superior *(nachalnik)* of the Russian colony in his district," the consul was advised to display "personal accessibility" and "attentive and considerate attitude" to the needs of the emigrants.[32] However, as before, treatment received by help-seekers very much depended on the character or social status of the current holder of the consular office. Many Russian consuls, often recruited from the ranks of the nobility, looked down on their illiterate and rough-mannered emigrant clients, believing that most aid seekers had brought their troubles upon themselves through gullibility and ignorance. A Russian traveler

M. Bernov, who visited Montreal in the summer of 1913 during Count Passek's tenure as consul general, found the consular staff utterly wanting in attention to the needs of their compatriots: "[The consul] is never in office and obviously has his own understanding of service so far from the eyes of his superiors. . . . I called in twice, between one and three o'clock, and all I saw both times was some cipher clerk of Polish origin, who did not even speak proper Russian."[33] Seasoned bureaucrats, the consuls were not easily impressed by sycophancy or hyperbolized patriotism. Reporting to Petrograd in 1915, Likhachev wrote, for instance, that the true purpose of many of the requests for ticket money was simply to get a free ride home rather than to enlist in the Russian army.[34] Consular reply letters presented a notable contrast to the often wordy and emotionally embellished emigrant petitions. Short, dry and formal, they sent a clear message to their recipients that every subject of the tsar was entitled to an equal measure of attention and nobody should expect special treatment. Unless the supplicants belonged to a higher rank than peasantry or townspeople, they did not even merit a title of "Mr." or "Mrs." Instead, the correspondent was simply addressed by his or her full name.

The nature of the paternalist czarist state left the emigrants with few avenues for contesting the consul's actions. Filing a complaint with a superordinate Russian authority was about the only way of doing this, but few seemed to be willing to take this rather onerous and time-consuming route. Aside from logistical difficulties involved, the dependence of the supplicant on the consul's benevolence was obviously not conducive to adopting a defiant posture. When an emigrant did complain to higher authorities, it was normally done after returning to his home village. If such complaints managed to make their way through the multiple circuits of the Russian bureaucracy, they were forwarded to the Second Section of the Ministry of Foreign Affairs, which oversaw the consular service. The consul was then requested to submit a formal report on the matter, which normally closed the case.[35]

The fall of the Romanov monarchy in February 1917 and the subsequent installation of the Soviet government in Petrograd in October of the same year signaled an end to the paternalist state, replacing it (or so it seemed) with notions of popular sovereignty and civil rights. However, political transformations in the homeland, at least in the short term, brought few dramatic changes in the practice of emigrant-consul relationships other than the decreasing use of old titles and salutations and sycophantic or overly paternalistic language (thus, "Dear Sir" or "Dear Mr. Consul" in emigrant letters gradually replaced "Your Excellency"). Russian émigré socialists may have denounced the consuls as relics of the old czarist regime, but at least until 1919 the latter seem to have retained a considerable degree of legitimacy with ordinary peasant emigrants, who continued to write petitions and letters asking for various forms of assistance and employing much the same strate-gies they had used before 1917 (as a number of examples cited earlier demon-strate). The spirit of the revolution, however, did introduce some new themes into the language of the emigrant letters, equipping the more politically edu-cated writers with new strategies of self-empowerment based on the notion of citizens' rights. A Ukrainian emigrant whose application for a passport was turned down by Konstantin Ragosine, the Russian consul in Vancouver, wrote a complaint to the Russian Consulate General in the United States, alleging that Ragosine refused to issue passports to Russian emigrants on the grounds that he served "not the interests of the Russian people but A.F. Kerensky [the head of Russia's Provisional Government]" and would not admit the fact that Kerensky was no longer in power and "the country [was] apparently ruled by the Soviet of Workers', Soldiers', and Peasants' Deputies, which should be obeyed in every way."[36] At the opposite end of the emigrant political spectrum a few self-styled "patriots," apparently aware of the political stance of the con-suls, who in 1918 had sworn their loyalty to the White government of Admiral Kolchak, attempted to request favors on account of their anti-Bolshevik atti-tudes. In one somewhat unusual case, several Russian emigrants sentenced to capital punishment for murder wrote to Likhachev, asking the consul to obtain an extradition order for them so that they could redeem themselves by fighting against the Bolsheviks in Siberia.[37]

Through writing letters and petitions to the consular officials, early twentieth-century Russian emigrants engaged in a dialogue with their home state, probing the degree of its avowed commitment to the protection of its subjects regardless of their current whereabouts. The writers consid-ered themselves to be entitled to such protection even despite their absence (temporary, as most hoped) from the homeland and in some cases even regardless of the fact that they had adopted British citizenship. As this essay has attempted to show, the source of this sense of entitlement was, how-ever, not a legal norm but the moral code of the paternalist state, which obliged the rulers to take care of the ruled. In making an appeal for assis-tance, the petitioners used different strategies of moral self-empowerment and adopted a variety of public identities, such as a pauper, victim, or loyalist, with a view of obtaining consular assistance. In many letters, the line between the public and the private appears blurred, as the writers attempted to take their relationship with the czarist state out of the public realm and put it on a personal basis. While contesting mistreatment through the Canadian legal system or appealing for help with Canadian public agencies was beyond the ability of most emigrant laborers, the con-suls were part of the familiar world of czarist bureaucracy that could be manipulated to one's advantage using ways and methods tested and found working in the old land. Although it is difficult to say precisely how typical such attitudes toward state authority were for the Russian emigrant population, they were probably more common, especially among eastern Slav emigrants, than it would appear from standard notions of emigration from Russia as motivated by political and religious oppression or from multiple contemporary references to Russian émigré radicals.

Notes

1. Alejandro Portes, Luis E. Guarnizo, and Patricia Landolt, "The Study of Transnationalism: Pitfalls and Promises of an Emergent Research Field", *Ethnic and Racial Studies* 22, no. 2 (March 1999): 223.
2. P. Tizenko, *Emigratsionnyi vopros v Rossii, 1820–1910* (Libava: Libavskii vestnik, 1909), p. 34.
3. For a brief history of the Russian consular records see Bruce Ashkenas, *Records of Imperial Russian Consulates in Canada, 1898–1922* (Washington, DC: National Archives and Records Administration, 1992). Library and Archives Canada holds a full microform copy of these papers.
4. Four individuals held the post of Russian consul (later consul general) in Montreal in successive terms: Nicholas Struve (1899–1912); Mikhail Ustinov (1912–1913, Acting Consul General); Count Nicholas de Passek (1913–1914) and Sergey Likhachev (also spelled as Likacheff) (1914–1922). The Vancouver consulate was headed by Konstantin Ragosine during the whole period of its existence.
5. With the important exception of the Doukhobors, there is little published literature on Russian immigration to early twentieth-century Canada. The best, yetdated source is Grigorii Okulevich, *Russkie v Kanade: Istoriia russkikh raboche-fermerskikh klubov imeni M. Gor'kogo (1930–1940) i Federatsii russkikh kanadtsev (1941–1952)* (Toronto: Federation of Russian Canadians, 1952). For general English-language surveys of early twentieth-century emigration from czarist Russia, see V.V. Obolensky-Ossinsky, "Emigration from and Immigration into Russia," in *Interpretations*, vol. 2, *International Migrations*, ed. Imre Ferenczi and Walter F. Willcox (New York: Gordon and Breach, 1969), pp. 521–579; and Ralph Melville, "Permanent Emigration and Temporary Transnational Migration: Jewish, Polish and Russian Emigration from Czarist Russia, 1861–1914," in *Overseas Migration from East-Central and Southeastern Europe, 1880–1940*, ed. Julianna Puskás (Budapest: Akadémiai Kiadó, 1990), pp. 133–142.
6. Annual Reports of the Superintendent of Immigration, Department of the Interior, Sessional Paper No. 25, *Canada. House of Commons. Sessional Papers, 1901–1915*.
7. See on this Ben Eklof, *Russian Peasant Schools: Officialdom, Village Culture, and Popular Pedagogy, 1861–1914* (Berkeley: University of California Press, 1986).
8. Vadim Kukushkin, "Peasants on the Move: Early Twentieth-Century Labour Migration from Russia's Western Frontier to Canada." Unpublished PhD thesis, Carleton University, Ottawa, Canada, 2004, p. 90.
9. Adam Shpiruk to the consul, August 18, 1918, Library and Archives Canada, Ottawa, Likacheff-Ragosine-Mathers Collection (hereafter, Li-Ra-Ma Collection), MG30 E406, vol. 78, file 8449. I have tried to do my best to preserve the flavor of the original letters in the translated quotations. Grammatically incorrect constructions found in the original, however, are translated into standard English.
10. For an excellent discussion of Russian nationality policies see Andreas Kappeler, *The Russian Empire: A Multiethnic History* (Harlow: Pearson Education Ltd., 2001).

11. The U.S. data show that between 1908 and 1924, the rate of return migration among individuals classified as "Russians" stood at 65 percent, which was one of the highest among all ethnic groups. See Thomas J. Archdeacon, *Becoming American: An Ethnic History* (New York: Macmillan, 1983), p. 139. The Canadian authorities did not collect statistics of return migration.
12. See, for instance, Krasutsky, Gofman, Demidovich and others to the consul, May 25, 1914, Li-Ra-Ma Collection, vol. 21, file 664.
13. See David A. Gerber, "Epistolary Ethics: Personal Correspondence and the Culture of Emigration in the Nineteenth Century," *Journal of American Ethnic History* 19, 4 (Summer 2000): 10.
14. Sheila Fitzpatrick, "Editor's Introduction: Petitions and Denunciations in Russian and Soviet History", *Russian History* 24, 1–2 (1997): 4.
15. William I. Thomas and Florian Znaniecki, *The Polish Peasant in Europe and America*, 2nd edn. (New York: Dover Publications, 1958), p. 141.
16. Emily Pyle, "Peasant Strategies for Obtaining State Aid: A Study of Petitions during World War I," *Russian History* 24, 1–2 (1997): 42.
17. Adam Kostiuk to the consul, December 1914 (precise date unknown), Li-Ra-Ma Collection, vol. 8, file 261.
18. Dmitry Burdiuzhan to the consul, November 7, 1914, Li-Ra-Ma Collection, vol. 8, file 261.
19. Pavel Kozak to the consul, December 19, 1917, Li-Ra-Ma Collection, vol. 24, file 821.
20. The Ivan Bespalko case, Li-Ra-Ma Collection, vol. 6, file 216.
21. The Dudchenko case, Li-Ra-Ma Collection, vol. 6, file 217.
22. Panteley Vakulchik to the consul, June 22, 1918, Li-Ra-Ma Collection, vol. 99, file 11691.
23. Paraskeva Shumovich to Likhachev, January 19, 1918; R.C. Vincent to Likhachev, February 14, 1918, Li-Ra-Ma Collection, vol. 22, file 719.
24. Anton Syvak to the consul, November 11, 1915, Li-Ra-Ma Collection, vol. 7, file 227.
25. Li-Ra-Ma Collection, vol. 10, file 303.
26. Li-Ra-Ma Collection, vol. 11, file 365.
27. Ibid.
28. Li-Ra-Ma Collection, vol. 96, file 11170.
29. Semion Tryn and others to the consul, March 20, 1915, Li-Ra-Ma Collection, vol. 12, file 376.
30. Li-Ra-Ma Collection, vol. 7, file 251.
31. Ibid.
32. Ministerstvo inostrannykh del, Departament lichnogo sostava i khoziaistvennykh del—gg. Imperatorskim rossiiskim generalnym konsulam, konsulam i vitse-konsulam, January 9, 1912, Li-Ra-Ma Collection, vol. 1, file 3.
33. *Kievlianin*, July 27, 1913. It should be said in Passek's defense that by the time of Bernov's visit the 64-year-old consul was seriously ill. He would die in office in February 1914.
34. "Kratkaia dokladnaia zapiska o sodeistvii, okazannom Imperatorskim Konsulstvom v Kanade russkim poddannym, nakhodiashchimsia v strane i obrashchavshimsia za takovym iz-za voiny (1914–1915)," Li-Ra-Ma Collection, vol. 15, file 399.
35. See, for instance, the case of Petr Pokoruk: Likhachev to the 2nd Section of the Ministry of Foreign Affairs, March 12, 1915, Li-Ra-Ma Collection, vol. 6, file 226.
36. Timofey Fedyk to the Russian Consulate General in the United States, January 19, 1918, Li-Ra-Ma Collection, file 11170.
37. Aleksandr Martyniuk and others to the consul, October 29, 1919, Li-Ra-Ma Collection, vol. 7, file 237.

Index